The Law Commission
Consultation Paper No 197

UNFITNESS TO PLEAD

A Consultation Paper

ISBN: 9780118405041

Printed in the UK for The Stationery Office Limited
on behalf of the Controller of Her Majesty's Stationery Office

ID PO02395755   10/10

Printed on paper containing 75% recycled fibre content minimum.

THE LAW COMMISSION – HOW WE CONSULT

About the Law Commission
The Law Commission was set up by section 1 of the Law Commissions Act 1965 for the purpose of promoting the reform of the law.

The Law Commissioners are: The Rt Hon Lord Justice Munby (*Chairman*), Professor Elizabeth Cooke, Mr David Hertzell, Professor David Ormerod and Miss Frances Patterson QC. The Chief Executive is: Mr Mark Ormerod CB.

Address for correspondence: Steel House, 11 Tothill Street, London SW1H 9LJ.

Topic of this consultation
This consultation paper deals with the law on unfitness to plead. A summary of the main points can be found in Part 1.

Scope of this consultation
The purpose of this consultation is to generate responses to our provisional proposals.

Geographical scope
The contents of this consultation paper refer to the law of England and Wales.

Impact assessment
An impact assessment is included.

Previous engagement
N/A

Duration of the consultation
We invite responses to our provisional proposals and questions from 27 October 2010 to 27 January 2010.

How to respond
Send your responses either –

By email to: criminal@lawcommission.gsi.gov.uk OR   **By post to:**   address above
                    Tel: 020-3334-0271 / Fax: 020-3334-0201

If you send your comments by post, it would be helpful if, whenever possible, you could send them to us electronically as well (for example, on CD or by email to the above address, in any commonly used format).

After the consultation
In the light of the responses we receive, we will decide our final recommendations and we will present them to Parliament. We hope to publish our report by summer 2012. It will be for Parliament to decide whether to approve any changes to the law.

Code of Practice
We are a signatory to the Government's Code of Practice on Consultation and carry out our consultations in accordance with the Code criteria (set out on the next page).

Freedom of information
We will treat all responses as public documents in accordance with the Freedom of Information Act and we may attribute comments and include a list of all respondents' names in any final report we publish. If you wish to submit a confidential response, you should contact us before sending the response. PLEASE NOTE – We will disregard automatic confidentiality statements generated by an IT system.

Availability of this consultation paper
You can view/download it free of charge on our website at: **http://www.lawcom.gov.uk/docs/cp197.pdf**.

CODE OF PRACTICE ON CONSULTATION

○ **THE SEVEN CONSULTATION CRITERIA**

Criterion 1:   When to consult

Formal consultation should take place at a stage when there is scope to influence the policy outcome.

Criterion 2:   Duration of consultation exercise

Consultations should normally last for at least 12 weeks with consideration given to longer timescales where feasible and sensible

Criterion 3:   Clarity and scope of impact

Consultation documents should be clear about the consultation process, what is being proposed, the scope to influence and the expected costs and benefits of the proposals.

Criterion 4:   Accessibility of consultation exercises

Consultation exercises should be designed to be accessible to, and clearly targeted at, those people the exercise is intended to reach.

Criterion 5:   The burden of consultation

Keeping the burden of consultation to a minimum is essential if consultations are to be effective and if consultees' buy-in to the process is to be obtained.

Criterion 6:   Responsiveness of consultation exercises

Consultation responses should be analysed carefully and clear feedback should be provided to participants following the consultation.

Criterion 7:   Capacity to consult

Officials running consultations should seek guidance in how to run an effective consultation exercise and share what they have learned from the experience.

○ **CONSULTATION CO-ORDINATOR**

The Law Commission's Consultation Co-ordinator is Phil Hodgson.

○ You are invited to send comments to the Consultation Co-ordinator about the extent to which the criteria have been observed and any ways of improving the consultation process.

○ **Contact:**   Phil Hodgson, Consultation Co-ordinator, Law Commission, Steel House, 11 Tothill Street, London SW1H 9LJ – Email: phil.hodgson@lawcommission.gsi.gov.uk

Full details of the Government's Code of Practice on Consultation are available on the BIS website at http://www.bis.gov.uk/policies/better-regulation/consultation-guidance.

THE LAW COMMISSION

UNFITNESS TO PLEAD

CONTENTS

PART 1
INTRODUCTION

1.1 In this consultation paper ("CP") we discuss the law on unfitness to plead or to be tried in criminal proceedings. The law on unfitness to plead is concerned with whether or not an accused is able to stand trial and, if not, the procedure that should be used to deal with that accused. Where the issue of unfitness to plead arises, the court does not consider the accused's guilt, but rather two distinct issues. First, there is the question of whether the accused is "under a disability" which renders it inappropriate for him or her to be tried. This can be due to a disability caused by a physical impairment or a mental disorder. An example would be an accused who as a result of very low intellectual ability is unable to follow the process of his or her trial. Secondly, if the court finds that the accused is under such a disability, the jury must determine whether or not the accused did the act or made the omission charged.

1.2 In this CP, our analysis of the modern law on unfitness to plead is set within the broader context of the law relating to vulnerable defendants,[1] the Mental Health Act 1983 as amended by the Mental Health Act 2007, and the Mental Capacity Act 2005.

1.3 We think that this is necessary because, as a cursory look at the history shows, those aspects of law that govern criminal process and mental health have been shaped in a piecemeal way to address specific difficulties.[2] One consequence of this is that the laws are disparate and do not take sufficient account of each other. Previous reforms to the law on unfitness to plead have been made without sufficient consideration of the long term implications of the way in which they will work across the spectrum of criminal law, and without consideration of commensurate reforms of the test for establishing unfitness to plead.[3] Any further reform of the law in this area should be coherent.

THE LAW GOVERNING THE PRESENT PROCEDURE

1.4 The present procedure for determining whether an accused person is unfit to plead is governed by sections 4 and 4A of the Criminal Procedure (Insanity) Act 1964 ("the 1964 Act"), as amended by the Criminal Procedure (Insanity and Unfitness to Plead) Act 1991 ("the 1991 Act") and the Domestic Violence, Crime and Victims Act 2004.

---

[1] Now summarised in Practice Direction (Criminal Proceedings: Consolidation), para III.30, as inserted by Practice Direction (Criminal Proceedings: Further Directions) [2007] 1 WLR 1790.

[2] The Criminal Procedure (Insanity and Unfitness to Plead) Act 1991 addressed some of the problems highlighted in the Report of the Committee on Mentally Abnormal Offenders (1975) Cmnd 6244. For example, the s 4A procedure was introduced to allow for an examination of the facts of the case where an accused was found to be unfit to plead: see paras 2.25 to 2.27 below. A further example of piecemeal reform are the amendments made in the Domestic Violence, Crime and Victims Act 2004, which were intended to address the difficulties that had arisen in relation to article 5 of the European Convention on Human Rights: see paras 2.32 to 2.41 below.

[3] The legal test for establishing unfitness to plead is known as the *Pritchard* test. As we explain in Part 2 below, the test is outdated and inconsistent with modern psychiatry.

1.5   The procedure under the 1964 Act applies to trial on indictment only.[4] We explain this procedure in detail in Part 2 of this CP but, in brief, section 4 is concerned with an assessment of the accused's mental or physical state to determine whether he or she is "under a disability" which prevents him or her from being tried (in other words, is unfit to plead). This is often referred to as the "trial of the issue". If it is determined that the accused is under such a disability, then section 4A provides for a hearing as to the facts of the case. This hearing is aimed at ascertaining whether or not the accused "did the act or made the omission" with which he or she is charged. This is often referred to as the "trial of the facts" or the "section 4A hearing". In this CP we refer to it as the "section 4A hearing".

1.6   Section 4 of the 1964 Act provides:

    (1)   This section applies where on the trial of a person the question arises (at the instance of the defence or otherwise) whether the accused is under a disability, that is to say, under any disability such that apart from this Act it would constitute a bar to his being tried.

    (2)   If, having regard to the nature of the supposed disability, the court are of opinion that it is expedient to do so and in the interests of the accused, they may postpone consideration of the question of fitness to be tried until any time up to the opening of the case for the defence.

    (3)   If, before the question of fitness to be tried falls to be determined, the jury return a verdict of acquittal on the count or each of the counts on which the accused is being tried, that question shall not be determined.

    (4)   Subject to subsections (2) and (3) above, the question of fitness to be tried shall be determined as soon as it arises.

    (5)   The question of fitness to be tried shall be determined by the court without a jury.

    (6)   The court shall not make a determination under subsection (5) above except on the written or oral evidence of two or more registered medical practitioners at least one of whom is duly approved.

1.7   Section 4A provides:

    (1)   This section applies where in accordance with section 4(5) [of the 1964 Act] it is determined by a court that the accused is under a disability.

    (2)   The trial shall not proceed or further proceed but it shall be determined by a jury –

        (a)   on the evidence (if any) already given in the trial; and

---

[4]   This means that it applies only to proceedings in the Crown Court. In summary proceedings the law is governed by s 37(3) of the Mental Health Act 1983 which permits the magistrates' court to impose a hospital order or a guardianship order in certain circumstances in the absence of a trial and by s 11(1) of the Powers of Criminal Courts (Sentencing) Act 2000. We discuss the law in relation to summary proceedings in Part 8 below.

> (b)   on such evidence as may be adduced or further adduced by the prosecution, or adduced by a person appointed by the court under this section to put the case for the defence,
>
> whether they are satisfied, as respects the count or each of the counts on which the accused was to be or was being tried, that he did the act or made the omission charged against him as the offence.
>
> (3)   If as respects that count or any of those counts the jury are satisfied as mentioned in subsection (2) above, they shall make a finding that the accused did the act or made the omission charged against him.
>
> (4)   If as respects that count or any of those counts the jury are not so satisfied, they shall return a verdict of acquittal as if on the count in question the trial had proceeded to a conclusion.
>
> (5)   Where the question of disability was determined after arraignment of the accused, the determination under subsection (2) is to be made by the jury by whom he was being tried.

1.8   There is no statutory provision for the legal test of whether or not an accused person is unfit to plead. The test itself, known as the *Pritchard* test, is covered by the common law.[5] We discuss the *Pritchard* test in detail at paragraphs 2.43 onwards below. In short, the *Pritchard* test requires that the accused must be able to: plead to the indictment; understand the course of the proceedings; instruct a lawyer; challenge a juror; and understand the evidence.[6] If the accused is unable to do any one of these five things then he or she is unfit to plead.

THE THINKING BEHIND THE CURRENT UNFITNESS TO PLEAD PROCEDURE

1.9   It is important to consider the rationale for or thinking behind the current law which protects an unfit accused from being tried. Professor R A Duff has argued that the reason why an unfit accused should not be tried is that the trial would be a "travesty: we would be attempting or pretending to treat as a rational agent, answerable for his actions, someone who *cannot* answer for them".[7] Professor Duff has argued that the capacity of the "rational agent" includes the ability "to understand the moral dimensions of the law and his own actions". Whereas it has been pointed out rather more pragmatically by Professor R D Mackay that "this may be to go too far, for there are many defendants who have warped standards of morality but who are clearly fit to plead",[8] there remains a great deal of sense in Professor Duff's proposition. If because of his or her mental disorder a person lacks the mental capacity to link his or her alleged criminal behaviour with his or her trial and (if convicted) punishment then little is achieved by trying him or her according to ordinary principles. This is because:

---

[5]   The legal test for unfitness to plead is the *Pritchard* test: see paras 2.43 to 2.87 below.

[6]   RD Mackay, *Mental Condition Defences in the Criminal Law* (1995) p 224.

[7]   RA Duff, *Trials and Punishments* (1986) p 119.

[8]   RD Mackay, *Mental Condition Defences in the Criminal Law* (1995) p 217.

The proper persuasive purpose of a conviction ... is not to make criminal conduct imprudent, but to bring home to the offender and to others the wrongness of his conduct, by condemning it; like moral blame, a conviction should appeal to an offender's moral understanding, not merely to his self-interest.[9]

1.10   There are several reasons why those who are unfit to plead should not be tried. First, it is not seemly and cannot reflect well on any civilised legal system to force someone who has little understanding of the trial process to be subjected to it. The trial process itself is demonstrative of our respect for the law because, as Professor Duff argues:

> In trying alleged offenders we show that we take seriously the question of whether they have broken the law; in convicting and condemning proven offenders we show that we care for the law's demands as being both justified and important, and are not prepared to let breaches of these demands go unnoticed and uncondemned. We do this not simply in order to induce or reinforce a proper regard for and obedience to the law in ourselves or others; but because our concern for the law and its purposes itself requires us to take notice of illegality, just as our regard for the demands of morality requires us to take notice of immorality. In providing authoritative determinations of guilt and innocence – authoritative condemnations of the guilty and acquittals of the innocent – a system of criminal trials gives formal expression to our regard for the law.[10]

1.11   That being so, it would be an abuse of the process of the law to subject someone to a trial when he or she is unable to play any real part in that trial. This goes further than merely requiring that a person understands the trial process; it is concerned with whether or not he or she can meaningfully engage in the trial. We return to the issue of participation later in this CP, and it lies at the heart of the provisional proposals that we make for reform.

1.12   Secondly, if unfit accused are subject to trial then there is a very obvious danger of convicting those who might be innocent because they may not have the ability to rebut the allegations against them.

1.13   The procedure under the current law ensures that an accused who lacks understanding of the trial process is not unfairly subjected to a trial which he or she cannot follow. It also provides an opportunity for the case to be brought to a conclusion. This has many benefits. An accused has the opportunity of being acquitted if he or she is found not to have done the act charged. If the accused is found to have done the act or made the omission there is an opportunity for him or her to begin receiving appropriate treatment. From the witnesses' perspective matters are not left in abeyance: witnesses are able to give their evidence.

1.14   That is not to say however that the current procedure does not have limitations. Both limbs of the present process may be deficient. In relation to the issue of fitness, it is unclear to what extent the present test of unfitness directly attacks

---

[9]   RA Duff, *Trials and Punishments* (1986) p 125.

[10]   Above, p 126.

the mischief at which it is aimed. There is the possibility that some accused who, having regard to their medical and or mental condition, ought not to be tried will nevertheless pass the test and be subjected to a trial. Equally, it may be that some accused are classified as unfit and subjected to a process that is inappropriate having regard to their condition. For example, the process forces those who are classified as unfit and who have some prospect of becoming fit[11] into a trial of the facts when it may be more appropriate for such an individual to have a full trial once they are fit. In relation to the trial of the facts, there is also an underlying concern. This process is applied to someone who is unfit to be tried. Logically, it might be argued that once someone has been classified as unfit to be tried, the appropriate question should be what to do with that person until they are fit to be tried. That may involve a much broader question as to whether they pose a potential danger to the public if released pending an improvement of their condition such that they can be tried. The current law circumvents this question by focusing on the issue of whether the accused has done the act or made the omission charged. That is an imperfect guide as to whether he or she is dangerous or safe until he or she is tried.

THE SCOPE OF THIS CONSULTATION PAPER

1.15   This CP addresses the law on unfitness to plead and makes proposals for reforming the law in a way which is consistent with modern psychiatric thinking and with the modern trial process. We do not address the issue of insanity[12] save for the way in which it is likely to impact on the question of fitness.[13]

The difference between unfitness to plead and insanity

1.16   Unfitness to plead differs from insanity in that it is concerned with the question of an accused's mental state at the time of his or her trial and not at the time of the offence. There are two fundamental differences. First, in relation to procedure, if a person is unfit to plead, he or she cannot be tried in the same way as a person who is fit. An unfit accused is therefore subject to a section 4A hearing after which he or she can either be acquitted or found to have done the act or made the omission charged. A person who pleads insanity is subjected to the normal criminal trial process. Secondly, in terms of outcome, an unfitness hearing does not lead to a verdict of guilty. A trial in which a plea of insanity is raised, on the other hand offers the prospect of a special verdict: not guilty by reason of insanity.[14]

TERMINOLOGY

1.17   When we refer in this CP to the present law, we use the term "unfitness to plead". For an accused to be unfit to plead under the present law there must be a finding

---

[11]   Some people may never be fit to be tried because of the nature of their disability.

[12]   Our intention is that insanity will be addressed by the Law Commission in a separate paper.

[13]   There is an obvious overlap in circumstances where a mental disorder which an accused has at the time of his or her hearing may have pre existed at the time of the commission of the offence. We address this matter in more detail in the course of our discussion as to the possibilities for reform of the present s 4A hearing in Part 6 below.

[14]   It is discharged on the balance of probabilities: see s 2(1) of the Trial of Lunatics Act 1883.

that an accused is "under a disability" such that it would constitute a bar to trial.[15] We refer to an accused under such a disability as being "unfit to plead".[16]

1.18   However, the language of the current law is somewhat misleading. "Unfitness to plead" is not a particularly apt description of the criteria used (referred to as the "*Pritchard* criteria") to determine whether an accused person is unfit to plead because, as will be seen below, the ability to enter a plea is only one aspect of the legal test.[17] In our view, "unfitness to plead" describes a "global" state of competence[18] which involves more than the accused's ability to enter a plea. The term "unfitness to plead" conflates the issues of the accused's ability to enter a plea to the charge and his or her ability to stand trial.[19]

1.19   In relation to our proposals, we have considered whether use of the terms "unfit for trial" or "unfit to participate in a trial" would represent an improvement of nomenclature but we have concluded that they would also be unsatisfactory. These terms do not, we believe, adequately describe the nature of inquiry into an accused's capacity to be tried. Under article 6, the European Convention on Human Rights[20] jurisprudence requires the accused to be capable of taking an active role as opposed to having merely a passive comprehension of the proceedings.[21] In practice, in order for participation to be meaningful the accused would have to be capable of making certain decisions in relation to his or her trial. Accordingly, in this CP we propose that the current test for unfitness to plead should be replaced by a test which assesses what we refer to as the "decision-making capacity" of the accused.[22] Thus instead of referring to an accused as "unfit to plead", he or she would be said to "lack decision-making capacity". In essence, decision-making capacity is informed by the principle of effective participation and requires the ability to have an active as opposed to a passive

[15]   See s 4 of the 1964 Act.

[16]   The headnote to s 4 of the 1964 Act provides "Finding of unfitness to plead".

[17]   See para 2.46 below.

[18]   "Global" is a technical term which reflects the fact that unfitness to plead does not relate to one specific task that the accused must be capable of doing (namely, to enter a plea). Instead it relates to a more general ability to do a range of tasks. For a discussion of the difference between "decision-relative" and "global" concepts of competence, see AE Buchanan, *Deciding for Others* (1989) pp 18 to 23.

[19]   See the recent Court of Appeal decision in *Ghulam* [2009] EWCA Crim 2285, [2010] 1 WLR 891 where the court appeared to use the terms "fit to plead" and "fit to be tried" interchangeably.

[20]   Article 6 establishes that everyone is entitled to "a fair and public hearing within a reasonable time and by an independent and impartial tribunal established by law." It also establishes that everyone charged with a criminal offence is to be presumed innocent until proven guilty and that everyone charged with a criminal offence has minimum rights including, (a) to be informed promptly and in detail of the nature and cause of the accusation, in a language which he or she understands, (b) to have adequate time and facilities to prepare a defence, (c) to be able to defend him or herself or, to be given free assistance if the individual has insufficient means of paying for assistance him or herself, (d) to examine or have examined witnesses, and (e) to have the assistance of an interpreter where necessary.

[21]   The jurisprudence on effective participation is discussed further at paras 2.89 to 2.102 below.

[22]   By "decision-making capacity" we mean the ability of the accused to make the range of decisions that will be required in the trial. This test is discussed in greater detail in Part 3 below.

involvement in the trial. The focus is on the decision-making process as opposed to the (often superficial) quality of the actual decision itself.[23]

1.20 We refer to case law in the USA and to the work of various commentators on the US material (both legal and psychiatric). When we do this we use the American terminology – "competence" for trial.

1.21 As we explain further in Part 2, a person who is found unfit to plead is not subjected to a trial. Rather he or she undergoes a hearing under section 4A which is intended to ascertain whether or not he or she has done the act or made the omission charged (in other words, committed the conduct element of the offence in question). When we refer to a section 4A hearing we have chosen to use the term "the accused". We only refer to a person as a "defendant" when we refer to an accused in the context of a trial or when (under our proposals) he or she has been found to have decision-making capacity with the assistance of special measures if necessary.

STRUCTURE OF THIS CONSULTATION PAPER

1.22 In Part 2 of this CP we discuss the history of the law on unfitness to plead, and the statutory developments over the last 45 years which have resulted in the procedure outlined in paragraphs 1.6 to 1.7 above.

1.23 As we shall see in Part 2, although the procedure for determining unfitness to plead is covered by statute, the statute does not address the legal test for unfitness to plead. The legal test – known as the *Pritchard* test – was developed through case law, and we consider this case law in Part 2. We go on to provide a detailed analysis of the problems with the current legal test and discuss what we believe to be its shortcomings. We also look at the concepts of capacity and participation, and consider in detail the jurisprudence on effective participation which has developed as a result of the need for the courts to comply with article 6 of the European Convention on Human Rights. Finally we consider how the concept of participation has influenced the current law relating to vulnerable defendants.

1.24 In Part 3 we propose that the common law *Pritchard* test should be replaced. We suggest that there should be a new legal test for what is presently referred to as unfitness to plead. We explain why we think that the new test should be based on the decision-making capacity of the accused. This test would focus on the decision-making abilities of the accused, and assess these abilities in the context of the requirements of a trial. We believe that the test should be informed by the concept of effective participation in the trial. This is because in our view it is not possible for a defendant to have any meaningful participation in his or her trial unless he or she can make relevant decisions. In Part 3 we give examples of how the decision-making capacity test would apply and consider the relevance of the civil test for capacity under the Mental Capacity Act 2005. We also explore the way in which a capacity based test could operate in criminal proceedings.

---

[23] See further the discussion of whether or not it should be required that any decision is rational at paras 3.48 to 3.57 below.

1.25   In Part 4 we look closely at the law on special measures for vulnerable defendants in criminal trials. We explain why we support the continued development and application of special measures. We propose that the availability of special measures should form part of the new test of decision-making capacity which we have provisionally proposed in Part 3.

1.26   In Part 5 we look at the interface between law and psychiatry and, in particular, the need for psychiatric input in determination of the issue. We explain the benefit of having a standardised psychiatric test which would assist in the determination of whether or not a person is unfit to plead (or under our proposals, lacks decision-making capacity). We also consider the current requirements relating to the medical evidence which is necessary for a finding of unfitness to plead to be made, and propose that an equivalent requirement should be included in our reformed process.

1.27   In Part 6 we discuss the problems with the present section 4A hearing for the determination of the facts of the charge once a person has been found by the court to be unfit to plead. In essence, the main problem is that it is only possible to assess the conduct element of the offence with which the accused is charged. We set out the reasons why we think that this procedure is problematic and make proposals for its reform.

1.28   In Part 7 we look at a range of miscellaneous issues, such as the court's powers of disposal pursuant to a finding that the accused has done the act or made the omission charged; an area which we feel is covered satisfactorily by the present law. We also look at the Secretary of State's power to remit an accused who has been found to have done the act and subjected to a hospital order with a restriction order to court for trial. We consider the question of whether or not it is right to try defendants in a criminal trial and hear the case against an unfit accused at the same time and in the course of the same proceedings. We also address the fact that at present, where a finding under section 4A is quashed, the Court of Appeal does not have any power to remit an unfit accused for a re-hearing other than a retrial.

1.29   Finally in Part 8, we look at how issues of decision-making capacity are addressed in the adult magistrates' court and the youth court.

1.30   In Appendix A we provide a summary of mental health law which explains the changes made to the Mental Health Act 1983 by the Mental Health Act 2007.

1.31   In Appendix B we provide a recent case study[24] for a section 4A hearing. This case study has been referred to in Part 6 because it is illustrative of some of the issues which can arise in the context of the section 4A hearing.

1.32   In Appendix C we provide the details of some research by Professor Mackay. Professor Mackay has already carried out empirical research in relation to unfitness to plead and we asked him to carry this work forward for the purposes of this project. We draw on Professor Mackay's research in Parts 5, 6 and 7 of this CP.

---

[24] *Patrick Sureda* Central Criminal Court 2008. We are grateful to His Honour Judge Jeremy Roberts QC for all his help.

1.33 In Appendix D we provide an impact assessment of our provisional proposals for the reform of the law on unfitness to plead.

PROVISIONAL PROPOSALS IN THIS CONSULTATION PAPER

1.34 We have made the following provisional proposals on which we wish to consult:

> **Provisional Proposal 1: The current *Pritchard* test should be replaced and there should be a new legal test which assesses whether the accused has decision-making capacity for trial. This test should take into account all the requirements for meaningful participation in the criminal proceedings . (Paragraph 3.41)**
>
> **Provisional Proposal 2: A new decision-making capacity test should not require that any decision the accused makes must be rational or wise. (Paragraph 3.57)**
>
> **Provisional Proposal 3: The legal test should be a revised single test[25] which assesses the decision-making capacity of the accused by reference to the entire spectrum of trial decisions he or she might be required to make. Under this test an accused would be found to have or to lack decision-making capacity for the criminal proceedings. (Paragraph 3.99)**
>
> **Provisional Proposal 4: In determining the defendant's decision-making capacity, it would be incumbent on the judge to take account of the complexity of the particular proceedings and gravity of the outcome. In particular the judge should take account of how important any disability is likely to be in the context of the decision the accused must make in the context of the trial which the accused faces. (Paragraph 3.101)**
>
> **Provisional Proposal 5: Decision-making capacity should be assessed with a view to ascertaining whether an accused could undergo a trial or plead guilty with the assistance of special measures and where any other reasonable adjustments have been made. (Paragraph 4.27)**
>
> **Provisional Proposal 6: Where a defendant who is subject to a trial has a mental disorder or other impairment and wishes to give evidence then expert evidence on the general effect of that mental disorder or impairment should be admissible. (Paragraph 4.31)**
>
> **Provisional Proposal 7: A defined psychiatric test to assess decision-making capacity should be developed and this should accompany the legal test as to decision-making capacity. (Paragraph 5.17)**

---

[25] As we explain further in Part 3, criticism has focused in part on the fact that the present test is a "unitary construct", which takes into account fitness for plea and participation and which means that there would be a single assessment of the accused's decision-making capacity, normally at the outset of the proceedings.

Provisional Proposal 8: The present section 4A hearing should be replaced with a procedure whereby the prosecution is obliged to prove that the accused did the act or made the omission charged and that there are no grounds for an acquittal. (Paragraph 6.140)

Provisional Proposal 9: If the accused is acquitted provision should be made for a judge to hold a further hearing to determine whether or not the acquittal is because of mental disorder existing at the time of the offence. (Paragraph 6.140)

Provisional Proposal 10: The further hearing should be held at the discretion of the judge on the application of any party or the representative of any party to the proceedings. (Paragraph 6.152)

Provisional Proposal 11: The special verdict should be determined by the jury on such evidence as has been heard or on any further evidence as is called. (Paragraph 6.152)

Provisional Proposal 12: Where the Secretary of State has referred a case back to court pursuant to the accused being detained under a hospital order with a section 41 restriction order and it thereafter becomes clear beyond doubt (and medical evidence confirms) that the accused is still unfit to plead,[26] the court should be able to reverse the decision to remit the case. (Paragraph 7.21)

Provisional Proposal 13: In the event of a referral back to court by the Secretary of State and where the accused is found to be unfit to plead,[27] there should not be any need to have a further hearing on the issue of whether the accused did the act. This is subject to the proviso that the court considers it to be in the interests of justice.[28] (Paragraph 7.21)

Provisional Proposal 14: In circumstances where a finding under section 4A is quashed and there has been no challenge to a finding in relation to section 4 (that the accused is under a disability) there should be a power for the Court of Appeal in appropriate circumstances to order a re-hearing under section 4A. (Paragraph 7.59)

1.35   In addition to the above proposals, we also ask the following questions:

---

[26] Or lacks decision-making capacity under our proposed legal test.

[27] Or lacks decision-making capacity.

[28] We assume that this would involve consent on the part of the representative of the accused.

Question 1: Do consultees agree that we should aim to construct a scheme which allows courts to operate a continuum whereby those accused who do not have decision-making capacity will be subject to the section 4A hearing[29] and those defendants with decision-making capacity should be subject to a trial with or without special measures depending on the level of assistance which they need? (Paragraph 4.27)

Question 2: Can consultees think of other changes to evidence or procedure which would render participation in the trial process more effective for defendants who have decision-making capacity but due to a mental disorder or other impairment require additional assistance to participate? (Paragraph 4.31)

Question 3: Do consultees agree that we have correctly identified the options for reform in relation to the section 4A hearing? If not, what other options for reform would consultees propose? (Paragraph 6.153)

Question 4: If consultees do not agree that option 5 is the best option for reform, would they agree with any other option? (Paragraph 6.153)

Question 5: Should a jury be able to find that an unfit accused has done the act and that there are no grounds for acquittal in relation to an act other than that specifically charged? (Paragraph 6.159)

Question 6: Are there circumstances in which an accused person who is found to have done the act and in respect of whom there are no grounds for an acquittal should be able to request remission for trial? (Paragraph 7.26)

Question 7: Should an accused who is found to be unfit to plead (or to lack decision-making capacity) be subject to the section 4A hearing in the same proceedings as co-defendants who are being tried? (Paragraph 7.44)

Question 8: Do consultees think that the capacity based test which we have proposed for trial on indictment should apply equally to proceedings which are triable summarily? (Paragraph 8.37)

Question 9: Do consultees think that if an accused lacks decision-making capacity there should be a mandatory fact-finding procedure in the magistrates' court? (Paragraph 8.37)

---

[29] As it exists at present (see para 1.7 above and paras 2.25 to 2.26 below) or as amended under our proposals (see Part 6 below).

Question 10: If consultees think that there should be a mandatory fact-finding procedure, do they think it should be limited to consideration of the external elements of the offence or should it mirror our provisional proposals 8 and 9? (Paragraph 8.37)

Question 11: Do the matters raised in questions 8, 9 and 10 merit equal consideration in relation to the procedure in the youth courts? (Paragraph 8.68)

Question 12: How far if at all, does the age of criminal responsibility factor into the issue of decision-making capacity in youth trials? (Paragraph 8.69)

ACKNOWLEDGEMENTS

1.36   We would like to record our thanks to a number of individuals who have given us invaluable assistance in our work on this project to date. In particular we have had the benefit of an expert advisory group. They are: the Right Honourable Lord Justice Hughes, His Honour Judge Jeremy Roberts QC, Gillian Harrison (Better Trials Unit) and Nicola Padfield (Fitzwilliam College, Cambridge).

1.37   We are also grateful to the following members of our working party who have provided us with assistance: Professor Ronnie Mackay (De Montford University, Leicester), Toby Long (barrister), Professor Don Grubin (Newcastle University), Dr Tim Exworthy (Consultant Forensic Psychiatrist), Mark Ashford (solicitor), Professor Michael Farrell (Institute of Psychiatry), Dr Ian Hall (Consultant Psychiatrist), Dr Rob Poole (Honorary General Adult Psychiatrist), Lucy Scott-Moncrieff (solicitor) and Peter Wilcock (barrister).

1.38   We would also like to thank Elizabeth Moody (PPO), Nigel Shackleford (NOMS), Clare Connelly (University of Glasgow), Christine Magill (CPS), Susan Sutherland (Scottish Law Commission) and Nan Mousley (solicitor) for their assistance.

1.39   We are also grateful to Dr Nigel Blackwood (Honorary Consultant Forensic Psychiatrist), Dr Tim Rogers (Consultant Forensic Psychiatrist), Professor Jill Peay (LSE), Dr Michael Watts (UCL), Rebecca Brewer (Institute of Psychiatry) and all other delegates who attended the Law Commission conference on 19 March 2009.

PART 2
THE EXISTING LAW

INTRODUCTION

2.1 In this Part we discuss the existing law. We start with the history of the law on fitness to plead to show that the process has not developed in a coherent way. This is in part because the statutory procedure and the legal test for unfitness to plead have developed separately. We will first look at the statutory procedure which has undergone significant developments since 1964. We then turn our attention to the legal test which has remained unchanged since the early to mid-nineteenth century. Later in this Part, we go on to discuss the right of effective participation under article 6 of the European Convention on Human Rights, which has developed outside the context of unfitness to plead.

THE HISTORY OF THE LAW ON UNFITNESS TO PLEAD

2.2 For many years the English legal system did little more than pay lip service to the need for a procedure for processing those accused who were unfit to plead. The situation began to change in the nineteenth century, during which time the emphasis was on developing criteria to ascertain whether or not an accused was unfit. Thereafter much of the focus has been on the unfairness of an inflexible disposal procedure for those accused found unfit to plead.

2.3 Until the time of Hale,[1] it appears that the rationale behind establishing whether or not an accused was unfit to plead to the indictment was rooted in the possibility of the Crown being able to seize his or her property in the event of a conviction[2] as opposed to any concept of the seemliness of the trial of a person who was unable to defend him or herself properly. One of the most notable aspects of what has been described by Nigel Walker as a "reverence for the ritual of law"[3] was the necessity of being able to distinguish whether an accused was mute by malice or mute by visitation of God. If an accused was found to be mute by malice, he or she was subjected to the *peine forte et dure*,[4] a process which amounted to being confined in a narrow cell, starved and gradually crushed under an increasing weight until such time as he or she either reconsidered the decision not to enter a plea or died.[5]

---

[1] Sir Matthew Hale (1609-1676). Hale's *Pleas of the Crown* was first published in 1736.

[2] Which was the real advantage in so far as the Crown was concerned.

[3] By which Walker means the importance that was attributed to basic procedure such as the entering of a plea by an accused.

[4] Which essentially means "under the pain of death".

[5] N Walker, *Crime and Insanity in England and Wales* (1968) p 220.

2.4 By the time Hale[6] was writing, a trial judge could exercise his discretion to empanel a jury to decide whether or not an accused was unfit to plead and decide on the veracity of his or her condition.[7]

> If a man in his sound memory commits a capital offence, and before his arraignment, he becomes mad, he ought not by law to be arraigned during such his phrenzy, but be remitted to prison until that incapacity be removed; the reason is, because he cannot advisedly plead to the indictment … . But because there may be great fraud in this matter … the judge before such respite of trial … may do well to impanel a jury to enquire *ex officio* touching such insanity, and whether it be real or counterfeit.[8]

2.5 As Walker has pointed out however, it was not "until the middle of the eighteenth century that the insane prisoner had any real chance of being found unfit for trial".[9] To support this proposition, Walker cites Lord Chief Justice Keynon, "No man shall be called upon to make his defence at a time when his mind is in that situation as not to appear capable of so doing".[10]

STATUTORY DEVELOPMENTS

2.6 Statutory provision for determining the question of whether an accused was unfit to plead was introduced by section 2 of the Criminal Lunatics Act 1800 which provided:

> if any person indicted for any offence shall be insane, and shall upon arraignment, be found so to be by a jury lawfully impanelled for that purpose, so that such a person cannot be tried upon such indictment, or if upon the trial of any such person so indicted such person shall appear to the jury charged with such indictment to be insane, it shall be lawful for the court before whom any such person shall be brought to be arraigned or tried as aforesaid to direct such finding to be recorded, and thereupon to order such person to be kept in strict custody until his Majesty's pleasure shall be known.

In 1963, the Criminal Law Revision Committee ("the CLRC") was asked by the Home Secretary to consider what if any provision should be made for revision to the Criminal Lunatics Act 1800.[11]

---

[6] Hale, *Pleas of the Crown* 1, cited in N Walker, *Crime and Insanity in England and Wales* (1968) p 220.

[7] In capital cases at least.

[8] Hale, *Pleas of the Crown* 1, cited in N Walker, *Crime and Insanity in England and Wales* (1968) p 221.

[9] N Walker, *Crime and Insanity in England and Wales* (1968) p 222.

[10] Proceedings in the case of John Frith, for High Treason at Justice Hall in the Old Bailey on Saturday, April 17 (1790): see Howell's *State Trials*, Vol 22 (1783-1794), cols 307, col 318.

[11] Criminal Law Revision Committee Third Report: Criminal Procedure (Insanity) (1963) Cmnd 2149, para 2.

The Criminal Procedure (Insanity) Act 1964

2.7 The review by the CLRC was prompted by a number of procedural uncertainties,[12] and by the evolving understanding of mental disorder. The CLRC found that the criteria for determining unfitness to plead were satisfactory,[13] as was the use of the jury to determine the issue.[14] The CLRC's primary recommendations concerned provision for a right of appeal against a finding of unfitness,[15] and for a procedure under which the latest stage at which unfitness could be raised was the opening of the case for the defence.[16]

2.8 The CLRC proposed that the right to appeal should apply to defendants found unfit to plead later than on arraignment.[17] An appeal would be allowed on the ground that, even though the finding of unfitness may have been properly reached, the defendant ought to have been acquitted before the issue was considered because there was no case to answer. In other words, there was insufficient evidence on which a properly directed and reasonable jury could convict. The result of a successful appeal would be that the appellant would be tried for the offence[18] unless the Court of Appeal considered that he or she should have been acquitted before the issue arose and therefore returned a verdict of not guilty.[19]

2.9 Noting that practice varied regarding when the issue of unfitness should be determined, the CLRC concluded that allowing it to be left until the opening of the case for the defence was the best way to allow a possibility of acquittal on the facts. It would then be open to the court to direct an acquittal, or to the trial jury to stop the case at "any appropriate time",[20] in other words at any time after the close of the prosecution case.[21]

---

[12] As late as 1958 there still seemed to be uncertainty for example about where the burden of proof in unfitness to plead hearings should lie: see S Prevezer, "Fitness to plead and the Criminal Lunatics Act 1800" [1958] *Criminal Law Review* 144, 150. In *Podola* [1960] 1 QB 325, it had been held that if the issue was raised by the defence the court had to be satisfied as to that issue on the balance of probabilities. It was also not until *Podola* was decided that it became clear that there was a right of appeal from unfitness to plead hearings.

[13] We discuss these criteria (known as the *Pritchard* criteria) at paras 2.44 to 2.87 below.

[14] Criminal Law Revision Committee Third Report: Criminal Procedure (Insanity) (1963) Cmnd 2149, paras 14 to 15.

[15] Above, para 29.

[16] Above, para 28.

[17] Arraignment being when the defendant is asked to enter his or her plea. Arraignment is generally considered to be the start of the trial: see s 30 of the Criminal Procedure and Investigations Act 1996.

[18] In which case the Court of Appeal would record a verdict of acquittal: see s 4(6)(b) of the 1964 Act as originally enacted.

[19] Criminal Law Revision Committee Third Report: Criminal Procedure (Insanity) (1963) Cmnd 2149, para 29.

[20] Above, para 28.

[21] It has long been the case that a jury may acquit but cannot convict any time after the close of the prosecution case and before retiring to consider the verdict.

2.10   The CLRC further recommended that it should be possible for the issue of unfitness to plead to be raised by "the prosecution or the defence, by the court or by a [third party] … because we regard it as right that any available information on such an important question … should be before the court".[22]

2.11   The CLRC's Third Report was accepted and implemented in the 1964 Act with virtually no dissent.

2.12   Section 4 of the 1964 Act introduced a procedure for a finding of unfitness to plead together with a right of appeal against a finding of unfitness. Section 4 of the 1964 Act is set out at paragraph 1.6 above.

2.13   Subsections 4(2) and 4(3) gave effect to the recommendations of the CLRC discussed at paragraphs 2.8 to 2.9 above. It was therefore possible for the accused to avoid a finding of unfitness to plead if the jury returned a verdict of acquittal at the close of the prosecution case, because they were directed to do so on the basis that there was insufficient evidence for a properly directed jury to convict.[23] This was significant because it provided an opportunity for the accused to avoid the outcome of a disposal under section 5.

2.14   Section 5 of the 1964 Act provided that, where a finding was made that the accused was unfit to plead, the court was compelled to order indefinite hospitalisation. The 1964 Act did not provide for a hearing as to the facts of the offence with which the accused was charged in the event of him or her being found unfit to plead. In effect, this meant that the accused was subject to detention without proof that he or she had committed the offence charged. The CLRC observed:

> The question whether to recommend any, and if so what, provision on the subject has taken up by far the greatest part of our time, and we have not been able to reach a unanimous conclusion.[24]

The Butler Report[25]

2.15   Notwithstanding the 1964 Act reforms, a number of problems remained. Despite the possibility of delaying determination of the issue until the start of the case for the defence, the opportunity to examine the facts was still limited to effectively putting the prosecution to proof before the close of the prosecution case. This limitation on considering the facts was of particular concern given that a hospital order was mandatory following a finding of unfitness to plead.[26]

---

[22]   Criminal Law Revision Committee Third Report: Criminal Procedure (Insanity) (1963) Cmnd 2149, para 15.

[23]   *Galbraith* [1981] 2 All ER 1060.

[24]   Criminal Law Revision Committee Third Report: Criminal Procedure (Insanity) (1963) Cmnd 2149, para 18.

[25]   Report of the Committee on Mentally Abnormal Offenders (1975) Cmnd 6244.

[26]   See para 2.14 above.

2.16   The next review of the law regarding unfit accused, the Report of the Committee on Mentally Abnormal Offenders ("the Butler Report") was published in 1975. The Butler Report noted several problems with the existing procedure and made a number of provisional proposals for change.

2.17   As we indicated in paragraph 2.15 above, one of the main problems with the law as it stood was the concern that there was still no procedure for examining the facts of the case in the event that an accused had been found unfit to plead under the provisions of section 4 of the 1964 Act. Even where the prosecution evidence had been heard, there was no provision for hearing evidence from the defence. On a finding of disability (unfitness) the accused had to be committed to hospital under an indefinite order, and remain there until the Home Secretary decided otherwise.[27] In the words of the Butler Committee, "it might become too easy for people to be put away, perhaps for long periods, without proper justification".[28] This problem stemmed from the fact that an accused may have been entitled to an acquittal on the facts. As the Committee noted:

> There will often be no justification for putting him in hospital if he did not commit the offence charged against him. He may, for example, be a mentally handicapped person living peaceably with his mother, and a grievous wrong would be done to him if he were committed to hospital on a charge that could not be substantiated. If he is so committed the hospital doctor and the advisers of the Home Secretary must naturally act on the assumption that the patient committed the offence charged against him, and this may affect the estimation of when he is safe to be released.[29]

As a result it was only in the interests of the accused on a very serious charge to seek a finding of disability.

2.18   In light of these observations, the Committee concluded that the 1964 Act was problematic and made a number of recommendations for reform. Some of these recommendations were uncontentious but others were controversial. The recommendations included the following:

(1)   The question whether the defendant is under a disability should be decided at the outset of trial, or as soon as it is raised. If medical advice indicates that recovery is possible within six months, proceedings may be adjourned up to this time and subsequently re-opened.[30]

(2)   The trial judge should have power to decide the question of disability:

---

[27]   Professor Mackay points out that research on unfitness cases between 1976 and 1989 showed that there were eight acquittals following remission for trial from hospital under s 5(4) of the 1964 Act as originally enacted; a fact that he observed was "disquieting": see RD Mackay, *Mental Condition Defences in the Criminal Law* (1995) p 233.

[28]   Report of the Committee on Mentally Abnormal Offenders (1975) Cmnd 6244, para 10.12.

[29]   Above, para 10.13.

[30]   Above, para 10.19.

(a) where the medical evidence is unanimous; or

(b) where the medical evidence is disputed but the defence does not specifically request that a jury decides the question.[31]

(3) If the defendant is found to be under a disability there should be a trial of the facts in which the normal rules of evidence and burden of proof must apply. Therefore if the jury is not satisfied that the defendant did the act with the necessary mental state they must find the defendant not guilty. Intention should be proved by inference from the evidence of what the defendant did. If a finding of not guilty cannot be returned the jury should be directed to find that the defendant should be dealt with as a person under disability, which should not count as a conviction or carry any punishment.[32]

(4) The court should be given discretion as to disposal following a finding that a defendant under a disability did the act charged, with options including a hospital order, out-patient treatment, or a guardianship order.[33]

(5) Two medical practitioners should give supporting evidence before a defendant may be found to be under a disability.[34]

2.19 The proposal at (2) above contrasted with the recommendation of the CLRC that the determination of unfitness to plead should remain a matter for the jury.

Owing to the great importance of the issue from the point of view of the accused and of the public ... it would be in accordance with the established principles as to the respective functions of the judge and jury in criminal cases that it should continue to be determined in all cases by a jury.[35]

---

[31] Report of the Committee on Mentally Abnormal Offenders (1975) Cmnd 6244, para 10.20.

[32] Above, paras 10.24 to 10.27.

[33] Above, para 10.29.

[34] Above, para.10.41.

[35] Criminal Law Revision Committee Third Report: Criminal Procedure (Insanity) (1963) Cmnd 2149, para 15.

2.20 The Butler Committee acknowledged this discrepancy and attributed the CLRC's recommendation to the fact that it had been made at a time when capital punishment had not yet been abolished, and concluded that this was probably a factor in their reluctance to withdraw the issue of unfitness from the jury. In deciding that the judge was in some cases more suitably placed to decide the issue, the Butler Committee were influenced by a number of factors. The involvement of the jury in the decision was seen as an "historical survival"[36] from the days when it was necessary to determine whether the defendant was mute by malice or by visitation of God, before subjection to the *peine forte et dure*.[37] Insofar as the decision as to whether the trial should proceed, or whether the untried defendant should be committed to hospital, juries were not normally involved in these kinds of decisions. Furthermore it was already the practice in the USA to leave the decision to the judge, and in Scotland in the majority of cases.[38]

The Criminal Procedure (Insanity and Unfitness to Plead) Act 1991

2.21 The recommendations of the Butler Committee led eventually to the 1991 Act. The 1991 Act provided for a flexibility of disposal in relation to those who had been found unfit to plead.[39]

2.22 The 1991 Act also inserted the present section 4A into the 1964 Act. Section 4A provides for a mandatory hearing of the facts of the case (which is not a trial) once an accused has been found to be unfit to plead. Broadly speaking, section 4A serves the purpose of enabling an unfit accused to be acquitted if there is insufficient evidence that the accused has done the act or made the omission with which he or she is charged.

[36] Report of the Committee on Mentally Abnormal Offenders (1975) Cmnd 6244, para 10.22.

[37] The violent means which were used to extract a plea from an accused who was thought to be "mute of malice" as opposed to "mute by visitation from God": see para 2.3 above.

[38] The Butler Committee reported that in Scotland it was possible for either the judge or the jury to decide the issue but in practice it was decided by the judge in the vast majority of cases, even where there was disagreement between psychiatrists: see para 10.23 of the Report of the Committee on Mentally Abnormal Offenders (1975) Cmnd 6244.

[39] See para 2.36 below.

2.23 The 1991 Act however did not fully implement the recommendations contained in the Butler Report. Some of these recommendations were controversial – in particular, the recommendation at paragraph 2.18(3) above.[40] Professor Griew for example commented on the proposal to make provision for a trial of the facts and said "those ideas have, I believe, been felt in official circles to present serious difficulties, as I agree they do; and there is a danger that these difficulties may stand in the way of implementation".[41] The suggestion that this procedure, as proposed in the Butler Report, was thought to be unworkable is underlined by the introduction of a "trial of the facts" limited to the external elements of the offence by the 1991 Act.[42] This was contrary to the recommendations of the Butler Committee which, as can be seen from paragraph 2.18(3) above, explicitly anticipated a trial of the facts which included consideration of the fault element.

> It might be misleading for the jury simply to be directed to report that the facts have been proved, because the word "facts" might be understood to refer only to the external facts, the act done or omission made, whereas the issues to be established by the prosecution include the defendant's state of mind. If this were not so, the defendant would not obtain his verdict of not guilty even though there was insufficient evidence that he had the requisite intention or other mental state for the crime – indeed, he would not obtain it even though it was clear that the affair was an accident. This would clearly be unsatisfactory.[43]

2.24 Furthermore, a consultative document issued by the Home Office in 1978[44] referred to doubts regarding a number of the Butler Report's proposals. For example, it was felt that there were "serious difficulties attached to the proposal" that the courts should only have power to make a hospital order if the conditions imposed by the Mental Health Act 1959 for such an order were met.[45] As we see later,[46] this is in effect what the law is now.

---

[40] E Griew, "Let's Implement Butler on Mental Disorder and Crime!" [1984] *Current Legal Problems* 47, 48 to 49.

[41] Above, at 49.

[42] Discussed in more detail below at paras 2.26 to 2.27 and Part 6 below.

[43] Report of the Committee on Mentally Abnormal Offenders (1975) Cmnd 6244, para 10.24.

[44] Home Office, *Butler Report – disposal in cases of disability and the special verdict* (1978).

[45] Above, para 7.

[46] See paras 2.39 to 2.41 below.

Procedure in section 4A for determining the facts

2.25 If the court determines that the accused is under a disability then it is bound to follow the procedure in section 4A of the 1964 Act. The first thing that the court must do is formally appoint a representative "to put the case for the defence".[47] Until the Court of Appeal decision in *Norman*,[48] it was thought that this would always be defence counsel. A failure to appoint a representative[49] however will not amount to a material irregularity and will not jeopardise the ultimate finding of the court.[50] The main advantage of the appointment of a person to represent the accused is that this representative has the power to make decisions on behalf of the accused.

2.26 Section 4A is designed to facilitate a finding as to whether or not the accused did the act[51] or made the omission complained of in the charge that he or she faces on the indictment while simultaneously protecting him or her from being convicted of any offence.[52] This is because it would be wrong for an accused to be found guilty and sentenced when he or she is not in a position to be able to meet the charge either by defending him or herself or by providing instructions as to mitigation. It also has another equally, if not more important function, which is that it enables the defence to test the evidence in the proper way so that if it is not proved to the requisite standard that the accused did the act complained of then he or she can be acquitted. In short, the procedure enables the accused to be acquitted but prevents him or her from being *convicted*.

2.27 Section 4A(2) provides that in the event of a finding that the accused is under a disability so that he or she cannot be tried, the trial must stop and the jury or a jury (if it has yet to be sworn) will determine whether or not the accused did the act or made the omission charged.

Summary of the distinction between a trial and a section 4A hearing

2.28 A trial involves, as Professor Duff[53] has pointed out, treating the accused as a rational agent who is responsible for his or her actions. As such it is presumed that he or she will participate in it and the trial procedure itself underlines this assumption.

---

[47] Criminal Procedure (Insanity) Act, s 4A(2)(b).

[48] [2008] EWCA Crim 1810, [2009] 1 Cr App R 192. In *Norman* it was held that a specialist in mental health issues should be appointed. We refer to this case again in Part 7, which was actually decided in relation to whether or not the act in question could be said to have been made out on the established facts.

[49] In practical terms such a failure will mean that the defence advocate continues to represent the accused.

[50] *Egan* [1998] 1 Cr App R 121, where it was held to be a matter of form and not of substance.

[51] Broadly speaking "the act" consists of the conduct element of the offence only: see *Antoine* [2000] UKHL 20, [2001] 1 AC 340. We look at this issue in detail in Part 6 below.

[52] The Butler Report noted that the pre-1991 procedure was inadequate because it gave the defence no opportunity to present evidence or to test the facts of the allegation: see para 2.17 above.

[53] RA Duff, "Fitness to plead and fair trials: Part 1: a challenge" [1994] *Criminal Law Review* 419, 420.

The charge is that *"you"* committed the offence; and though the jury's verdict is expressed in the third person, telling the court that they find the defendant guilty (or not), the court must then address the defendant directly, speaking on behalf of the law or the community whose law it is.[54]

2.29   The trial "is a process of argument and judgment which is meant to be conducted *with* the defendant".[55] A fit defendant has a right to be tried and the trial is his or her opportunity of engaging in "a communicative process of argument and justification".[56] The proposition that the accused not only has the right to participate in the trial process but is expected to do so is, for example, reflected in the fact that if a defence case statement is not signed by the accused then the judge[57] can require a defendant to satisfy him or her that he or she has complied with his or her obligations under the Criminal Procedure and Investigations Act 1996.[58] Further, trial procedure is predicated on the assumption that the defendant will give evidence because "the jury ... may draw such inferences as appear proper from the failure of the accused to give evidence or his refusal, without good cause, to answer any question".[59] Where this subsection applies the court is obliged to:

> satisfy itself ... *that the accused is aware* that the stage has been reached at which evidence can be given for the defence and that he can, if he wishes, give evidence and that, if he chooses not to give evidence, or having been sworn, without good cause refuses to answer any question, it will be permissible for the court or jury to draw such inferences as appear proper from his failure to give evidence or his refusal, without good cause, to answer any question.[60]

---

[54]   RA Duff, "Fitness to plead and fair trials: Part 1: a challenge" [1994] *Criminal Law Review* 419, 420 (emphasis in original).

[55]   RA Duff, *Trials and Punishments* (1986) p 35 (emphasis in original).

[56]   Above, p 122.

[57]   Either the trial judge or the judge managing the Plea and Case Management Hearing (PCMH).

[58]   See *R (Sullivan) v Maidstone Crown Court* [2002] EWHC 967 (Admin), [2002] 1 WLR 2747. Section 5(5) of the Criminal Procedure and Investigations Act 1996 provides that once disclosure has been completed by the prosecution then "the accused must give a defence statement to the court and the prosecutor". Section 6A provides that the contents of the defence statement should set out such matters as the nature of the accused's defence and any particular defence on which he or she intends to rely as well as indicate the matters of fact on which he or she takes issue with the prosecution.

[59]   Criminal Justice and Public Order Act 1994, s 35(3).

[60]   Above, s 35(2) (emphasis added).

2.30   Whereas a trial holds an accused to account, the issue being whether he or she is guilty or not guilty of the charge on the indictment, the section 4A hearing is designed to test the evidence to the extent that it exists either way. An accused person is not expected to participate in the hearing and his or her interests are protected by the person appointed to put his or her case in so far as this is possible. There is no issue as to guilt and the means of disposal provided for in section 5 of the 1964 Act are not intended to be punitive.[61]

2.31   The distinction therefore really lies in the different issues involved. In a trial, the issue is the general issue of whether the defendant is guilty or not guilty, whereas in the section 4A hearing the issue is whether the accused did the act or made the omission charged. Unlike the section 4A hearing, a trial requires participation on the part of the accused. To subject an accused to a trial when he or she cannot participate will be unfair[62] and any conviction resulting from a trial which is unfair may well be unsafe.[63] Conversely, an accused who is subject to section 4A proceedings does not enjoy the full protection of article 6.[64] This is a matter which we address further in Part 6.

The Domestic Violence, Crime and Victims Act 2004

Who determines the trial of the issue under the current law?

2.32   As a result of the Domestic Violence, Crime and Victims Act 2004, section 4(5) of the 1964 Act now states that it is the court which has to determine whether an accused is unfit to plead.[65] This was previously a matter which had to be determined by a jury.[66] If it was decided on arraignment[67] and the jury found that the accused was fit to plead then the trial proceeded with a fresh jury. If however the question of unfitness fell to be determined at any other time in the trial then the court had the power to direct that the question could be decided by either a separate jury or by the jury by which the accused was already being tried.

2.33   The requirement that the issue of whether the accused is "under a disability" is now to be determined by the court was endorsed by Lord Justice Auld in his 2001 Review of the Criminal Courts of England and Wales.[68]

---

[61]   See our discussion at paras 6.47 and 6.48 below that whether or not they are punitive is a moot point.

[62]   The right to a fair trial in article 6 has been held by the European Court of Human Rights to include the right to participate effectively in criminal proceedings (*Stanford v United Kingdom* App No 16757/90). See further the discussion at paras 2.89 to 2.102 below.

[63]   *Togher* [2001] 3 All ER 463.

[64]   *H and others* [2003] UKHL 1, [2003] 1 WLR 411.

[65]   Section 22 (1) to (3) replaced the requirement for a jury to determine the unfitness of the accused except in cases where the accused was arraigned before 31 March 2005. See the transitional provisions of the Domestic Violence, Crime and Victims Act 2004, s 59 and Sch 12, para 8.

[66]   Section 4(4) of the 1964 Act before amendment.

[67]   Arraignment being when the accused is asked to plead to the indictment.

[68]   This is something which was recommended by the Butler Committee on a more limited basis: see the Report of the Committee on Mentally Abnormal Offenders (1975) Cmnd 6244, para 10.20.

In the majority of cases the jury's role on the issue of unfitness to plead is little more than a formality because there is usually no dispute between the prosecution and the defence that the defendant is unfit to plead. However, the procedure is still cumbrous, especially when the issue is raised, as it mostly is, on the arraignment, because it can then require the empanelling of two juries. More importantly it is difficult to see what a jury can bring to the determination of the issue that a judge cannot. He decides similar questions determinative of whether there should be a trial, for example, whether a defendant is physically or mentally fit to stand or continue trial in applications to stay the prosecution or for discharge of the defendant.[69]

2.34 Debate during the Bill's passage reveals that the Government was persuaded by Lord Justice Auld's reasoning. In response to Opposition concern about the erosion of jury trials in general, Vera Baird QC MP cited the statistic that in 90% of cases where unfitness to plead was an issue, there was no dispute between the prosecution and the defence.[70] Furthermore it would still be necessary to have the agreement of two registered medical practitioners for there to be a finding of unfitness.[71] In these circumstances the Government felt that the expense and time taken to empanel a jury to determine the issue were not justified by any possible advantage.

2.35 As indicated in the previous paragraph, the court cannot make a determination under section 4(5) that the accused is under a disability except on the written or oral evidence of two or more registered medical practitioners at least one of whom is duly approved.[72] We address this matter in detail in Part 5 of this CP.[73]

---

[69] RE Auld, Review of the Criminal Courts of England and Wales (2001), chapter 5, para 213 (footnote omitted).

[70] *Hansard* (HC), 27 October 2004, vol 425, col 1525.

[71] As required by s 4(6) of the 1964 Act.

[72] Section 4(6) of the 1964 Act. Under s 8(2) of the 1964 Act, "duly approved" means approved for the purposes of s 12 of the Mental Health Act 1983 by the Secretary of State as having special experience in the diagnosis or treatment of mental disorder. In practice, a finding of unfitness is likely to be based on evidence from at least one psychiatrist.

[73] See paras 5.18 to 5.21 below.

Disposal of the case in the event that the accused is found to have done the act

2.36   Flexibility of disposal in section 5 of the 1964 Act[74] was first introduced by the 1991 Act and later amended by the Domestic Violence, Crime and Victims Act 2004. If an accused is found to have done the act with which he or she is charged then sections 5 and 5A of the 1964 Act now provide for various disposals. The provisions are the same for a finding of not guilty by reason of insanity. The court has the power under section 5 to make a hospital order[75] with or without a restriction order,[76] a supervision order or an order for the accused's absolute discharge.

2.37   Research conducted by Professor Mackay and further research which he has conducted for us since the inception of this project, suggests that the flexibility of disposal, which was brought about by the 1991 Act and which is now operative, has removed what may have been a disincentive to rely on unfitness to plead.[77]

2.38   An accused who is detained in pursuance of a hospital order because of (1) a finding of unfitness to plead and (2) that he or she did the act or made the omission charged against him or her and who is also subject to a section 41 restriction order under the Mental Health Act 1983 can be remitted for trial by the Secretary of State after consultation with the responsible clinician.[78]

Hospital orders under the Mental Health Act 1983

2.39   The provisions for disposal in the 1964 Act were brought into line with article 5 of the European Convention on Human Rights by the Domestic Violence, Crime and Victims Act 2004.[79] "Hospital order" under section 5 of the 1964 Act is now to be given the same meaning as hospital order under section 37 of the Mental Health Act 1983.[80] A result of this change is that admission to hospital with a restriction order[81] in cases of murder is no longer mandatory, but can only be made in circumstances where the court has the power to make a hospital order under the Mental Health Act 1983.

---

[74]   As we have seen at para 2.14, s 5 originally provided that the accused who had been found unfit to plead should be detained indefinitely in hospital.

[75]   "Hospital order" has the meaning given to it under s 37 of the Mental Health Act 1983: see s 5(4) of the 1991 Act.

[76]   See s 41 of the Mental Health Act 1983.

[77]   See for example RD Mackay, "A continued upturn in unfitness to plead – more disability in relation to trial under the 1991 Act" [2007] *Criminal Law Review* 530. This is also true of insanity.

[78]   Section 5A(4) of the 1964 Act. The "responsible clinician" is the person with overall responsibility for the patient's case, and does not necessarily have to be a medical practitioner: see further paras 5.20 below and Appendix A.

[79]   Section 24 of the Domestic Violence, Crime and Victims Act 2004 inserts new ss 5 and 5A into the 1964 Act.

[80]   See s 5(4) of the 1964 Act as inserted by s 24(1) of the Domestic Violence, Crime and Victims Act 2004.

[81]   A restriction order is provided for by s 41 of the Mental Health Act 1983.

2.40   Section 37 requires that the court must be satisfied, on the evidence of two registered medical practitioners,[82] that the offender has a mental disorder of a nature or degree which makes it appropriate for him or her to be detained in hospital for medical treatment and that appropriate medical treatment is available.[83] A court can therefore only make a hospital order in relation to an unfit accused found to have done the act on the basis of "objective medical expertise", as required by article 5 of the European Convention.[84]

2.41   The provisions of the Mental Health Act 1983, which were amended by the Mental Health Act 2007, are discussed in greater detail in Appendix A of this CP. Most significantly, the Mental Health Act 2007 amended the definition of mental disorder to "any disorder or disability of the mind".[85] This in effect broadened the definition for the purpose of longer-term detention powers. It also removed as a criterion for the longer-term powers of detention the requirement that medical treatment must be "likely to alleviate or prevent a deterioration of [the patient's] condition" (the "treatability" test). Instead, it must now be shown that "appropriate medical treatment" is available, where the purpose of such treatment is to "alleviate, or prevent a worsening of, the disorder or one or more of its symptoms or manifestations".[86] This emphasis on the availability of the treatment rather than its efficacy may widen the scope of the Mental Health Act 1983 in relation to the use of longer-term powers.[87]

Summary of the statutory developments

2.42   It is clear that the 1991 Act did not provide for a root and branch reform of the law on unfitness to plead. From the above, it can be inferred that the purpose of its amendments to the 1964 Act were as follows:

(a)   to ensure that the trial of the issue is addressed as soon as a question as to the accused's unfitness is determined, subject to the proviso that:

(i)   the accused against whom there is no evidence can be discharged as soon as possible without any question as to his or her unfitness being determined;

---

[82]   At least one of whom must be a practitioner approved for the purposes of s 12 of the Mental Health Act 1983 by the Secretary of State as having special experience in the diagnosis or treatment of mental disorder: see s 54(1) of the Mental Health Act 1983.

[83]   See s 37(2)(a)(i) of the Mental Health Act 1983.

[84]   *Winterwerp v Netherlands* (1979) 2 EHRR 387 (App No 6301/73). See further paras 5.30 to 5.33 below and Appendix A.

[85]   Section 1(2) of the Mental Health Act 1983, as amended by the s 1 of the Mental Health Act 2007.

[86]   Section 145(1)(c) of the Mental Health Act 1983 sets out the definition of "medical treatment" for the purposes of the Act.

[87]   D Hewitt, "Treatment shock" [2007] *New Law Journal* 157. Although the emphasis is now on the purpose of the treatment rather than its likely effect, Hewitt suggests that the weakening of the treatability test is not as great as some may have feared.

(b)   thereafter, to provide for a means of determining whether the evidence against the accused amounts to proof that he or she did the act or omission with which he or she is charged whilst protecting him or her from criminal conviction;

(c)   to ensure that the possibility of an acquittal is maintained and that the accused is adequately represented in this regard;

(d)   to protect the accused from sentence if he or she is found to have done the act or made the omission charged and thereafter;[88] and

(e)   to provide flexibility of disposal.

THE LEGAL TEST FOR UNFITNESS TO PLEAD

2.43   None of the statutory reforms to which we have referred above dealt with the legal test for unfitness to plead.[89] We now analyse the criteria (known as the *Pritchard* criteria) which are used to judge whether an accused is unfit to plead and consider whether these criteria are a suitable modern basis for determining the issue. We explain why, in our view, they are not. We think that an analysis of the case law shows that, at best, the criteria are not comprehensive and place a disproportionate emphasis on low intellectual ability. At worst, the criteria simply set too high a threshold for finding an accused to be unfit to plead and are inconsistent with the modern trial process.

The foundation of the *Pritchard* criteria

2.44   The legal test of whether an accused is under a disability (unfit to plead) is still that which was established in *Pritchard*.[90] Although the definition of "disability" is any disability, whether that is mental or physical, the legal test employs specific criteria for determining whether the accused is under such a disability.

---

[88]   As Duff argues:
> For punishment aims, and must aim, if it is to be properly justified, to *address* the offender as a rational and responsible agent: if she cannot understand what is being done to her, or why it is being done, or how it is related as a punishment to her past offence, her punishment becomes a travesty.

RA Duff, *Trials and Punishments* (1986) p 27 (emphasis in original).

[89]   It is important not to confuse the legal test with any defined psychiatric test for assessing whether or not a person is unfit to plead. The whole question of using a psychiatric test is addressed in Part 5 below.

[90]   (1836) 7 C & P 303.

2.45   In *Pritchard* the accused, who was deaf and could not speak, was indicted for bestiality. Alderson B, relying on *Dyson*,[91] empanelled a jury to determine whether the accused "was mute of malice or by visitation from God". The jury found the latter and were then sworn to inquire whether the accused could plead to the indictment. There was evidence that he could read and write and the jury found that he was able to plead and he pleaded not guilty. The jury were then directed to determine whether the accused was sane or not.[92] Alderson B directed the jury that in order to be sane the accused must be:

> Of sufficient intellect to comprehend the course of proceedings in the trial so as to make a proper defence, to know that he may challenge any of you to whom he may object and to comprehend the details of the evidence.[93]

2.46   *Pritchard*, together with *Davies*,[94] lay down the following criteria for deciding the question of whether or not an accused is unfit to plead: the ability to plead to the indictment, to understand the course of the proceedings, to instruct a lawyer, to challenge a juror and to understand the evidence.[95] Expert witnesses who speak to the issue of whether the accused is unfit to plead therefore now have to give evidence on the questions of whether the accused is able to meet these criteria. An inability to meet any one of the criteria is sufficient to render an accused person unfit to plead. The fact that the court may take the view that the accused is not capable of making decisions which are in his or her best interests is not enough to conclude that he or she is unfit to plead.[96]

[91]   (1831) 7 C & P 305. The accused, who was deaf and could not speak, was charged with having murdered her illegitimate child. A jury found her to be mute by visitation from God. Although a plea of not guilty was recorded with the assistance of an interpreter and through the use of sign language, it was not possible for the accused to understand the more complex procedure of challenging jurors. Parke J relied on Hale's authority as to arraignment during a "phrenzy" to instruct the jury to find her insane.

[92]   If the accused was not sane then he or she had to be dealt with under the provisions of section 2 of the Criminal Lunatics Act 1800.

[93]   (1836) 7 C & P 303, 304.

[94]   (1853) Car & Kir 328. The concept of being unable to instruct legal advisors arose later in *Davies* and so has been subsequently added to the criteria. In *Davies* an accused who was thought to be "mad" reacted to arraignment in a confused manner. The issue for the jury was whether the defendant was incapable of properly instructing his counsel because of his "madness".

[95]   RD Mackay, *Mental Condition Defences in the Criminal Law* (1995) p 224.

[96]   *Robertson* [1968] 3 All ER 557.

2.47 The *Pritchard* test really only addresses extreme cases of a particular type (usually bearing on cognitive deficiency)[97] and, as we explain in paragraph 2.60 below, it continues to set a high threshold for finding an accused unfit to plead. It also fails to cover all the aspects of the trial process (for example, the ability to give evidence) and therefore has the practical effect of limiting the number of people who are found to be unfit to plead. The *Pritchard* test was nonetheless approved by the Court of Appeal in *Friend (No 1)*[98] in the context of a decision concerning the application of section 35 of the Criminal Justice and Public Order Act 1994.[99]

2.48 The *Pritchard* test was also left intact by the statutory developments in the 1964 Act and the 1991 Act. The CLRC was mainly concerned with what happened to an accused who had been found to be unfit to plead. Consequently, the 1964 Act did not define new criteria[100] for a finding of "disability in relation to trial".

2.49 The Butler Committee did address the legal test. Along with the recommendations listed at paragraph 2.18 above, it also recommended that the criteria which comprise the legal test should be reformulated to include the ability to:

   (a)   understand the course of the proceedings at the trial
         so as to make a proper defence;

   (b)   understand the substance of the evidence;

   (c)   give adequate instructions to his legal advisers; and

   (d)   plead with understanding to the indictment.

2.50 The omission of the requirement of the ability to challenge a juror, and the addition of the ability to instruct legal advisors and plead with understanding, were reportedly made on the recommendation of the judiciary.[101]

---

[97] Although the case of *Pritchard* was decided in relation to a person who was a deaf-mute and could not speak, it has since been applied to many different conditions: see RD Mackay, *Mental Condition Defences in the Criminal Law* (1995) p 216. However, it has been found to exclude amnesia regarding the events of the alleged offence: see *Podola* [1960] 1 QB 325.

[98] [1997] 1 WLR 1433. However, in *Friend (No 2)* [2004] EWCA Crim 2661, [2004] All ER (D) 140, on a referral from the Criminal Cases Review Commission, the Court of Appeal held that the conviction was unsafe because of fresh evidence which showed that the appellant had attention deficit hyperactivity disorder which had not been diagnosed at the time of trial. This would have affected the appellant's ability to give evidence. The question of whether it would have rendered him unfit to plead was not addressed on appeal.

[99] Section 35(1)(b) in effect provides that no adverse inference may be drawn from a failure of the accused to give evidence where the judge directs that it is undesirable for the accused to give evidence because of a physical or mental health condition.

[100] In other words it did not create a new legal test for unfitness to plead.

[101] Report of the Committee on Mentally Abnormal Offenders (1975) Cmnd 6244, para 10.3.

2.51 The Butler Committee's recommendations in relation to the legal test however were not addressed by the 1991 Act. Arguably, the 1991 Act should have introduced a statutory framework setting out factors to which the court should (at the very least) have regard in determining the legal test for the trial of the issue. Not only is there no statutory framework stating factors which ought to be taken into account but there is no guidance or code of practice on this matter.

Recent interpretation of the *Pritchard* criteria

2.52 To some extent, judges and psychiatrists make the best of these dated criteria for the determination of unfitness to plead – expanding them where possible. For example, the criteria were expounded in *John M*[102] in a way that attempted to make them consistent with the modern trial process. In that case the appellant had been convicted of rape, indecent assault on a female, indecency with a child and taking indecent photographs of a child. At trial, the defence contended that the defendant suffered from a serious impairment to his short term memory, known as anterograde amnesia, which rendered him incapable of following the proceedings and giving evidence in his own defence, and that he was therefore unfit to plead. The issue was contested before the jury. There was evidence from various witnesses on the issue including that of three psychiatrists. Two of the psychiatrists had concluded that the defendant was unfit to plead and one of whom was of the view that he was fit, although this psychiatrist had previously noted that special steps would be required in order to deal with his memory problems.

2.53 The trial judge directed the jury as follows. It was sufficient for the defence to persuade the jury on the balance of probabilities that any one of the following things was beyond the defendant's capability: (1) understanding the charges; (2) deciding whether to plead guilty or not; (3) exercising his right to challenge jurors; (4) instructing solicitors and counsel; (5) following the course of proceedings; and (6) giving evidence in his own defence.[103] The judge then proceeded to explain what was meant by each of these items in detail.

2.54 In so far as instructing solicitor and counsel was concerned he said:

> This means that the defendant must be able to convey intelligibly to his lawyers the case which he wishes them to advance on his behalf and the matters which he wishes them to put forward in his defence. It involves being able (a) to understand the lawyers' questions, (b) to apply his mind to answering them, and (c) to convey intelligibly to the lawyers the answers he wishes to give. It is not necessary that his instructions should be plausible or believable or reliable, nor is it necessary that he should be able to see that they are implausible, or unbelievable or unreliable. Many defendants put forward cases and explanations which are implausible, unbelievable or unreliable ... .[104]

---

[102] *M (John)* [2003] EWCA Crim 3452, [2003] All ER (D) 199.

[103] This is a good example of an expansion designed to make the test consistent with the trial process of which giving evidence tends to be an important part.

[104] *M (John)* [2003] EWCA Crim 3452, [2003] All ER (D) 199 at [21].

2.55   As to item (5) on the list, "following the course of the proceedings", the trial judge expounded as follows:

> This means that the defendant must be able ... (a) to understand what is said by the witness and by counsel in their speeches to the jury and (b) to communicate intelligibly to his lawyers any comment which he may wish to make on anything that is said by the witnesses or counsel. Few defendants will be able to remember at the end of a court session all the points that may have occurred to them about what has been said during the session. It is therefore quite normal for the defendant to be provided with pencil and paper so that he can jot down notes and pass them to his lawyers either as and when he writes them or at the end of the session.
>
> ...
>
> It is not necessary that the defendant's comments on the evidence ... should be valid or helpful to his lawyers or helpful to his case. It often happens that a defendant fails to see what is or is not a good point to make in his defence. The important thing is he should be able to make whatever comments he wishes.[105]

2.56   In so far as item (6) "giving evidence if he wishes in his own defence" was concerned, the following directions were given:

> This means that the defendant must be able (a) to understand the questions he is asked in the witness box, (b) to apply his mind to answering them, and (c) to convey intelligibly to the jury the answers which he wishes to give. It is not necessary that his answers should be plausible or believable. Nor is it necessary that he should be able to see that they are implausible or unbelievable or unreliable. Many defendants and other witnesses give evidence which is either in whole or in parts implausible, unbelievable or unreliable. The whole purpose of the trial process is to determine what parts of the evidence are reliable and what parts are not ... . Nor is it necessary that the defendant should be able to remember all or any of the matters which give rise to the charges against him. He is entitled to say that he has no recollection of those events, or indeed of anything that has happened during the relevant period.[106]

2.57   The jury found that the defendant was fit to plead and therefore to stand trial. He was convicted and appealed. The first ground of appeal was that the judge had misdirected the jury by setting the test for fitness to plead too low with the result that it was too easily met. In addition it was argued[107] that the first two of the six items (understanding the charges and deciding whether or not to plead guilty) should not have been included.

---

[105] *M (John)* [2003] EWCA Crim 3452, [2003] All ER (D) 199 at [22] to [23].

[106] Above, at [24].

[107] In the skeleton, *M (John)* [2003] EWCA Crim 3452, [2003] All ER (D) 199 at [27].

2.58 Having considered *Pritchard, Robertson*[108] and *Berry*[109] the court stated that:

> When we consider the judge's directions in the present case in the light of those authorities we can find no deficiency in them. Indeed this Court regards them as admirable directions. They do not set the test of fitness to plead at too low a level.[110]

2.59 The court pointed out that the question of whether the appellant had been fit to be tried was a question for the jury who could take whatever view they wished of the evidence. As we have seen above,[111] the question of unfitness is now a matter for the court and not for the jury. There is no reason however why a judge tasked with determining the issue would not address him or herself to the issues as outlined above.

Problems with the *Pritchard* criteria

2.60 The *Pritchard* criteria have been widely criticised for failing to provide an adequate legal test for unfitness to plead, and for setting too high a threshold for a finding of unfitness. Although empirical research does show that the number of findings of unfitness to plead is rising,[112] the conclusion of research into the suitability of the *Pritchard* criteria was that "formal findings of unfitness under the ... test are extremely rare."[113] This means that "significant numbers of the mentally ill continue to undergo trial and may be doing so unfairly."[114] It is also thought that:

> There is a widespread belief among forensic psychiatrists that many mentally ill defendants in the current system may not be receiving a fair trial.[115]

---

[108] [1968] 3 All ER 557.

[109] (1978) 66 Cr App R 156.

[110] *M (John)* [2003] EWCA Crim 3452, [2003] All ER (D) 199 at [31].

[111] See para 2.32 above.

[112] The results of Professor Mackay's latest research can be found in Appendix C. He observes that, "the annual number of findings of UTP [unfitness to plead] for the research period [2002 to 2008] 725 [gives] an annual average number of UTP findings ... over one hundred for the first time", p 207 below.

[113] TP Rogers, NJ Blackwood, F Farnham, GJ Pickup, MJ Watts, "Reformulating fitness to plead: a qualitative study" (2009) 20(6) *Journal of Forensic Psychiatry and Psychology* 815, 816.

[114] Above, 817.

[115] Dr Tim Rogers, Specialist Registrar in Forensic Psychiatry (now Consultant Forensic Psychiatrist), letter to the Law Commission dated 21 August 2007.

2.61　In a study by Dr Tim Rogers and others, it was claimed that the numbers of people who are found to be unfit to plead are "startlingly low" when it is considered that 10% of men on remand had shown signs of psychotic illness in the previous year.[116] Although this is disturbing it is perhaps inevitable given the criteria which make up the present test. The situation contrasts with the one in the USA where approximately one fifth of the estimated 60,000 evaluations of competency every year find that the defendant lacks competence to stand trial.[117] In the USA the Supreme Court decision in *Dusky*[118] determined a more comprehensive test than that offered in Pritchard, and importantly that test incorporates capacity.[119]

2.62　It was suggested in the study by Dr Rogers and others that the low number of findings of unfitness to plead is due to the absence of a standardised procedure for the screening of defendants in England and Wales.[120] In England and Wales there is a degree of arbitrariness in whether the process of determining the issue happens at all. This is because it depends on either solicitor or counsel for the accused recognising mental abnormality and obtaining prior authority from the Legal Services Commission for the preparation of psychiatric reports. It is generally unlikely that the court will pick up on unfitness in respect of a defendant who is represented and in respect of whom no such representations are made. It is claimed that:

> the potential for unfit defendants to 'slip through the net' may contribute to the estimated 3000-3700 men so severely mentally ill in prison that they require immediate NHS transfer.[121]

---

[116] TP Rogers et al, "Reformulating the law on fitness to plead: a qualitative study" (2009) 20(6) *Journal of Forensic Psychiatry and Psychology* 815, 816 citing Singleton et al (1998).

[117] Above, 816 citing RJ Bonnie and T Grisso (2000) and D Mossman et al (2007).

[118] *Dusky v United States* (1960) 362 US 402 held that the standard for competence to stand trial is whether the defendant has "sufficient present ability to consult with a lawyer with a reasonable degree of rational understanding and has a rational as well as a factual understanding of the proceedings against him".

[119] Although it should be remembered that in the USA once defendants are found to lack competence to be tried there is no procedure for examination of the facts.

[120] TP Rogers et al "Reformulating the law on fitness to plead: a qualitative study" (2009) 20(6) *Journal of Forensic Psychiatry and Psychology* 815, 816.

[121] Above, 816 to 817, citing the Prison Reform Trust, *Troubled inside: responding to the mental health needs of men in Prison* (2005).

2.63   The research by Dr Rogers and others was conducted using a semi-structured interview which was devised to study the views of experienced criminal barristers. The results highlighted several problems with the current approach to unfitness to plead, including the deficiencies of the *Pritchard* test. Five key themes emerged by way of the results[122] which help to define the true construct of fitness and document current assessment and procedural difficulties.[123] Below we concentrate on what was considered to be one of the difficulties, namely the assessment of fitness to plead.

2.64   The difficulties with the assessment of fitness to plead were numerous. First, it was felt that "legal criteria are applied inconsistently (by different psychiatrists and on different occasions)".[124] Secondly, it was thought that "fitness often changes over time", in other words that an accused may have been fit at the time of assessment but may have become unfit by the time of trial.[125] Thirdly, it was thought to be a problem that "psychiatrists assess young people differently" in the sense that "the test for young people is slightly different in practice but not in law ... psychiatrists are more able to be firm in saying no trial in the very young".[126] Fourthly, "psychiatrists make assessments without consulting the legal team", in other words it was felt that there should be a more collaborative approach.[127] Fifthly, it was thought that there was the potential for clients to deceive their barristers by feigning illness.[128]

2.65   The research also showed that barristers considered that there were a number of specific omissions in the *Pritchard* criteria. These omissions take into account the practicalities of the trial process.

    (1)   The absence of any reference to the ability to give evidence. This was described by one barrister in the following terms:

---

[122]   These themes were classified as (1) defining the ideal construct of fitness, (2) procedural problems, (3) difficulties with the assessment of fitness, (4) issues specific to judges, and (5) suggested procedural solutions.

[123]   TP Rogers et al, "Reformulating the law on fitness to plead: a qualitative study" (2009) 20(6) *Journal of Forensic Psychiatry and Psychology* 815.

[124]   Above, 827.

[125]   Above, 827.

[126]   Above, 827.

[127]   Above, 827.

[128]   Above, 827.

> One of the ridiculous difficulties about *Pritchard* is that it doesn't even address the most crucial part – going into the witness box and telling the jury what you did or didn't do ... they are often swayed to acquit somebody who may or may not be innocent, because their explanation makes sense, because they like them ... there is no substitute ... if someone is not able to do that because cross examination will be meaningless, it may well be that that person should not be standing trial ... .[129]

(2)   Suggestibility, in other words the extent to which a defendant will agree with leading questions.

(3)   A reference to memory, particularly as memory can be affected by some mental disorders.

(4)   A reference to decisional competence. The difficulties that this could afford were described by one barrister:

> It's a very difficult situation to have someone who cannot understand what is good for them, even after advice ... they are at great risk of alienating the jury, alienating the judge or being convicted where they might not otherwise be.[130]

(5)   The possible relation between physical illness and unfitness. An example was given of a defendant who was profoundly affected by the fact that she was suffering from cancer.[131]

(6)   The relation between psychosis and unfitness. Some barristers referred to problems arising in finding psychotic patients unfit by using the *Pritchard* criteria which were not designed with them in mind. One example in this regard was of a defendant who had "deep-seated delusions, which weren't enough to give him a legal defence. On the basic *Pritchard* test he was okay. He decided that he would rather plead guilty than give evidence or be found guilty – he had the capacity to plead guilty but none of it was fair".[132]

(7)   The fact that the *Pritchard* test made no reference to cultural background. In this regard the following example was given by one barrister:

---

[129] TP Rogers et al, "Reformulating the law on fitness to plead: a qualitative study" (2009) 20(6) *Journal of Forensic Psychiatry and Psychology* 815, 823. The essence of this comment is that the ability to give evidence is a crucial part of the trial process, which reflects the point we made at para 2.29 above where we suggested that trial procedure is predicated on the assumption that a defendant will give evidence.

[130] Above, 824.

[131] Above, 824. A physical illness may, for example, result in mental distress and mean that the accused is unable to follow the evidence. In *R v B and Others* [2008] EWCA Crim 1997, [2009] 1 WLR 1545 a defendant was unfit to plead as a result of his recent stroke.

[132] As we go on to explain below at paras 2.75 to 2.87, the case law (which has been decided since this research was conducted) demonstrates that this is indeed a problem which has arisen as a result of a disproportionate emphasis on cognitive ability.

One young man that raised anxiety in my mind was 17, from Eastern Europe and had seen his parents murdered. He had literally lived on his own from the age of 11, on a hillside tending goats. He got an A for intelligence, was deemed fit to plead but there was a huge vacuum in his cultural understanding ... he could not give evidence because either his answers or the questions asked were being misconstrued.[133]

2.66 Barristers were asked to consider which aspects of the *Pritchard* criteria they considered irrelevant and most (although not all) considered that the ability to challenge a juror was irrelevant.[134]

2.67 By way of contrast, those aspects of the *Pritchard* criteria which barristers believed should be retained were:

   (a)   the ability to plead;

   (b)   the ability to understand proceedings; and

   (c)   the ability to instruct counsel.

2.68 Some of the observations at paragraph 2.65 above as to the omission of specific matters from the *Pritchard* criteria, namely (1) (2) (3) and (4), bear directly on the question of the accused's capacity to make decisions. Others, such as (6), refer explicitly to the disproportionate emphasis on cognitive ability.[135] This is something we now consider.

---

[133] TP Rogers et al, "Reformulating the law on fitness to plead: a qualitative study" (2009) 20(6) *Journal of Forensic Psychiatry and Psychology* 815, 824.

[134] Above, 824.

[135] By which we mean what the accused can be said to know or understand.

The disproportionate emphasis on cognitive ability

2.69 The principal problem with *Pritchard* is that it represents a determination to focus on the intellectual abilities of the accused as opposed to his or her capacity to make decisions. The emphasis is therefore on cognitive ability.[136] In *Robertson*,[137] for example, the accused was able to comprehend the court proceedings but was found to be unfit to plead on the basis that he suffered from a paranoid illness and was thought to be unable to defend himself. The medical evidence was that "delusional thinking might cause him to act unwisely or otherwise than in his own best interests". The Court of Appeal overturned the finding of unfitness. It relied on *Pritchard* and held that the mere fact that the accused was not capable of doing things which were in his own best interests was an insufficient basis for a finding of unfitness. In other words an accused's capacity to understand proceedings is separated in law from the question of whether he or she is capable of sound decision-making in relation to the conduct of those proceedings. These concepts have been thought to be sufficiently discrete for the courts to be able to say that only the former will have any bearing on the fitness to plead of the accused.[138] The position in England and Wales in this regard contrasts with the position which now exists in Jersey where it has recently been held that these two concepts cannot readily be divorced from one another[139] and that accordingly, the capacity to make rational decisions is of relevance to the determination of the issue.

2.70 Since the Butler Committee reported,[140] there has been a good deal of academic criticism of the *Pritchard* criteria. This criticism centres on the fact that the criteria focus on intellectual ability rather than disorders of mood and other aspects of mental illness. Professor Grubin has argued that:

> these nineteenth century criteria, which associate intellectual ability with insanity, were fundamentally flawed from the beginning, blurring what had been a well recognised distinction between mental deficiency and madness.[141]

---

[136] In other words what the accused can be said to know or comprehend.

[137] [1968]1 WLR 1767.

[138] In civil law, there are links between whether a person makes an unwise decision and capacity. While an unwise decision cannot be taken as proof that someone lacks capacity, it can trigger the need for an assessment of that person's capacity: see the Mental Capacity Act 2005 Code of Practice, para 2.11.

[139] *A-G v Gemma Harding* [2009] JRC 198, [2009] Jersey Law Review Note 52 held, applying *A-G v O'Driscoll* [2003] Jersey Law Review 390, that impairment by way of borderline personality disorder which caused fluctuation in rational decision making was sufficiently substantial to render the accused incapable of participating effectively over the course of her trial.

[140] See paras 2.18 onwards above. The Butler Committee did not address the fact that the criteria have in reality been limited to a consideration of cognitive ability.

[141] D Grubin, "What constitutes fitness to plead" [1993] *Criminal Law Review* 748, 748.

2.71 Professor Grubin points out that the decision to equate unfitness to plead with insanity was arguably a misconstruction of Hale.[142] It has not been tested and the criteria have not been challenged in the courts,[143] although the courts have obviously debated the meaning of the criteria. He points out that *Dyson*[144] established "intelligence as the foundation on which future decisions about fitness to plead were to be made".[145]

The failure to take capacity and participation into account as part of the legal test

2.72 As has been seen above, the *Pritchard* criteria place emphasis on an ability to understand rather than the ability to function or to do something (in other words, mental capacity). Fitness to plead, as we have said earlier, is a global concept which can be said to cover a general state, and is not context-specific or time-specific. It has tended to be construed as being about the accused's cognitive ability which is, to all intents and purposes, seen in the abstract.

2.73 Capacity on the other hand, involves the capacity to do something or to perform the task of making a particular decision in relation to a particular set of circumstances.[146] As such, it is part of an equation and can have no real meaning in the abstract.

---

[142] D Grubin, "What constitutes fitness to plead" [1993] *Criminal Law Review* 748, 752:

> Two crucial precedents, both questionable, were thus set in *Dyson*. First, it brought idiocy under the umbrella of insanity by establishing that those found unfit to plead were "not sane". This linkage however appears to have been a misconstruction of Hale, confounding his comments on idiocy and insanity: in the passage quoted to the jury Hale is referring to the madman in his phrenzy, not to the idiot with no possibility of understanding. The leap from Dyson's mental deficiency to insanity is not a straightforward one, and it is not clear that disposal under the 1800 Act was legally correct.

See para 2.4 above for the relevant extract from Hale.

[143] Above, 749.

[144] (1831) 7 C & P 305. In *Dyson*, the trial of a "deaf-mute" indicted for murder, the jury was instructed that if they were "satisfied that the defendant had not then, from the defect of her faculties, intelligence enough to understand the nature of the proceedings against her, they ought to find her not sane."

[145] D Grubin, "What constitutes fitness to plead" [1993] *Criminal Law Review* 748, 752.

[146] See AE Buchanan, *Deciding for Others* (1989) p 18:

> The statement that a particular individual is (or is not) competent is incomplete. Competence is always competence for some task – competence *to do something*. The concern here is with competence to perform the task of making a decision. Hence competence is to be understood as decision-making capacity. But the notion of the decision-making capacity itself is incomplete until the nature of the choice as well as the conditions under which it is to be made are specified. The competence is decision relative not global (emphasis in original).

2.74 In our view, capacity is linked directly to the question of participation which we explore below. We believe that an accused cannot participate meaningfully in his or her trial unless he or she has the capacity to make decisions. For example, meaningful participation in terms of giving evidence is predicated on the ability of the accused to decide to give evidence. Such a decision involves an understanding of the advantages and disadvantages of giving evidence in the circumstances of the particular case.

The practical effect of a failure to take capacity into account

2.75 It is clear that the capacity to make decisions is excluded from the present test for unfitness to plead and that in a worst case scenario, this can lead to considerable injustice with both legal advisors and the courts (at first instance) being unable to do anything to remedy a flawed decision on the part of a defendant who, although he or she clearly lacks capacity, is nevertheless fit to plead under the *Pritchard* test. The problems which can ensue were highlighted in *Erskine*.[147]

2.76 In *Erskine*, the appellant was charged with seven counts of murder and one count of attempted murder. The trial took place in 1988. There was evidence at the time of the trial that at the date of the offences, the appellant was suffering from an abnormality of mind so as to be able to plead to manslaughter by way of diminished responsibility. The appellant chose to instruct his representatives, however, that he was not involved in the killings and was convicted. On an application for leave to appeal out of time, the appellant contended that he had been suffering from schizophrenia and psychopathic disorder which had the effect of substantially diminishing his responsibility pursuant to section 2 of the Homicide Act 1957. It was submitted that his failure to run this defence at trial was attributable to his mental disorder.

2.77 The application was granted and the appeal was allowed.

> There was unequivocal contemporaneous evidence that his mental responsibility for his actions at the time of the killing was substantially impaired. In addition, there was contemporaneous evidence which suggested that as a result of reduced mental acuity, not amounting to unfitness to plead, but part and parcel of his illness, the decision not to advance the defence was irremediably flawed. There was nothing his legal advisors could do about it, and in reality nothing he could do about it himself.[148]

2.78 There is a strong case for regarding such an accused person as unfit to plead, because the accused's mental disorder[149] means that he or she lacks the capacity to assess the strengths and weaknesses of his or her legal position, even though his or her understanding of the law and of legal process may be very good. However, at present, if the accused has such an understanding, then he or she is regarded in law as fit to plead.

---

[147] [2009] EWCA Crim 1425, [2010] 1 WLR 183.

[148] Above at [95].

[149] Which may but does not necessarily mean that he or she is delusional.

2.79 There is a line of authorities addressing the problems that can occur when illness affects an accused's capacity to make decisions.[150] In essence, it may mean, as was the case in *Erskine*, that the accused's mental state itself is responsible for a particular decision to do with his or her trial. An example would be where an accused who is charged with murder, and who has a mental disorder, rejects the offer of a plea of guilty to manslaughter by way of diminished responsibility and goes on to be convicted of murder. If he or she had not been suffering from mental disorder at the time of the trial, he or she would have accepted the offer of the plea. The difficulties that are encountered in this respect and in extreme cases[151] have been explored by Professor Bonnie in the context of a discussion of the decision of the United States Court of Appeals for the Ninth Circuit in *Moran v Godinez*.[152] In that case, the Ninth Circuit held that the standard of competency required to plead guilty and to waive the right to counsel[153] was higher than the standard required to stand trial. However, the Supreme Court later held that the Ninth Circuit erred in applying two different competency standards.[154]

---

[150] Cited in detail in *Erskine* [2009] EWCA Crim 1425, [2010] 1 WLR 183 at [41] to [62].

[151] In the USA where the defendant may face the death penalty.

[152] 972 F 2d 263 (9th Cir 1992), where the accused decided to plead guilty to murder. In discussing this case, Professor Bonnie said:

> Wholesale capitulation by remorseful capital defendants is not unusual. Such defendants typically insist on pleading guilty against counsel's advice and instruct counsel to refrain from introducing any evidence in mitigation or like Richard Moran, they discharge their attorneys and plead guilty while unrepresented. These defendants also frequently request sentences of death. This behaviour presents puzzling and controversial questions regarding the ethical and legal obligations of defence attorneys and trial judge … They file appeals or habeas petitions seeking to nullify the convictions and death sentences they so ardently sought. The possibility of strategic behaviour in such cases cannot altogether be ruled out, but the most likely explanation is that medication, counselling, and the passage of time alleviate the prisoners' acute distress and they eventually come to prefer life, even with suffering and guilt, to death.

> RJ Bonnie, "The competence of criminal defendants: beyond Dusky and Drope" (2003) 47(3) *University of Miami Law Review* 539, 588.

[153] It should be borne in mind that pleading guilty in the USA has more extreme ethical implications due to the existence of plea bargaining. Here there is no such concept. Rather there is only the Goodyear direction – the process by which the defendant can request a formal indication as to sentence from the judge prior to plea: *Goodyear* [2005] EWCA Crim 888, [2005] 1 WLR 2532.

[154] *Godinez v Moran* (1993) 509 US 389 at p 397. Professor Bonnie's discussion of the decision focuses on the potential advantages of having different standards of competence for different stages of the trial process which have distinct consequences. A plea of guilty where a defendant faces the death penalty has a more serious consequence than undergoing the trial where a defendant is represented and may have a chance of being acquitted. We address this disaggregated approach at paras 3.64 to 3.78 below, but for the moment, the point we wish to make is that the mental disorder from which the defendant suffers may lead him or her to make decisions which are fundamentally flawed.

2.80   *Murray*[155] provides a good example of the proposition that the present dichotomy between understanding and capacity can lead to injustice.[156] In *Murray* the appellant who suffered from paranoid schizophrenia had killed her five-year-old daughter by stabbing her with a kitchen knife more than fifty times. She insisted on pleading guilty to the offence of murder even though she had a defence of diminished responsibility. Her insistence on pleading guilty was as a result of the overwhelming guilt she felt at having killed her child. The defendant's conviction for murder was quashed by the Court of Appeal and a conviction for manslaughter substituted, on the grounds of diminished responsibility. In this case the consensus among the psychiatrists involved in the trial was that the defendant was not unfit to plead in the legal sense of the term, but, as one of them observed:

> Psychiatric understanding and the law in relation to mentally ill defendants do not always sit together comfortably.[157]

2.81   In other words, the law as its stands did not make sufficient allowance for the fact that the defendant's memory of her thoughts and emotions at the time of the killing were such that she did not wish to discuss them with anyone and simply wished to be punished for what she saw as 'murder'. The system does not have any regard for the process by which a defendant comes to the decision to plead guilty.[158] Lord Justice Toulson observed:

> This case … illustrates in acute form the problems of the potential mismatch between the legal test and psychiatric understanding in these matters.[159]

2.82   We think that the fact that an accused can have a serious degree of mental abnormality,[160] a mental disorder or actually be delusional[161] and still be fit to plead is worrying and this anomaly has been further highlighted by a series of recent cases.

---

[155] [2008] EWCA Crim 1792.

[156] For additional examples see *Diamond* and *Moyle* below at paras 2.83 to 2.86 below.

[157] *Murray* [2008] EWCA Crim 1792 at [5].

[158] We think that it ought to have such a regard and that this is consistent with the thinking of Professor Duff to which we referred in Part 1.

[159] *Murray* [2008] EWCA Crim 1792 at [6].

[160] *Berry* (1978) 66 Cr App R 156.

[161] *Taylor* (1992) 77 CCC (3d) 551.

2.83 In *Moyle*[162] the defendant was found guilty of murder having declined to plead guilty to manslaughter on the grounds of diminished responsibility, despite a history of psychiatric problems and a diagnosis of paranoid schizophrenia at the time of the trial. The issue of unfitness to plead was not raised during the trial, despite the recommendation of a consultant psychiatrist.[163]

2.84 On appeal the court held that the defendant had been fit to plead at the time of the trial.[164] This was despite evidence that his delusions would have, "significantly impaired his ability to take a proper or valid part in his trial, and significantly affected his capacity to be properly defended in legal proceedings"[165] and that his mental disorder "might have affected his ability correctly to appraise, believe, weigh up and validly use information relating to the legal proceedings".[166]

2.85 *Diamond*[167] is a similar case. The defendant had pleaded not guilty to murder rather than avail himself of the partial defence of diminished responsibility, and had been found guilty. The Court of Appeal found that he was fit to plead at the time of the trial. However, the court acknowledged that one of the psychiatrists who gave evidence had identified a gap in the law in that:

> On the established test, a defendant is fit to plead in cases where his mental condition may well enable him to advance successfully the plea of diminished responsibility, yet his mental condition is still such that it may also prevent rational or sensible decision making as to the conduct of his defence. Once it is concluded that the defendant is fit to plead, although it may be apparent to everyone else that there is an issue as to whether his decision making is materially affected by his mental condition, he is entitled to refuse to have his mental condition assessed.[168]

---

[162] [2008] EWCA Crim 3059, [2009] *Criminal Law Review* 586.

[163] The reason for this was (among other things) the nature of the present test:
> Clearly, beliefs, one hopes always delusional, that the court is biased cannot extinguish a person's right to be tried or the public's right to have that person tried. A false belief about the punishment liable to be inflicted does not impair the defendant's ability to be tried.

[2008] EWCA Crim 3059, [2009] *Criminal Law Review* 586 at [39].

[164] According to the *Pritchard* criteria.

[165] *Moyle* [2008] EWCA Crim 3059, [2009] *Criminal Law Review* 586 at [27].

[166] Above at [27]. However, the Court of Appeal quashed the conviction for murder and substituted a conviction for manslaughter on the grounds of diminished responsibility, on the basis that the defendant's decisions at the time of trial were "affected by the illness itself".

[167] [2008] EWCA Crim 923, [2008] All ER (D) 401.

[168] *Diamond* [2008] EWCA Crim 923, [2008] All ER (D) 401 at [46].

2.86 As cases such as *Diamond* show, the unfairness of the present situation[169] is demonstrated by the fact that a defendant may, for example, be delusional and yet fit to plead because he or she has an underlying cognitive understanding. Yet his or her delusional state may well be such as to impair his or her capacity to make decisions. This makes a mockery of what we know of the concept of participation because although the defendant may appear to be engaging with the trial process,[170] the participation – such as it is – is not on the required level and is ultimately a sham in which legal professionals and the courts are forced to collude.

2.87 These difficulties (which result from having a legal test which does not take account of decision-making ability) have, as *Diamond, Moyle* and *Murray* show, to some extent been obscured by the way in which the Court of Appeal has so far been able to deal with them. This has been attributable to the fact that the cases have involved the appellant being charged with murder and the court has therefore been able to quash the conviction and substitute a conviction of manslaughter by reason of diminished responsibility.[171]

THE RELATIONSHIP BETWEEN CAPACITY AND PARTICIPATION

2.88 In our view, an accused's capacity to make decisions touches on the question of whether an accused is able to participate effectively in his or her trial. Participation as a jurisprudential concept is a relatively recent phenomenon, which may explain why it was not considered by either the CLRC or the Butler Committee. It has developed as a result of case law dealing with the right to a fair trial under article 6 of the European Convention on Human Rights.

The accused's right to participate effectively in the trial

2.89 The European Court of Human Rights has made it clear that article 6 of the Convention, read as a whole, "guarantees the right of an accused to participate effectively in a criminal trial".[172] In summary, the cases show that a defendant needs to have some level of active involvement in his or her trial which, in our view, would in practice require the accused to be able to make certain decisions.

---

[169] It is tempting to think that the unfairness only exists in relation to defendants but in fact, if justice is not done, then the criminal justice system is brought into disrepute and this is unfair to witnesses, victims of crimes and the public at large.

[170] RA Duff, *Trials and Punishments* (1986) p 119 to 120

[171] Section 2 of the Homicide Act 1957, which provides:
  (1) Where a person kills or is a party to a killing of another, he shall not be convicted of murder if he was suffering from such abnormality of mind (whether arising from a condition of arrested or retarded development of mind or any inherent causes or induced by disease or injury) as substantially impaired his metal responsibility for his acts or omissions in doing or being a party to the killing …
  (3) A person who but for this section would be liable, whether as a principal or as accessory to be convicted of murder shall be liable instead to be convicted of manslaughter.
  Section 52 of the Coroners and Justice Act 2009 which makes new provision for diminished responsibility is now in force in England and Wales.

[172] *Stanford v United Kingdom* App No 16757/90 at [22].

2.90   In *Stanford v United Kingdom*,[173] the applicant complained that he did not have a fair trial because he was unable to hear the proceedings. The applicant's solicitor and counsel were aware of this problem but no complaint was made to the trial judge. Although the court interpreted article 6 as providing for a right to effective participation, it held that there had not been a breach of article 6 in this case.[174] The court noted that the decision to remain silent about the applicant's hearing difficulties was made for tactical reasons and there was nothing to suggest that he disagreed with this decision at the time.[175] Moreover, the applicant was represented by solicitor and counsel who had no difficulty in following the proceedings and would have been able to discuss with the applicant any evidence which did not already appear in the witness statements.[176]

2.91   In *Stanford*, the court stated that the right to participate effectively in the trial included, amongst others, the right of an accused to be present and to hear and follow the proceedings.[177] Effective participation was also the general principle behind the specific rights of the accused listed in article 6(3) of the European Convention – "to defend himself in person", "to examine or have examined witnesses", and "to have the free assistance of an interpreter if he cannot understand or speak the language used in court".[178] For the court, the right to effective participation is "implicit in the very notion of an adversarial procedure".[179]

2.92   The principle of effective participation in *Stanford* was further developed in the joint cases of *T v United Kingdom* and *V v United Kingdom*.[180] T and V were 11 years old when they were tried and convicted of murder and abduction in circumstances which attracted considerable media and public interest. Their trial took place in the Crown Court and was conducted with the full formality of an adult trial – for example, gowns and wigs were worn. Court procedures were however modified to a certain extent given the defendants' ages at the time. Measures taken included taking the defendants to the courtroom prior to trial and giving them a "child witness pack" to introduce them to court procedures; seating them next to social workers in a specially raised dock so they could see the courtroom; having their parents and lawyers seated nearby; shortened hearing times to reflect the school day; and regular breaks.

---

[173] App No 16757/90.

[174] Above at [32].

[175] Above at [23].

[176] Above at [30].

[177] Above at [26]. The court observed that the right of an accused to be present at his or her trial was already protected under English common law, which covered both his or her physical presence and ability to understand the nature of the proceedings: see Lord Reading CJ in *Lee Kun* (1916) 1 Kings Bench Reports 337 at 341, cited by the court in *Stanford* at [17].

[178] *Stanford v United Kingdom* App No 16757/90 at [26].

[179] Above at [26].

[180] *T v United Kingdom* App No 24724/94 and *V v United Kingdom* App No 24888/94, reported as a joint decision in (2000) 30 EHRR 121.

2.93 Part of the applicants' claim before the European Court of Human Rights was that they were denied a fair trial in breach of article 6 because they had not been able to participate effectively in the criminal proceedings against them. In relation to T, there was psychiatric evidence that he was suffering from post-traumatic stress disorder and that this, combined with the lack of therapeutic work after the offence, meant that he had limited ability to instruct his lawyers and to testify in his own defence.[181] In V's case, there was evidence that he had the emotional maturity of a younger child; that he was too traumatised and intimidated to give his account of events to his lawyers or the court; and that he was not able to follow or understand the proceedings. The court (with one judge dissenting) found that the applicants were unable to participate effectively in the proceedings and were denied a fair trial as guaranteed by article 6.

2.94 The court once again emphasised that article 6 guarantees the "right of an accused to participate effectively in his criminal trial".[182] This was the first case in which the court had to consider how this guarantee applies to children. The general rule, reiterated in the later case of *SC v United Kingdom*,[183] is that:

> It is essential that a child charged with an offence is dealt with in a manner which takes full account of his age, level of maturity and intellectual and emotional capacities, and that steps are taken to promote his ability to understand and participate in the proceedings.[184]

2.95 This general idea can be extended to apply to any vulnerable defendant, in that in order for article 6 to be satisfied, consideration must be given to the accused's vulnerability and steps taken to ensure that he or she can understand and participate in the proceedings. Indeed, it is a result of cases such as *T* and *V* that there is now a Practice Direction which applies in the Crown Court and magistrates' courts to children or adults with a mental disorder or significant impairment of intelligence and social functioning (referred to collectively as "vulnerable defendants").[185]

---

[181] *T v United Kingdom* App No 24724/94 and *V v United Kingdom* App No 24888/94, reported as a joint decision in (2000) 30 EHRR 121 at [80].

[182] Above at [85].

[183] *SC v United Kingdom* (2005) 40 EHRR 10 (App No 60958/00) at [28].

[184] *T v United Kingdom* App No 24724/94 and *V v United Kingdom* App No 24888/94, reported as a joint decision in (2000) 30 EHRR 121 at [86].

[185] Practice Direction (Criminal Proceedings: Consolidation), para III.30 (as inserted by Practice Direction: Criminal proceedings: Further Directions) [2007] 1 WLR 1790). See further the discussion of special measures in Part 4 below.

2.96   In finding that the applicants in this case had been denied a fair trial, the court felt that, unlike in *Stanford*, it was not sufficient that they had been represented by skilled and experienced lawyers.[186] This was because, in the circumstances of the trial, it was unlikely that the applicants would have felt sufficiently uninhibited to have consulted with their lawyers during the trial.[187] Moreover, their immaturity and disturbed emotional state meant that they would have not been capable of cooperating with their lawyers outside the courtroom and giving them information for the purposes of their defence.[188] Such reasoning suggests that the court views effective participation as requiring some form of active involvement from the accused in his or her trial.

2.97   In *SC v United Kingdom*,[189] the court gave further examples of what the right to effective participation requires. The applicant in this case was again a child, who was 11 years old when he was tried and convicted for attempted robbery. There was evidence that he had limited intellectual ability, a poor attention span and would be unlikely to follow the proceedings. The psychiatrist who examined him had concluded that, while he was fit to enter a plea, the court would have to ensure that the procedure was explained to him in terms that he could understand.[190] The judge had rejected the submission that to try the accused in the Crown Court would be an abuse of process given that procedures were now habitually adopted in the Crown Court to reduce the formality of the trial. During his trial, the applicant was not made to sit in the dock and was accompanied by his social worker. Regular breaks were also taken and the judge and counsel did not wear wigs or gowns.[191]

2.98   The applicant appealed to the Court of Appeal on the basis of new evidence from the social worker who had sat with him during the trial which suggested he had been confused and had not understood what was going on, particularly when he was sentenced to custody. The Court of Appeal however rejected this evidence on the basis that the trial judge had taken into account the defendant's age, level of maturity and intellectual and emotional capacities, and that steps had been taken to promote his ability to understand and participate in the proceedings.[192]

2.99   The European Court of Human Rights, however, found that the applicant was not able to participate effectively in the proceedings and therefore was denied a fair trial. It recognised that the measures taken were consistent with the Practice Direction concerning the trial of children and young persons in the Crown Court, although this had not been in force at the time of the applicant's trial. The court also accepted that a child defendant, as with an adult, did not need to be able to understand every point of law or evidential detail. However, it went on to say:

[186] *T v United Kingdom* (App No 24724/94) and *V v United Kingdom* (App No 24888/94), reported as a joint decision in (2000) 30 EHRR 121 at [90].

[187] Above. The court gave particular weight to the public attention that the case attracted – for example, there was a full public gallery – and also that some measures, such as the raised dock, may have heightened the applicants' feelings of discomfort during the trial: at [88].

[188] Above at [90].

[189] *SC v United Kingdom* (2005) 40 EHRR 10 (App No 60958/00).

[190] Above at [13].

[191] Above at [15].

[192] Above at [18].

"Effective participation" in this context presupposes that the accused has a broad understanding of the nature of the trial process and of what is at stake for him or her, including the significance of any penalty which may be imposed. It means that he or she, if necessary with the assistance of, for example, an interpreter, lawyer, social worker or friend, should be able to understand the general thrust of what is said in court. The defendant should be able to follow what is said by the prosecution witnesses and, if represented, to explain to his own lawyers his version of events, point out any statements with which he disagrees and make them aware of any facts which should be put forward in his defence.[193]

2.100 From this, the court concluded that the applicant was not capable of participating effectively in his trial, giving particular emphasis to the fact that he had not grasped the fact that he could face a custodial sentence.[194] Importantly, the decision in *SC* suggests that a child defendant will only be able to participate effectively if he or she is tried in a youth court:[195]

> where the decision is taken to deal with a child who risks not being able to participate effectively because of his young age and limited intellectual capacity, by way of criminal proceedings ... [then] it is essential that he should be tried in a specialist tribunal which is able to give full consideration to and make proper allowance for the handicaps under which he labours, and adapts its procedure accordingly.[196]

---

[193] *SC v United Kingdom* (2005) 40 EHRR 10 (App No 60958/00) at [29].

[194] Above at [32] to [34].

[195] It was on this basis that the High Court dismissed an application for judicial review of the decision not to stay proceedings in a youth court for an abuse of process: *R (TP) v West London Youth Court* [2005] EWHC 2583 (Admin), [2006] 1 WLR 1219. The High Court reasoned that the youth court would be able to make the necessary adjustments in order to increase the accused's (who had limited intellectual capacity) involvement in the proceedings and that a number of steps could be taken. It reasoned that the conclusion in *SC* was that a child should be tried in a specialist tribunal, which was the youth court: see *SC v United Kingdom* (2005) 40 EHRR 10 at [26] to [27]. We look at *R (TP) v West London Youth Court* (2005) EWCH 2583 (Admin), [2006] 1 WLR 1219 at para 8.40 below.

[196] *SC v United Kingdom* (2005) 40 EHRR 10 (App No 60958/00) at [35].

2.101   The court also noted that while a psychiatrist had found that the applicant had sufficient intelligence to understand what he had done was wrong and therefore was fit to plead,[197] it did not follow from this that he was capable of participating effectively in his trial to the extent required by article 6.[198] This suggests that effective participation goes beyond the cognitive abilities of the accused. In this regard, the Mental Health Act Commission has raised concerns that if the *Pritchard* test "is interpreted literally as a test of cognition, it is possible that persons without mental capacity to participate effectively in criminal proceedings could still progress to trial, which could lead to a breach of ECHR article 6".[199]

2.102   In summary, the case law of the European Court of Human Rights provides examples of specific things that an accused must be able to do in order to participate effectively in criminal proceedings. For example, he or she must be able to consult with lawyers or give them information in order to conduct the defence. However, in our view, the underlying reasoning in the cases gives rise to a broader principle – namely, that effective participation requires active involvement on the part of the accused rather than just a passive presence.[200] We believe this is also reflected in some of the specific requirements for effective participation. For example, in order to give meaningful instructions an accused will have to be able to make certain decisions. However, it is also clear from the case law that where the accused's abilities are limited, he or she may still be able to participate effectively in the trial as long as certain steps are taken.

---

[197] In fact, an understanding on the part of the defendant that what he or she had done was wrong is not part of the legal test for unfitness to plead. This suggests some conflation between the concepts of insanity and unfitness to plead.

[198] *SC v United Kingdom* (2005) 40 EHRR 10 (App No 60958/00) at [36].

[199] Mental Health Act Commission, *In place of fear? Eleventh Biennial Report* (2005) at para 5.19.

[200] In *R (TP) v West London Youth Court* [2005] EWHC 2583 (Admin), [2006] 1 WLR 1219 the High Court also seemed to suggest that effective participation requires the accused's active involvement in the trial, in that it agreed at [7] with the district judge's interpretation of the right to a fair trial as follows:

> [The accused had] to be able to give proper instructions and to participate by way of providing answers to questions and suggesting questions to his lawyers in the circumstances of the trial as they arose [and] had to have the opportunity to consider what representations he wished to make once he understood the issues involved.

Vulnerable defendants

2.103   The issue of participation in the trial has arisen in the context of vulnerable defendants.[201] There is a difficult area between being unfit to plead and being fit to plead but, due to an impairment or condition, needing assistance to participate effectively in the trial process. The concept of the right to effective participation has been developed, both in the jurisprudence of the European Court of Human Rights and now in domestic case law, mainly in relation to child defendants.[202] The general principles have however been extended in domestic law to vulnerable adults. Such developments, however, have occurred outside the context of unfitness to plead. In our view, there needs to be greater coherence between the development of effective participation and special measures and reform of the legal test for unfitness to plead.

2.104   There have been improvements in terms of facilitating participation in the trial process for vulnerable defendants through the imposition of special measures. Special measures are measures which the court can adopt to assist the defendant to understand, follow and properly participate in his or her trial.[203] Such measures include giving a vulnerable accused the opportunity of giving evidence through a live link.[204] Recent studies have revealed that there is still considerable progress which needs to be made.[205] Other studies have shown that special measures do not necessarily always have the desired effect.[206] This tends to be because although they are put into place at the outset of the trial, they do not last throughout the proceedings because it is all too easy for the legal profession and the judiciary to forget that the measures are in place.

---

[201] Defendants who have some mental or social impairment but who are not classified as unfit to plead.

[202] See discussion at paras 2.89 to 2.102 above.

[203] See for example, Practice Direction (Criminal Proceedings: Consolidation) para III.30 as inserted by Practice Direction (Criminal Proceedings: Further Directions) [2007] 1 WLR 1790.

[204] See s 33A of the Youth Justice and Criminal Evidence Act 1999, as amended by s 47 of the Police and Justice Act 2006.

[205] See the recent paper published by the Prison Reform Trust: J Jacobson with J Talbot , *Vulnerable defendants in the criminal courts: a review of the provision for adults and children* (Prison Reform Trust 2009).

[206] See TP Rogers et al, "Reformulating fitness to plead: a qualitative study" (2009) 20(6) *Journal of Forensic Psychiatry and Psychology* 815, 828.

2.105   It seems to us that the effects of the distinction between the trial and the section 4A hearing which we have referred to at paragraphs 2.28 to 2.31 is underlined in the context of vulnerable defendants because many vulnerable defendants could, with the assistance of special measures, be able to effectively participate in a trial. Article 6 of the European Convention on Human Rights was not something which was specifically considered by Professor Duff to whose views we have already referred to in Part 1. For Professor Duff, who was writing in 1986, the choice was a stark one between a trial with no special measures or being found unfit to plead. Advances concerning vulnerable defendants and the possibility of further advances in the area of special measures may mean that the choice need not be quite so stark in the future. The importance of developing inclusion for vulnerable defendants has been noted elsewhere with the caveat that such developments should not be allowed to derogate from the importance of unfitness to plead.[207] As we explain in Part 4 of this CP, we agree with this proposition.

CONCLUSIONS

2.106   We think that in light of the problems we have described in relation to the *Pritchard* criteria, a new legal test is needed to replace the current test for unfitness to plead. This is particularly so given the developments in relation to participation and vulnerable defendants. A new concept is needed which takes into account these developments and which is in line with modern psychiatric thinking. In the next Part, we discuss our provisional proposals for a new legal test which is based on decision-making capacity.

---

[207] TP Rogers, NJ Blackwood, F Farnham, GJ Pickup, MJ Watts, "Fitness to plead and competence to stand trial: a systematic review of the constructs and their application" (2008) 19(4) *Journal of Forensic Psychiatry and Psychology* 576, at 585 where it is recognised that special measures have been adopted to help "borderline" unfit defendants to cope with the trial, but that "this should not diminish the importance of re-evaluating our approach to the mentally ill in court".

PART 3
A NEW LEGAL TEST

INTRODUCTION

3.1 In Part 2, we analysed the problems with the current common law test for unfitness to plead (the *Pritchard* test). Given these problems, and given the developing concept of effective participation in relation to article 6 of the European Convention on Human Rights, we believe that it is necessary to have a new legal test. We therefore provisionally propose that the current common law test for unfitness to plead (the *Pritchard* test) should be replaced. In this Part we discuss what the new legal test should be. In our view, it should be a test which is based on, or takes into account, the decision-making abilities of the accused. We refer to this proposed new test as the "decision-making capacity" test.

What we mean by "decision-making capacity"

3.2 Later in this Part we explore the concept of capacity in greater detail and the way in which it could apply in the criminal context. However, it is useful at the outset to give an overview of what we think a decision-making capacity test would require.

3.3 In this regard, we have considered the capacity test under various branches of the civil law and the capacity test which is provided for by the Mental Capacity Act 2005. There is little difference in civil law between the test for capacity which exists pursuant to common law and that which exists under the Mental Capacity Act 2005. For example, in *Re MM*[1] it was held, amongst other things, that there was no distinction between the common law test for capacity and the statutory test:

> *Re MB*[2] and *Masterman-Lister*[3] … reflect a general theory which … has now been given statutory force in section 3 of the [Mental Capacity Act 2005] … The test in its statutory form applies to all the aspects of 'personal welfare' referred to in section 17 of the [Mental Capacity Act 2005]. It would be most unfortunate if the common law were to draw distinctions alien to a statutory scheme which is, in significant part, built on common law foundations. And it would be worse than unfortunate if a judge of the Family Division exercising the inherent jurisdiction had to adopt an approach significantly different

---

[1] [2001] EWHC 2003 (Fam), [2009] 1 FLR 443. In this case, MM suffered from paranoid schizophrenia, had an IQ of 56, a moderate learning disability and poor cognitive functioning. The local authority had applied for declarations as to MM's lack of capacity to conduct litigation on her own behalf; to decide where and with whom she would reside; to determine with whom she should have contact; to manage her financial arrangements and to enter into a contract of marriage. Further declarations were sought that it was in the best interests of MM that she reside in supported accommodation provided by the local authority and that she had no contact with KM (a person with whom she was having a relationship which was believed to be damaging to her safety and to her health). The local authority also asked for orders regulating MM's contact with KM. In making final declarations as to MM's capacity, and interim orders as to her placement and contact with KM and directing that the local authority file a care plan setting out proposals for contact including resumption of MM's sexual relationship with KM, the court held that the common law and the Mental Capacity Act 2005 were to be read consistently: see [78] to [80].

[2] [1997] FLR 426.

[3] [2002] EWCA Civ 1889, [2003] 1 WLR 1511.

51

from the approach to be adopted by the same judge when sitting in the Court of Protection exercising the statutory jurisdiction.[4]

3.4 The civil test takes a functional approach to capacity in that it assesses a person's ability to make a particular decision at a particular moment in time, and not a person's ability to make decisions more generally.[5] In civil law therefore capacity is "issue specific" so for example, a litigant (P) may have capacity to marry but lack capacity to make a will. The Family Division or the Court of Protection may therefore make a multi-limb declaration covering a number of different "issues" in relation to which P does or does not have capacity.[6]

3.5 There is a distinction between "litigation capacity" and "subject matter capacity". This distinction is consistent with the principle that capacity in civil law is "issue specific" so there can be, and are, cases where P has capacity to do something but lacks the capacity to litigate about the subject of the proceedings. An example would be where the question arises of a parent consenting to the making of an adoption order. This is a process which (because adoption is always a judicial act) requires litigation. There may be cases where although a parent has capacity to give consent to adoption he or she nevertheless does not have the capacity to act in the litigation without a litigation friend.[7]

3.6 Under the civil law, a person is not found to lack capacity simply because he or she has a mental disorder or disability (a "status" approach to capacity). Moreover, a person cannot be found to lack capacity on the basis that he or she has made a decision which is inconsistent with conventional values or with which the person assessing capacity disagrees or which is irrational (an "outcome" approach).[8] However, while an unwise or irrational decision cannot be taken as proof that someone lacks capacity, under the Mental Capacity Act 2005 it can trigger the need for an assessment of that person's capacity.[9]

3.7 The civil law's approach to capacity also involves the application of the concept of "proportionality".[10]

3.8 By "proportionality" we mean that the threshold of capacity varies depending on the decision which has to be made. The more serious the possible consequences of the decision or the more complex the issue which is the subject of that decision, then the higher the threshold of capacity required. The application of the principle of proportionality to an issue specific approach means that the question

---

[4] *Re MM* [2007] EWHC 2003 (Fam), [2009] 1 FLR 443 at [78] by Munby J.

[5] See paras 3.27 to 3.29 below for a discussion of the Mental Capacity Act 2005 Code of Practice.

[6] As was the case in *Re MM* [2007] EWHC 2003 (Fam), [2009] 1 FLR 443: see n 1 above. See also *Re PS* [2007] EWHC 623 (Fam), [2007] 2 FLR 1083 at [4].

[7] *Sheffield City Council v E* [2004] EWHC 2808 (Fam), [2005] Fam 326 at [40] to [42].

[8] The different approaches to capacity are highlighted in D Powell, "House of Lords: sexual offences and the Mental Capacity Act" (2010) 74(2) *Journal of Criminal Law* 104, 106.

[9] See the Mental Capacity Act 2005 Code of Practice, para 2.11. See *Sidaway v Board of Governors of Bethlem Royal Hospital* [1985] AC 871 for discussion of the rights of patients with capacity to make irrational and self-endangering decisions.

[10] Although the word "proportionality" adequately describes that to which we refer in para 3.8 below, it is not a term which is used in the civil law.

is "does P have the capacity[11] to conduct this particular piece of litigation?" or "does P have the capacity to consent to this particular medical intervention?" as opposed to "does P have the capacity to litigate or consent generally?"[12]

3.9   So the litigant, P, might have capacity to consent to a medical procedure but lack capacity to litigate about that very procedure if the circumstances are such that the litigation was likely to be complex. How capacity is measured in proportional terms will typically include considerations of matters such as gravity and complexity. Gravity itself is measured by reference to implications and consequences.[13] Later in this part we discuss the implications of such a test for criminal trials.[14]

3.10   The level of forensic complexity is peculiar to each specific case. This is true of both the civil context and the criminal context. So in the latter, a case which involves more than one defendant (each of whom are running mutually exclusive defences) is likely to be more complex than a case where there is only one defendant or where there is more than one defendant but all defendants are running the same defence. If one of the defendants in a multi-handed trial has relevant previous convictions then it may be more complex than a case where all defendants are of good character. Similarly, a case where the prosecution rely on admissible background evidence in addition to the evidence going directly to the counts on the indictment, is likely to prove more complex than a case which only requires scrutiny of specific counts on the indictment and so forth.

3.11   We believe that the functional approach under civil law is preferable to a status or outcome approach to capacity in the context of unfitness to plead. In this Part we provisionally propose that there should be a test of decision-making capacity which considers whether the accused has the capacity to do the range of tasks or make the range of decisions which are involved in his or her trial. As we have seen, in civil law, this is referred to as litigation capacity. This is informed by the functional approach in civil law in that the focus is on the decision-making process of the accused. Importantly, this means that an accused should not be presumed to lack capacity simply because he or she has a particular mental disorder or disability, or has made an unwise decision. However, if the civil approach to capacity was to be wholly adopted in the criminal context then the principle of proportionality would become central to determinations of capacity as

---

[11]   We do not use the term "sufficient capacity" because in our view, a person either does have capacity or does not have capacity *in relation to an issue*.

[12]   See *Sheffield City Council v E* [2004] EWHC 2808 (Fam), [2005] Fam 326 at [38] to [39].

[13]   See *Re T (Adult: Refusal of Treatment)* [1993] Fam 95, 113: "what matters is that the doctors should consider whether at that time he had a capacity which was commensurate with the gravity of the decision which he purported to make" by Lord Donaldson MR, cited in *Sheffield City Council v E* [2004] EWHC 2808 (Fam), [2005] Fam 326 at [29]. For an analogous discussion in the context of children's capacity see *Gillick v West Norfolk and Wisbech Area Health Authority* [1986] AC 112, Lord Fraser at 169 and Lord Scarman at 189. The issue has also arisen in the context of what capacity is required in the civil law to consent to sexual intercourse: see *X City Council v MB* [2006] EWHC 168 (Fam), [2006] 2 FLR 968 at [70] to [74]. See also *Masterman-Lister v Jewell* [2003] 1 WLR 1511 at [27], [29] and *Re MB (Medical treatment)* [1977] 2 FLR 426.

[14]   See para 3.83 and onwards below.

it is under civil law.[15] This is an issue to which we return below.[16] Although it is our provisional view that the concept of proportionality as we discussed in paragraph 3.8 above should not apply in the criminal context, and this view forms the basis of our provisional proposal 3, we are also inviting consultees to respond to an alternative proposal in this regard. Provisional proposal 4 is an alternative to provisional proposal 3 which takes the concept of proportionality into account.

3.12 The test which we provisionally propose is also informed by the principle of effective participation discussed in Part 2. We believe that a decision-making capacity test in criminal proceedings would ensure that the necessary requirements for participation were met.

3.13 A person would therefore lack decision-making capacity if he or she is unable to make decisions for him or herself in relation to his or her trial. In establishing whether a person is unable to make such decisions, we think that section 3 of the Mental Capacity Act 2005 is useful. We provisionally propose that an accused should be found to lack capacity if he or she is unable:

(1) to understand the information relevant to the decisions that he or she will have to make in the course of his or her trial,[17]

(2) to retain that information,[18]

(3) to use or weigh that information as part of decision making process, or

(4) to communicate his or her decisions.

3.14 As we discuss further below, this decision-making capacity test would involve a single assessment of decision-making capacity, which will usually occur at the

---

[15] See further para 3.29 below.

[16] See paras 3.83 and onwards below.

[17] We would also provisionally propose that (as under s 3(2) of the Mental Capacity Act 2005) a person should not be regarded as unable to understand the information relevant to a decision if he or she is able to understand an explanation of it given to him or her in a way that is appropriate to his or her circumstances (using simple language, visual aids or any other means). Relevant information also includes information about the reasonably foreseeable consequences of making a decision one way or another, or of failing to make a decision (see s 3(4) of the Mental Capacity Act 2005).

[18] For as long as it would be necessary to make the decision as under s 3(3) of the Mental Capacity Act 2005, the fact that a person is able to retain the information for a short period only would not prevent him or her from being regarded as having decision-making capacity.

outset of the trial or when the issue is raised[19] (sometimes referred to as a unitary test).[20]

3.15   It is useful at the outset to give a few examples of how this new decision-making capacity test could apply in different situations.

Example 3A

A was involved in a motorcycle accident when he was younger. He suffered head injuries and sustained lasting brain damage. As a result, he has the mental age of a five-year-old and a very low cognitive ability. He does not understand much of what is said to him and finds unfamiliar surroundings frightening.

3.16   We think the facts of example 3A illustrate a lack of decision-making capacity as contemplated in paragraph 3.13(1) because A will not be able to understand new and unfamiliar information, or relate such information to what he needs to think about or needs to do in the course of his trial.

Example 3B

A is suffering from severe depression. He has no interest in interacting with other people and says that he does not care what happens to him. He has a disturbed sleep pattern, poor concentration and is unable to remember things. He has difficulty focusing on specific matters and has a poor ability to express himself verbally.

3.17   We think that the facts of example 3B illustrate a lack of decision-making capacity as contemplated in paragraph 3.13(2). This is because A will not be able to retain information or retain sufficient information to be able to focus on a decision or on subsequent decisions which may be related to his initial decision.

---

[19]   Subject, of course, to the fact that, if it is raised at the outset, it would still be possible to postpone the determination of the issue up until the opening of the defence case. However s 51 of the Crime and Disorder Act 1998 and s 41 of and Sch 3 to the Criminal Justice Act 2003, which provide for transfer for trial in the case of offences which are triable either way, may mean that in the main, the issue will be dealt with at the outset. This is because applications to dismiss are dealt with before arraignment.

[20]   Broadly speaking, the issue is how we can establish a legal test which covers all the decisions which are likely to arise in the context of a trial and which accommodates the wide spectrum of difficulties likely to be encountered without the result of that test being unduly limiting for particular defendants who may be able to make some decisions but not others.

<blockquote>

Example 3C

A is a 13-year-old male who suffers from severe Attention-Deficit Hyperactivity Disorder (ADHD). This is at its worst when he is anxious. He cannot focus and is impulsive. He finds it almost impossible to remember any new information he is given.

</blockquote>

3.18 We think that the facts of example 3C also illustrate a lack of decision-making capacity as contemplated in paragraph 3.13(2) as A's condition will prevent him from retaining information. This example also illustrates a lack of decision-making capacity as envisaged in paragraph 3.13(3). This is because he will not be able to use or weigh the information that he will be given to make the decisions which are necessary because of his inability to retain it. His impulsiveness will prevent him from considering information properly or from responding to it in an appropriate way.

<blockquote>

Example 3D

A suffers from paranoid schizophrenia. He understands the charge but indicates to the court that he wants to plead guilty because "there is no point" pleading not guilty as everyone in the court including the judge and the jury are out to "get him". He is convinced that his counsel and his solicitor are part of this conspiracy and he believes they are making the evidence up to make his predicament worse than it is. He has no insight into his condition.

</blockquote>

3.19 We think that the facts of example 3D illustrate a lack of decision-making capacity as envisaged in paragraph 3.13(3) because A is unable to use or weigh information to make a decision. His decisions are being made as a result of his mental disorder and are consequently flawed.[21] The delusions from which he is

---

[21] We have said in example 3D that A has no insight into his condition. In our view, this alone would not necessarily mean that he lacks capacity. The relationship between capacity and insight has been discussed in the context of decisions as to medical treatment and whether or not it is possible for a person who lacks insight into his or her condition to retain capacity to refuse treatment for that condition. In other words, where a person chooses to believe, contrary to what has been said by his or her doctors, that he or she is mentally well, is he or she still capable of making decisions as to medical treatment? Although true understanding and belief are closely linked, a requirement for belief could mean that a person may be found to lack capacity simply because he or she makes a decision with which the person assessing capacity disagrees. Allen for example has argued that if we are not able to understand anything that we do not believe in, this would "make it impossible to disbelieve a doctor and retain capacity": see N Allen, "Is capacity 'in sight'" [2009] *Journal of Mental Health Law* 165 at 169. In *Re C* [1994] 1 WLR 290, [1994] 1 All ER 819 a patient suffering from paranoid schizophrenia was found to have capacity to refuse amputation after developing gangrene in his foot. The court reasoned that there was no evidence of a link between C's refusal and his delusions: see p 823. He did not, for example, believe that he would die because of the gangrene, despite being told that without amputation he only had a 15% chance of survival. However, although his general capacity was impaired by his mental disorder, it was not established that he did not "sufficiently understand the nature, purpose and effects of the treatment". At p 824, Thorpe J went onto say: "He has understood and retained the relevant information, that in his own way he believes it, and that in the same fashion he has arrived at a clear choice". This case suggests that a person can have capacity even though he or she does not accept the medical evaluation.

suffering do not, without more, mean that there is an absence of decision-making capacity. Rather, it is the fact that A's decision is being made on the basis of his delusion which means that he lacks capacity.

Example 3E

A suffers from obsessive compulsive disorder which is at its worst whenever he is stressed or anxious. Whenever he is asked a question, he feels compelled to consider the question from all angles and ruminates obsessively about the underlying meaning of the words or phrases in the question. He finds it impossible to come to a clear conclusion and make a decision.

3.20 We think that the facts of example 3E could also illustrate a lack of decision-making capacity as envisaged in paragraph 3.13(3) as when A is in this state of mind, he cannot use or weigh information to make decisions because all his decisions are subject to his compulsion.[22]

Example 3F

A is autistic and is unable to communicate with others. He can understand information and process lots of it, but does not acknowledge others and tends to "live in his own world".

3.21 We think that example 3F illustrates a lack of capacity as envisaged in paragraph 3.13(4) because A has such difficulty communicating.

3.22 Whereas the above examples show a range of conditions which may render an accused unfit (or demonstrate a lack of decision-making capacity), we are unable to say at this stage how many people passing through the criminal justice system would qualify under our proposed test. Neither are we yet in a position to extrapolate figures from that proportion of the population who suffer from such conditions.

A CAPACITY BASED TEST

3.23 We have given an overview of our provisional decision-making capacity test. It is clear from Part 2 that there are two problems in so far as the current legal test for unfitness to plead (the *Pritchard* test) is concerned. First, it places a disproportionate emphasis on cognitive ability, and does not take any or sufficient account of factors such as emotion or volition. Secondly, it does not take account of the capacity of the accused to make decisions relating to his or her trial.

3.24 The second of these factors is often a result of the first. Commentators have drawn attention to the distinction between the tests for unfitness to plead in criminal law and for capacity in civil law and in doing so, they have highlighted the inadequacy of the criminal law.[23]

---

[22] We are grateful to Dr Tim Exworthy for his assistance.

[23] L Scott-Moncrieff and G Vassall-Adams, "Yawning gap: capacity and fitness to plead" *Counsel Magazine*, October 2006, 14.

The capacity test under civil law

3.25 The Mental Capacity Act 2005 definitions of capacity apply for the purpose of the Act.[24] As we have stated at paragraph 3.3 there is very little difference between the definition in the Mental Capacity Act and the definition at common law.

3.26 The Mental Capacity Act 2005 is based on the Law Commission's recommendations on mental capacity[25] and is intended to provide a legislative scheme to ensure that decisions and actions can be lawfully made on behalf of people who lack capacity to take the action or make the decision for themselves.[26] Section 2 provides the following definition of capacity:

(1) For the purposes of this Act, a person lacks capacity in relation to a matter if at the material time he is unable to make a[27] decision for himself in relation to a matter because of an impairment of, or a disturbance in the functioning of, the mind or brain.

(2) It does not matter whether the impairment or disturbance is permanent or temporary.

(3) A lack of capacity cannot be established merely by reference to –

    (a) a person's age or appearance, or

    (b) a condition of his, or an aspect of his behaviour, which might lead others to make unjustified assumptions about his capacity.

(4) In proceedings under this Act or any other enactment, any question whether a person lacks capacity within the meaning of this Act must be decided on the balance of probabilities.

(5) No power which a person ("D") may exercise under this Act –

    (a) in relation to a person who lacks capacity, or

    (b) where D reasonably thinks that a person lacks capacity, is exercisable in relation to a person under 16.

3.27 There is, therefore, a basic diagnostic threshold which has to be reached in order to establish a lack of capacity (this being that there has to be an impairment of, or a disturbance in the functioning of, the mind or brain). Although it may not be immediately apparent from a reading of section 2, the test for capacity for which it provides is one which assesses the individual's ability to make a decision given

---

[24] Most of the Act was implemented in October 2007.

[25] See Mental Incapacity (1995) Law Com No 231.

[26] The Mental Capacity Act 2005 is accompanied by a Code of Practice which provides detailed guidance on implementation whilst simultaneously protecting the autonomy of the vulnerable subjects.

[27] The wording focuses on a single decision because capacity is determined on an issue-specific basis.

the specific demands of a particular situation. This is evidenced by the Mental Capacity Act 2005 Code of Practice which explicitly states:

> In this chapter, as throughout the Code, a person's capacity (or lack of capacity) refers specifically to their capacity to make a particular decision at the time it needs to be made.[28]

3.28 We explained what we mean by this in paragraphs 3.4 to 3.8 above.

3.29 The Code also states, for example, that "an assessment of a person's capacity must be based on their ability to make a specific decision at the time it needs to be made, and not their ability to make decisions in general".[29] This principle is reiterated in respect of every aspect of the civil test. Another example is that the Code highlights that "for a person to lack capacity to make a decision, the Act says their impairment or disturbance must affect their ability to make the specific decision when they need to".[30] It is clear therefore that the approach is context and time specific.

3.30 Section 3 of the Mental Capacity Act 2005 defines what is meant by "inability to make decisions":

(1) For the purposes of section 2, a person is unable to make a decision for himself if he is unable –

(a) to understand the information relevant to the decision,

(b) to retain that information,

(c) to use or weigh that information as part of the process of making the decision, or

(d) to communicate his decision (whether by talking, using sign language or any other means).

(2) A person is not to be regarded as unable to understand the information relevant to a decision if he is able to understand an explanation of it given to him in a way that is appropriate to his circumstances (using simple language, visual aids or any other means).

(3) The fact that a person is able to retain the information relevant to a decision for a short period only does not prevent him from being regarded as able to make the decision.

(4) The information relevant to a decision includes information about the reasonably foreseeable consequences of –

(a) deciding one way or another, or

---

[28] Mental Capacity Act 2005 Code of Practice, p 19.

[29] Above, para 4.4.

[30] Above, para 4.13.

(b)   failing to make the decision.

3.31   As we indicated at paragraph 3.13, we believe that factors similar to those listed in section 3 should be relevant to determining whether an accused lacks decision-making capacity. It is section 3 that ensures a focus on the decision-making process rather than, for example, the content of a person's decision.

3.32   In proposing a test based on a model that works in civil law, we are assuming that in criminal proceedings the judge's ability to predict the likely events as to which a defendant will have to make decisions during the course of a trial is no more onerous than in civil proceedings and that this is so notwithstanding that there can be some unpredictability about how a criminal trial might progress.

3.33   It has been argued that the true basis of the capacity test in civil law is one of proportionality.[31] We accept that proportionality is an intrinsic aspect of civil capacity. As we have already explained at paragraph 3.8, this principle means that the circumstances surrounding and consequent to the decision to which the question of capacity attaches bear on the threshold for capacity. In other words, the more serious the possible consequences of a particular decision, the higher the threshold for a person to be found to have the capacity to make that decision.[32] Equally, the more complex the facts of the case and any other matters which are likely to arise during the case itself, then the higher the threshold for capacity should be. This is an integral aspect of civil law.[33] Although it is not referred to expressly in the Mental Capacity Act 2005, it is a concept which has long been considered part of the common law.[34] For reasons which we explain below,[35] our provisional view is that civil capacity and a decision-making capacity test for criminal proceedings cannot be analogous in this respect.

Capacity in criminal proceedings

3.34   At the beginning of this Part we gave an overview of what we mean by a test of decision-making capacity for criminal proceedings. We now discuss in further detail the justifications for having such a test and consider the way in which it could apply in the context of a criminal trial.

---

[31]   L Scott-Moncrieff and G Vassall-Adams, "Yawning gap: capacity and fitness to plead" *Counsel Magazine*, October 2006, 14. See also T Exworthy, "Commentary: UK perspective on competency to stand trial" (2006) 34 *Journal of the American Academy of Psychiatry and the Law* 466, where at 471 Dr Exworthy writes:

> The principle of proportionality is now firmly embedded in case law concerning the level of capacity required for health care decisions, and this general approach can also be discerned in the procedures scheduled to arrive in 2007 with the implementation of the Mental Capacity Act.

[32]   A Buchanan, "Competency to stand trial and the seriousness of the charge" (2006) 34(4) *Journal of the American Academy of Psychiatry and the Law* 458, 460:

> There have been suggestions that the criminal law should adopt this principle of proportionality with respect to competence to stand trial. The commentary accompanying the ABA's [American Bar Association] Mental health standard 7-4.1, for instance, states that along with the complexity of the case, the "severity" of the charge should inform the assessment of competence.

[33]   *Masterman-Lister v Jewell* [2002] EWHC 417, [2003] 1 WLR 1511 at [21].

[34]   See *Re MB (Medical Treatment)* [1977] 2 FLR 426.

[35]   See paras 3.83 and onwards below.

3.35 We believe that the concept of decision-making capacity builds upon the need to ensure that the accused is able to participate effectively in the trial.[36] This is because, in our view, it is not possible for an accused to have meaningful participation in his or her trial unless he or she can perform certain tasks or make decisions.

3.36 The concept of capacity focuses on the ability to *do something*. It therefore cannot exist in the abstract. We believe that a decision-making capacity test can be formulated so as to be broad enough to cover a range of matters such as plea, what instructions to give, whether to give evidence or not, and so on. In short, capacity in the criminal context of unfitness to plead would reflect an appreciation of what is at stake in a trial and what the likely consequences (for the defendant) of a decision one way or the other will be.[37]

3.37 We provisionally propose in this CP that the current legal test for unfitness to plead should be replaced with a test of decision-making capacity. If this were so, then paradigmatic cases such as *Moyle*,[38] *Diamond*[39] and *Murray*[40] would presumably result in a finding that the accused lacks decision-making capacity. This is because the accused's psychiatric symptoms can significantly interfere with his or her capacity to make decisions. So in our example 3D, discussed at paragraph 3.18 above, A would probably be fit to plead under the *Pritchard* test because he has sufficient intellectual ability to understand the proceedings. However, under a capacity-based test he lacks decision-making capacity. This is because he is unable to use or weigh information as part of the decision-making process. This example is similar to the problem that arose in *Erskine*, which was discussed in Part 2.[41]

3.38 A properly devised capacity-based test of fitness to plead/be tried in criminal proceedings should be broad enough to cover reasoning difficulties which are caused by matters other than cognitive deficiency or mental illness. As has been argued with reference to civil capacity:

> [A sophisticated capacity test] should address the interplay between cognition (knowing), emotion (evaluating) and volition (acting). A person's 'reasoning defect' may be linked to any of these "capacities" and perhaps is more likely to result from an emotional or psychological deficit than any obvious failure in cognitive function. Impairment of decision-making ability is often a result of diminished or absent emotion such as embarrassment, sympathy and guilt, this

---

[36] See paras 2.89 to 2.102 above.

[37] However, as we discuss further below, although in order to be able to make decisions we believe the accused should have to understand the implications of making a decision one way or another (as is required in the civil context under s 3(4) of the Mental Capacity Act 2005), we do not necessarily think that the threshold of capacity should vary depending on the seriousness of the consequences of a particular decision. We realise that this may be controversial and have therefore made an alternative proposal on this subject.

[38] [2008] EWCA Crim 3059, [2008] All ER (D) 205.

[39] [2008] EWCA Crim 923, [2008] All ER (D) 401.

[40] [2008] EWCA Crim 1792 (unreported).

[41] See paras 2.76 to 2.79 above.

may be related to an impairment of emotion related signals and the failure to activate an emotion related memory.[42]

3.39   It can be seen that, for example, there could be circumstances where a person with a personality disorder[43] would be found to lack decision-making capacity.[44]

3.40   In our view, if an accused has decision-making capacity this would ensure that all the requirements for meaningful participation are met (for example, plea, giving instructions, understanding the purpose of the proceedings, deciding whether to give evidence, what witnesses to call and so on). A decision-making capacity test would ensure greater fairness for vulnerable defendants and remedy the problems that have been identified with the current *Pritchard* test in this regard.[45]

3.41   It follows that we would provisionally propose replacement of the *Pritchard* (common law legal) test. Indeed the abolition of some of the aspects of the test, such as the reference to an ability to challenge a juror, is unlikely to be controversial.[46] If an accused has decision-making capacity, then it follows that he or she would satisfy the requirements of the current *Pritchard* test because they are less than the requirements for decision-making capacity.[47] In our view,

[42]   C Heginbotham and M Kinton, "Developing a capacity test for compulsion in mental health law" [2007] *Journal of Mental Health Law* 72, 78.

[43]   A personality disorder is defined in the ICD-10 Classification of Mental and Behavioural Disorders as being capable of being diagnosed when:

> There is evidence that the individual's characteristic and enduring patterns of inner experience and behaviour as a whole deviate markedly from the culturally expected and accepted range…Such deviation must be manifest in more than one of the following areas:
>
> (1)   cognition (ie ways of perceiving and interpreting things, people, and events; forming attitudes and images of self and others);
>
> (2)   affectivity (range, intensity, and appropriateness of emotional arousal and response);
>
> (3)   control over impulses and gratification of needs;
>
> (4)   manner of relating to others and of handling interpersonal situations.
>
> The deviation must manifest itself pervasively as behaviour that is inflexible, maladaptive, or otherwise dysfunctional across a broad range of personal and social situations…
>
> There is personal distress, or adverse impact on the social environment, or both, clearly attributable to the behaviour referred to…
>
> The deviation cannot be explained as a manifestation or consequence of other mental disorders …

See: World Health Organisation, *The ICD-10 Classification of Mental and Behavioural Disorders: diagnostic criteria for research* (1993) p 123.

[44]   As was the case in *A-G v Gemma Harding* [2009] JRC 198, [2009] Jersey Law Review Note 52.

[45]   See paras 2.60 and onwards above.

[46]   This was in fact recommended by the Butler Committee: see the Report of the Committee on Mentally Abnormal Offenders (1975) Cmnd 6244, para 10.3. In our view, it makes sense to abandon the reference to the ability to challenge a juror given that jurors cannot now be challenged except for cause: see s 12(1) of the Juries Act 1974. A challenge for cause is either a challenge to the array, ie the make-up of the group, which is unlikely as the responsibility for summoning jurors has been invested with the Lord Chancellor since 1971, or to the polls ie to the individual juror on say, the basis of partiality or on the basis that he or she is for some reason disqualified.

[47]   Namely, the ability to plead, to understand the proceedings, to instruct a lawyer and to understand the evidence.

the requirements of trial are predicated on the defendant being able to make a decision. For example, in our examples 3B and 3C above, A would be unable to participate because he is not able to focus sufficiently to make a decision.

> **Provisional Proposal 1: The current *Pritchard* test should be replaced and there should be a new legal test which assesses whether the accused has decision-making capacity for trial. This test should take into account all the requirements for meaningful participation in the criminal proceedings.**

3.42 An additional advantage of adopting a capacity based test is that it will be clear that the basis of the test is the accused's decision-making capacity. In other words, it is limited to the ability to make particular decisions. As such, it deals with the mischief which the unfitness to plead procedure aims to address. The test is flexible and does not necessarily reduce a person to being "unfit" simply because of a low cognitive ability or learning disability. It has been observed that a procedure which did automatically do that would run the risk of inducing a lack of self-esteem[48] or sense of inadequacy in people with learning disabilities.

3.43 This is important as there will obviously be cases where it is appropriate to try people who could be said to come into this category.

Example 3G

A has a very low IQ. He cannot read and write because of his learning difficulties. He understands, however, that he is accused of assault, which he states he did not do. With assistance, A may be able to understand the trial process. His working memory is poor, however, and so he has difficulty answering questions and understanding the purpose of those questions. These difficulties mean that he can appear suggestible.

3.44 In example 3G, A may come into the category we have discussed at paragraph 3.42. The question will be whether he is able to make the relevant decisions, possibly with assistance.[49]

3.45 Another advantage of having a decision-making capacity test is that it will be more in line with the civil test of capacity. The discrepancy between the civil test for capacity and the criminal test for unfitness to plead is arguably problematic for the following reasons.

3.46 First, a person can be more readily deemed to lack capacity (because there is a more sophisticated and appropriate test) when his or her civil rights and obligations are at stake but not deemed unfit when his or her liberty and reputation are at stake (because he or she faces criminal proceedings). Lucy Scott-Moncrieff and Guy Vassall-Adams have argued that:

> It is astonishing and possibly unlawful, that the civil law test for capacity and the criminal law test for unfitness to plead are contradictory. A person who would not have capacity under the

---

[48] See AE Buchanan, *Deciding for Others* (1989) p 64.

[49] We discuss the role of special measures within a decision-making capacity test in Part 4.

Mental Capacity Act, to take relatively trivial decisions about his life might be found fit to plead in the criminal law context and be expected to make such important decisions as to whether to plead guilty or not guilty ... .[50]

3.47 Furthermore it is argued by the authors that the criminal defendant is in a worse position than the civil litigant.[51] We believe that the difficulties are demonstrated when it is considered that there may also be cases where D could face criminal and civil trials in relation to the same conduct.[52] This is one perspective, but we think that at this stage it is also important to note that it could equally be argued that the right to self-determination is of immense importance where a person risks a conviction and possibly loss of liberty as in the criminal context. Although there are also very serious family cases where what is at stake could be, for example, the permanent loss of children to adoption to which the principle of the right to self-determination also applies, the process of litigation by a next friend means that in civil law, the proceedings in question will nevertheless go ahead as a trial even where the litigant lacks capacity. As we have seen in Part 2, this is not the case in the criminal context where a finding that the accused is unfit will mean that the trial will stop and the general issue will not be resolved in full.[53]

The need for decision-making capacity to be rational

3.48 In the course of a preliminary discussion with specialists during the research for this CP, a number of legal and medical professionals thought that there should be no requirement that any decision called for in the course of the plea or trial proceedings should be "rational" because it would be unduly prescriptive. The justification for this standpoint is that there should be a right to self-determination. Moreover, as has been pointed out by Allen Buchanan, "'rationality' is a term both in wide common use and without any clear and fixed, agreed-upon meaning, not a technical term whose meaning and application is easily restricted".[54] This approach would also be consistent with the capacity test contained in the Mental Capacity Act 2005.

3.49 Whereas the ability to form a rational judgement was a factor in our recommendation in 2006 for reform of the law on diminished responsibility,[55] there is an issue as to whether or not the ability to form a rational decision ought to be a factor in a revised test for capacity.

3.50 Generally speaking, there should be a discernible line between a decision which is irrational and one which is simply unwise or ill advised which the right to self-determination means a person is entitled to make. However, there is no express

---

[50] L Scott-Moncrieff and G Vassall- Adams, "Yawning gap: capacity and fitness to plead" *Counsel Magazine*, October 2006, 14.

[51] Above, 14. It is argued that the unfairness is particularly apparent in cases where the mentally incapacitated defendant is charged with murder and given the opportunity of pleading guilty to voluntary manslaughter by way of diminished responsibility when not capable of making that decision: see p 15.

[52] For example, child abduction.

[53] See Part 6 for a discussion on the limitations of the present fact-finding (s 4A) process where an accused has been found to be unfit to plead and for our proposals for reform.

[54] AE Buchanan, *Deciding for Others* (1989) p 69.

[55] Murder, Manslaughter and Infanticide (2006) Law Com No 304, para 9.20.

requirement in the Mental Capacity Act 2005 that the decision in question has to be rational in order for a person to be held to have the capacity to make it. Instead, for a person to lack capacity he or she must first meet the diagnostic test set out in section 2 and secondly be "unable to make a decision" because he or she is unable to do one of the following things listed in section 3: (a) understand the information relevant to the decision; (b) retain that information; (c) use or weigh that information as part of the process of making the decision; or (d) communicate the decision.

3.51 The focus under the Mental Capacity Act 2005 is therefore on the decision-making process rather than the content of the decision which is made. We believe that in the criminal context an evaluation of decision-making capacity should similarly focus on the process of understanding and reasoning as opposed to the content of the decision which is eventually arrived at. It is important not to conflate the capacity of the decision maker with the rationality of the choice he or she makes.[56] In our example 3E at paragraph 3.19, A will not be considered to have decision-making capacity. This is not because of the content of his decisions if he is able to make them at all, but because any decisions which he makes are not based on a rational process.

3.52 Conversely, there may be reasons for one person making a particular decision which on the face of it does not appear to be objectively rational but which is rational when the subjective context is considered. An example of this would be the peace campaigner who is tried for criminal damage to Ministry of Defence property and who wishes to be convicted by a jury (before whom he or she can give evidence) in order to draw attention to the cause he or she supports.

3.53 Ultimately, the critical divide between the decisions we think the law should permit and what we think it should not permit is not between irrational decisions and unwise decisions but between decisions taken by those who do and those who do not have capacity to function rationally.[57]

3.54 To this end, we believe that there should not be an undue focus on the decision itself. There should not be a blanket requirement, for example, that the accused must make "rational" decisions. This is not to say, however, that the rationality or otherwise of a decision is irrelevant. As in the civil context, if an accused makes an unwise or irrational decision this could trigger the need for an assessment of his or her decision-making capacity.[58] Obviously if the process of making decisions discloses an irrationality which cannot be justified objectively, then this will raise questions as to capacity.[59]

3.55 Further, under section 3(4) of the Mental Capacity Act 2005, information relevant to a decision includes information about the reasonably foreseeable consequences of (a) deciding one way or another, or (b) failing to make a

---

[56] See AE Buchanan, *Deciding for Others* (1989) p 65.

[57] See *Sidaway v Board of Governors of Bethlem Royal Hospital* [1985] AC 871, 904 by Lord Templeman. See also, *Masterman Lister v Jewell* [2002] EWHC 417, [2003] 1 WLR 1511 at [29] by Wright J.

[58] See para 3.6 above.

[59] See Part 6 as to how (in the context of unfitness) the s 4A procedure successfully provides for an accused to be represented and therefore obviates this type of problem.

decision. This therefore reinforces the idea that rationality is an important but not determinative aspect of capacity.

3.56 We think that such a focus on the process employed to make a particular decision ought, in practice, to avoid the sort of flawed decisions which have resulted in wrongful convictions. This may alleviate the problem which was identified by the Court of Appeal in *Erskine*,[60] which we have discussed in Part 2.[61] It will also assist in identifying those who have capacity and those who do not.

3.57 The result should be that there is a test which allows for self-determination but does not contemplate unlimited bad choices,[62] as in our example 3D where the choice which A makes is attributable to a mental disorder (paranoid schizophrenia) which he cannot help.[63] It should also mean that personal morals and values are accommodated within the system.

> **Provisional Proposal 2: A new decision-making capacity test should not require that any decision the accused makes must be rational or wise.**

The application of a capacity based test to criminal proceedings

3.58 There seems to have been little discussion of the mechanics and of the practical advantages or disadvantages of the direct application to criminal proceedings of the civil law test which we have described above.

The approach which has been adopted in the clinical literature

3.59 In academic clinical literature, there has been some discussion of two possible approaches in assessing unfitness to plead: the "unitary construct" and the "disaggregated test". These terms have been used to distinguish between the two different forms that a capacity based test could take in criminal proceedings. As we hope to explain, however, there does not necessarily need to be a strict dichotomy between the unitary and the disaggregated approach. We therefore do not think that the terminology is particularly helpful.

A TRADITIONAL UNITARY CONSTRUCT

3.60 Under a traditional unitary construct,[64] there would be one test as to decision-making capacity which is, in so far as is possible, decided at the outset of the proceedings. This test would determine whether the accused has decision-making capacity for all purposes in relation to trial.[65] English law currently employs an (outdated) traditional unitary construct in the *Pritchard* test, under

---

[60] [2009] EWCA Crim 1425, [2010] 1 WLR 183 at [95] by Lord Judge CJ.

[61] See paras 2.76 to 2.79 above.

[62] AE Buchanan, *Deciding for Others* (1989) p 62.

[63] See para 3.18 above.

[64] A term we use as a general label for the sort of test of which *Pritchard* is an example.

[65] As is discussed further in Part 4, the decision as to whether the accused has decision-making capacity should take into account the possibility of increasing participation through special measures.

which the accused is either fit or unfit for all purposes. In the USA, the Supreme Court has ensured that there is a unitary construct in the form of the *Dusky* test.[66]

3.61 There are some obvious advantages to the traditional unitary construct. First, there is the theoretical advantage that it reflects the thinking behind or underlying rationale for having any form of unfitness to plead procedure namely, that because of the accused's mental or physical condition, a criminal trial is in itself an inappropriate process. A comprehensive all-or-nothing approach takes account of the fact that it is not just the reliability of the verdict which is crucial but rather, the emphasis is on the fact that the defendant "is asked to understand and accept it as a proper judgment on his past conduct".[67] In short, he or she is being asked to take responsibility for his or her conduct.

3.62 Secondly, as long as decision-making capacity is assessed by reference to a comprehensive construct of the relevant abilities, then a unitary construct would not need to be overly prescriptive. A clear delineation of the threshold would mean less divergence in clinical opinion as to whether it is met.[68] It would effect certainty within the law.

3.63 From a legal point of view, a traditional unitary construct makes for simplicity.

A DISAGGREGATED TEST

3.64 A disaggregated test would involve breaking down the trial into particular sections for which decision-making capacity would be required.

3.65 Rather than labour on terminology, we think that we can illustrate the difference between the two types of test (unitary and disaggregated) by virtue of the fact that the disaggregated test would allow for a person to be considered to be fit for one purpose in relation to the trial but not fit for another. The Ninth Circuit in the USA (erroneously) held in *Moran v Godinez*[69] that there is a different standard of competence for different stages of the process. The accused may well be able to

---

[66] *Dusky v United States* (1960) 362 US 402. In *Godinez v Moran* (1993) 509 US 389 (1993) the US Supreme Court held that *Dusky* was a single construct test in that there was no difference between the standard of competence required to plead guilty and the standard required to undergo trial.

[67] See RA Duff, *Trials and Punishments* (1986) p 35.

[68] As we discuss in Part 5, the *Pritchard* test has not been applied consistently by psychiatrists. We provisionally propose that a standardised psychiatric test could be useful for assessing decision-making capacity and lead to more consistency in assessments.

[69] 972 F.2d 263 (9th Cir 1992). This decision was reversed by the US Supreme Court which ruled in a favour of a unitary test: *Godinez v Moran* (1993) 509 US 389, which is discussed at para 2.79 above. Prior to the Supreme Court decision, it was unclear whether the same standard of competency applied to pleading guilty and waiving the right to counsel as to standing for trial. Federal courts of appeals were undecided on the matter. There was on-going debate in US academia as to whether there should be a disaggregated test in place, see for example: RJ Bonnie, "The competence of criminal defendants: beyond *Dusky* and *Drope*" (1992-1993) 47 *University of Miami Law Review* 539. The decision in the Supreme Court did not end this debate, and the decision has attracted a substantial amount of criticism. See for example, JW Corinis, "A reasoned standard for competency to waive counsel after *Godinez v Moran*" (2000) 80 *Boston University Law Review* 265, "Due process – mental competency to waive counsel and to plead guilty: *Godinez v Moran*" (1993) 107 *Harvard Law Review* 155, JR Marshall, "Two standards of competency are better than one: why some defendants who are not competent to stand trial should be permitted to plead guilty" (2003-2004) 37 *University of Michigan Journal of Law Reform* 1181.

communicate to legal advisors that he or she is guilty of the offence with which he or she is charged and legal advisors are well placed to ensure that the accused is seeking to plead guilty on the basis of admissible evidence and to advise as to sentence. The accused may not, however, be able to understand the more complex decisions relating to trial and which may arise in the course of the proceedings, for example, that his or her bad character might be revealed under the provisions of section 101(1) of the Criminal Justice Act 2003 if certain accusations are made by him or her. Under a unitary test, if he or she lacked the capacity to participate in all aspects of a criminal trial then there would be a blanket ban on any form of participation.[70] In contrast, the proponents of the disaggregated test would not prevent the accused from entering what would otherwise be a safe plea of guilty.

3.66 We should point out at this stage that we are provisionally in favour of a unitary test but one which provides a considerable improvement on the current *Pritchard* test. As the civil law shows, there is no problem with a unitary test being broad enough to take into account all the different factors which are likely to arise in a trial. As we said at paragraph 3.32 above we are assuming that civil law and criminal law are analogous in this respect. We do not think that breaking down different aspects of the process to allow, for example, a decision that the accused has capacity to plead guilty but does not have capacity to undergo a trial is a workable approach. It could prove to be complex and time-consuming. This has been recognised in the USA where it has been observed that the "administration of justice becomes more complicated if defendants are able to participate in some parts of the process but not in others".[71]

3.67 The traditional unitary construct (in the form of the current *Pritchard* test) has however been criticised on the basis that it fails to take into account that there are two separable factors which underpin unfitness to plead: "a foundational concept of competence to assist counsel[72] and a contextualised concept of decisional ability".[73] Broadly speaking, this could be described as the giving of instructions and the decision-making capacity necessary for participation in the trial. The fact that the *Pritchard* test is a single test means that it fails to recognise that a person's ability to enter a plea can be distinct from his or her ability to stand trial. So in example 3G discussed at paragraph 3.43, D may be able to pass the *Pritchard* test but without more, he will not necessarily be able to participate in the trial process.

3.68 In contrast to the traditional unitary construct, a disaggregated approach would break down the test into discrete abilities.

3.69 From the preliminary discussions with specialists that we conducted in the course of researching this project, we know that there is a great deal of support for the idea of a disaggregated test from legal and medical professionals.

---

[70] As at present, see s 4A(2) of the1964 Act, which provides that "the trial shall not proceed" after a finding of unfitness to plead.

[71] A Buchanan, "Competency to stand trial and the seriousness of the charge" (2006) 34(4) *Journal of the American Academy of Psychiatry and the Law* 458, 461.

[72] That is to say, instructions and plea.

[73] TP Rogers et al, "Reformulating fitness to plead: a qualitative study" (2009) 20(6) *Journal of Forensic Psychiatry and Psychology* 815, 817.

3.70   Some judges have also indicated that they believe there should be two tests concerning unfitness to plead, namely, a test as to whether a defendant is unfit to plead and a test as to whether a defendant is unfit to stand trial.[74] Our understanding of the law is that section 4 of the 1964 Act taken together with the legal (*Pritchard*) test[75] means there is only one test. Further, in our view the statute[76] clearly contemplates the issue can be raised before or after arraignment – the stage at which the accused is asked to enter a plea. However, we wish to consider why it is felt appropriate to construct the law as providing for separate tests.

3.71   Research suggests that some barristers are also dissatisfied with a traditional unitary construct (in the form of the *Pritchard* test), first because it fails to take into account that unfitness can vary depending on the complexity of the case, and secondly, as we have mentioned above, because it fails to separate unfitness to plead from unfitness to stand trial.[77] It is important to consider what people see as the practical advantages of a disaggregated application of capacity in criminal proceedings.

3.72   If disaggregation is taken to extremes then it would require a separate consideration of each decision which would need to be made in the trial at the time at which the need to make that decision arose. That approach produces the real possibility that the accused may be found to lack capacity in relation to a particular aspect of the trial only. Adopting such an approach, it may be argued, may be unnecessarily time consuming and of no real benefit to an accused. At paragraph 3.79 we explain that such an extensive disaggregation is not a feature of civil law. The perceived advantage, in practical terms, of a disaggregated test is that it would enable a court to determine capacity as to the single issue of pleading guilty. Thus an accused might, if found to have capacity to do so, plead guilty even if there might have been doubts about his or her ability to engage in some aspects of the full trial process. This might be thought to be expedient where, for example, an accused is charged with a minor offence having been arrested immediately, with reliable witnesses available to testify and where the offending conduct was recorded unambiguously on CCTV.

3.73   There are, we believe, potential problems with the concept that an accused who is unfit for trial is nevertheless fit to plead guilty.

3.74   This is because if the accused decided to plead guilty, this plea would be accepted, notwithstanding the fact that, because of his or her mental or physical

---

[74]   We have anecdotal evidence that some judges believe that there are two tests and have dealt with cases accordingly.

[75]   Under which the ability to enter a plea of guilty or not guilty is only one aspect.

[76]   Section 4A(5) of the 1964 Act provides:
        Where the question of disability was determined *after* arraignment of the accused, the determination under subsection (2) is to be made by the jury by whom he was being tried.
        (Emphasis added.)

[77]   T P Rogers et al, "Reformulating fitness to plead: a qualitative study" (2009) 20(6) *Journal of Forensic Psychiatry and Psychology* 815, 822.

condition, the accused would not be capable of participating in other aspects of a trial.[78]

3.75 We believe that entering a plea of guilty is not therefore necessarily a simple matter which can be attenuated from other parts of the trial or sentence. There can be a need to give instructions in relation to confiscation hearings after sentence.[79] A convicted person may need to instruct counsel on other sentencing issues. If a convicted person is assessed as being dangerous[80] then he or she may be sentenced to an indeterminate sentence of imprisonment for public protection. We are aware of research which has demonstrated that the effect of the imposition of such sentences has been to increase the incidence of mental illness or disorder within our prisons. This is already a problem and we would not wish to contribute to its increase.[81]

3.76 More generally, we believe that the attenuation of trial and sentence is contrary to the thinking behind the need for any form of an unfitness to plead procedure, namely that the trial itself (in the broad sense of taking responsibility) is an inappropriate process for those accused who have a mental or physical condition which means that they are unable to understand the process or make all of the decisions necessary for meaningful participation. As Professor Duff has argued, the trial itself is a rational process involving responsibility for wrongdoing.[82]

3.77 However, we believe that the decision-making capacity test which we are proposing will accommodate the concerns of those who think that the present test fails to have regard to the separable factors of plea and trial. In this way we obviate the need for a disaggregated test. This is because as we explain in Part 4 of this CP, the proposed legal test will include consideration of the extent to which special measures will assist the accused. In other words, whether an accused will be able to participate if special measures are ordered will be an integral factor in determining his or her decision-making capacity. We envisage the development of the law in relation to special measures on a case by case basis.[83] As consideration of the use of special measures will be obligatory, a judge who is aware that an accused wishes to plead guilty will be able to consider all the circumstances which would facilitate this. We think that the simplicity of the

---

[78] In the recent case of *Walton* [2010] All ER (D) 33, (2010) 174 CL & J 528, the Court of Appeal quashed the conviction of an accused who had been allowed to plead guilty despite the evidence that he was unfit to plead.

[79] Proceeds of Crime Act 2002, s 6.

[80] Under the provisions of the Criminal Justice Act 2003, ss 225 to 229.

[81] Sainsbury Centre for Mental Health, *In the dark: the mental health implications of Imprisonment for Public Protection* (2008).

[82] We referred to these arguments in Part 1.

[83] As we go on to explain in Part 4, although many special measures are fixed by statute, there is no limit to a judge's common law powers to ensure that a defendant is able to participate effectively in his trial: see *Ukpabio* [2007] EWCA Crim 2108, [2008] 1 WLR 728.

potential proceedings would factor into any decision as to what special measures were needed.[84]

3.78 We have therefore concluded that we can reject the need for a disaggregated test.

3.79 An application of the civil understanding of capacity does not require an assessment of the accused's capacity in relation to each specific decision which needs to be taken in the course of his or her trial[85] but an overall approach[86] (something which could be referred to as "litigation capacity"), with a higher threshold for capacity where the possible consequences of the decision are more serious or when the case is forensically complex as opposed to being straight-forward. In civil law, the context and issue specific approach of the Mental Capacity Act 2005 and the common law means that there can be a single test which is broad enough to consider the range of abilities that will be required for litigation.

3.80 Therefore a revised unitary test which assesses all aspects of litigation capacity and which exists in conjunction with our provisional proposals on special measures could address the practical problems which are perceived as underlying the traditional unitary construct.

3.81 A revised unitary test (in other words, a single test)[87] could be sufficiently wide to take into account the range of different decisions and tasks required as part of a trial. Thus, unlike under the *Pritchard* test, the requirements of the trial would be broken down fully and the decision-making capacity test would therefore inevitably bear some of the characteristics of a more disaggregated approach. This is because different decision-making abilities are required for different

---

[84] We also think that the Practice Direction on vulnerable defendants assists in this regard. In particular see, paras III.30.3 to III.30.5 and III.30.10 to III.30.12: Practice Direction (Criminal Proceedings: Consolidation), para III.30, as inserted by Practice Direction (Criminal Proceedings: Further Directions) [2007] 1 WLR 1790.

[85] A criminal trial comprises a number of decisions such as the decision to plead guilty or not guilty, to instruct on and deploy a particular defence, to give comments on prosecution evidence, to give evidence or not give evidence, to call witnesses in support of a defence, and this does not include all the various and more unusual matters which may arise during the course of the trial itself. This needs to be read in conjunction with our proposal for a defined psychiatric test (Part 5) which will in fact test all these abilities at the outset of the trial.

[86] *Re W (Care Proceedings: Litigation Capacity)* [2008] EWHC 1188 (Fam), [2010] 1 FLR 1176 at [80] where it was stated by McFarlane J, who held that there was no evidential basis that a man lacked litigation capacity:

What is it I am assessing? It is not issue specific in the sense that I have to look at whether he can give instructions and has capacity to be a litigant on particular parts of the case, for example, in due course, whether contact is to be on a Saturday afternoon or a Sunday morning or whatever the practical issues might be, it is to take part in the proceedings as a whole. The analogy that I offered yesterday was of someone being put into the driving seat of a car and the question for the court is whether he has sufficient capacity to be the driver for the whole leg of the procedural journey at least, through the fact-finding process, and not simply for different stretches of that journey. It has to be established on the balance of probability that he lacks capacity to undertake that task and to make the necessary decisions.

[87] Which is applied once.

aspects of the trial process and the single test would have to encompass them all.

3.82 A test of this sort would provide for considerable flexibility.

The principle of proportionality

3.83 So far, we have not considered the application of what we have previously referred to as "proportionality".[88] If our revised test was to mirror civil law entirely, then it would entail the same proportionality considerations which are central to capacity assessments under civil law. It has been argued that this would mean that whether an accused is fit to stand trial would depend on the nature of the charge and complexity of the proceedings. As Lucy Scott-Moncrieff and Guy Vassall-Adams have argued, an accused may be fit to plead in an uncomplicated shoplifting trial but not fit to plead in a more complicated trial where, for example, the evidence is more complex.[89] The argument in support of this proposition is that in the more complex proceedings, there will be numerous issues and witnesses on which the accused is required to give instructions and in relation to which he or she may be expected to give evidence.

3.84 So in a trial, whether the accused had capacity to plead, to instruct counsel, to give evidence, and to call evidence would have to be separately weighed up as against the overall gravity and complexity. If we return to the examples at paragraph 3.83, we see that the results may be different in relation to different decisions in different trials. There is therefore no fixed standard by which any one case can be assessed. The test is "does D have the capacity to plead, instruct counsel, and follow the proceedings in this *particular* trial?"

3.85 The proportionality approach has been debated extensively in the USA where the test for adjudicative competence has been criticised for attributing too passive a role to the accused.[90] Notwithstanding the on-going debate,[91] however, it is hard to conceive of practical models on which to base a reformed test. Neither has it been decided what factors would be relevant to the threshold for capacity with factors such as the seriousness of the charge and even the personality of the

---

[88] Disaggregation (which we have rejected) and proportionality are separate concepts but we touch on the interface between them in para 3.100 where we acknowledge that our proposed test in conjunction with the special measures aspect of that test (see Part 4) is open to the criticism that it is a proportionality based test in disguise.

[89] L Scott-Moncrieff and G Vassall-Adams, "Yawning gap: capacity and fitness to plead" *Counsel Magazine*, October 2006, 14 at 15.

[90] RJ Bonnie and T Grisso, "Adjudicative competence and youthful offenders" in R Schwartz and T Grisso, *Youth on Trial* (2000) p 75:

> In the picture that emerges [from the case law] the defendant responds, consults and assists, but the active adversaries in the litigation are the prosecutor and the defense attorney. This may be an accurate picture of many, if not most, criminal proceedings, but it is an incomplete picture of the *rights* accorded to the defendant under the Constitution and of the values embedded in the requirement of adjudicative competence. (Emphasis in original).

[91] See n 69. See further NG Poythress et al, "Client abilities to assist counsel and make decisions in criminal cases: findings from three studies" (1994) 18 *Law and Human Behaviour* 437. The authors point to the fact that *Godinez v Moran* 509 US 389 (1993) clarified aspects of the law on this matter, but "the Court's silence regarding the criteria for decision-making capacity invites further conceptual development and continuing controversy" p 438.

defence advocate "because sympathetic attorneys require less mental capacity of their clients"[92] being suggested as potentially relevant. Such factors could themselves be problematic as the seriousness of the charge, for example, cannot necessarily be assessed objectively.

3.86 Therefore, although the civil test for capacity under the common law and the Mental Capacity Act 2005 could provide something of a precedent for an improved approach to the question of capacity in criminal proceedings, it also raises questions and presents practical difficulties.

3.87 The principle of proportionality, namely that the circumstances surrounding and consequent to the decision to which the question of capacity attaches should bear on the threshold for capacity, is clearly inherent within a functional test. It may be that notwithstanding that we have assumed that a trial judge can assess the likely issues at the start of the criminal trial, the principle lends itself more readily to the civil jurisdiction than it does to a criminal trial.

3.88 A criminal trial involves a series of decisions. At their most minimal these decisions comprise plea or basis of plea if that plea is in some way qualified, for example if the defendant admits part of the offence or a lesser offence,[93] or he or she admits being a secondary party to robbery but claims not to have known for example that the co-defendant was carrying a knife. They will also include deciding on instructions regarding cross-examination, whether to give evidence and whether to call witnesses.

3.89 This, however, is not the main reason why we think that the principle of proportionality is not, or might not be, consistent with criminal proceedings.[94] The reasons for our concern are first, that if proportionality is to be a factor in criminal proceedings then there will be a lack of certainty in the procedure which will generate its own problems. Secondly, the method of dealing with a case (in terms of the way in which the hearing on the issues proceeds) once a person has been found to lack capacity or to be unfit to plead differs in civil and criminal law. Thirdly, civil law and criminal law are fundamentally different because of the important role of sentencing which exists in criminal law.

A POTENTIAL LACK OF CERTAINTY

3.90 The main problem with the application of proportionality is first, that an approach based on the principle of proportionality may lead to a lack of certainty in terms of what a particular result will be. Under a proportionality approach, the threshold for capacity depends on the circumstances surrounding and consequent to the particular decision. However, those circumstances which surround the matter for decision will not always be objectively measureable. For example, what is serious for one person may not be serious for another. Whereas this is accepted within the civil jurisdiction where, as stated above, capacity can arise in "subject matter

---

[92] A Buchanan, "Competency to stand trial and the seriousness of the charge" (2006) 34(4) *Journal of the American Academy of Psychiatry and the Law* 458, 459.

[93] For example, the accused admits an offence contrary to s 20 of the Offences Against the Person Act 1861 (causing grievous bodily harm) as opposed to s 18 of that Act (causing grievous bodily harm with intent).

[94] Civil and family trials often also involve a series of decisions of equal or similar weight and complexity.

capacity" or in "litigation capacity", it is unusual (if not unique) within criminal procedure. Generally, it does not seem that there is potential for such uncertainty about a particular result.[95] Complexity may be something which is difficult to predict.[96] In any trial there may be evidential issues which are not immediately apparent. For example, in a case involving more than one accused, some unexpected disclosure by the prosecution may lead to the defence case becoming cut-throat[97] as between the accused. In our view, the question which needs to be considered is whether the degree of uncertainty about which we are concerned will go to make a proportionality test unworkable in criminal law.

3.91 If proportionality is a factor in decision-making then there is a danger that it will lead to a greater likelihood of inconsistent decision making across the board. Defendants who have been found fit to plead (or under our proposed test, to have capacity) on the basis of a test applied when it was anticipated that the trial would not be a complex one and who were subsequently convicted, would point to factors which had occurred in the course of the trial in order to claim that the decision was wrong by virtue of matters which had not been foreseen at the time of the decision. In other words, it would be argued that the threshold had been set too low.

Example 3H

A is found to have decision-making capacity at the outset of the proceedings after raising the issue as a preliminary matter. He is later convicted by the jury on the basis of what appears to be a poor performance in cross-examination. He appeals on the basis that the threshold was set too low and the difficulties which he experienced in the course of the cross-examination were not anticipated. Further, he argues that he was not in a position to make a proper decision as to whether to give evidence because he had not appreciated what it would involve.

3.92 Example 3H aims to show the way in which a defendant may attempt to appeal a conviction on the basis that the finding of capacity was wrong simply because he or she cannot accept that he or she made an erroneous decision.

3.93 On the other hand, these arguments could be similarly deployed in the family law context where the concept of proportionality is an integral factor. The main distinction is that in criminal law the long term consequences of a finding of unfitness (lack of decision-making capacity) is that the accused is not convicted and a finding of fitness (decision-making capacity) could ultimately result in a prison sentence. A loss of liberty (in other words, the severity of the

---

[95] It seems to us that the lack of a proper legal test and the uncertainty about what will trigger a legal test in summary proceedings has led to uncertainty in that jurisdiction. This seems to have led to inconsistency in the case law. This is a matter which we explore in Part 8.

[96] Although as we have already observed, judges and experienced counsel should be able to anticipate much of what will occur.

[97] A term used to describe the situation where one defendant will seek to be acquitted by ensuring that another defendant is convicted for example, by leading evidence of his or her previous convictions. In other words, it is a term used to describe a situation where each accused is blaming the other.

consequences) is likely to make a defendant[98] more disposed to query the initial finding as to his or her capacity.

3.94 Another distinction between civil law and criminal law is that in the former jurisdiction, a lack of capacity on the part of the applicant or the defendant will not mean that the trial will not go ahead as is the case in the criminal jurisdiction. The applicant or defendant who lacks capacity can still litigate by his or her litigation friend and the issues are determined as they would have been if he or she had had capacity. The issues at the heart of the case will not necessarily change by virtue of a finding of lack of capacity. In criminal law once an accused is found to be unfit "the trial shall not proceed"[99] and the general issue of whether the defendant is guilty or not guilty is replaced with an issue as to whether the accused has or has not done the act.[100] Accordingly, there is an inherent flexibility in civil law which plays no part in criminal law where the emphasis is entirely on individual accountability. Although this is a distinction which does not necessarily bear directly on the question of proportionality, it is indicative of a flexibility which has no real role in criminal responsibility.[101] The potential variability of the results of individual capacity proceedings is consistent with this flexibility.

THE ROLE OF SENTENCING

3.95 The role of the sentencing process in criminal procedure differentiates it from civil law. Modern sentencing, in particular, increases the emphasis on individual responsibility which should co-exist with the right to self-determination. In the case of all discretionary sentences or sentences other than hospital orders under Part 3 of the Mental Health Act 1983, the court must have regard to the following purposes of sentencing: (a) the punishment of offenders; (b) the reduction of crime (including its reduction by deterrence); (c) the reform and rehabilitation of offenders; (d) the protection of the public; and (e) the making of reparation by offenders to persons affected by their offences.[102] Sentencing is becoming increasingly complicated, particularly for serious crimes where, as we have already pointed out, a conviction may mean that dangerousness is in issue.[103] If this is the case then the court may have the power to impose a life sentence or a sentence of Imprisonment for Public Protection,[104] the aim of which is to be

---

[98] Or applicant.

[99] See s 4A(2) of the 1964 Act.

[100] This may change however if our provisional proposal 8 was to be adopted. See Part 6 where we explore the options for change.

[101] This is a distinction which has been referred to elsewhere and in terms of potential injustice. The Royal College of Psychiatrists has observed that children who are subject to care proceedings or who are undertaking litigation may have the support of a Children's Guardian or a Litigation friend but there is no equivalent for a child defendant (who because of emotional immaturity may be unfit to plead). The Royal College has called for "new measures to be set up [as far as child defendants are concerned] to ensure the mandatory integration of the criminal justice system with the civil justice system, bearing in mind that the very young child defendant is often a 'child in need' in terms of the Children Act 1989. See Royal College of Psychiatrists, *Child Defendants* (March 2006) p 9.

[102] Criminal Justice Act 2003, s 143 (1), (2).

[103] See para 3.75 above.

[104] Criminal Justice Act 2003, s 225(3). Mental disorder does not preclude a finding of dangerousness.

preventative rather than punitive.[105] If such a sentence is to work, therefore, it involves cooperation on the part of the defendant who is expected to participate in enhanced thinking skills courses and similar schemes.

3.96 How does this affect any consideration of the application of the principle of proportionality? In civil law it is conceivable that a person would have the capacity to litigate and to accept an award but thereafter not have the capacity to administer that award.[106] In other words, the question of capacity can properly be reassessed to meet the circumstances. In criminal law it is not so easy to separate questions of sentence from trial.

3.97 Finally, we are proposing that there should be a defined psychiatric test to measure decision-making capacity in criminal law. This is for the reasons which we explore in Part 5 of this CP. This is not something which exists in civil law but research suggests that such a test may indeed be beneficial.[107]

Overcoming the potential problems with a unitary construct

3.98 It would seem to us that the potential problems in having a traditional unitary construct (like the *Pritchard* test, as outlined at paragraph 3.60 above) can in part be overcome by setting parameters for the required standard of decision-making capacity which are sufficiently wide to encompass a number of scenarios presented by the entire spectrum of trial decisions. We believe that within a revised unitary construct, the capacity of the accused to make a range of decisions relevant to the trial can be assessed and this may enable us to ascertain what a particular accused can and cannot do. However, we believe that an accused should not stand trial unless he or she has the decision-making capacity which would allow for participation in all its aspects. This should be the basis of the legal test.

3.99 For the reasons outlined at paragraphs 3.90 to 3.97 we are presently of the view that this test should not involve proportionality.

> **Provisional Proposal 3: The legal test should be a revised single test which assesses the decision-making capacity of the accused by reference to the entire spectrum of trial decisions he or she might be required to make. Under this test an accused**

---

[105] *Johnson* [2006] EWCA Crim 2486, [2007] 1 All ER 1237.

[106] See *Masterman-Lister v Jewell* [2002] EWCA Civ 1889, [2003] 1 WLR 1511 in the judgment of Kennedy LJ at [27]. Although it was not something which the court had to decide in this case as it was held that the complainant was a patient within the meaning of RSC Order 80 throughout the relevant period.

[107] See R Cairns, A Buchanan, A S David, P Hayward, G Richardson, G Szmukler, "Reliability of mental capacity assessments in psychiatric in-patients" (2005) 187 *British Journal of Psychiatry* 372 which records research which ascertained that the MacCAT-T (MacArthur Competence Assessment Tool for Treatment) in combination with a clinical interview could be used to provide highly reliable binary judgements on capacity to consent to treatment which were obtained in separate interviews.

This study has shown that two clinicians can reliably agree about capacity to decide about treatment in the early stages of admission to a psychiatric hospital, using a combination of the MacCAT-T and a clinical interview.

would be found to have or to lack decision-making capacity for the criminal proceedings.

3.100 This obviously stops short of any proposal on proportionality and we are aware that, notwithstanding the arguments which we have put forward in this Part, consultees may think that the above proposal for a revised test does not go far enough. We have therefore decided to include an alternative provisional proposal which aims to incorporate what we have called the proportionality issue into a revised decision-making test. There are two reasons for doing this. First, it may be the case that the civil and criminal jurisdictions are more analogous than we think. Secondly, our reasons for rejecting a disaggregated approach namely, that the special measures aspect of the test will suffice to address the perceived problems,[108] may be considered to be a proportionality based test by another name. In these circumstances consultees may think that it would not make sense to preclude a further proportionality based test in relation to trial.

3.101 This alternative proposal contemplates a unitary test in which the judge's evaluation of the accused's decision making capacity should take account of the anticipated complexity of the trial and the gravity of the offence. It would be for the judge to assess how important the accused's capacity to make each decision was in relation to a particular matter and to assess how important that matter was in the context of the trial.

> **Provisional Proposal 4: In determining the defendant's decision-making capacity, it would be incumbent on the judge to take account of the complexity of the particular proceedings and gravity of the outcome. In particular the judge should take account of how important any disability is likely to be in the context of the decision the accused must make in the context of trial which the accused faces.**

CONVERTING A TRIAL TO A SECTION 4A HEARING

3.102 A further matter which needs to be considered is that of how readily (if at all) a trial could, in the event that it were to become necessary, be converted to a fact finding under section 4A.[109] Under our provisional proposals, there would be a single test to determine whether the accused has decision-making capacity. Although an accused may have been found to have decision-making capacity, unforeseen circumstances may arise during a trial which may mean that the accused no longer meets the threshold of the decision-making capacity test. Therefore, while our provisional proposals are based on the idea of a single test for capacity, this does not mean that a finding that the accused has decision-making capacity at the beginning of the trial necessarily means that the issue cannot be reconsidered at a later stage. The issue can be reconsidered in exactly the same way that unfitness to plead can be reconsidered in trials at the moment.

3.103 This is not to be confused with a pure disaggregated approach, which would require an assessment of capacity in relation to each specific decision or task

---

[108] See para 3.77 above.

[109] A trial and a section 4A hearing should however remain mutually exclusive. It is just that circumstances may arise in a trial which afford a doubt as to decision-making capacity which was not previously apparent.

that the accused has to do in the course of his or her trial, taking into account the possible consequences of that decision or task.

CONCLUSIONS

3.104   In summary, for the reasons highlighted in Part 2 we think that the present legal test for unfitness to plead is outdated and inappropriate in light of modern psychiatric science. This means that the criteria for determining whether an accused is unfit to plead are sometimes distorted or simply ignored by the courts and those expert witnesses involved in the assessment of unfitness to plead.[110] The criteria place a disproportionate emphasis on cognitive deficiencies at the expense of incorporating other forms of mental or physical conditions which could affect the accused's decision-making ability. The present legal test fails to take decision-making ability into account.

3.105   We think that decision-making capacity as we have defined it should be the new legal test. It should be a unitary test which, in so far as is possible, takes place at the outset of the proceedings.[111] Under this test an accused would be found to either have or to lack decision-making capacity for all purposes in relation to his or her trial. It is a test which focuses on the decision-making process rather than the content of any decision made, and in that respect would require the accused to be able to do similar things to those which he or she is required to do under section 3 of the Mental Capacity Act 2005. The test should also be informed by the concept of effective participation which has so far developed independently of the law on unfitness to plead, so that an accused who is found to have decision-making capacity is capable of meaningful participation in his or her trial.

3.106   As far as our alternative proposals for the role of proportionality are concerned, we have provisionally concluded that proportionality should not play a part in our new test as to decision-making capacity because we are concerned that it is likely that there are differences between criminal procedure and civil procedure which will make it unworkable. However we recognise that consultees may think there are compelling reasons for introducing a proportionality-based test in criminal proceedings and have therefore made an alternative proposal in this regard.

3.107   In the next Part, we consider whether the availability of special measures should be a factor in the legal test for decision-making capacity which we have provisionally proposed. This is relevant to our rejection of the disaggregated test. We then go on to consider in Part 5 whether there needs to be a standardised psychiatric test to assess decision-making capacity in accordance with the legal test.

---

[110] We discuss further in Part 5 how the *Pritchard* test has been used by psychiatrists.

[111] Or as soon as the issue is raised.

PART 4
THE ROLE OF SPECIAL MEASURES

INTRODUCTION

4.1 We have already referred to the development of special measures for vulnerable accused in Part 2 of this CP. In this Part, we explain the following:

(1) what special measures are, including the way in which they have been developed;

(2) what the problems have been with special measures so far; and

(3) the options as regards the role of special measures in our proposed legal test of decision-making capacity. In brief the possibilities are whether:

(a) they should form part of the legal test – in other words, when considering whether the accused has decision-making capacity, the availability of special measures to enhance participation for those with a mental or physical disorder should be taken into account; or

(b) they should not form part of the legal test, but notwithstanding this, whether more must be done to ensure they are used properly. This is because a finding of decision-making capacity does not preclude the accused from requiring additional assistance as a result of his or her mental or physical disorder.

4.2 Special measures are measures which are put into place to assist vulnerable defendants to participate in the proceedings. The aim of providing for special measures is to make proceedings compliant with article 6 of the European Convention on Human Rights. Special measures, in so far as defendants are concerned, have been developed in conjunction with the concept of effective participation, which was discussed in Part 2. This case law, which has largely developed in relation to child defendants, was applied in relation to vulnerable defendants[1] generally by virtue of the Practice Direction (Criminal Proceedings: Consolidation), as inserted by the Practice Direction (Criminal Proceedings: Further Directions).[2] The Practice Direction aims to assist the judiciary in making the trial process more accessible to vulnerable defendants. The overriding principle in the Practice Direction is that the ordinary trial process should "so far

---

[1] "Vulnerable defendants" are defined in the Practice Direction (Criminal Proceedings: Consolidation), para.III.30 (as inserted by Practice Direction (Criminal Proceedings: Further Directions) [2007] 1 WLR 1790) at III.30.1 as "(a) children and young persons under 18 or (b) adults who suffer from a mental disorder within the meaning of the Mental Health Act 1983 or who have any other significant impairment of intelligence and social function".

[2] [2007] 1 WLR 1790.

as necessary" be adapted and "all possible steps" taken to "assist a vulnerable defendant to understand and participate" in criminal proceedings.[3]

4.3   Special measures have, however, been developed outside the context of unfitness to plead, and there has been little consideration of the difficult relationship between those accused who are unfit to plead and those accused who are fit to plead but nonetheless require additional assistance because of a mental or physical disorder. We think that special measures should play a greater role within the overall capacity structure which we envisage. This is particularly so in relation to our rejection of a fully "disaggregated" test for unfitness to plead.[4]

THE USE OF SPECIAL MEASURES

4.4   As stated previously, the Practice Direction on vulnerable defendants[5] serves the purpose of extending the rules on special measures concerning children (which were forged through the development of the Convention jurisprudence)[6] to cover all vulnerable defendants. The definition of "vulnerable" in this context is "adults who suffer from a mental disorder within the meaning of the Mental Health Act 1983 or who have any other significant impairment of intelligence and social function".[7] This may include those defendants who suffer from learning disability.[8]

4.5   The Practice Direction makes it clear that at each step of the proceedings the implications of what is happening should be explained.[9] If the procedure is

---

[3]   Practice Direction (Criminal Proceedings: Further Directions) [2007] 1 WLR 1790, para III.30.3.

[4]   See paras 3.72 to 3.78 above.

[5]   Practice Direction (Criminal Proceedings: Consolidation), para III.30, as inserted by Practice Direction (Criminal proceedings: Further Directions) [2007] 1 WLR 1790. III.30.3 provides "All possible steps should be taken to assist a vulnerable defendant to understand and participate in those proceedings. The ordinary trial process should, so far as necessary, be adapted to meet those ends". III.30.18 states "Where the court is called upon to exercise its discretion in relation to any procedural matter falling within the scope of this practice direction but not the subject of specific reference, such discretion should be exercised having regard to the principles in paragraph III.30.3."

[6]   To which we have referred in Part 2 above.

[7]   See para III.30.1 of the Practice Direction (Criminal Proceedings: Consolidation) as inserted by Practice Direction (Criminal proceedings: Further Directions) [2007] 1 WLR 1790.

[8]   Learning disability is not a mental illness for the purpose of the Mental Health Act 1983 as amended by the Mental Health Act 2007 unless it can be said to be associated with abnormally aggressive conduct (see s 1(2A) of the Mental Health Act 1983). As we explain below at paras 4.10 to 4.11, it has been observed that the definition in section 1(2) of the Mental Health Act 1983 is itself problematic because it marginalises people who suffer from learning disabilities.

[9]   Practice Direction (Criminal Proceedings: Consolidation), para. III.30, as inserted by Practice Direction (Criminal Proceedings: Further Directions) [2007] 1 WLR 1790. Para III.30.11 provides that the court:
      should ensure in particular that the role of the jury has been explained. It should remind those representing the vulnerable defendant and the supporting adult of their responsibility to explain each step as it takes place, and at trial to explain the possible consequences of a guilty verdict. Throughout the trial the court should continue to ensure by any appropriate means, that the defendant understands what is happening and what has been said by those on the bench, the advocates and witnesses.
      See also n 5 above.

followed properly, then in this respect it is analogous to a disaggregated approach to capacity which is also based on a step-by-step, context-specific approach.[10] This is because if at any stage it is thought that there is insufficient comprehension, there is the possibility of raising the issue of unfitness to plead (lack of decision-making capacity).

4.6   In addition to the guidance in the Practice Direction there are statutory provisions which exist to assist vulnerable adult defendants. For example, an accused who is aged 18 or over and who has been classified as being vulnerable can give evidence to a court by a live television link as long as certain conditions have been met.[11] The Coroners and Justice Act 2009 also provides the right to support from an intermediary for the purpose of giving evidence.[12] This is likely to be a speech and language therapist.[13] We consider that the role of an intermediary for a vulnerable defendant will work in the same way that it works for a vulnerable witness.[14]

4.7   Although the Practice Direction seeks to consolidate the procedure in relation to vulnerable defendants, a number of other practices have been developed in the courts on a more or less ad hoc basis.

---

[10]   See para 3.72 above.

[11]   Section 33A of the Youth Justice and Criminal Evidence Act 1999, as amended by s 47 of the Police and Justice Act 2006.

[12]   Section 104(1) of the Coroners and Justice Act 2009 will insert s 33BA after s 33B of the Youth and Criminal Evidence Act 1999. S 33BA(3) provides [for a direction]:

> For any examination of the accused to be conducted through an interpreter or other person approved by the court for the purposes of this section ("an intermediary").

Section 33BA(4) provides that the function of an intermediary is to communicate –
> (a) to the accused, questions put to the accused, and
> (b) to any person asking any questions, the answers given by the accused in reply to them,
> and to explain such questions or answers so far as necessary to enable them to be understood by the accused or the person in question.

At the time of writing there is no date for when this provision will come into force.

[13]   The provision has been criticised however as only being applicable to the giving of evidence and not entitling the defendant to help with communication throughout the trial: see J Jacobson with J Talbot, *Vulnerable defendants in the criminal courts: a review of provision for adults and children* (Prison Reform Trust 2009) p 15.

[14]   See A Middleton, "A voice for vulnerable witnesses" (2010) 66(1) *Magistrate* 6:
> The role of the intermediary [in relation to vulnerable witnesses] is to facilitate communication between the vulnerable witness and the criminal justice practitioners … at trial, whether youth, magistrates' or Crown Court. Facilitating communication means assessing levels of receptive and expressive language, identifying types of questions or style of communication a witness will or will not understand.

4.8 The trial judge has common law powers to ensure that the accused is able to participate effectively in his or her trial.[15] A qualifying adult defendant is also able to participate in his or her trial via a live link.

4.9 A trial where special measures are used to ensure participation serves to protect the accused's rights under article 6 of the European Convention on Human Rights.[16] Under the current law, an accused found to be unfit to plead under the *Pritchard* test and who is therefore subject to a section 4A hearing is not entitled to the protection of article 6.[17] In Part 6, we ask consultees whether they think that an accused who is subject to a section 4A hearing should in fact be protected by article 6.[18]

Problems with special measures in practice

4.10 One problem is that, notwithstanding the definition of vulnerable defendants in the Practice Direction, the provisions for vulnerable defendants do not focus on the specific needs of those defendants with learning difficulties. Rather, they focus on the broader issue of mental disorder.[19] One such example of this broad approach is evident in the Crown Prosecution Service guidance on mentally disordered offenders.[20] It has been said that:

---

[15] *Ukpabio* [2007] EWCA Crim 2108, [2008] 1 WLR 728 where it was held that there are no limits on a judge's common law discretion to ensure an accused's participation in his trial. In *H* [2003] EWCA Crim 1208, [2003] All ER (D) 436, in a non-binding part of the judgment the Court of Appeal held that there was no reason why in certain circumstances a person with severe learning disabilities should not be able to have the assistance of an interpreter or be asked leading questions based on a detailed defence case statement in the course of examination-in-chief.

[16] It is worth, however, emphasising that the European Court of Human Rights has found a breach of art 6 in cases where special measures were used, illustrating that the use of special measures in itself will not necessarily ensure compatibility unless such measures ensure that the accused is able to effectively participate in the proceedings (see the discussion of the case law on effective participation at paras 2.89 to 2.102 above). These cases were however decided in relation to child defendants, where the central concern of the court appears to have been that the defendants should have been tried in a youth court.

[17] *H* [2003] EWCA Crim 1208, [2003] All ER (D) 436.

[18] Since the procedure which we are proposing should replace the present s 4A procedure is far more akin to an actual trial, we think that there is an argument that the accused should be protected. However, this is arguably counter-balanced by the proposition (which we think some consultees may support, but which we do not ourselves support) that a person who has been found to have done the act should, in the event that he or she becomes well, be able to apply to stand trial. This is something that we will consider further in Part 7.

[19] Section 1(2) of the Mental Health Act 1983 makes it clear that for the purpose of the Act, learning disability is only to be classed as mental illness if it is associated with abnormally aggressive conduct.

[20] Crown Prosecution Service, *Mentally Disordered Offenders* (March 2010) http://www.cps.gov.uk/legal/l_to_o/mentally_disordered_offenders/ (last visited 10 September 2010). See J Jacobson with J Talbot, *Vulnerable defendants in the criminal courts: a review of provisions for adults and children* (Prison Reform Trust 2009) p 7. The focus of the objection to the guidance is that it relies on the definition of mental disorder in the Mental Health Act 1983 which as we have seen, excludes learning disability unless it is associated with "abnormally aggressive or seriously irresponsible conduct".

The conflation of learning disability with mental illness, under the broad heading of 'mental disorder' is problematic to the extent that it masks the more specific needs of defendants with learning disabilities. However, the reality is that many individuals who appear before the courts do not have a single or clearly delineated form of intellectual or psychological difficulty. Mental illness and learning disability (or learning difficulty) may co-exist; or defendants may be cognitively impaired because of the effects of acute mental health problems and/ or substance abuse, rather than a pre-existing learning disability or difficulty.[21]

4.11 This problem is compounded when it is considered that "learning disabilities and difficulties are largely 'hidden disabilities' with few visual or behavioural clues. Many people with such disabilities try hard to hide their impairments in order to appear competent, to protect themselves, to avoid ridicule, or to enhance their sense of self-esteem".[22] If an accused's difficulties are not apparent to the court, or to those who are responsible for representing him or her, they may not be picked up on.

4.12 A further practical point is that recent research shows that participation for vulnerable defendants is often compromised. Notwithstanding the provisions we have referred to above,[23] a degree of public concern has been expressed, for example about the failure of the criminal justice system to protect the article 6 rights of people with learning disabilities.[24] Dr Nigel Blackwood's research has also shown that judicial decisions to invoke special measures at the outset of a trial often lapse well before its conclusion.[25]

What more could be done in relation to special measures

4.13 In this regard, it is important to note that specific measures aimed at assisting learning disabled defendants could easily be formally adopted. For example, the Prison Reform Trust cites the measures referred to in the Care Service Improvement Partnership Handbook for Criminal Justice Professionals, namely: the use of visual aids, the avoidance of jargon, emphasising key words and the use of concrete rather than abstract terms, the breaking of large chunks of information into smaller chunks, preparing the individual for each new phase of the communication, being patient and calm while communicating, the use of open-ended rather than closed questions, and avoidance of double negatives

---

[21] J Jacobson with J Talbot, *Vulnerable defendants in the criminal courts: a review of provisions for adults and children* (Prison Reform Trust 2009) p 7.

[22] Above, p 14.

[23] See paras 4.4 to 4.8 above.

[24] See J Jacobson with J Talbot, *Vulnerable defendants in the criminal courts: a review of provisions for adults and children* (Prison Reform Trust 2009) p 8 citing the Joint Committee on Human Rights:

> We are concerned that the problems highlighted by this evidence could have potentially very serious implications for the rights of people with learning disabilities to a fair hearing, as protected by the common law and by Article 6 ECHR. Some of this evidence suggests that there are serious failings in the criminal justice system, which give rise to the discriminatory treatment of people with learning disabilities (JCHR, 2008, para 212).

[25] See para 2.104 above.

and vague questions.[26] Although these are well recognised measures, we suspect that some of them are often compromised because of the time involved in applying them.

4.14 The Prison Reform Trust's report on vulnerable defendants in the criminal courts has made a number of recommendations which are intended to improve the situation for vulnerable adult defendants in the courts. These recommendations include revising the unfitness to plead criteria[27] and having learning disability specialists to offer expert advice to courts on measures for supporting vulnerable adults in the courtroom and to contribute to the development and implementation of court disposals.[28] Further recommendations by the Trust include improved systems for screening and assessing defendants' needs, which would include screening when any party raises a concern about a defendant at any stage in the court process.[29]

4.15 In total there are seven recommendations (many of which are founded on the recommendations of the Bradley Report),[30] all of which we would endorse.

> (1) There should be a review of the policy framework for supporting vulnerable defendants, with the aims of: developing clearer principles for determining the circumstances under which the criminal prosecution of a defendant should and should not be continued, revising the fitness to plead criteria, establishing parity in statutory support for vulnerable witnesses and vulnerable defendants, ensuring the policy responses to mentally disordered defendants can take into account specific concerns relating to learning disability as well as mental health problems.

---

[26] J Jacobson with J Talbot, *Vulnerable defendants in the criminal courts: a review of provisions for adults and children* (Prison Reform Trust 2009) pp 18 to 19 citing Care Services Improvement Partnership (CSIP) handbook for criminal justice professionals (2007).

[27] Above, p 3, although there is no recommendation as to how the present criteria should be revised. The report is underpinned by the idea that there should be a greater focus on inclusion of vulnerable people within the criminal justice system and so we assume that a capacity based test such as the one which we have proposed will be welcomed.

[28] Preliminary discussions with specialists carried out during the work on this CP supports this. Dr Ian Hall, a consultant psychiatrist with particular knowledge and expertise in treating people who suffer from learning disability, has indicated that part of the problem for people with learning disabilities is an unfamiliarity with court proceedings and that it is possible to develop a person's fitness by preparing him or her for the experience: meeting of Law Commission working group on unfitness to plead, 14 December 2009.

[29] J Jacobson with J Talbot, *Vulnerable defendants in the criminal courts: a review of provisions for adults and children* (Prison Reform Trust 2009) p 3. Screening is aimed at identifying any possible impairments and whether or not a full assessment is required.

[30] K Bradley, *The Bradley Report: Lord Bradley's Review of People with Mental Health Problems or Learning Disabilities in the Criminal Justice System* (Department of Health 2009).

(2)   Every court should have access to a local liaison and diversion scheme. All liaison and diversion schemes should have input from, or at a minimum direct access to, learning disability specialists and should perform the following functions: screening and assessment / referral for assessment of defendants' needs, facilitate access to health and social care services (alongside or as an alternative to criminal prosecution, as appropriate), advise courts on measures for supporting vulnerable defendants in the court room, contribute to the development and implementation of court disposals.

(3)   Improved systems for screening and assessing defendants' needs should be introduced. These systems should be implemented by liaison and diversion schemes as above and entail: screening when any party raises a concern about a defendant, at any stage in the court process; referral for timely, full assessments (including psychiatric assessments) as required; systematic reporting of screening/assessment findings to the courts including pre-sentence reports.

(4)   Judges and magistrates should receive training on the range of impairments (including learning disabilities) that defendants can display, the implications of these impairments for the criminal justice process and methods by which vulnerable defendants' participation in court proceedings can be enhanced.

(5)   HMCS should ensure that all its provision complies with the Disability Discrimination Act, such that courts are fully accessible to vulnerable defendants (as well as to all other court users who are vulnerable) and these defendants receive the practical support and assistance they require in order to participate effectively in proceedings. Monitoring of the Courts Service's compliance with the Disability Discrimination Act should be undertaken.

(6)   In order to minimise the use of custodial remand for vulnerable defendants, healthcare and other support services for defendants on bail, provision for hospital remands, should be extended. Improved access to psychiatric and other assessments (see recommendation 3) should also help to reduce custodial remands of vulnerable defendants.

(7)   There should be greater and more flexible use of the community order in sentencing vulnerable defendants, ensuring full compliance with the Disability Discrimination Act and particularly the Disability Equality Duty. This can be achieved by making 'activity' and 'programme' requirements fully accessible to offenders with learning disabilities and mental health needs, and broadening the scope of the mental health treatment requirement.[31]

---

[31]   J Jacobson with J Talbot, *Vulnerable defendants in the criminal courts: a review of provisions for adults and children* (Prison Reform Trust 2009) pp 3 to 4.

SPECIAL MEASURES AND CAPACITY

4.16 In Part 3, we proposed that the current legal test for unfitness to plead (the *Pritchard* test) should be replaced by a decision-making capacity test which is informed by the full spectrum of trial decisions and the requirements for effective participation. We have expressed concern elsewhere in this CP that developments in the area of vulnerable defendants through the principle of effective participation and the use of special measures have occurred outside the context of the law on unfitness to plead.[32] We therefore think that it is important that any reform of the legal test should consider the role that special measures should play.

4.17 We think that special measures could play a role in one of two different ways.

(1) The availability of special measures could be a factor in the new legal test. This would mean that in determining whether the accused has decision-making capacity, consideration should be given to the extent to which special measures could assist the accused to participate in his or her trial.

(2) The availability of special measures would not be relevant to the legal test for decision-making capacity. However, an accused who has decision-making capacity may still be vulnerable because of a mental or physical disorder and therefore the deployment of special measures at trial may be appropriate. This would be similar to the current position, where the availability of special measures is not part of the *Pritchard* test.

4.18 In essence, under our provisional proposal we envisage a continuum whereby some accused will be deemed to lack decision-making capacity and will be dealt with in a reformed section 4A hearing. Others will be found to have decision-making capacity, but some of these accused will still require additional assistance using special measures if they are to participate effectively in their trial. We think that it is important to emphasise, however, that the system should be mindful of the defendant's mental or physical condition throughout the proceedings and should focus on assisting him or her to be able to participate in the criminal proceedings. As we discussed in Part 3, circumstances may arise so that the accused can no longer be said to have the required capacity, for example, if he or she suffers a deterioration in his or her particular condition. In such circumstances, it should be possible to convert to a hearing under section 4A.[33]

Special measures as a factor in the legal test

4.19 Option 1 set out at paragraph 4.17 would include the availability of special measures in the legal test as to decision-making capacity. As we envisage it, this will mean that courts and those who have a duty to the court (such as counsel, solicitors and experts) will need to consider how (if at all) an accused's ability to participate in a trial will be served by the availability of special measures. This is our preferred option.

---

[32] See para 2.103 above.

[33] See para 3.102 above.

4.20 The main advantage to including consideration of the existence and effects of special measures as part of the legal test for decision-making capacity is that it puts the availability of special measures at the forefront of the capacity determination. The primary disadvantage of special measures not being considered (option 2 above) as part of the legal test for decision-making capacity is that there will be a risk of replicating the present situation in which their availability is frequently overlooked.[34] We have already observed that the law on special measures has developed independently of unfitness to plead and that the disparate provision of measures for those who are vulnerable is something which we would wish to remedy.

4.21 Including special measures in the decision-making capacity test may also serve to ensure that appropriate measures are adopted on the basis of the defendant's specific needs. This could remedy some of the problems highlighted at paragraphs 4.10 to 4.11 where the provisions for vulnerable defendants have been criticised for failing to ensure those defendants with learning difficulties are able to participate effectively in their trials.

4.22 As we explained in Part 3, one of the perceived practical problems with the present test for unfitness to plead is that it does not recognise the separate components of plea and participation in the trial. This has led to debate as to the advantages of a more disaggregated approach which would enable the courts to accept a plea of guilty in appropriate circumstances.[35] If the application of special measures is a factor to which the court must have regard in determining capacity, then in an appropriate case[36] a court would be able to adopt the procedures referred to in paragraph.30.3 of the Practice Direction on vulnerable defendants[37] to ascertain whether an accused has capacity to enter a guilty plea.

4.23 Furthermore, in the Crown Court a practice has developed of counsel seeking a *Goodyear*[38] indication in relation to sentence. This could possibly be developed in the context of any consideration as to capacity with an indication being sought on the basis of the prosecution case on the papers.[39]

---

[34] TP Rogers et al, "Reformulating fitness to plead: a qualitative study" (2009) 20(6) *Journal of Forensic Psychiatry and Psychology* 815, 828.

[35] See paras 3.64 to 3.78 above.

[36] An example of an appropriate case is referred to at para 3.72 above.

[37] Practice Direction (Criminal Proceedings: Consolidation), para III.30, as inserted by Practice Direction (Criminal proceedings: Further Directions) [2007] 1 WLR 1790. Para III.30.3 provides "All possible steps should be taken to assist a vulnerable defendant to understand and participate in those proceedings. The ordinary trial process should, so far as necessary, be adapted to meet those ends". Para III.30.18 states "Where the court is called upon to exercise its discretion in relation to any procedural matter falling within the scope of this practice direction but not the subject of specific reference, such discretion should be exercised having regard to the principles in paragraph III.30.3."

[38] *Goodyear* [2005] EWCA Crim 888, [2005] 1 WLR 2532 outlines the process whereby a defendant may instruct his counsel to seek an indication from the judge of his or her current view of the maximum sentence which would be imposed on the defendant in the event of a guilty plea.

[39] The usual practice being that an indication is sought on an agreed written basis of plea.

4.24 The inclusion of the consideration of special measures as part of the test will serve to further the development of special measures on a case by case basis and ensure that the courts adapt to the needs of a particular defendant.

4.25 Under the current *Pritchard* test, the role of special measures is not considered. If a factor in the reformed legal test for the decision-making capacity of the accused is the possibility of having special measures to assist the accused, this will presumably increase the prospects of some defendants who would currently be found unfit to plead being able to stand trial.

4.26 For these reasons we think that the availability of special measures should form part of the legal test as to capacity.

4.27 However, taking account of the availability of special measures as part of the decision making capacity test will not remove the possibility of an accused being found to lack decision-making capacity. There will always be accused who are not going to be susceptible to the assistance which can be offered by way of special measures. It is these accused who would be subject to a reformed section 4A hearing.

> **Provisional Proposal 5: Decision-making capacity should be assessed with a view to ascertaining whether an accused could undergo a trial or plead guilty with the assistance of special measures and where any other reasonable adjustments have been made.**
>
> **Question 1: Do consultees agree that we should aim to construct a scheme which allows courts to operate a continuum whereby those accused who do not have decision-making capacity will be subject to the section 4A hearing[40] and those defendants with decision-making capacity should be subject to a trial with or without special measures depending on the level of assistance which they need?**

FURTHER PROPOSALS ON SPECIAL MEASURES

The relevance of expert evidence

4.28 As we have seen, special measures tend to have been developed on a fairly piecemeal basis. Given our provisional proposals for a legal test based on decision-making capacity which will include the availability of special measures, we would expect special measures to continue to develop. We have therefore asked ourselves what other proposals could reasonably be made in relation to special measures.

4.29 One issue is whether or not, in a trial, evidence can be properly admitted on issues relating to any condition from which the accused suffers with the aim of preventing the jury from possibly drawing an adverse inference. There is authority on the admissibility of such evidence in relation to a vulnerable prosecution witness where the Court of Appeal held that the prosecution were entitled to

---

[40] As it exists at present (see Part 1 above) or as amended under our provisional proposals (see Part 6 below).

adduce evidence of a psychiatrist to the effect that a child suffering from autism was likely to present herself in a particular way.[41] We can see no reason as to why this principle should not be equally applicable to, say, a defendant who has Asperger's Syndrome[42] or some other disability which may be outside the general knowledge of the jury and may affect the way in which the defendant presents him or herself and therefore cause the jury to draw an adverse inference in respect of his or her evidence.

4.30   At the moment, the trial judge has a discretion not to give a direction under section 35[43] of the Criminal Justice and Public Order Act 1994[44] in the event that the accused does not give evidence and has in fact answered questions in interview.[45] This power is often relied upon as a concession to those defendants who are fit to plead but who have a mental or physical condition which would make it difficult or disadvantageous to them to give evidence in a trial.[46] We think that the principle of full inclusion[47] should apply, by which we mean that every effort should be made to receive the evidence of a defendant who may be disabled.

---

[41]   *S (VJ)* [2006] EWCA Crim 2389. In this case, expert evidence was allowed to the effect that the witness's behaviour and demeanour (in evidence-in-chief) was by no means unusual or surprising. It must be regarded against the background of her autistic condition and did not amount to bolstering her credibility.

[42]   Where for example there may be a lack of eye contact when the sufferer is exposed to stress, or a literal-mindedness which could be misconceived by the jury.

[43]   As to the drawing of an inference "as appear[s] to be proper from the failure of the accused to give evidence, or his refusal without good cause, to answer any question": see s 35(3) of the Criminal Justice and Public Order Act 1994 which provides:

> Where this subsection applies, the court or jury, in determining whether the accused is guilty of the offence charged, may draw such inferences as appear proper from the failure of the accused to give evidence or his refusal, without good cause, to answer any question, it will be permissible for the court or jury to draw such inferences as appear proper from his failure to give evidence or his refusal, without good cause, to answer any question.

[44]   This discretion applies if it appears to the court that the "physical or mental condition of the accused makes it undesirable for him to give evidence": see s 35(1)(b) of the Criminal Justice and Public Order Act 1994.

[45]   Which in reality often amounts to a concession that that there is a case to answer.

[46]   See *Friend (No1)* [1997] 2 All ER 1011, 1019.

[47]   In the spirit of the Bradley Report (K Bradley, *The Bradley Report: Lord Bradley's Review of People with Mental Health Problems or Learning Disabilities in the Criminal Justice System* (Department of Health 2009)) and the report for the Prison Reform Trust (J Jacobson with J Talbot, *Vulnerable defendants in the criminal courts: a review of provisions for adults and children* (Prison Reform Trust 2009)), over recent years inclusion has been an important public policy goal aimed at ensuring equality for people with disabilities and eliminating discrimination. In the report by the Prison Reform Trust, it was suggested that the concept of inclusion in relation to criminal justice policy means that when individuals with mental health problems, learning disabilities or other disabilities are prosecuted, "the criminal justice process should be adapted and appropriate support made available so as to make it possible for them to participate effectively": see J Jacobson with J Talbot, *Vulnerable defendants in the criminal courts: a review of provisions for adults and children* (Prison Reform Trust 2009) p 28.

4.31 We think that the policy behind such a reform is broadly consistent with the policy behind the use of intermediaries provided for by section 104 of the Coroners and Justice Act 2009.[48]

> **Provisional Proposal 6: Where a defendant who is subject to a trial has a mental disorder or other impairment and wishes to give evidence then expert evidence on the general effect of that mental disorder or impairment should be admissible.**
>
> **Question 2: Can consultees think of other changes to evidence or procedure which would render participation in the trial process more effective for defendants who have decision-making capacity but due to a mental disorder or other impairment require additional assistance to participate?**

---

[48] Which we referred to in para 4.6 above.

PART 5
ASSESSING THE CAPACITY OF THE ACCUSED

INTRODUCTION

5.1 As indicated in Part 3, we think that a decision-making capacity test should replace the present test for determining the issue of whether an accused is unfit to plead. Alongside this we have proposed that the test should take into account the various decisions that an accused will be required to make during the course of his or her trial and ensure that he or she is able to participate effectively. Whilst we have avoided proposing that decisions made by the accused must be rational, we have proposed that the emphasis should be on the decision-making process as opposed to the content of any decision ultimately reached. We think that this will make for a certain degree of rationality whilst maintaining the right to self-determination. We have stated in Part 4 that the legal test for decision-making capacity should specifically include the availability and extent of special measures.

5.2 At present, English law lacks a defined psychiatric test for assessing decision-making capacity in relation to criminal proceedings. In the USA there have been a number of different tests used for assessing competence to stand trial and to plead. Generally speaking, they appear to be intended to cover an assessment of the various things which an accused will be expected to do in the course of a trial.[1]

---

[1] For example the McGarry test, referred to as the "competency to stand trial assessment instrument", contains 13 items for assessment:
  (1) ability to appraise the legal defences available;
  (2) level of unmanageable behaviour;
  (3) quality of relating to lawyer;
  (4) ability to plan legal strategy and to instruct a lawyer as to defence;
  (5) ability to appraise roles of various participants in courtroom proceedings;
  (6) understanding of court procedure;
  (7) appreciation of charges;
  (8) appreciation of range and nature of possible penalties;
  (9) ability to appraise likely outcomes;
  (10) capacity to disclose and to instruct a lawyer of pertinent facts surrounding offence;
  (11) capacity to challenge prosecution witnesses realistically;
  (12) capacity to give evidence;
  (13) evidence of self-serving as opposed to self-defeating motivation.
This test has been identified as the most often used: see PA Zapf and JL Viljoen, "Issues and considerations regarding the use of assessment instruments in the evaluation of competency to stand trial" (2003) 21 *Behavioural Sciences and Law* 351, 355.

5.3 However some of the tests have been criticised[2] and it is arguable that there is still a need to develop a model which is not overly prescriptive but broad enough to incorporate any condition which can reasonably be said to bear on the question of decision-making capacity.[3] It has been pointed out that between 1965 and 2005, some 19 psychiatric tests have been constructed in North America for the assessment of competence or fitness.[4] The tests have been variously and specifically criticised in terms of their particular limitations. Psychiatrists in England and Wales have not adopted the MacArthur Competence Assessment Tool-Fitness to Plead[5] which was adapted for use in England and Wales.

THE RELATIONSHIP BETWEEN LAW AND PSYCHIATRY

5.4 In this CP we propose that whether an accused has or does not have decision-making capacity under our reformed legal test should be assessed using a standardised psychiatric test. One of the problems with the present *Pritchard* test (the legal test) is what has been described by the Court of Appeal as the "mis-match" between law and psychiatry.[6] In our view, it is necessary for reform to take account of the relationship between the disciplines of law and psychiatry.

5.5 Later in this Part we consider whether or not the law should require psychiatric evidence or whether or not evidence from a wider range of practitioners such as psychologists, nurses, social workers and occupational therapists, would be sufficient. We conclude that to be compliant with article 5 of the European

---

[2] The Competency Screening Test (PD Lipsitt, D Leloss and AL McGarry 1971) was said to give high false positive rates and to have an inconsistent factor structure. The Competency to Stand Trial assessment instrument (AL McGarry and WJ Curran 1973) was said to have a limited range and a lack of focus on the link with symptoms/legal impairment. The Georgia Court Competency Test (R Wildman et al 1979) was said to have too great a focus on foundational competencies. The Competence Assessment for Standing Trial - Mental Retardation (C Everington and C Dunn 1995) was said to create problems because the legal standards were not lower or different for mentally retarded defendants. See TP Rogers et al, "Fitness to plead and competence to stand trial: a systematic review of the constructs and their application" (2008) 19(4) *Journal of Forensic Psychiatry and Psychology* 576, 588 to 589.

[3] AA Akinkunmi cites T Grisso, *Evaluating Competencies: Forensic Assessments and Instruments* (1986) as describing the following four important characteristics that must be considered in developing an instrument for evaluating competence to stand trial:

> The evaluation procedure should: (1) ensure that each of the relevant legal constructs must be captured; (2) have quantitative measures that reflect performance in discrete legal domains; (3) include flexible, in-depth enquiries on legal issues that are guided by coherent legal theory; and (4) be administered in a standardized fashion that promotes inter- and intrarater reliability.

See AA Akinkunmi, "The MacArthur Competence Assessment Tool- Fitness to Plead: a preliminary evaluation of a research instrument for assessing fitness to plead in England and Wales" (2002) 30 *Journal of the American Academy of Psychiatry and the Law* 476, 477.

[4] TP Rogers et al, "Fitness to plead and competence to stand trial: a systematic review of the constructs and their application" (2008) 19(4) *Journal of Forensic Psychiatry and Psychology* 576, 587.

[5] This is an American test which was developed in 1997. A scenario is read to the person being tested and questions are asked so that the researcher is able to rate capacity for understanding, reasoning and appreciation of matters relevant to the impending trial.

[6] *Murray* [2008] EWCA Crim 1792 at [6]; see discussion at paras 2.80 to 2.81 above.

Convention on Human Rights[7] the opinion of at least two medical practitioners, one of whom is duly approved as having special expertise in the diagnosis or treatment of mental disorder, should be required. First, however, we consider the justifications for having a standardised psychiatric test to assess decision-making capacity in criminal proceedings.

The absence of a defined psychiatric test to assess unfitness to plead

5.6 Currently there is no defined psychiatric test used to assess unfitness to plead. The MacArthur Competence Assessment Tool-Fitness to Plead ("MacCAT-FP") was adapted for use in England and Wales,[8] however it has not been adopted by clinicians.[9] In the civil context, there is no single clinical test used to assess capacity according to the legal test laid out under the Mental Capacity Act 2005. However, the time- and context-specific nature of the civil test arguably requires a more flexible approach to assessing capacity than would be necessary in the criminal context. The civil test does not employ a defined psychiatric test for the assessment of litigation capacity. Further, assessments as to capacity apply to a wide range of decisions, from day-to-day decisions to more serious decisions such as whether to undergo medical treatment. Capacity is usually assessed by the person directly concerned with the individual at the time that he or she needs to make a particular decision, meaning that a wide range of people need to be able to assess capacity, such as family members, carers and doctors.[10] However, the Code of Practice recognises that more serious or complex decisions may require professional input before an assessment of capacity is made.[11] Medical opinion is also viewed as an important element in any decision by a court as to whether a person has capacity.[12]

5.7 Although a new decision-making capacity test for criminal proceedings could be adopted without also adopting a standardised psychiatric test, the arguments in favour of having a suitable psychiatric test for assessing capacity are compelling. An analysis of the way in which psychiatrists have worked in the past demonstrates this. It is claimed that psychiatrists "are inconsistent in their

---

[7] Which allows for the detention of persons of "unsound mind" (article 5(1)(e)) only where there is "objective medical expertise" which establishes that a person has a mental disorder: see *Winterwerp v Netherlands* (1979) 2 EHRR 387 (App No 6301/73) at [39].

[8] AA Akinkunmi, "The MacArthur Competence Assessment Tool-Fitness to Plead: a preliminary evaluation of a research instrument for assessing fitness to plead in England and Wales" (2002) 30 *Journal of the American Academy of Psychiatry and the Law* 476. The original American test was adapted for use in England and Wales by making such changes as omitting reference to the involvement of juries in sentencing.

> It has been subjected to review by both experienced forensic psychiatrists and legal practitioners with a view to ensuring that its content captures all the relevant legal and clinical criteria (at 478)… in determining fitness to plead [trials showed that the test] is able to distinguish between fit and unfit patients (at 481).

[9] TP Rogers et al, "Reformulating fitness to plead: a qualitative study" (2009) 20(6) *Journal of Forensic Psychiatry and Psychology* 815, 817.

[10] Mental Capacity Act 2005 Code of Practice, para 4.38.

[11] Above, para 4.53.

[12] See *Masterman-Lister v Jewell* [2002] EWHC 417, [2002] All ER (D) 247 at [16], although the court emphasised that ultimately "it is for the court to decide whether or not a person has capacity – not the medical profession".

application of the *Pritchard* criteria".[13] At present, the *Pritchard* criteria leave a lot to the discretion of medical practitioners who will, of course, have the initial input. This reliance on discretion may well be because there is no formal standardised clinical test for assessing unfitness to plead.[14] It may of course also be attributable to the fact that the *Pritchard* criteria are outdated and that medical practitioners are therefore making the best of an unsatisfactory situation.[15]

5.8 Empirical research into the way in which psychiatrists arrive at their judgments on unfitness to plead has shown that it is rarely the case that all five of the *Pritchard* criteria are considered in assessing unfitness. For example in a research sample which covered findings of unfitness during the period 1976 to 1989 (in which there was a total of 302 findings of unfitness) an examination of the psychiatric reports "revealed that in only nine cases was mention made in any single report of all five criteria".[16]

5.9 Between 1992 and 1993 (out of 125 cases of unfitness to plead) an analysis of the court file in each of the cases resulted in 197 pre-trial reports. Again, in only 21 reports did the psychiatrist address all five criteria for the purpose of giving an opinion as to unfitness to plead. In 28 reports the accused was considered to be unfit to plead by virtue of the diagnosis alone and the report did not address the accepted criteria at all.[17] Professor Mackay and Gerry Kearns report that other "criteria" in addition to or instead of those which are the recognised *Pritchard* criteria were frequently mentioned. These included:

> He does not understand the nature and possible consequences of the charge. If a witness said something with which he did not agree he would not be able to cope with this.

> I do not believe that he would be able to cross-examine a witness.

> He has very little understanding of his predicament and his decision to plead guilty to the alleged offence appears to be formed by a desire to go to prison where he can lie in bed all day. He does not understand that he may be cross-examined and he has little understanding of the nature and function of a jury. His thought processes are particularly rigid and naïve and he is quite capable of entertaining logically incompatible positions.[18]

---

[13] TP Rogers et al, "Reformulating the law on fitness to plead: a qualitative study" (2009) 20(6) *Journal of Forensic Psychiatry and Psychology* 815, 817.

[14] The MacCAT-FP not having been adopted by clinicians: see para 5.6 above.

[15] In much the same way as they have done for the purposes of diminished responsibility as defined by s 2 of the Homicide Act 1957: see Partial Defences to Murder (2004) Law Com 290, para 5.50.

[16] RD Mackay, *Mental Condition Defences in the Criminal Law* (1995) p 224.

[17] For a full breakdown see G Kearns and RD Mackay, "An upturn in unfitness to plead? Disability in relation to the trial under the 1991 Act" [2000] *Criminal Law Review* 532, 538.

[18] G Kearns and RD Mackay, "An upturn in unfitness to plead? Disability in relation to the trial under the 1991 Act" [2000] *Criminal Law Review* 532, 539.

5.10 More recently an analysis of the impact of the 1991 Act between 1997 and 2001 was made of 329 cases.[19] There were 606 reports which made express mention of fitness to plead and six made implied reference to the same.[20] There were 29, however, that failed to address the issue. In only 58 reports did the psychiatrist address all five of the criteria for the purpose of the finding of unfitness to plead.

5.11 In 89 of the reports the defendant was thought to be fit to plead or to be unfit by virtue of the diagnosis and/or by relying on other criteria without the psychiatric report addressing the established *Pritchard* criteria.

5.12 Professor Mackay notes that, as in the previous years, criteria were used which were distinct from those recognised as part of the *Pritchard* test. Broadly, they reflect the examples that were cited at paragraph 5.9.

> It is my opinion that he is unable to understand the seriousness of the situation facing him or the implications of his offence. It is my opinion that he is not fit to plead due to his psychiatric illness.[21]

> He does not comprehend the gravity of his offence and has limited understanding of what his lawyer does. He could give no reasonable account of the role of the court, the judge or the jury.[22]

> On balance I would consider that she is unfit to plead since she is unable to address the issues or events on the night in question, lacks insight into her mental disorder … and the fluctuating nature of her attention and concentration along with particular preoccupations which at times prevent her following and responding logically to questions would suggest that she remains unfit to plead.[23]

5.13 Professor Mackay has now completed a study of formal findings of unfitness to plead during the seven year period between 2002 and 2008, during which there was a total of 725 findings of unfitness.[24] Unlike the previous three studies however, there was no access to court files and therefore there was no access to the relevant psychiatric reports. It is thus not possible to ascertain which of the relevant criteria were addressed by the psychiatrists in recent years. We have set out the results of this research at Appendix C.

The role of a defined psychiatric test to assess capacity in the criminal context

5.14 Although the inconsistent application of the *Pritchard* test by psychiatrists is probably a reflection upon the inadequate nature of the criteria, it is just as likely

---

[19] RD Mackay et al, "A continued upturn in unfitness to plead – more disability in relation to trial under the 1991 Act" [2007] *Criminal Law Review* 530, 536.

[20] In 41 of the cases there were no reports.

[21] RD Mackay et al, "A continued upturn in unfitness to plead – more disability in relation to trial under the 1991 Act" [2007] *Criminal Law Review* 530, 537 (in relation to a 33-year-old male suffering from schizophrenia).

[22] Above, 537 (in relation to a 74-year-old male with dementia).

[23] Above, 537 (in relation to a 55-year-old female suffering from schizophrenia).

[24] This is equal to an annual average of 103.6 findings of unfitness.

95

to be a reflection of the fact that there is no standard test for psychiatrists to use. We think that if there was a sound psychiatric test for assessing decision-making capacity in criminal proceedings, this would lead to consistency in assessments. Research on the use of particular tests for ascertaining consent to psychiatric treatment supports the view that a test coupled with an interview with a clinician will lead to consistency of outcome.[25]

5.15 The use of a purpose-made (as opposed to an adapted) test also has the advantage of ensuring that opinion as to capacity is not founded purely on the subjective judgment of the clinician.[26]

5.16 In our view, the role of the psychiatric test is to provide a standard means of assessing whether the accused has decision-making capacity in accordance with the legal test. However, this does not mean that this standardised psychiatric test would be the only part of the assessment process. We would expect that in most cases the test would also be accompanied by a clinical interview. Moreover, while our provisional view is that the gravity and complexity of the proceedings should not be a factor in the legal test,[27] this information would be part of the factual matrix within which the expert would make an assessment of the accused's decision-making capacity. In other words, the gravity and complexity of the proceedings should be treated by experts as a matter of fact – they are not part of the legal test itself. This information would of course be highly relevant if our alternative provisional proposal 4 at paragraph 3.101 were to be supported by consultees.

5.17 By adopting such a psychiatric test, the approach to decision-making capacity in criminal proceedings would again differ from the approach taken in the civil context. As was discussed above, the time- and context-specific nature of the civil test requires a wider approach to capacity assessments.[28]

Provisional Proposal 7: A defined psychiatric test to assess decision-making capacity should be developed and this should accompany the legal test as to decision-making capacity.

---

[25] On this point see R Cairns et al, "Reliability of mental capacity assessments in psychiatric in-patients" (2005) 187 *British Journal of Psychiatry* 372 that recorded research, which ascertained that the MacCAT-T (MacArthur Competence Assessment Tool for Treatment) in combination with a clinical interview could be used to provide highly reliable binary judgements on capacity to consent to treatment which were obtained in separate interviews.

This study has shown that two clinicians can reliably agree about capacity to decide about treatment in the early stages of admission to a psychiatric hospital, using a combination of the MacCAT-T and a clinical interview (at 377).

[26] This has led to problems in the civil jurisdiction. See G Richardson, "Mental capacity at the margin: the interface between two acts" (2010) 18 *Medical Law Review* 56 at 65 to 66:

For present purposes, lack of insight can be understood as a lack of awareness of illness, but even this reduced definition harbours tensions within it. At its core lies a judgment about the patient's ability to accept certain experience or behaviour as pathological, thus giving it an inherently subjective character.

[27] See para 3.99 above.

[28] See para 5.6 above.

WHO SHOULD ASSESS CAPACITY?

5.18 Under the current law on unfitness to plead, section 4(6) of the 1964 Act provides that a court cannot make a determination as to the accused's unfitness to plead "except on the oral or written evidence of two or more registered medical practitioners at least one of whom is duly approved".[29] This statutory requirement for medical evidence was a result of amendments made in the 1991 Act[30] and was recommended by the Butler Committee.[31] The CLRC did not recommend legislation requiring evidence from two doctors on the basis that it was invariable practice to have such evidence.[32] The Butler Committee was, however, of the opinion that there should be a statutory requirement as there were cases, albeit rare, where there was not evidence from two doctors.[33]

5.19 "Registered medical practitioner" is defined in the 1964 Act as a "fully registered person within the meaning of the Medical Act 1983 who holds a licence to practice".[34] "Duly approved" means "approved for the purposes of section 12 of the Mental Health Act 1983 by the Secretary of State as having special experience in the diagnosis or treatment of mental disorder".[35] Although the 1964 Act does not therefore specifically require that the evidence comes from a psychiatrist,[36] in practice a finding of unfitness to plead has required a consensus of psychiatric opinion.[37]

---

[29] The Court of Appeal held in *Ghulam* [2009] EWCA Crim 2285, [2010] 1 WLR 891 that while the court must have evidence from two registered medical practitioners (at least one of whom is duly approved) in order to find the accused unfit to plead, s 4(6) does not preclude a finding that the accused is fit to plead where there is no such evidence: see [16]. It reasoned that subsection (6) should be confined to determinations that the accused is unfit to plead because otherwise whenever unfitness was asserted, even where there was inadequate evidence, the court could not proceed until the requisite medical evidence was obtained.

[30] See s 2 of the 1991 Act.

[31] Report of the Committee on Mentally Abnormal Offenders (1975) Cmnd 6244, para 10.41.

[32] Criminal Law Revision Committee Third Report: Criminal Procedure (Insanity) (1963) Cmnd 2149, para 16.

[33] Report of the Committee on Mentally Abnormal Offenders (1975) Cmnd 6244, para 10.41.

[34] Section 8(2) of the 1964 Act.

[35] Section 8(2) of the 1964 Act. Section 12 of the Mental Health Act 1983 sets out general requirements as to medical recommendations for admission to hospital under Part 2 of the Act (civil admission) but is also relevant to provisions providing for the detention in hospital of persons involved in criminal proceedings, including a hospital order under s 37 under Part 3 of the same act. The Mental Health Act 2007 inserted a new subsection 2A into s 12 which provides that an approved clinician is to be treated as approved for the purposes of s 12 as having special experience in the diagnosis or treatment of mental disorder. This however only applies to registered medical practitioners who are also approved clinicians.

[36] The Butler Committee specifically recommended that only one of the registered medical practitioners should need to be duly approved and not both, on the basis that it would be undesirable to "exclude the evidence of the defendant's own doctor who would already have knowledge of his history and, therefore, might well be the most suitable witness as to the defendant's ability to comprehend the proceedings": see Report of the Committee on Mentally Abnormal Offenders (1975) Cmnd 6244, para 10.42.

[37] TP Rogers et al, "Fitness to plead and competence to stand trial: a systematic review of the constructs and their application" (2008) 19(4) *Journal of Forensic Psychiatry and Psychology* 576, 587.

5.20 However, a significant change under the Mental Health Act 2007 was to allow many of the roles under the Mental Health Act 1983 to be performed by a wider range of professionals by replacing the role of the "responsible medical officer" with that of the "responsible clinician". Responsible medical officers were in practice usually consultant psychiatrists[38] whereas the responsible clinician, who has overall responsibility for a patient's case, can be any practitioner who has been approved for that purpose. Approval is not intended to be restricted to medical practitioners – it can extend to practitioners from other professions, such as psychology, occupational therapy and social work.[39] The Mental Health Act 1983 therefore now recognises a broader range of mental health professionals as having the necessary expertise to take clinical responsibility for a particular patient.

5.21 Despite this broader approach to professional roles under the Mental Health Act 1983, and the provision under the Mental Capacity Act 2005 for a wide range of people to make capacity assessments,[40] we believe for the reasons which we discuss below[41] that there should remain the requirement in criminal proceedings that an accused cannot be found to lack decision-making capacity except on the oral or written evidence of two registered medical practitioners, at least one of whom is duly approved under section 12 of the Mental Health Act 1983. In practice we therefore envisage that a determination as to decision-making capacity will continue to require evidence from at least one psychiatrist, particularly if, as we propose, there is a standardised psychiatric test to assess decision-making capacity.

An example of a legal test which does not necessarily contemplate psychiatric input

5.22 Although it is our preferred view that there should be a psychiatric test to assess decision-making capacity, it is possible to have a legal test which is not predicated on psychiatric input. The Scottish model provides an example of a unitary legal test which does not contemplate a particular psychiatric test or that there will even necessarily be any psychiatric input. It is based on the recommendations of the Scottish Law Commission.[42]

5.23 The Scottish Law Commission sought to restate the general nature of insanity as a plea in bar of trial (unfitness) with the intention of giving expression to the rationale behind the law. The Commission recommended:

---

[38] Explanatory notes to the Mental Health Act 2007, para 47. See also W Bingley, "The Mental Health Act 2007" [2007] 9 *Archbold News* 6, 7.

[39] Explanatory notes to the Mental Health Act 2007, para 48.

[40] See para 5.6 above.

[41] See paras 5.29 to 5.36 below.

[42] The recommendations have been incorporated into the Criminal Justice and Licensing (Scotland) Act 2010, which received Royal Assent on 6 August 2010.

The test for the plea of unfitness in bar of trial should be that as a consequence of the accused's mental or physical condition at the time of the trial he lacks the capacity to participate effectively in the proceedings against him. The test should include a non-exhaustive list of activities which would indicate such lack of capacity.[43]

5.24 This definition sets out a general rationale for the plea of unfitness as well as a non-exhaustive[44] list of factors which indicate unfitness. The Scottish Law Commission was of the opinion that the "general rationale of the plea in bar in the existing law is that because of a person's mental or physical condition a criminal trial is an inappropriate process for that person."[45] However, it thought that it was better to express this general rationale in terms of "effective participation",[46] as this was the formulation used by the European Court of Human Rights.[47] For the Scottish Law Commission, effective participation captured the "notion of full or rational appreciation by the accused of the proceedings".[48]

5.25 The Scottish Commission recommended that the court should have regard to the following factors when determining whether a person is unfit for trial:

    (a)   the ability of the person to –

        (i)   understand the nature of the charge;

        (ii)   understand the requirement to tender a plea to the charge and the effect of such a plea;

        (iii)   understand the purpose of, and follow the course of, the trial;

        (iv)   understand the evidence that may be given against the person;

        (v)   instruct and otherwise communicate with the person's legal representative; and

    (b)   any other factor which the court considers relevant.[49]

---

[43] Insanity and Diminished Responsibility (2004) Scottish Law Commission Report No 195, recommendation 19 at para 4.19.

[44] The Scottish Law Commission thought that if the list was exhaustive then it would not be possible to identify all the appropriate skills: Insanity and Diminished Responsibility (2004) Scottish Law Commission Report No 195, recommendation 19 at para 4.11.

[45] Insanity and Diminished Responsibility (2004) Scottish Law Commission Report No 195, recommendation 19 at para 4.12.

[46] As to which see paras 2.89 to 2.102 above.

[47] Insanity and Diminished Responsibility (2004) Scottish Law Commission Report No 195, para 4.14.

[48] Above, para 4.14.

[49] Above, Appendix A, cl 4 of the Draft Criminal Responsibility and Unfitness for Trial (Scotland) Bill, which would add new s 53F(1) and (2) to the Criminal Procedure (Scotland) Act 1995.

5.26   In recommending that the court should have regard to the above factors, the Scottish Law Commission took account of Professor Bonnie's reformulation of the *Dusky* test[50] which was as follows:

> A defendant is competent to proceed to [adjudication] [trial] if he has a rational understanding of the charge against him, the nature and purpose of the proceedings and the adversary process, is able to assist counsel in his defence, and has the capacity for rational decision-making in relation to the defense and disposition of the case.[51]

5.27   Section 170 of the Criminal Justice and Licensing (Scotland) Act 2010[52] inserts a new section 53F into the Criminal Procedure (Scotland) Act 1995. Subsection (2) lays out the same list of non-exhaustive factors as recommended by the Scottish Law Commission, and the general principle (as expressed in subsection (1)) is that a person "is incapable, by reasons of a mental or physical condition, of participating effectively in a trial".

5.28   The Scottish Law Commission also recommended the repeal of the requirement in section 54(1) of the Criminal Procedure (Scotland) Act 1995 that there must be written or oral evidence of two medical practitioners in order for the court to find that the accused is unfit for trial.[53] This recommendation has been adopted in the Criminal Justice and Licensing (Scotland) Act 2010.[54] The Commission expressed concern that the requirement in section 54(1), taken alongside section 61(1)(a) which requires that at least one of the medical practitioners must have been approved under the Mental Health (Care and Treatment) (Scotland) Act 2003, meant that "evidence from other experts, such as clinical psychologists, would not be sufficient basis for establishing insanity in bar of trial".[55] It highlighted the fact that under the existing law in Scotland, the plea in bar of trial dealt with more conditions than just mental illness and that the effect of section 54(1) could be to "duplicate evidence which is relevant to the determination of the plea in bar in cases which deal with conditions outwith the expertise of psychiatrists". Thus the Commission concluded that there should be no restrictions, except on the basis of relevance, on the type of evidence that could be admitted to establish the plea.[56]

---

[50]   Professor Bonnie provided direct assistance to the Scottish Law Commission.

[51]   Insanity and Diminished Responsibility (2003) Scottish Law Commission Discussion Paper No 122, para 4.15. However the recommendations as set out at para 5.25 above do not actually refer to the capacity for rational decision making. We wonder whether if this was referred to, there would in fact be an *a priori* requirement of psychiatric input.

[52]   Yet to come into force.

[53]   Insanity and Diminished Responsibility (2004) Scottish Law Commission Report No 195, para 5.63.

[54]   Section 170(2)(a)(i).

[55]   Insanity and Diminished Responsibility (2004) Scottish Law Commission Report No 195, para 5.60.

[56]   Above, para 5.62.

Establishing a lack of decision-making capacity

5.29   It is our view however that there should continue to be restrictions on the type of evidence that is admissible to establish that an accused lacks decision-making capacity. As we discuss further in Part 7, under the current law if it is found that an unfit accused did the act or made the omission charged against him or her, the court has the power to make a hospital order. Moreover, under our provisional proposals for a revised section 4A hearing,[57] we think that where an accused who lacks decision-making capacity is acquitted after a section 4A hearing there could be a further hearing to consider a special verdict on the question of whether the acquittal was because of a mental disorder existing at the time of the alleged offence. If there is such a special verdict, then the same options for disposal, including a hospital order, would be available as are currently available under section 5 of the 1964 Act.[58]

5.30   A finding that an accused lacks decision-making capacity (or under the current law, is unfit to plead) could therefore result in a loss of his or her liberty. Thus, as the Court of Appeal in *Ghulam*[59] observed:

> It is perfectly understandable that Parliament should have required that a finding that a defendant is indeed unfit to plead should not be made except on substantial medical evidence, given the potential consequences for the defendant.[60]

5.31   This thinking is also reflected in the Butler Committee's report, where it justified its recommendation for a statutory requirement as to medical evidence on the basis that "the defendant should not be put in jeopardy of loss of his liberty unless there is an agreed opinion by two doctors"[61] that he or she is unfit to plead.

5.32   Further, the potential for an unfit accused to be detained in hospital raises an issue under article 5 of the European Convention on Human Rights which protects the right to liberty. Under article 5(1)(e), an exception to this right is the lawful detention of "persons of unsound mind". The European Court of Human Rights has emphasised, however, that in order to establish mental disorder for the purposes of article 5(1)(e), there must be "objective medical expertise".[62] The Domestic Violence, Crime and Victims Act 2004 amended the 1964 Act so that a hospital order can only be made under section 5 where it could be made under section 37 of the Mental Health Act 1983.

---

[57]   See Part 6 below.

[58]   See Part 7 below for a discussion of the various disposals.

[59]   [2009] EWCA Crim 2285, [2010] 1 WLR 891.

[60]   Above at [18].

[61]   Report of the Committee on Mentally Abnormal Offenders (1975) Cmnd 6244, para 10.41.

[62]   *Winterwerp v Netherlands* (1979) 2 EHRR 387 (App No 6301/73) at [39].

5.33   The purpose of this change was to ensure that any detention of an unfit accused in hospital would be compatible with article 5. This is because section 37(2) of the Mental Health Act 1983, read in conjunction with section 54(1), precludes the making of a hospital order unless there is written or oral evidence from two registered medical practitioners, at least one of whom is duly approved under section 12 as having special experience in the diagnosis or treatment of mental disorder, that the offender is suffering from a mental disorder of a nature and degree that makes detention in hospital appropriate.

5.34   Although section 5 of the 1964 Act now only allows a hospital order where the conditions under section 37 of the Mental Health Act 1983 are satisfied, and therefore ensures that there is "objective medical expertise" as required under article 5, we believe that substantial medical evidence should still be required before a finding that the accused lacks decision-making capacity can be made. Article 5 provides a strong protection of the right to liberty and any exceptions to it are to be interpreted narrowly.[63] It would appear contrary to such thinking to weaken the evidential requirements for a finding that could ultimately lead to the accused's loss of liberty. It would also be contrary to the thinking behind the statutory requirement of evidence from two or more doctors, one of whom is approved as having experience in the diagnosis or treatment of mental disorder.[64] Moreover, if a hospital order is to be made, the evidence required to make such an order under section 37 of the Mental Health Act 1983 is likely to be more easily available if there has been evidence from at least one psychiatrist at the point when the accused's decision-making capacity was determined.

5.35   We also think it is important to note the concerns raised by the Joint Committee on Human Rights in relation to the wider range of practitioners who are now able to carry out many of the functions under the Mental Health Act 1983 which were previously reserved to responsible medical officers.[65] Of particular concern to the Committee was the Government's view that objective medical expertise "means relevant medical expertise, and not necessarily that of a registered medical practitioner" and could therefore extend to, for example, evidence from a psychologist with the relevant skills and ability to identify the presence of a mental disorder.[66] The Joint Committee however disagreed with this broad interpretation, emphasising that the European Court of Human Rights had given "every indication ... that objective medical expertise involved reports from psychiatrists who are doctors" and that "the opinion of a medical expert who is a

---

[63]   *Litwa v Poland* (2001) 33 EHRR 53 (App no 26629/95).

[64]   See paras 5.29 to 5.30 above.

[65]   See Joint Committee on Human Rights, Legislative Scrutiny: Mental Health Bill, Fourth Report of Session 2006-07, HL Paper 40, HC 288.

[66]   Above, para 9.

psychiatrist is necessary for a lawful detention on grounds of unsoundness of mind".[67]

5.36 We therefore believe that restrictions should remain on the type of evidence that is capable of supporting a finding that an accused lacks decision-making capacity. Although we recognise that an accused may lack capacity as a result of a condition outside the experience of psychiatrists as experts,[68] we believe that the majority of cases which come (or ought to come) before the courts in the context of unfitness to plead concern conditions in relation to which psychiatric opinion is relevant. We think this is the case even in circumstances where that opinion may be secondary to the conclusions of other mental health professionals such as clinical psychologists, educational psychologists or speech and language therapists. A decision that may ultimately result in an accused being deprived of his or her liberty should be based on substantial medical evidence. We would therefore retain the current requirement in section 4(6) of the 1964 Act so that, under our proposed new legal test, the court cannot make a determination as to the decision-making capacity of the accused except on the oral or written evidence of two or more medical practitioners, at least one of whom is approved under section 12 of the Mental Health Act 1983 as having special experience in the diagnosis or treatment of mental disorder. This would ensure compliance with the requirements of article 5. It would also ensure consistency between the evidential requirements for finding that an accused lacks decision-making capacity and those for making a hospital order under section 37 of the Mental Health Act 1983.

FINDING A SUITABLE PSYCHIATRIC TEST

5.37 In this regard, we support the work of Dr Blackwood and his colleagues[69] who are presently analysing a test which they have devised.[70] This effectively forms the third tranche of the work to which we have referred to elsewhere in this CP.[71] The published work of Dr Blackwood has focused, amongst other things, on the deficiencies of the unitary construct.[72]

5.38 In essence, the current research is intended to show what people of various different capacities do and do not understand about legal proceedings. From a

---

[67] Above, para 25. The Joint Committee relied on the case of *Varbanov v Bulgaria* App No 31365/96, where the European Court of Human Rights said at [47] that "no deprivation of liberty of a person considered to be of unsound mind may be deemed in conformity with article 5(1)(e) … if it has been ordered without seeking the opinion of a medical expert". The court went on to say that "in the absence of an assessment by a psychiatrist" there was no justification for the applicant's detention: see *Varbanov v Bulgaria* App No 31365/96 at [48].

[68] Such as a physical condition.

[69] Dr Nigel Blackwood, Rebecca Brewer, Professor Jill Peay and Mike Watts.

[70] The research is being carried out at the Institute of Psychiatry at King's College London and is being funded by the Nuffield Foundation.

[71] See TP Rogers et al, "Fitness to plead and competence to stand trial: a systematic review of the constructs and their application" (2008) 19(4) *Journal of Forensic Psychiatry and Psychology* 576 and "Reformulating the law on fitness to plead: a qualitative study" (2009) 20(6) *Journal of Forensic Psychiatry and Psychology* 815.

[72] TP Rogers et al, "Reformulating the law on fitness to plead: a qualitative study" (2009) 20(6) *Journal of Forensic Psychiatry and Psychology* 815.

psychiatric point of view, the questions are: what cognitive abilities are central to the ability to comprehend court proceedings and to follow evidence? How does depressive and psychotic symptamatology impact on these abilities? How does learning disability impact upon these abilities?[73] In other words, what will be the likelihood of a particular diagnosis (say, depression) affecting the relevant degrees of capacity necessary for trial?

5.39   A suitably devised psychiatric test would assist in measuring the capacity of the accused to do the various things required by the legal test.[74] It would need to test the accused's ability to retain information and to use this information to weigh up competing factors and their implications. The psychiatric test which Dr Blackwood and his colleagues are working on consists of a short video scenario of court proceedings which demonstrates the role of the various participants in those proceedings as well as the purpose of cross examination and giving evidence. It is played to the subject (the accused) who is then asked a series of questions about what has been shown. The answers which are elicited then assist in determining the level of capacity of the subject.

5.40   We have had the benefit of seeing the draft test and await the results of the ongoing research. We assume that the result of the test itself would be accompanied in any given case by a clinical interview.[75]

Capacity to do some things but not others

5.41   We think that it will follow from a psychiatric test such as that designed by Dr Blackwood and his colleagues that an accused may be found to have decision-making capacity in relation to some matters but not others.[76] He or she may be able to enter a plea but not have sufficient capacity to participate in the trial or in some of the more demanding aspects of the trial. These participatory aspects include comprehending the role of solicitors, barristers, the judge, jury and witnesses as well as the purpose and process of the trial including the giving of instructions, the purpose of examination in chief, cross-examination and re-examination. They also include the implications of giving or not giving evidence and an appreciation of the possible outcome of the proceedings.

5.42   Under our unitary but nevertheless functional approach to the legal test, an accused should not stand trial unless he or she has the capacity to participate in *all* aspects of his or her trial.[77] A psychiatric test which breaks down the elements of the trial and considers the accused's capacity in relation to these elements is compatible with such an approach. We do not believe, however, that a psychiatric test should be used as a basis for a disaggregated approach which would, for

---

[73]   Talk given by Dr Nigel Blackwood to the Law Commission on 19 March 2009 and to the Criminal Appeal Lawyers Association in October 2009.

[74]   In essence, such tasks would involve the decision to enter a plea, understanding of the procedure, an understanding of the implications of the evidence in chief and cross-examination, and the decision to give evidence.

[75]   This may be confirmed when the research is complete.

[76]   This is of course subject to the proviso that until Dr Blackwood's research has been completed, we cannot actually know what degree of capacity is required.

[77]   In our view, the determination of capacity should (as we explained in Part 4) take into account special measures.

example, allow the accused to enter a plea of guilty (because he or she has the capacity to enter a plea) even though he or she does not have the capacity to make other decisions or do other tasks in relation to his or her trial unless such an opinion is formed for the basis of the special measures aspect of the test referred to in Part 4 of this CP. We discussed earlier the theoretical problems with a fully disaggregated approach in this respect, namely that it goes against the whole thinking behind having any form of an unfitness to plead procedure.[78]

---

[78] See para 3.74 to 3.76 above.

PART 6
THE SECTION 4A HEARING

INTRODUCTION

6.1 So far we have been concerned with the procedure and legal test to determine whether a person is unfit to plead, which is often referred to as the "trial of the issue". We now turn to the second part of the existing unfitness to plead procedure which takes place when an accused is found to be under a disability so that he or she is unfit to plead.

6.2 The procedure which is to be followed in these circumstances is, as we explained in Part 2 of this CP, provided for by section 4A of the 1964 Act. This is sometimes referred to as the "trial of the facts" or, as we refer to it in this CP, as the "section 4A hearing". Section 4A effectively allows for a hearing as to the facts following which the accused can be acquitted but not convicted. Instead he or she can be found to have done the act or made the omission with which he or she is charged. As such, the section 4A hearing is wholly distinct from a trial.[1]

6.3 In this Part we analyse the way in which the current procedure under section 4A works. It is important to state at the outset that the present procedure, whereby counsel or a solicitor is appointed by the court to represent the accused and to present his or her case, works well in terms of assisting an unfit accused. Until the enactment of section 4A, a defendant in a trial of any kind was always entitled to decide for him or herself how his or her case was to be conducted and his or her representatives were obliged to act on his or her instructions. We have seen in *Erskine*[2] the sort of difficulties which can occur in cases where counsel have to follow the instructions of a defendant who is not capable of making decisions and whose decisions are irrational and flawed as a result of mental disorder.[3] The great advantage of the section 4A hearing is that the appointed legal representative, although he or she will obviously discuss the case with the accused, is not bound to follow the accused's instructions about the way in which the case should be run if he or she does not agree that those instructions are in the accused's interests. In other words, the appointed legal representative is not limited in the same way as counsel in an ordinary trial. This is obviously subject to the facts, circumstances and evidence in any one particular case. In this way the section 4A hearing is conducted in a manner calculated to achieve the fairest possible outcome for the accused.

6.4 This procedure provided for by section 4A was intended to counter the problems which arise when an accused cannot participate effectively in his or her trial by giving appropriate instructions to his or her lawyers, following the proceedings and, if he or she wishes, giving evidence in his or her own defence.

6.5 The section 4A hearing, which was entirely novel at the time it was introduced by Parliament in the 1991 Act, has more or less consistently succeeded in achieving

---

[1] We discussed the differences between the s 4A hearing and a trial at paras 2.28 to 2.31 above.

[2] [2009] EWCA Crim 1425, [2010] 1 WLR 183.

[3] See paras 2.76 to 2.79 above.

that objective. Broadly speaking, it does what it was intended to do which is to enable the prosecution's evidence to be properly tested and to allow any points which can be properly made in the accused's favour to be put before the jury for their consideration.

6.6 We think, however, that there are a number of problems with the section 4A hearing. In essence, these problems flow from a tension between the need to allow the accused a fair hearing as to the facts of the alleged offence and the need to protect the public from an accused who may be dangerous. The present legislation aims to provide for a fair hearing by giving the accused an opportunity to be acquitted following a section 4A hearing if the prosecution is unable to prove that the accused did the act. It aims to protect the public by ensuring that if there is evidence on which it can be proved that the accused has done an injurious or dangerous act then he or she can be found to have done that act and he or she will be subject to the disposal of the courts.

6.7 The principal problem is that the section 4A hearing, whereby the jury is asked to determine whether the accused "did the act", depends on it being possible to divide the conduct element from the fault element of a criminal offence.[4] The case law has shown, however, that this is not always possible.[5] There are problems when the lawfulness or the unlawfulness of the accused's act depends on his or her state of mind. A guilty state of mind may render unlawful what would otherwise be lawful, and an innocent state of mind may render lawful what would otherwise be unlawful. An example of this is the offence of possession of an offensive weapon contrary to section 1 of the Prevention of Crime Act 1953. Section 1(4) provides that the defendant does the act of "having an offensive weapon in a public place" if he or she *intends* to use it to cause injury.

6.8 We conclude that there is a principled case for reform of the present procedure as well as a need to address the problems which, the case law suggests, may arise in distinguishing between the conduct and fault elements, particularly if the section 4A hearing is used more frequently.[6]

6.9 In this Part, therefore, we discuss possible options in relation to the reform of the section 4A hearing.

(1) Do nothing and allow the law to develop on a case-by-case basis.

(2) Adopt the recommendation of the Butler Committee, namely, that all the elements of the offence must be proved without qualification.

---

[4] As we discuss below, the House of Lords in *Antoine* [2000] UKHL 20, [2001] 1 AC 340 held that the reference to the "act" in s 4A means that the prosecution has to prove only the conduct element of the offence.

[5] *R (Young) v Central Criminal Court* [2002] EWHC 548 (Admin), [2002] 2 Cr App Rep 178: see para 6.25 below.

[6] We think that it would be likely, as a result of the broader test of decision-making capacity which we provisionally proposed in Part 3, that more accused would be dealt with through a s 4A hearing. The possible impact of our provisional proposals in this respect is discussed in our impact assessment, at Appendix D.

(3)   Abolish the section 4A hearing altogether and allow the accused to stand trial. This would be subject to the proviso that once an accused has been found to lack decision-making capacity, then a legal representative would be appointed by the court to represent his or her interests in the trial.

(4)   Adopt the Scottish procedure under which the prosecution must prove: (a) beyond reasonable doubt that the accused did the act or made the omission constituting the offence; and (b) on the balance of probabilities that there are no grounds for acquitting the accused. If the accused is acquitted, the court can make a further finding that the acquittal is on grounds of insanity.

(5)   Replace the section 4A hearing with a procedure whereby the prosecution is obliged to prove all elements of the offence. However, if the accused is acquitted there would be scope for a further hearing to determine whether or not the acquittal is on the basis of mental disorder existing at the time of the offence. If there is such a qualified acquittal, then the accused is subject to the disposal of the court.

6.10   We recognise that each of these five options has its advantages and disadvantages. However, for reasons which we go on to explain below, option 5 is our preferred option, and we make our provisional proposals for reform on this basis.

THE CASE FOR REFORM: PROBLEMS WITH THE SECTION 4A HEARING

6.11   Before going on to consider these five options, it is first necessary to discuss what we believe to be the problems with the current section 4A hearing. The most difficult issue is what the prosecution must prove in order for an accused who is unfit to plead[7] to be subject to the disposal of the court.[8] Section 4A requires the jury to determine whether the accused "did the act or made the omission" charged against him or her as the offence. This has been held by the House of Lords in *Antoine*[9] to mean that the prosecution only has to prove the conduct element of the offence in question. Although this was clearly the intention behind the legislation,[10] the reasoning in *Antoine* is not always easy to follow, and this has led to uncertainty and inconsistency in the law. As we explain further below, we believe this provides a strong case for reform of the section 4A hearing.

---

7   Or, under our proposals, lacks decision-making capacity.

8   Under s 5 of the 1964 Act, these disposals are a hospital order (with or without a restriction order), a supervision order or an order for absolute discharge. We discuss these disposals in greater detail in Part 7 below.

9   [2000] UKHL 20, [2001] 1 AC 340, which overturned *Egan* [1998] 1 Cr App R 121 on this point. In *Egan*, the Court of Appeal had held that in order to prove that the accused had done the act it was essential that all the ingredients of the offence (in that case theft) were proved: see pp 124 to 125.

10   See the second reading of the Criminal Procedure (Insanity and Unfitness to Plead) Bill where John Greenway MP said that it would not make sense for the courts to look at the mental element: *Hansard* (HC), 1 March 1991, vol 186, col 1272.

6.12   We also go on to discuss a further issue that has arisen in the case law, namely, the way in which the section 4A hearing has been construed for the purposes of article 6 of the European Convention on Human Rights.[11]

The decision of the House of Lords in *Antoine*[12]

6.13   In *Antoine* the accused was charged with murder and manslaughter and had been found to be under a disability under section 4(5) of the 1964 Act. The trial judge ruled that the accused could not rely on the defence of diminished responsibility at a hearing under section 4A.[13] His ruling was upheld by the Court of Appeal and the accused appealed to the House of Lords. The point of law certified for the opinion of the House of Lords was:

> Where pursuant to section 4A(2) of the Criminal Procedure (Insanity) Act 1964 a jury has to determine whether an accused person has done the act of murder, is it open to the accused to rely on section 2 of the Homicide Act 1957?

6.14   The House of Lords dismissed the appeal. It was held that once a jury had determined that the accused was under a disability pursuant to section 4(5) of the 1964 Act, then the defence of diminished responsibility could not arise as he was no longer liable to be convicted of murder. It could not therefore be raised for the purposes of a section 4A hearing.

6.15   The decision in *Antoine*, however, was not confined to whether an accused was able to assert that he or she was guilty or had done the act of voluntary manslaughter by way of diminished responsibility (in which respect the opinion of the House of Lords is undoubtedly right).[14] The House of Lords also considered the following wider question:

> Where, pursuant to section 4A(2) of the Criminal Procedure (Insanity) Act 1964, a jury has to determine whether an accused did the act or made the omission charged against him as the offence, must the jury be satisfied of more than the actus reus of the offence? Must the jury be satisfied of mens rea?

6.16   The House of Lords held that the use of the word "act" as opposed to "offence" was consistent with the purpose of section 4A, which was that the jury should consider only the conduct element of the offence and should not be concerned with any mental element.

6.17   Lord Hutton outlined several policy reasons behind his opinion that the word "act" should only amount to the conduct element of the offence. First, he said that the purpose of the section 4A hearing is:

---

[11]   See para 6.42 to 6.54 below.

[12]   [2000] UKHL 20, [2001] 1 AC 340.

[13]   Under s 2 of the Homicide Act 1957.

[14]   In the sense that it is consistent with s 4(3) of the 1964 Act, the thinking in the Butler Report, and with the principle that both trial and conviction are a rational process in which the accused must be able to participate, as to which see RA Duff, *Trials and Punishments* (1986) p 119.

To strike a fair balance between the need to protect a defendant who has, in fact, done nothing wrong and is unfit to plead at his trial and the need to protect the public from a defendant who has committed an injurious act which would constitute a crime if done with the requisite *mens rea*. The need to protect the public is particularly important where the act done is one which has caused death or physical injury to another person and there is a risk that the defendant may carry out a similar act in the future.[15]

6.18 Secondly, where an accused was insane at the time of the killing then if the construction of "act" was not confined to the conduct element, it would mean that "a very serious risk to the public would arise which Parliament could not have intended".[16] For example, if an accused charged with murder was insane at the time of the killing and was unfit to plead at the time of the trial by reason of that insanity, then it would not be possible to prove the fault element for murder because of the insanity existing at the time of the alleged offence. The jury would therefore have to acquit an accused who would be released to the danger of the public.[17]

6.19 In his exposition of how a balance between the need to protect an innocent accused and the public interest is to be achieved, Lord Hutton endeavoured to give some guidance. In circumstances where an accused was charged with an offence which could be negated by an arguable defence of accident, mistake or self-defence, which he or she could have raised but for the fact that he or she was unfit to plead then:

> If there is objective evidence which raises the issue of mistake or accident or self-defence, then the jury should not find that the defendant did the "act" unless it is satisfied beyond reasonable doubt on all the evidence that the prosecution has negatived that defence.[18]

6.20 For example, if there was evidence in the case of an assault from an independent witness that the victim had hit the accused first then it would be open to the jury to acquit the accused under section 4A(4) of 1964 Act. However, the defence would not be free to raise this defence in the absence of such a witness. In other words, there must be some extraneous evidence which raises the defence. This approach seems to presuppose an absence of instructions from the accused, therefore suggesting that Lord Hutton thought that the accused would not have any decision-making capacity concerning the section 4A hearing.

---

[15] *Antoine* [2000] UKHL 20, [2001] 1 AC 340, 375.

[16] Above, 373.

[17] Section 5(3) of the 1964 Act (which addresses disposal) refers to sentences which are "fixed by law". At the time of the decision in *Antoine*, this presented a further problem in the case of offences for which the sentence was fixed by law which extended beyond murder, ie, certain offences under s 5 of the Firearms Act 1968 pursuant to s 51A of the same Act. It is conceivable that a hospital order may not be appropriate as it would not be justifiable under s 37 of the Mental Health Act 1983. However, now see s 37(1A) of the Mental Health Act 1983.

[18] *Antoine* [2000] UKHL 20, [2001] 1 AC 340, 376.

6.21   The decision in *Antoine* has since been applied in relation to the partial defence of provocation.[19] In *Grant*,[20] the trial judge ruled that, in relation to the question of whether the accused did the act of murder, the defences of lack of intent and provocation could not be put before the jury. The Court of Appeal (dismissing the appeal) held that both defences related to the fault element for murder and so were not a matter for the jury to consider under section 4A.

6.22   Given that provocation is, like diminished responsibility, a partial defence to murder it is both consistent and sensible that, at present, it cannot be asserted and relied on by the accused in the course of a section 4A hearing. A successful plea would lead to a conviction and it would defeat the purpose of section 4A[21] for an unfit accused to be convicted of voluntary manslaughter.

6.23   However, as we discuss further below,[22] under our provisional proposals for reform it may be possible to consider defences in so far as this is consistent with the fact that decisions about the section 4A hearing are made by the accused's appointed legal representative. In other words, as long as there is a sufficient evidential basis to raise the defence or partial defence then the representative of the accused can do so if he or she thinks that it is in the accused's best interest. On the basis of our provisional proposals, therefore, the decision in *Antoine* would be reversed.

Problems with the decision in *Antoine*

6.24   The reasoning in *Antoine* essentially requires a strict division between the conduct and fault elements of the offence, so that the jury focus only on whether the accused committed the conduct element of the offence when determining whether he or she did the act. This line of reasoning, however, cannot always be strictly adhered to in cases where the offence charged does not lend itself readily to a division of conduct and fault elements. The reality is that it is not always possible to disregard the mental state of the accused for the purpose of ascertaining whether he or she has done the "act".

6.25   For example, in *R (Young) v Central Criminal Court*[23] it was held that the accused's intention was a "material fact" for the purpose of the conduct element of the offence of dishonestly concealing material facts contrary to section 47(1) of the Financial Services Act 1986. Further, in the late Professor Smith's commentary on that decision he observed:

---

[19]   *Grant* [2001] EWCA Crim 2611, [2002] QB 1030 at [42] to [47]. In *Antoine*, Lord Hutton had reserved his opinion on whether the defence could call witnesses to raise the issue of provocation in a section 4A hearing. He did, however, observe that "the defence of provocation to a charge of murder is only relevant when the jury are satisfied that the defendant had the requisite mens rea for murder": see [2000] UKHL 20, [2001] 1 AC 340, 377.

[20]   [2001] EWCA Crim 2611, [2002] QB 1030.

[21]   Section 4A is intended to protect the accused from a conviction.

[22]   See para 6.154 to 6.159 below.

[23]   [2002] EWHC 548 (Admin), [2002] 2 Cr App R 178 at [34], [35].

In other cases it appears that the verb used to describe the act necessarily implies a mental element – "possesses" and "permits" are common examples.[24]

6.26 As such, it is necessary, in order to determine whether the accused did the act, to consider a degree of fault in some cases but not in others. Where the conduct and fault elements of the offence are readily divisible, the fault element will not be considered. This means that the result in any given case could, to some extent, be arbitrary as it will depend on the nature of the charge. This can lead to a lack of consistency in different cases.

6.27 It also leads to other problems of coherence. Is it not anomalous that fault cannot be considered in a case as serious as murder but must be considered for an offence of, for example, having an offensive weapon in a public place?[25] The fact that there will be something approximating to a consideration of any fault element in the less serious offence means that there could be an increased scope for an acquittal under section 4A. We believe that this is demonstrative of a fundamental unfairness in the current law.

6.28 This is not a problem which is confined to only a few offences. In recent years, a large number of offences have been created which would be likely to cause problems if an accused was found to be unfit to plead and there was accordingly a section 4A hearing, where section 4A was construed as it was in *Antoine*. Examples of such offences include the following offences under the Terrorism Act 2000:

(1) supporting proscribed organisations contrary to section 12;[26]

(2) raising funds for terrorism contrary to section 15;[27]

(3) money laundering for the purpose of terrorism contrary to section 18;[28]

---

[24] [2002] *Criminal Law Review* 588, 589.

[25] Section 1(4) of the Prevention of Crime Act 1953 provides that the defendant does the act of "having an offensive weapon in a public place" if he or she intends to use it to cause injury.

[26] Section 12(1) creates an offence of inviting support for a proscribed organisation. Section 12(2) creates an offence of arranging, managing or assisting in arranging or managing a meeting knowing that it is either to support a proscribed organisation, to further the activities of a proscribed organisation or is to be addressed by a person who belongs or professes to belong to a proscribed organisation. Section 12(3) provides for an offence of addressing a meeting where the purpose of the address is to encourage support for a proscribed organisation or to further its activities.

[27] Section 15(1) and (2) provide for offences of inviting another to provide money or property, or of receiving money or property, if the person intends that it should be used, or has reasonable cause to suspect that it may be used, for the purposes of terrorism. Section 15(3) creates the offence of providing money or property if the person knows or has reasonable cause to suspect that it will or may be used for the purposes of terrorism.

[28] Section 18(1) provides for an offence of entering into or becoming concerned in an arrangement which facilitates the retention or control by or on behalf of another person of terrorist property by concealment, by removal from the jurisdiction, by transfer to nominees or in any other way. It is a defence for a person charged with an offence under s 18(1) to prove that he or she did not know and had no reasonable cause to suspect that the arrangement related to terrorist property.

(4)   failure to disclose a belief or suspicion that another person has committed an offence under sections 15 to 18 contrary to section 19;

(5)   failure to disclose information that could assist in preventing an act of terrorism or apprehending a terrorist contrary to section 38B;[29] and

(6)   possession of an article for a purpose connected with an act of terrorism contrary to section 57.[30]

6.29   These are clear examples of offences where it is impossible to determine whether the conduct element has been committed without having regard to the mental state of the accused. Additional examples can be found in sections 1[31] and 2[32] of the Terrorism Act 2006 and in sections 327 to 329 of the Proceeds of Crime Act 2002.[33]

Defences

6.30   The unfairness to which we have referred in paragraph 6.27 above is also apparent in the context of defences, many of which are inextricably linked with the elements of the offence which are in issue. Self-defence is an obvious example of where it is difficult to disengage the conduct element from the fault element. A defendant is legally entitled to use force to defend him or herself if he or she genuinely, even if mistakenly, believes him or herself to be under attack, as long as the force used is reasonable in the circumstances. If he or she does so this negates the fault element for the offence in question.[34] In deciding whether the force which the defendant used was reasonable in the circumstances, the jury are instructed to proceed on the basis of the

[29]   Section 38B applies where a person has information which he or she knows or believes might be of material assistance in preventing the commission by another person of an act of terrorism, or in securing the apprehension, prosecution or conviction of another person in the United Kingdom, for an offence involving the commission, preparation or instigation of an act of terrorism. The offence is committed where the person does not disclose the information as soon as reasonably practicable.

[30]   Section 57(1) provides that it is an offence for a person to possess an article in circumstances which give rise to a reasonable suspicion that his or her possession is for a purpose connected with the commission, preparation or instigation of an act of terrorism. Section 57(3) provides for an assumption in circumstances where it is proved that the article was on the premises at the same time as the accused that the accused possessed the article for the proscribed purpose unless it is proved by the accused that he or she did not know of its presence on the premises or that he or she had no control over it.

[31]   Section 1(2) provides that an offence is committed if the person publishes a statement intending or being reckless at the time of publication as to whether members of the public will be directly or indirectly encouraged or induced to commit, prepare or instigate acts of terrorism.

[32]   Section 2 provides for an offence of disseminating terrorist publications if the person intends an effect of his or her conduct to be a direct or indirect encouragement or other inducement to the commission, preparation or instigation of acts of terrorism, or is reckless as to whether his or her conduct has such an effect.

[33]   Section 327 provides for an offence of concealing, disguising, converting, transferring or removing criminal property. Criminal property is defined in s 340(3) as property which constitutes a person's benefit from criminal conduct or if it represents such a benefit (in whole or in part and whether directly or indirectly) and the alleged offender knows or suspects that it constitutes or represents such a benefit. This definition of "criminal property" applies to each of the principal money laundering offences referred to above.

[34]   *Williams (Gladstone)* [1987] 3 All ER 411.

circumstances as the defendant genuinely, even if mistakenly, believed them to be.

6.31 However, in *Antoine* their Lordships held that, in a section 4A hearing, it was only if there was "objective evidence" of self-defence that the issue should be left to the jury. Accordingly the jury should ignore anything which may have been in the accused's mind at the time of the offence.

6.32 In *Antoine*, their Lordships were not required to decide what kind of objective evidence might be sufficient. It seems likely that they had in mind the relatively straightforward and common case where a fight between the accused and the alleged victim was witnessed by one or more independent witnesses whose evidence suggests that the victim was or may have been the aggressor and the accused's response, judged objectively, was (or may have been) a reasonable one.

6.33 Of course, the reality is that much more complex issues can arise in self-defence cases. For example, the accused may have killed or injured the victim whilst labouring under a genuine but mistaken belief that the victim was attacking him as the result of a delusion caused by mental illness.[35]

6.34 If an unfit accused's state of mind at the time of the offence is to be ignored altogether (as is currently the position under *Antoine*), then he or she is placed at a significant disadvantage compared with a "fit" defendant who may be able to obtain an acquittal on the basis that he or she was acting lawfully.[36]

6.35 In other jurisdictions, attempts have been made to disengage the requisite elements of the offence from the requisite elements of a defence to that offence but this has not been thought to be sustainable.[37]

Secondary participation

6.36 Secondary participation is the common law doctrine which allows a person who encourages or assists or, in some circumstances, causes another person to perpetrate a criminal offence to be liable to the same extent as the perpetrator. It can be of particular importance in the context of murder cases because a person who is secondarily liable will receive the mandatory life sentence.

---

[35] As was the case in *Sureda*, set out in Appendix B.

[36] This would be particularly unfair in a joint trial between a fit defendant and an unfit accused. We explore this in detail in Part 7.

[37] See, for example, the observation of Crispin J in the decision of the Supreme Court of the Australian Capital Territory in *Morris* [2002] ACTSC 12 at [10]. Crispin J resolved the problem in s 317 of the Crimes Act 1900, as amended by the Crimes Amendment Act 2004 (the court must be "satisfied beyond reasonable doubt that the accused committed the acts that constitute the offence charged"), by finding it was not intended to exclude essential elements of the offence such as intention and knowledge but only the need for the jury to consider mental defences based on mental impairment of the accused: at [14], [16]. We discuss this further at paras 6.60 to 6.61 below.

> **Example 6A**
>
> D1 is the younger brother of D2, who has a very dominating personality. D2 persuades D1 to drive him to V's house so that D2 can "finish V off". V dies as a result of D2's attack. In these circumstances, D1 is guilty of murder if he knows of D2's intention.

6.37 The issue of secondary participation was recognised in *Antoine* as a potential problem in unfitness to plead cases[38] and has been further considered elsewhere.[39] If, under a true construction of section 4A, the court is precluded from looking at the accused's knowledge and his or her liability depends on what he or she *knew* the perpetrator intended to do, then it is not possible to ascertain whether the accused is secondarily liable.

6.38 Although the issue of secondary participation arose in *R v M*[40] it was not fully resolved. This was because the appeal was allowed on the basis that this evidence was wrongly admitted and that accordingly there was a breach of article 6(3)(d) of the European Convention on Human Rights. This is ironic given that, as we will see below, the House of Lords in *H*[41] held that the section 4A hearing does not amount to a determination of a criminal charge for the purposes of article 6.[42]

Inchoate offences

6.39 The exclusive focus on the conduct element of the offence is also potentially problematic if the accused is charged with an inchoate offence.[43] This is because the conduct element of this type of offence is often conduct which is not in itself unlawful, for example, the act of agreement to commit an offence in conspiracy.

---

[38] *Antoine* [2000] UKHL 20, [2001] 1 AC 340, 377.

[39] RD Mackay and WJ Brookbanks, "Protecting the unfit to plead: a comparative analysis of the 'trial of the facts'" [2005] *Juridical Review* 173, 182.

[40] [2003] EWCA Crim 357, [2003] 2 Cr App R 322. The accused, who was charged with murder, was said to have "the intellectual capacity of a young child and was so suggestible and lacking in understanding that he could not follow the court processes and [would have been] unable to give intelligent or coherent evidence". The facts were that the victim was surrounded by a group of youths and chased. At some point during the chase he sustained fatal stab wounds. Four of the co-defendants admitted that they were in the group who chased the victim. The prosecution relied upon evidence that the appellant was also in the group that had been found to have done the act of murder within the meaning of s 4A of the 1964 Act. The only evidence against the appellant was the evidence of a witness who was found to be in fear and whose evidence was read to the jury under s 23 of the Criminal Justice Act 1988.

[41] [2003] UKHL 1, [2003] 1 WLR 411.

[42] We discuss the whole question of article 6 in relation to the s 4A hearing at paras 6.42 to 6.54 below.

[43] Whether an increase in the number of inchoate offences dealt with under section 4A is likely to be proportionate to an increase in the number of cases of unfitness to plead is not known. Research conducted by Professor Mackay (see Appendix C) shows that between 2002 and 2008 there were 20 instances of attempted murder which were dealt with as unfitness to plead cases. We are precluded, however, from investigating any particular difficulties which may have arisen and whether any difficulties may have been attributable to the fact that the inchoate version of the offence was charged. In any event, it can be argued that attempt is in a different category from conspiracy and assisting and encouraging because by virtue of s 1(1) of the Criminal Attempts Act 1981, an attempt by definition involves the doing of an act which is more than merely preparatory.

This would have the potential to be grossly unfair and disproportionate and this has, to some extent, been recognised in other jurisdictions.[44]

6.40 There is also a potential problem with the new offences of encouraging and assisting crime contrary to sections 44 to 46 of the Serious Crime Act 2007.[45] The conduct involved may be conduct that, without the relevant intention or belief, is lawful. Yet the prohibition on the consideration of an accused's mental state could mean that an accused (who is not capable of forming the necessary fault element) is found to have done the act of encouraging or assisting for the purpose of section 4A. If an accused person is found to have done the act (and is exposed to the relevant disposal) which in the case of a fit defendant doing likewise would not amount to an offence, then this seriously undermines the protection from conviction that an unfit accused is afforded by the 1964 Act (as amended).

Conclusion

6.41 As we have seen above, it is not always possible to divide the conduct and fault elements of an offence for the purposes of a section 4A hearing, as is required by the decision in *Antoine*. In our view, this provides a theoretical justification for reform of the section 4A hearing. The decision in *Antoine* leaves considerable scope for uncertainty and the law has been left to develop on a piecemeal basis. If the problem is not confronted, there are likely to be further problems of coherence as well as considerable unfairness to accused in individual cases. This is so regardless of the practical impact of a revised test of unfitness to plead.[46]

The application of article 6 of the European Convention on Human Rights

6.42 Another problem with the present section 4A hearing is the way in which it has been construed for the purpose of article 6 of the European Convention on Human Rights.[47] In Part 2, we explained that the section 4A hearing is not a trial.

---

[44] See the decision of the Supreme Court of the Australian Capital Territory in *Ardler* [2003] ACTSC 24 at [23].

[45] These are the offences of: intending to encourage or assist the commission of an offence (s 44); believing that an offence will be committed and that his or her act will encourage or assist its commission (s 45); and encouraging or assisting offences believing that one or more will be committed (s 46).

[46] As we discuss in our impact assessment, we think it is reasonable to assume that our provisional test of decision-making capacity would lead to more section 4A hearings: see Appendix D.

[47] Article 6(3) provides for the following minimum rights for "everyone charged with a criminal offence":

(a) to be informed promptly, in a language which he understands and in detail, of the nature and cause of the accusation against him;

(b) to have adequate time and facilities for the preparation of his defence;

(c) to defend himself in person or though legal assistance of his own choosing or, if he has not sufficient means to pay for legal assistance, to be given it free when the interests of justice so require;

(d) to examine or have examined witnesses against him and to obtain the attendance and examination of witnesses on his behalf under the same conditions as witnesses against himself; and

(e) to have the free assistance of an interpreter if he cannot understand or speak the language used in court.

An essential difference is that a trial considers the general issue of whether the defendant is guilty or not guilty whereas the section 4A hearing has a far more limited remit. As we have seen above, the section 4A hearing is presently confined to a finding in relation to the conduct element of the offence. A finding that the accused has done the act does not amount to a conviction.

6.43 This has led the House of Lords to conclude that the section 4A hearing is not criminal in nature and that an unfit accused is therefore not entitled to claim the protection of article 6.[48] We do not suggest that the fact that article 6 has been held not to apply is a reason in itself for reforming the section 4A hearing. We do, however, think that any proposals for reform should take account of the fact that, at present, article 6 does not apply and that this is the subject of criticism.

The decision of the House of Lords in H[49]

6.44 In H, the 13-year-old accused was charged with two counts of indecent assault on a 14-year-old. Having been found to be unfit to plead, the accused was found to have done the act in accordance with section 4A of the 1964 Act. He was absolutely discharged and an order was made for him to be admitted on the sex offenders register. On appeal, his counsel contended that the procedure followed was incompatible with article 6(3).

6.45 The Court of Appeal dismissed the appeal and the accused appealed to the House of Lords.[50] The House of Lords held, dismissing the appeal, that the section 4A hearing did not constitute the determination of a criminal charge for the purposes of article 6. Applying the test in Engel,[51] Lord Bingham first addressed the way in which the section 4A hearing was classified in domestic law.[52] It was clear that the domestic law of England and Wales did not treat the procedure as involving the determination of a criminal charge. Lord Bingham observed that once there was a finding of unfitness to plead the 1964 Act provides that a criminal trial "shall not proceed or further proceed".[53] He also

---

[48] H [2003] UKHL 1, [2003] 1 WLR 411.

[49] Above.

[50] The certified question was:

Is the procedure defined by section 4A of the Criminal Procedure (Insanity) Act 1964 compatible with an accused person's rights arising under article 6 (1), 6(2) and 6(3)(d) of the ECHR? In particular, does the procedure in so far as:

(1) it provides for an acquittal of the accused person in the circumstances defined by the Act;

(2) it provides for a finding that the accused 'did the act' which constitutes the actus reus of the crime;

amount to the determination of a criminal charge for the purpose of article 6(1)?

Does a finding that an accused person "did the act" which constitutes the actus reus of the crime of indecent assault, being a crime of basic intent, violate the presumption of innocence afforded by Article 6(2)?

[51] Engel v The Netherlands (No 1) (1976) 1 EHRR 647 (App No 5100/71) where the test was said to be first, are the proceedings categorised as criminal under domestic law? Second, what is the nature of the offence? And third, what is the severity of the penalty?

[52] [2003] UKHL 1, [2003] 1 WLR 411 at [16].

[53] Section 4A(2).

noted that under section 4A(2), the jury had the power to acquit but not to convict.[54] The procedure could therefore result in an acquittal, but not in a conviction and not in punishment. Even an adverse finding (that the accused did the act) could lead to an absolute discharge, as was the outcome in *H* itself. If the finding led to a hospital order then there was nothing to preclude a full trial of the accused in the event that he or she recovered so as to be fit to plead.[55] Lord Bingham concluded that the section 4A hearing lacked the essential features of criminal process as identified in *Customs and Excise Commissioners v City of London Magistrates' Court*.[56]

6.46 The final limb of the *Engel* test (which involved taking into account the severity of the punishment) was not relevant because counsel for the accused had accepted that none of the orders consequent upon an adverse finding under section 4A were punitive. In this regard, Lord Bingham observed that:

> It was difficult if not impossible to conceive of a criminal proceeding which could not in any circumstances culminate in the imposition of any penalty, since it was the purpose of the criminal law to proscribe and, by punishing, to deter, conduct regarded as sufficiently damaging to the interests of society to merit the imposition of penal sanctions.[57]

6.47 The decision in *H* has, however, been criticised for not going behind the implications of a finding that an accused has done the act.[58] The fact that Lord Bingham considered the third aspect of the *Engel* test (the severity of the penalty) to be irrelevant does not seem to take into account that under sections 37 (hospital orders) and 41 (restriction orders) of the Mental Health Act 1983, hospital orders are in fact criminal disposals which can be imposed after conviction.[59] Detention in a hospital with indefinite restrictions must be regarded as severe.

6.48 Further, whereas Lord Bingham was of the view that registration on the sex offender's register was a non-punitive measure,[60] it has been argued that:

---

[54] [2003] UKHL 1, [2003] 1 WLR 411 at [16].

[55] This is only where the accused has been given a hospital order with a restriction order: see further Part 7 below.

[56] [2000] 1 WLR 2020, 2025, where it was held that these features are a formal accusation by the state or by a private prosecutor that a breach of the criminal law had been committed which might culminate in conviction or condemnation.

[57] [2003] UKHL 1, [2003] 1 WLR 411 at [19].

[58] RD Mackay and WJ Brookbanks, "Protecting the unfit to plead: a comparative analysis of the 'trial of the facts'" [2005] *Juridical Review* 173.

[59] We discuss the provisions of the Mental Health Act 1983 in greater detail in Appendix A.

[60] [2003] UKHL 1, [2003] 1 WLR 411 at [16].

He fails to point out that in *Welch v United Kingdom*[61] the court ruled that it "must remain free to go behind appearances and assess for itself whether a particular measure amounts in substance to a penalty".[62]

The decision of the Court of Appeal in *Chal*[63]

6.49 *H* was distinguished by the Court of Appeal in *Chal*. In *Chal*, the accused had made an apparently motiveless attack with a sledgehammer on a fellow employee at a building site. It was argued that the trial judge had wrongly admitted a hearsay account of the attack under section 116 of the Criminal Justice Act 2003. This evidence was the only eye-witness account. The issue on appeal was whether a court had the power to allow the introduction of hearsay evidence in proceedings under section 4A. It therefore fell to be determined whether criminal proceedings as defined by section 134 of the Criminal Justice Act 2003 included proceedings under section 4A. The trial judge had held that section 134 did apply to section 4A proceedings and that, even if it did not, then the statement was admissible under section 1 of the Civil Evidence Act 1995. The Court of Appeal held that although the proceedings under section 4A were not criminal in the sense that they culminated in a determination of criminal guilt or in the imposition of a criminal penalty, they were in fact criminal according to a general interpretation.

6.50 The substance of defence counsel's argument was that the proceedings under section 4A were not criminal proceedings as (relying on *H*) they did not lead to conviction and punishment. In dismissing the appeal, the Court of Appeal held that it was "axiomatic that the jury must be satisfied by evidence that would be admissible if the defendant were on trial".[64] This was because the purpose of section 4A was that:

> A person should not be detained unless a jury at a criminal trial would have found that he did the act charged and, conversely, that he should be eligible for detention if the jury is so satisfied.[65]

6.51 The Court of Appeal therefore concluded that the same rules of evidence and criminal procedure should be applied to proceedings under section 4A as would be applied if they were a "criminal trial in the strict sense".[66] The Court of Appeal also took support for this conclusion from the fact that the 1964 Act provides that if the issue of the defendant's unfitness happens to be raised during the course of a trial then the determination of whether he or she did the act is to be made on such evidence as has already been adduced. It could not be seriously contemplated that Parliament envisaged different rules of evidence should apply before and after the determination of disability.

---

[61] (1995) 20 EHRR 247 (App No 17440/90).

[62] See RD Mackay and WJ Brookbanks, "Protecting the unfit to plead: a comparative analysis of the 'trial of the facts'" [2005] *Juridical Review* 173, 176.

[63] [2007] EWCA Crim 2647, [2008] 1 Cr App R 247.

[64] Above at [26].

[65] Above.

[66] Above.

Classifying the section 4A hearing as either a criminal or a civil procedure

6.52 It has been observed that *H* and *Chal* were each decided on specific points of statutory interpretation. In the view of Professors Mackay and Brookbanks, the section 4A procedure is a "hybrid procedure" which has some characteristics which are criminal and some which are civil.[67] They observe that this was confirmed in *R (Julie Ferris) v Director of Public Prosecutions*.[68]

6.53 We agree with this view for two reasons. First, the disposals available in the event that an accused has done the act can be seen as punitive.[69] Secondly, the section 4A hearing is a unique procedure which is used to determine a criminal matter.[70] We think that this is, at least in part, the way in which it is contemplated in *Customs and Excise Commissioners v City of London Magistrates Court*,[71] namely because it involves a formal accusation as to the conduct element of an offence. The decision of the House of Lords that the section 4A procedure should not be categorised as a substantive criminal matter is consistent with only the conduct element being in issue. If all the elements of the offence were to be in issue[72] then the argument for categorising it as a criminal matter would be much stronger.

Conclusion

6.54 Below[73] we explain our provisional proposal that a revised section 4A procedure should involve a hearing as to all the elements of the offence (as proposed by the Butler Committee) but which is thereafter qualified by a special verdict.[74] Such a procedure would be to all intents and purposes akin to a formal charge and we think that this would justify the application of article 6.

OPTIONS FOR REFORM OF THE SECTION 4A HEARING

6.55 At the beginning of this Part we set out briefly five possible options in relation to the reform of the section 4A hearing.[75] In the light of the problems we have identified above, we now turn to discuss the five options in more detail before going on to make our provisional proposals.

---

[67] RD Mackay and WJ Brookbanks, "Protecting the unfit to plead: a comparative analysis of the 'trial of the facts'" [2005] *Juridical Review* 173, 177.

[68] *R (Julie Ferris) v Director of Public Prosecutions* [2004] EWHC 1221 (Admin) where it was held that s 4A proceedings shared aspects of both civil and criminal law. So, unless it was necessary to categorise the nature of the proceedings as either criminal or civil for a particular statutory purpose (as in *H* to ascertain whether article 6 applied) the temptation to do so should be resisted.

[69] See para 6.48 above.

[70] In the wide sense that there will be a victim, witnesses and so on who are affected by the resolution.

[71] [2000] 1 WLR 2020: see para 6.45 above.

[72] As we believe they should be and as they are, for example, in New South Wales, the Northern Territory and Victoria: see paras 6.75 to 6.82 below.

[73] See our discussion of option 5 for reform of the s 4A hearing at paras 6.128 to 6.140 below.

[74] A special verdict is one relating to an issue other than the general issue of guilty or not guilty.

[75] See para 6.9 above.

6.56   In our attempt to resolve the problems which we have identified in the present section 4A procedure, we have looked at various other jurisdictions. Our comparative research shows that the same issues and problems arise across the different jurisdictions. Where appropriate, we refer to this research in our discussion of the different options. In general, however, it appears that, with the exception of Scotland, there are in fact few jurisdictions which have a more advanced system for a hearing as to the facts of the case than the section 4A procedure.

Option 1 – do nothing

6.57   Although not an option for reform, the first option that has to be considered is to do nothing and leave the section 4A hearing as it stands. The scope of the hearing would therefore continue to be limited to determining whether the accused committed the conduct element of the offence, except in the limited circumstances envisaged in *Antoine*.[76]

6.58   In some Australian jurisdictions, the hearing as to the facts of the case following a finding of unfitness to plead is similarly limited to the conduct element of the offence.

Australian Capital Territory (ACT)

6.59   Following a finding that the accused is unfit to plead, section 316 of the Crimes Act 1900 provides for a "special hearing" before a jury, unless the Supreme Court is satisfied that the accused is capable of electing to have the hearing before a single judge. The accused is entitled to an acquittal if the court is not satisfied beyond reasonable doubt that the accused "engaged in the conduct required for the offence charged".[77]

6.60   The wording of section 316 was recently changed by the Crimes Amendment Act 2004. Prior to the amendment, section 317 of the Crimes Act 1900 had required that the court be satisfied beyond reasonable doubt that the accused "committed the acts that constitute the offence charged". Section 317 had been interpreted in a series of judicial decisions in a way that suggested that it did not prevent the jury from considering some mental elements. For example, in *R v Morris*[78] Justice Crispin observed that neither requiring the Crown to prove all elements of the offence nor requiring proof of only the objective elements was "wholly satisfactory".

---

[76]   These circumstances are where there is objective evidence of mistake, self-defence or accident: see para 6.19 above.

[77]   Section 316(9)(c), as amended by the Crimes Amendment Act 2004.

[78]   [2002] ACTSC 12.

He went on to find that section 317 was not intended to exclude any issues as to the knowledge or intention of the accused from consideration at a special hearing. The Crown was required to prove all the essential elements of an offence, but the defences of mental impairment or diminished responsibility could not be raised.[79]

6.61 These decisions were, however, regarded as unsatisfactory by the Government and the wording of the provision was changed to "engaged in the conduct required for the offence" so as to make clear that the prosecution was not required to prove the mental elements of the offence.[80]

South Australia

6.62 Section 269M.B of the Criminal Law Consolidation Act 1935 limits the inquiry to a trial of the "objective elements of the offence".[81] An objective element is defined as "an element of an offence that is not a subjective element".[82] Section 269A provides that "subjective element means voluntariness, intention, knowledge or some other mental state that is an element of the offence". In effect, the scope of the hearing under section 269M.B is therefore limited to the conduct element of the offence.

6.63 Section 269M.B also states that:

> On the trial of the objective elements of an offence, the court is to exclude from consideration any question of whether the defendant's conduct is defensible.[83]

---

[79] *Morris* [2002] ACTSC 12 at [19], [20] and [22]. This was applied at a special hearing before a judge without a jury in *Ardler* [2003] ACTSC 24. The Court of Appeal later gave a ruling in *Ardler* [2004] ACTCA 4 where it held that for the purposes of a special hearing:

> The prosecution is required to prove beyond reasonable doubt the physical acts of the offence charged which would constitute an offence done intentionally and voluntarily and with any particular intent or knowledge specified as an element of the offence but is not required to negative lack of mental capacity to act intentionally or voluntarily or to have the specific knowledge or intention specified as an element of the offence unless there is objective evidence which raises such an issue including mistake, accident, lack of any specific intent or knowledge of the particularity necessary to constitute the offence or self-defence in which case the prosecution must negative that issue beyond reasonable doubt.

> It also held that defences of mental impairment, provocation, or diminished responsibility could not be raised. See [90].

[80] See the statement of Mr Stanhope (Attorney General) during the passage of the Crimes Amendment Bill (No 2): *Hansard* (Legislative Assembly for the Australian Capital Territory), 2 March 2004, pp 484 to 485.

[81] As amended by the Criminal Law Consolidation (Mental Impairment) Amendment Act 2000.

[82] Section 269A.

[83] Section 269M.B(3).

6.64   The previous wording of this provision stated that:

> If the court is satisfied that – (a) the objective elements of the offence are established beyond reasonable doubt; and (b) there is, on the evidence before the court, no defence to the charge that could be established on the assumption that the defendant's mental faculties were not impaired at the time of the alleged offence, the court must record a finding that the objective elements of the offence are established and declare the defendant to be liable to supervision under this Part; but otherwise the court must find the defendant not guilty of the offence and discharge the defendant.[84]

6.65   In *R v T*[85] the Supreme Court of South Australia considered the ambit of the trial of the objective elements under this previous wording. Counsel for the appellant submitted that the court could not be satisfied that no defence to the charge could be established unless the court was satisfied that the appellant was aware of the consequences of his actions, and intended or was recklessly indifferent towards those consequences. Chief Justice Doyle rejected this analysis, holding that:

> In my opinion the provision cannot be read as requiring proof of the mental element of the offence in question. To so read the provision would be to require the court, in effect, to make a finding like a finding of guilt. If one thing is clear about the provision, it is that it is not intended to require proof of intention or other mental elements. As well, requiring the court to make a finding about intent, on the assumption that T's mental faculties were not impaired, would be to require the court to embark upon an almost impossible, and seemingly pointless enquiry.[86]

6.66   However, Chief Justice Doyle did go on to acknowledge that:

> The application of section 269M.B(2)(b) gives rise to some difficulty. The difficulty is inherent in the concept of a defence in the criminal law. The concept utilised by the criminal law, coupled with the obligation on the prosecution to prove guilt beyond reasonable doubt, combine to make it difficult to speak with any precision of defences in the criminal law. Nevertheless, that is often done … . Even some of the so-called defences such as provocation and self-defence raise mental elements. It is no answer to say that the provision must refer to defences like these defences, on the basis that they involve no consideration of mental elements, and that it is the absence of an issue relating to a mental element that identifies the defences to be considered under the provision.[87]

---

[84]   Section 269M.B(2).

[85]   [1999] SASC 429.

[86]   Above at [34].

[87]   Above at [37].

6.67   Notwithstanding these observations, the court remained convinced that the section did not oblige the prosecution to prove intent and the appeal was dismissed.

6.68   Shortly after *R v T,* the Government passed the Criminal Law Consolidation (Mental Impairment) Amendment Act 2000. This sought to amend section 269M.B(2)(b) in order to remove consideration of defences entirely, as part of a general clarification of the scope of the trial of objective elements. Under the Criminal Law Consolidation Act 1935 (both current and previous versions) the procedure is the same for determining whether a defendant is mentally competent to commit the offence as for determining whether a defendant is competent to stand trial.

Conclusion on option 1

6.69   Limiting the scope of the section 4A hearing to the conduct element of the offence appears to be largely justified on the basis that this strikes the most appropriate balance between protecting an unfit accused and the public interest.[88] Such considerations seem to have motivated changes to the law in some Australian jurisdictions to clarify that the hearing is limited to the conduct element of the offence only.[89] It should also be acknowledged that the introduction of the section 4A hearing in England and Wales was an important step forward in terms of protecting an unfit accused, in that it allows for an acquittal but not a conviction and requires a legal representative to be appointed to represent the accused's interests.

6.70   However, the division between the conduct and fault elements of the offence remains problematic. Indeed, in the Australian jurisdictions discussed above, judicial decisions prior to the changes to the legislation made by Government emphasised that it was not satisfactory to limit a special hearing to the "objective elements" of the offence.

6.71   We have already set out above the difficulties that could arise as a result of limiting the "act" for the purposes of section 4A to the conduct elements of the offence, except where the conduct is indivisible from the fault element.[90] Without reform, the law would have to develop on a piecemeal basis. This leaves considerable scope for uncertainty and could also mean that the law is applied inconsistently and somewhat arbitrarily. For these reasons, we believe that doing nothing in relation to the reform of the section 4A hearing would be unsatisfactory.

---

[88]   This was indentified by Lord Hutton in *Antoine* [2000] UKHL 20, [2001] 1 AC 340, 375: see para 6.17 above.

[89]   See the statement of Mr Stanhope (Attorney General) during the passage of the Crimes Amendment Bill (No 2): *Hansard* (Legislative Assembly for the Australian Capital Territory), 2 March 2004, p 485.

[90]   See the discussion at paras 6.24 to 6.40 above.

Option 2 – the recommendations of the Butler Committee

6.72   As we discussed in Part 2,[91] the Butler Committee was of the view that once an accused had been found to be unfit then "there should be a trial of the facts to the fullest extent possible having regard to the medical condition of the defendant".[92] Accordingly, mental elements should be inferred wherever possible from other evidence in the same way that they are in criminal proceedings generally. The policy behind this recommendation was the overriding need to avoid the possibility of a wrongful verdict. The fact that there would inevitably be circumstances where it would not be possible to make a finding concerning mental elements was not seen as a reason to dispense with the requirement for all the elements of the offence to be proved.

6.73   An option for reform would be to adopt the Butler Committee's approach so that all elements of the offence should be capable of being raised for the purpose of section 4A hearings. There are advantages to such an approach in that it would avoid having to make the sometimes difficult distinction between conduct and fault elements of the offence. It would lead to greater certainty and also greater fairness to the accused.

6.74   Some Australian jurisdictions have adopted a procedure whereby there is a special hearing which is akin to a full trial.

New South Wales

6.75   According to the Mental Health (Forensic Provisions) Act 1990,[93] if the Mental Health Tribunal has determined that the accused will not become fit to be tried during the period of 12 months following a finding of unfitness, a special hearing will take place.[94] The purpose of this hearing is to ensure that:

> Despite the unfitness of the person to be tried in accordance with normal procedures, the person is acquitted unless it can be proved to the requisite criminal standard of proof that, on the limited evidence available, the person committed the offence charged or any other offence available as an alternative to the offence charged.[95]

6.76   This clearly presupposes that all the elements of the offence, including mental elements, must be proved to the requisite standard. This is further supported by the requirement that the hearing is to be conducted "as nearly as possible as if it were a trial of criminal proceedings".[96] For the purposes of the hearing, the accused is assumed to have pleaded not guilty, he or she may "raise any

---

91   See para 2.18(3) above.

92   Report of the Committee on Mentally Abnormal Offenders (1975) Cmnd 6244, para 10.24.

93   Formerly known as the Mental Health (Criminal Procedure) Act 1990, amended by the Mental Health Legislation Amendment (Forensic Provisions) Act 2008 Schedule 1 para 2.

94   Mental Health (Criminal Procedure) Act 1990, s 19.

95   Above, s 19(2).

96   Above, s 21(1).

defence that could properly be raised if the special hearing were an ordinary trial of criminal proceedings" and he or she is entitled to give evidence.[97]

6.77   The following verdicts are available at a special hearing under section 22(1):

(a)   not guilty of the offence charged;

(b)   not guilty on the grounds of mental illness;

(c)   that on the limited evidence available, the accused person committed the offence charged; or

(d)   that on the limited evidence available, the accused person committed an offence available as an alternative to the offence charged.

6.78   The verdict under section 22(1)(b) is equivalent to the special verdict available in normal criminal proceedings that the accused is not guilty by reason of mental illness. A finding that the defendant committed the offence, or another offence available as an alternative, is a qualified finding of guilt and does not constitute a basis for a conviction, but does constitute a bar to further prosecution.[98] Furthermore, it is subject to appeal in the same way as a verdict in an ordinary criminal trial.[99]

6.79   It may be that this model provides an adequate solution to the problems with the current section 4A hearing. It offers the advantage of one hearing after which the court can reach the most satisfactory verdict on the facts and the evidence.

Northern Territory

6.80   Section 43V of the Northern Territory Criminal Code similarly makes provision for a special hearing to determine whether a defendant found not fit to stand trial is not guilty of the offence charged, not guilty of the offence charged because of mental impairment, or committed the offence charged or an offence available as an alternative. The jury must be satisfied beyond reasonable doubt "on the evidence that is available".[100]

6.81   The requirement that the jury find that the accused committed the "offence charged" implies that the prosecution must prove all elements of that offence, including the mental elements. Furthermore the hearing must be conducted as nearly as possible as if it were a criminal trial and the defendant may give evidence and raise any defence that would be available at a normal criminal trial.[101] As in New South Wales, any finding that the accused committed the offence is a qualified finding of guilt.[102]

---

[97]   Mental Health (Criminal Procedure) Act 1990, s 21(3).

[98]   Above, s 22(3).

[99]   Above, s 22(3)(c).

[100]   Criminal Code, s 43V(2).

[101]   Above, s 43W.

[102]   Above, s 43X.

Victoria

6.82 The Crimes (Mental Impairment and Unfitness to be Tried) Act 1997 also provides for a special hearing to determine whether the defendant is not guilty of the offence, not guilty of the offence because of mental impairment, or committed the offence charged or an available alternative offence.[103] This suggests that a full hearing of all the elements is intended. Furthermore, section 16 states that the hearing be conducted "as nearly as possible as if it were a criminal trial" and that at such a hearing "the defendant may raise any defence that could be raised if the special hearing were a criminal trial, including the defence of mental impairment".[104] The jury must be satisfied beyond reasonable doubt in order to make a finding that, on the evidence available, the defendant committed the offence charged or an offence available as an alternative.[105]

Conclusion on option 2

6.83 The Butler Committee envisaged that the section 4A hearing should be a trial to the fullest extent possible and our comparative research shows that such an approach is taken in other jurisdictions. This suggests that it is possible to consider the mental elements of the offence when dealing with an unfit accused. Further, these jurisdictions have continued to maintain a distinction between the trial and the "special hearing", particularly because a finding that the accused committed the offence following a special hearing is not equivalent to a normal finding of guilt.[106] As we explain below, we think that it is important to maintain such a distinction.

6.84 However, while the reasoning behind this recommendation in the Butler Report was undoubtedly sound, adopting its approach would lead (without more) to the problem that was referred to by Lord Hutton in *Antoine*:[107] that a dangerous offender might be acquitted to the detriment of public safety. This is because the accused's mental state may make it impossible for the prosecution to discharge the burden of proof as to the fault element of the offence. We recognise that requiring the prosecution to prove all elements of the offence could, without more, tip the balance too far in favour of the accused to the detriment of the public interest. In this regard, it is important to note that where the Australian jurisdictions have adopted a special hearing akin to a trial, the legislation makes provision for a special verdict of not guilty on grounds of mental illness.

6.85 It should also be remembered that the Butler Committee reported before the courts had the wider powers of disposal now available since the 1991 and 2004 amendments to the 1964 Act. At the time it made its recommendations, an accused found unfit to plead was subject to an indefinite hospital order. Against this backdrop, it may have been of greater importance to protect an accused through a full hearing as to the facts of the case.

---

[103] Crimes (Mental Impairment and Unfitness to be Tried) Act 1997, s 15.

[104] Above, s 16(2).

[105] Above, s 17(2).

[106] This is the underlying reason why we reject option 3 (abolishing the section 4A hearing).

[107] [2000] UKHL 20, [2001] 1 AC 340.

Option 3 – abolish the section 4A hearing

6.86 Another option would be to abolish the present section 4A hearing altogether. There would still be a hearing to determine whether an accused is unfit to plead or, under our proposed new test, lacks decision-making capacity. However, an accused found to lack decision-making capacity would be accommodated within the trial system.[108] This would be with the proviso that once the defendant had been found to lack decision-making capacity then a legal representative would be appointed to represent his or her interests in the trial.[109]

6.87 This trial would result in a verdict of one or other of the kinds arrived at in any other criminal trial:

    (a)   guilty; or

    (b)   not guilty; or

    (c)   not guilty by reason of insanity;[110]

        or, in a murder case

    (d)   not guilty of murder but guilty of manslaughter on the ground of provocation;[111] or

    (e)   not guilty of murder but guilty of manslaughter on the ground of diminished responsibility; or

    (f)   not guilty of murder but guilty of manslaughter by reason of being the survivor of a suicide pact.

6.88 With the exception of those trials where insanity is in issue, the jury would, as in any other trial, have to decide whether the prosecution have proved all the ingredients of the offence charged, including any mental element.

6.89 Under this approach, it would also follow that sentence could be passed as in any other criminal trial, save that on a conviction for murder for a person who lacks decision-making capacity there would be available, as an alternative to life imprisonment, an order for detention in a secure hospital with section 41 restrictions.[112]

6.90 Abolishing the section 4A hearing altogether seems, on the face of it, to be a radical proposal which, some may argue, negates all that has been achieved in

---

[108] We are grateful to His Honour Judge Jeremy Roberts QC for assistance which he has given us on this option.

[109] As is the case at present for a section 4A hearing.

[110] Assuming that the special verdict of insanity by virtue of s 2(1) Trial of Lunatics Act 1883 is retained when we come to consider insanity.

[111] The common law defence of provocation has now been replaced in England and Wales by the defence of loss of control: Coroners and Justice Act 2009, s 54.

[112] Under s 37(1) of the Mental Health Act 1983, the Crown Court currently cannot impose a hospital order in cases where the defendant is convicted of murder.

the area of unfitness to plead. There are however powerful arguments as to why it should be considered.

6.91   In order to address the theoretical justification for abolishing the section 4A procedure we need to remind ourselves of the thinking which underlies the 1964 Act as amended.[113] In essence, the current law is underpinned by the following three assumptions:

(1)   that it would be inappropriate for a person under a disability at the time of his or her trial to be found guilty of a criminal offence;

(2)   that it is possible to draw a clear distinction between the conduct element of a crime and the defendant's state of mind at the time of doing the act in question;

(3)   that a requirement that the prosecution must prove that the defendant had the necessary state of mind at the time of doing the relevant act would result in the possibility of a dangerous person having to be acquitted to the detriment of public safety.[114]

6.92   In relation to the first of these assumptions, we explained in Part 1 why it would be inappropriate for a person who is unfit to plead or who lacks decision-making capacity at the time of his or her trial to be held to account in the same way as a defendant who is fit.[115] This is because he or she is not in a position to properly defend him or herself and is not able to engage properly in the trial process. In addition, there is an obvious risk that the verdict could be considered unsafe.

6.93   It could be argued, however, that if the accused had the requisite mental state at the time of committing the crime then, although his or her present mental disorder could be regarded as being relevant to the sentence (particularly the need for a hospital order), he or she could still be subject to criminal liability and trial.

6.94   As we have seen in Part 2 of this CP, the reluctance of the law to subject a person under a disability to a criminal trial dates back to times when a defendant was unlikely to have had legal representation, he or she could not give evidence in his or her own defence and the courts did not have available to them the range of sentences which are available today. Further, many crimes were punishable by death.[116]

6.95   Criminal trial and sentencing procedures have now developed considerably. There is greater understanding of mental disorders and disabilities, their consequences and the possibilities for treatment. We also now have 18 years' experience of the way in which an accused's interests may effectively be protected in a section 4A hearing by counsel and/or solicitors appointed by the court to present the accused's case.

---

[113] We looked at this in detail in Part 2 above.

[114] See Lord Hutton in *Antoine* [2000] UKHL 20, [2001] 1 AC 340, 371: see para 6.17 above.

[115] See paras 1.9 to 1.13 above.

[116] See paras 2.2 to 2.5 above.

6.96 The proposition that an accused who has been found to be unfit should be subject to a trial (notwithstanding that he or she is relieved of the burden of having to give instructions) therefore needs further examination. This option for reform is arguably justifiable for the following reasons.

6.97 First, cases in which it is suggested that the defendant does not understand the nature of the charge (this may change if our provisional proposals become law) or lacks the capacity to make a decision as to his or her plea are rare in practice. Such cases could be dealt with quite simply by saying that, if there is any doubt as to the defendant's capacity in either of these respects, a plea of not guilty should be entered by the court and the prosecution should be required to prove their case against the defendant.

6.98 Secondly, juries in section 4A hearings are well able to understand and make allowance for the fact that it would be unreasonable to expect an accused under a disability to go into the witness box. They will always concentrate, as they should, on whether the prosecution proves beyond reasonable doubt that the accused "did the act". On the other hand, if they have to determine the fault element, then it is more likely that they would expect to hear from the defendant.

6.99 It is, however, not necessarily the case that the defendant is prejudiced in a trial by not being able to give evidence (because of his or her condition). There are many defendants who are fit to plead but whose evidence in the witness box is unhelpful to their case or positively assists the prosecution. Further, a defendant will not necessarily be disadvantaged by not being able to put forward a positive case[117] in the witness box. In some (if not most) cases the defendant will have given his or her account to the police or to others at the time of the alleged offence or shortly afterwards.[118] In addition, whether or not the defendant gave an account at the time, a written statement taken from him or her by his or her legal representatives could possibly be placed before the jury as hearsay evidence.[119]

6.100 Nonetheless, this in itself is not a convincing argument to support the proposition that an unfit accused should be subject to a normal trial. The crucial point is that a fit defendant is, if he or she wishes, able to participate through giving evidence; the same may not be the case for someone who is unfit to plead.

---

[117] For example, self-defence, accident or an entirely different version of events.

[118] As was the case in *Sureda* (the details of which were supplied by His Honour Judge Jeremy Roberts QC: see Appendix B). Mr Sureda had given his account of the killing of his mother to various civilian witnesses as well as to the police in interview. In the s 4A hearing evidence of these statements was, with the agreement of both counsel, put before the jury as it was relevant to issues which they had to decide.

[119] See s 114 of the Criminal Justice Act 2003. However, if this statement is wholly or partly adverse to the defendant then it will not be admissible unless it would be admissible under under s 76 of the Police and Criminal Evidence Act 1984: s 128(2) of the Criminal Justice Act 2003. A statement could still be admissible under s 116(2)(b), which allows for hearsay evidence to be admissible where the witness is unavailable because of a mental or physical condition. Notwithstanding this, the section is intended to deal with situations where the witness is unable to come to court, and in the case of an unfit defendant, he or she would be present in the court. It has been held that a proof of evidence taken before an accused became unfit should have been read to the jury in s 4A proceedings: see *Jagnieszko* [2008] EWCA Crim 3065.

6.101   In summary, the argument in favour of subjecting an unfit defendant to a trial in which he or she has an appointed representative is that this procedure has ensured fairness in section 4A hearings and could be adopted for the purpose of a trial. It would be explained to the jury that the defendant has been found to be under a disability and that is why (a) counsel have been appointed by the court to present his or her case and (b) he or she is not being called to give evidence.[120] An unfit defendant would therefore not necessarily be disadvantaged by being subject to a trial.

6.102   Next, it is necessary to address briefly the implications of assumption (2) at paragraph 6.91 above; namely, the assumption that it is always possible to draw a clear distinction between the conduct element and the defendant's state of mind (the fault element) at the time of doing that act.

6.103   We discussed above that this assumption has proved to be problematic following the decision of the House of Lords in *Antoine*. We emphasised that there are in fact cases where the distinction between conduct and fault is blurred.[121] The fact that the conduct and the fault elements of the offence cannot always readily be divided is one of the principal reasons for our provisional proposal that the section 4A hearing should be reformed. If the accused was subject to a trial where the issue was whether he or she was guilty or not guilty, then it would probably not matter that there are such difficulties involved in separating the conduct element from the fault element of a particular offence.

6.104   The third assumption (namely, that requiring the prosecution to prove all elements of the offence might result in a dangerous person having to be acquitted to the detriment of public safety) mirrors the policy justification identified by Lord Hutton in *Antoine* for limiting the scope of the section 4A hearing to the conduct element of the offence.[122] It is generally believed that if the prosecution had the burden of proving that the accused had the relevant fault element for the offence, then this may be a burden which is too difficult to discharge. This could mean that a potentially dangerous accused would be acquitted which would be detrimental to the public.

6.105   This concern seems to be linked to the idea that if a person is unfit at the time of trial because of mental disorder, then juries may be too quick to acquit an unfit accused because they would assume that he or she could not have been capable of forming the necessary fault element. It is important to highlight again at this point that unfitness to plead is concerned with the accused's condition *at the time of trial* and not at the time of the offence. However, it may be the case that an unfit accused was or may have been suffering from mental disorder at the time of the offence.

6.106   Nonetheless, this does not in itself mean that the prosecution would be unable to prove the fault element for the offence. There is no reason to believe that juries

---

[120] It should not necessarily be assumed that an unfit defendant will not give evidence. As we saw at paras 6.75 to 6.82 above, in the Australian jurisdictions which provide for a special hearing akin to a trial, the legislation specifically provides that the defendant can give evidence.

[121] See paras 6.24 to 6.29 above.

[122] See para 6.17 above.

are not fully capable of resolving difficult issues which involve an accused's state of mind at the time of the offence. Experience of cases where diminished responsibility[123] is relied upon as a defence shows that juries are able to understand that a person with a mental disorder at the time of the offence may still be capable of forming the necessary intent.

6.107 This may mean that there will not necessarily be a great risk of dangerous people being acquitted if the prosecution is required to prove all elements of the offence in a case involving an unfit accused. In other words, it may mean that the third assumption to which we have referred is unfounded.

6.108 In relation to the third assumption, it is also important to consider whether it could be said that if the prosecution had to prove all the elements of the offence then there would be a risk that some unfit accused would be found to have had the necessary intention when in fact they did not. We do not believe there would be such a risk. Intention (in a disputed case) can usually only be proved by circumstantial evidence, that is to say by drawing inferences from what the accused did and said in particular circumstances. Juries could be relied on to find the necessary intention proved where it provides the only sensible explanation for the defendant's acts and words.

Conclusion on option 3

6.109 It is possible to justify having a full trial for an accused who has been found unfit to plead subject to the proviso that he or she is represented in this trial by counsel and or solicitors appointed by the court as is presently contemplated by section 4A of the 1991 Act.

6.110 This approach has a number of possible advantages. First, it would not be necessary to separate the conduct and fault elements of the offence, thus avoiding the difficulties which we have identified with the reasoning in *Antoine*. Secondly, it would mean that article 6 of the European Convention on Human Rights would clearly apply to the proceedings.[124] As we discussed above,[125] the House of Lords has held that article 6 does not apply to proceedings under section 4A. In our view article 6 would apply where an unfit accused is subject to a normal trial. This is because the proceedings would be a criminal trial and the rights that article 6 confers would be exercised by the legal representative appointed to represent the accused. Option 3 also has the great advantage of simplicity.

6.111 However, it is our view that an accused who, because of a physical or mental condition, is unable to participate effectively in a trial should not be subject to the same proceedings and possible outcome (a finding of guilt) as an accused who is able to participate. We think that it is important to maintain a clear distinction between a normal trial and proceedings used to deal with an unfit accused.

---

[123] Diminished responsibility is an excusatory partial defence to murder which depends on the accused having the intent to kill: see s 2(3) of the Homicide Act 1957. Section 52 of the Coroners and Justice Act 2009 is now in force.

[124] As we explain below, however, we think that article 6 should in any event apply to section 4A hearings and to our proposed reform of the hearing.

[125] See paras 6.42 to 6.48 above.

Further, the protection from conviction that the section 4A hearing offers to an unfit accused is an important one, and we believe that this protection should be retained in any reform of the procedure. This protection would however be lost under option 3 as outlined above.

Option 4 – the Scottish procedure

6.112 A fourth option for reform of the present section 4A hearing would involve adopting the Scottish procedure for the "examination of the facts". This procedure is provided for by the Criminal Procedure (Scotland) Act 1995 ("the 1995 Act")[126] and is considered to be akin to the one that had been anticipated by the Butler Committee.[127]

6.113 The 1995 Act introduced changes similar to those that were effected in England and Wales by the 1991 Act.[128] The provisions introduced an examination of the facts in cases of "insanity in bar of trial".[129] Under section 55(1), the court must be satisfied:

(a) beyond reasonable doubt in respect of each charge against the accused, that he did the act or made the omission constituting the offence; and

(b) on the balance of probabilities that there are no grounds for acquitting the accused.

6.114 Where the court is satisfied as to both (a) and (b) it makes a finding to that effect. Importantly, where the court makes an acquittal, this is subject to section 55(4) of the 1995 Act. Section 55(4) provides that, where the court is satisfied that the person did the act or made the omission, but it appears to the court that the person was insane at the time of doing the act or making the omission constituting the offence, the court shall state whether the acquittal is on the ground of such insanity.

6.115 Under the Scottish procedure, the judge has a discretion to allow or refuse to allow the accused to give evidence and the discretion is exercisable with regard to the opinion of the psychiatrists. There is no formal verdict; rather, the judge makes a specific finding as to the facts.

---

[126] Which has been amended by the Criminal Justice and Licensing (Scotland) Act 2010, yet to come into force.

[127] RD Mackay and WJ Brookbanks, "Protecting the unfit to plead: a comparative analysis of the 'trial of the facts'" [2005] *Juridical Review* 173, 183. For a discussion of the Butler Committee's recommendation, see para 6.72 above.

[128] Section 54 is based largely on the recommendations of the Thomson Committee: see Criminal Procedure in Scotland: Second Report by the Committee appointed by the Secretary of State for Scotland and the Lord Advocate (Chairman: the Honourable Lord Thompson) (1975) Cmnd 6218. See also *Renton and Brown's Criminal Procedure,* para 26-06 for an exposition of the procedure.

[129] The term "insanity in bar of trial" was the term used for "unfitness for trial", and the latter term is used to replace it in the Criminal Justice and Licensing (Scotland) Act 2010.

6.116 Where the facts are held to have been established, this finding does not count as a conviction and it is possible for an accused so found to be subsequently charged on either a complaint or an indictment with an offence arising out of the same act or omission as was considered at the examination of the facts under section 55. There is therefore no question of double jeopardy in this respect. An acquittal at a section 55 hearing, however, would have the effect of barring any further hearing.

6.117 According to Professors Mackay and Brookbanks, the reference in section 55(1)(b) to "no grounds for acquitting" the accused encompasses consideration of mental elements as well as the act. This is an advantage of the Scottish procedure as it means that the conduct and fault elements of the offence do not have to be separated for the purposes of a finding under section 55. More importantly, however, by linking the examination of the facts with the possibility of an acquittal on the grounds of insanity, the Scottish procedure avoids the risk that was identified in *Antoine*. This risk was that if an accused charged with, for example, murder was insane at the time of the killing and was unfit to plead at the time of the trial by reason of that insanity, then it would not be possible to prove that he or she had the fault element for murder because of the insanity existing at the time of the alleged offence. The jury would therefore have to acquit the accused who would be released to the danger of the public.[130]

Problems with option 4

6.118 However, we believe that there are problems with the Scottish procedure. Section 55(1) states that the court must be satisfied "beyond reasonable doubt … that [the accused] did the act or made the omission constituting the offence", but the lack of grounds for acquittal need only be shown on the balance of probabilities. It has been argued that the fact that the prosecution are only obliged to show that there are no grounds for acquitting the accused on the balance of probabilities leaves the unfit accused more vulnerable than a fit defendant and therefore affords the unfit accused insufficient protection.[131]

6.119 A possible justification for having a lower standard of proof in relation to whether there are grounds for acquittal is that it reduces the burden on the prosecution in trying to prove the fault elements of the offence. However, this approach contrasts with the current position in England and Wales where, under the decision in *Antoine*,[132] once a defence is properly raised by objective evidence it is up to the prosecution to disprove it beyond reasonable doubt.

6.120 In our view, there does not seem to be any strong reason for the lower standard of proof in relation to any grounds for acquittal. The lower standard of proof means that the absence of the fault element of the offence and other defences which would be available to a fit defendant are diluted. This could be regarded as providing insufficient protection to those unfit accused who have a good defence to the charges. We believe that this cannot be justified, particularly when it is considered that section 55(4) provides for further consideration of whether any

---

[130] We have discussed this in relation to option 3 at paras 6.104 to 6.108 above.

[131] RD Mackay and WJ Brookbanks, "Protecting the unfit to plead: a comparative analysis of the 'trial of the facts'" [2005] *Juridical Review* 173, 184.

[132] [2000] UKHL 20, [2001] 1 AC 340.

acquittal was a result of "insanity" existing at the time of the offence. If so, the court can make a disposal[133] and the public is therefore protected from a potentially dangerous accused.

6.121 Neither the discrepancy between the required levels of proof nor the question of the scope of the examination of the facts appear to have produced much litigation in Scotland. A study by the Scottish Office Central Research Unit in 1999[134] found that:

> By and large ... the majority of the [examinations of the facts] proceeded fairly unproblematically. Evidence was led in much the same way as in a trial, that is, evidence-in-chief, followed by cross-examination and re-examination of witnesses. Indeed, the only visible way in which [examinations of the facts] were distinguishable from a criminal trial diet was the absence of the accused ... .[135]

6.122 Furthermore, interviews with judges, sheriffs, and defence and prosecution counsel found that all welcomed the reforms in the 1995 Act, and the examination of the facts procedure in particular.[136]

6.123 Research which was conducted at the time of the enactment of the 1995 Act and which has been taken further as part of this project[137] shows that the procedure under the 1995 Act is not used as frequently as we might have expected. The latest research focuses on the impact of the 1995 Act from 1999 to 31st March 2010 on cases involving "insanity in bar of trial". The results showed that there were 20 such cases in the High Court of Justiciary and 195 cases in the Sheriff Court.[138] A breakdown of the type of cases[139] which were heard in the High Court shows that out of the 20 cases where the accused was found to be insane so that his or her trial could not commence:

(1) six were dealt with by way of the imposition of interim compulsion orders (hospital orders) which ultimately led to compulsion orders;

(2) five were dealt with by way of compulsion orders (hospital orders);

(3) two resulted in the imposition of guardianship orders;

---

[133] Under s 57 of the 1995 Act, the court can make the following disposals in the event that it finds either (i) that the accused did the act and there are no grounds for acquittal or (ii) that the acquittal is on grounds of insanity: a hospital order (with or without a restriction order); a guardianship order; a supervision and treatment order; or no order.

[134] M Burman and C Connelly, "Mentally Disordered Offenders and Criminal Proceedings: the Operation of Part VI of the Criminal Procedure (Scotland) Act 1995" (1999).

[135] Above, p 25, para 11.5.

[136] Above, chapter 5.

[137] C Connolly, "Unfitness to Plead and Examination of the Facts Proceedings: A Report Prepared for the Law Commission of England and Wales" (March 2010).

[138] The High Court of the Justiciary sits as both a trial court (court of first instance) throughout Scotland and as an appellate court in Edinburgh. As a trial court, it hears solemn cases (more serious offences tried before a judge and jury). Sheriff Courts hear both solemn and summary cases (summary cases are heard without a jury).

[139] The breakdown includes charge and outcome.

(4)   three cases resulted in acquittals;[140]

(5)   in one case (involving lewd, indecent and libidinous practices)[141] no order was made;

(6)   two were deserted *pro loco et tempore*;[142] and

(7)   one was deserted *simpliciter*.[143]

6.124   Unfortunately the majority of cases were heard in the lower court (Sheriff Court) and these were not available for analysis, so we are unable to see (in terms of a breakdown) in what way that they were resolved.

6.125   The findings of the research do however appear to indicate that:

> The use of hospital remand reduces the number of accused found unfit to plead in Scotland. Of those who are found unfit to plead, less serious offences are generally deserted upon confirmation that the psychiatrist will seek to secure the person's detention using the civil law. It is mainly more serious offences, involving crimes of violence that proceed to [the examination of the facts].[144]

6.126   It is unclear to us why the examination of the facts procedure appears not to be used as much as it might. This could be seen as a potential disadvantage of the Scottish system.

Conclusion on option 4

6.127   From the limited information available, it appears that it is generally thought that the procedure in Scotland works well. By bringing together a finding as to both the conduct and fault elements of the offence with the possibility of an acquittal on grounds of insanity, the procedure avoids the difficulties with the decision in *Antoine* while ensuring that the public interest is protected. However, for the reasons that we discussed above, we do not think there is any strong reason for having a lower burden of proof in relation to whether or not there are grounds for acquittal.

Option 5 – our preferred option for reform of the section 4A hearing

6.128   As we have discussed above, the current law which limits the section 4A hearing to the conduct element of the offence has proven to be problematic. However, we recognise that requiring the prosecution to prove all elements of the offence could, without more, be detrimental to public safety. The key then is to try and formulate some middle ground between these approaches. The underlying

---

[140] In one of these cases, however, the person was still subject to a treatment order and the other to a compulsion order (hospital order) and treatment.

[141] Contrary to s 5 of the Sexual Offences (Scotland) Act 1976 and presumably less serious than the majority of cases with which this court was concerned.

[142] Meaning "without place or time". The case can still be taken up at some point in the future.

[143] This means that the case is abandoned and cannot be taken up in the future.

[144] This finding appears to be based on the results of semi-structured interviews with lawyers and psychiatrists.

objective for reform should be, in our view, to formulate a procedure which will produce in each case a fair outcome for both the accused and the wider public.

6.129   One way would be to have a procedure where, in so far as is possible, all the elements of the offence are considered. The prosecution would have the burden of proof in relation to this. In determining whether all elements of the offence are proved, it should be possible to consider defences in so far as this is consistent with the fact that decisions about the section 4A hearing are made by the accused's appointed legal representative. In other words, as long as there is a sufficient evidential basis to raise the defence or partial defence then the representative of the accused can do so if he or she thinks that it is in the accused's best interests. If the accused is acquitted (because, for example, there is no evidence of fault) then there may (but would not necessarily be)[145] a further hearing to consider whether or not the acquittal is because of mental disorder existing at the time of the offence.

6.130   As envisaged, there would be three possible outcomes to this procedure:

(1)   a finding that the accused has done the act or made the omission *and* that there are no grounds for acquitting him or her;[146]

(2)   an outright acquittal; or

(3)   an acquittal which is qualified by reason of mental disorder.[147]

6.131   Following a finding under either (1) or (3) the court would have available to it the same disposals as are currently available under the 1964 Act.

6.132   This procedure would have some of the qualities of a trial as opposed to a hearing as to the facts because it will effectively involve a special verdict – a qualified acquittal on the grounds of mental disorder existing at the time of the offence. This special verdict could take the form of a specific finding of facts (as in Scotland)[148] which would differ depending on the charge, or it could be a complete all or nothing verdict which is similar to the special verdict in cases of insanity by virtue of section 2 of the Trial of Lunatics Act 1883.[149]

---

[145]   See para 6.142 below.

[146]   See our discussion of the Scottish procedure at para 6.112 and following paras above. The difference would be that under our propsals, the prosecution would have to prove both aspects beyond reasonable doubt.

[147]   The Butler Committee proposed in relation to insanity that there should be a new defence of "not guilty on evidence of mental disorder": see the Report of the Committee on Mentally Abnormal Offenders (1975) Cmnd 6244, para 18.18.

[148]   See para 6.112 and following paras above.

[149]   Section 2 provides that if a defendant was insane at the time of committing the offence then he or she will be found "not guilty by reason of insanity", a verdict which provides the defendant with an exemption from criminal responsibility. It is not, however, an unqualified acquittal. Under s 5 of the 1964 Act the court must make an order for disposal. The disposals available are the same as those available where an unfit accused is found to have done the act: a hospital order (with or without a restriction order), a supervision order or an order for absolute discharge.

6.133 However, under option 5 it would remain the case that the accused could not be convicted of an offence. The hearing and the trial procedure – with its possibility of a guilty verdict – would therefore still be mutually exclusive.

6.134 The possibility of a special verdict would mean that the accused should be subject to the protections of article 6 of the European Convention on Human Rights. As explained above, the special verdict is in addition to the need for the prosecution to prove both elements of the offence. The procedure would therefore satisfy the "formal accusation" aspect of criminal proceedings.[150] This would mean that the decision in *H* would have to be overturned.[151]

Significance of the special verdict

6.135 If the prosecution is to prove all the elements of the offence, any consideration of the fault element of the offence will inevitably raise consideration of the accused's mental state at the time of the commission of the offence. Allowing for further consideration of whether an accused was acquitted because of mental disorder existing at the time of the alleged offence avoids the potential detriment to public safety identified by Lord Hutton in *Antoine*.[152] It also allows for the fact that an accused may only have become unfit since the time of the offence.

6.136 An obvious disadvantage of option 5 would be the danger of replicating the unsatisfactory procedure regarding a special verdict on insanity.[153] This could be counteracted in part by using the term "acquitted by reason of mental disorder".[154] It should also be borne in mind that, unlike the current procedure for a verdict of

---

[150] As referred to in *Customs and Excise Commissioners v City of London Magistrates' Court* [2000] 1 WLR 2020.

[151] We discussed the decision in *H* [2003] UKHL 1, [2003] 1 WLR 411 at paras 6.42 to 6.48.

[152] See para 6.17 above.

[153] The provision under s 2(1) of the Trial of Lunatics Act 1883 as amended by s 1(1) of the 1964 Act has long been thought to be unsatisfactory and the general reluctance to use the defence has been said to be demonstrative of this: see, for example, RD Mackay, *Mental Condition Defences in the Criminal Law* (1995) pp 142 to 143. Previous research conducted by Professor Mackay, and further research which he has conducted for the Law Commission since the beginning of this project, shows that although the number of insanity verdicts have increased since the introduction of the flexibility in the 1991 Act, the annual average number of verdicts remains relatively low. In the period 2002 to 2008, there were 143 findings of not guilty by reason of insanity; an annual average of approximately 20. This compares to an annual average of approximately 14 in the period 1997 to 2001, during which there was a total of 72 insanity verdicts.

[154] Section 168 of the Criminal Justice and Licensing (Scotland) Act 2010 inserts into the 1995 Act a new s 51A, which provides a special defence on the basis that "a person is not criminally responsible for his conduct constituting an offence, and is to be acquitted of the offence, if the person was at the time of the conduct unable by reason of mental disorder to appreciate the nature or wrongfulness of the conduct". Schedule 7, para 37, of the Act amends s 55 of the 1995 Act so that where an unfit accused is acquitted, the court must state whether this was because he or she was not "criminally responsible for the conduct" (in accordance with the defence set out in the proposed s 51A of the 1995 Act).

not guilty by reason of insanity,[155] the burden of proof in this process will be on the prosecution to the usual high standard.[156]

6.137 Further, research carried out by Professor Mackay shows that since the introduction of flexibility of disposal, the central disincentive to seeking a verdict of not guilty by reason of insanity has been removed. In addition, the number of findings of not guilty by reason of insanity has continued to rise since 1991.[157] It may therefore be the case that concerns about replicating some of the problems with section 2 of the Trial of Lunatics Act 1883 are unfounded.

Conclusion on option 5

6.138 In our view, option 5 strikes the most appropriate balance between protecting the accused and the public interest. By requiring the prosecution to prove all elements of the offence, it ensures greater fairness to an unfit accused. It also means that the difficulties resulting from the decision in *Antoine*[158] are avoided and would mean that an unfit accused would benefit from the protection of article 6 of the European Convention on Human Rights. The provision for a qualified acquittal, however, ensures that the public can be protected from an accused who may be dangerous.

6.139 There is, of course, the possibility that in a particular case the prosecution may fail to prove the fault element of the offence because the accused is unfit at the time of the hearing. If the jury finds that the acquittal was not because of mental disorder, then there is a chance that a person who has committed a dangerous act will be acquitted. However, we do not think that this risk is great enough to justify only requiring proof as to the conduct element. In our view, option 5 would provide for a procedure that minimises the risk to the public while ensuring that an unfit accused is not wrongly subjected to a disposal.

6.140 On this basis, we make the following provisional proposals:

> **Provisional Proposal 8: The present section 4A hearing should be replaced with a procedure whereby the prosecution is obliged to prove that the accused did the act or made the omission charged and that there are no grounds for acquittal.**

---

[155] Where the onus of proof is on the defence on the balance of probabilities.

[156] It is the need for medical evidence which means that insanity, as well as the partial defence of diminished responsibility, need to be raised by the defence: see s 2 of the Homicide Act 1957 and *Lambert, Ali and Jordan* [2002] QB 1112 at [18]. However, given that under option 5 it will have already been established that the accused lacks decision-making capacity and consequently there will have to have been the required medical evidence for this finding, the problem of obtaining medical evidence may not be relevant.

[157] Flexibility of disposal is a major change introduced by the 1991 Act. See RD Mackay, BJ Mitchell and L Howe, "Yet more facts about the insanity defence" [2006] *Criminal Law Review* 399, 410. This research has been continued as part of this Law Commission project and the findings are consistent with this upward trend.

[158] [2000] UKHL 20, [2001] 1 AC 340.

Provisional Proposal 9: If the accused is acquitted provision should be made for a judge to hold a further hearing to determine whether or not the acquittal is because of mental disorder existing at the time of the offence.

Other issues in relation to option 5

6.141   If consultees accept our provisional proposals 8 and 9, then there are further matters which need to be considered in relation to the procedure outlined under option 5.

The hearing to determine the special verdict

6.142   In relation to the further hearing provisionally proposed at paragraph 6.140 above, one issue that needs to be considered is whether it should be mandatory in every case to have a further hearing to determine whether an acquittal is because of mental disorder, or whether such a hearing should be held only at the discretion of the judge who presides over the case. There may be circumstances where it is clearly not necessary to consider whether the acquittal is on grounds of mental disorder and therefore there would be no need for a further hearing. This, in our view, is a strong argument for the further hearing only being held at the discretion of the judge.

6.143   We also think that it is necessary to address the question of whether there should be a further hearing to determine whether the acquittal is because of mental disorder, or whether that issue should be determined as part of the same proceedings by the same jury.

6.144   Technically, the second question for the jury (whether the acquittal is because of mental disorder existing at the time of the offence) constitutes further proceedings. This is because this second question is a separate issue from the question of whether the accused has done the act and whether there are any grounds for acquittal. The first question has two possible outcomes: that the accused did the act and that there are no grounds for acquittal, or an acquittal.

6.145   Section 11(4) of the Juries Act 1974 provides:

> Subject to subsection (5) below, the jury selected by any one ballot shall try only one issue (but any juror shall be liable to be selected on more than one ballot).

6.146   A single selected jury therefore cannot decide more than one issue. There are, however, exceptions to this rule.[159] In our view it would be consistent with these exceptions for another exception to be created for the purpose of determining whether an acquittal of an accused who lacks decision-making capacity is because of mental disorder existing at the time of the offence. This is because this special verdict is so closely linked with the initial issue of whether the accused did the act and whether there are any grounds for an acquittal. It would

---

[159] Section 11(5) provides that the trial of two or more issues by the same jury is permissible if the second or last issue begins within 24 hours from the time when the first issue was decided, or if the jury is the same as the one which tried the special plea (that is to say, insanity).

also save both time and money for a single jury to decide both issues. We think that this is consistent with the Court of Appeal decision in *B and others*[160] which is discussed in detail in Part 7 of this CP.

6.147 Although we think that it would be appropriate for the same jury to determine both issues, we have also considered whether the jury should be able to consider the matter of whether the acquittal is because of mental disorder at the same time as the other matters in issue. The alternative would be to have a subsequent hearing as to the qualified acquittal.

6.148 We think that there are circumstances when it would be problematic for the jury to consider all the issues at the same time. First, the accused ought (if his or her counsel thinks that it is in the accused's best interests) to have the opportunity of achieving an outright acquittal after which it is not thought appropriate to go to a special verdict hearing. The jury may acquit the accused because they are not sure that he or she has performed the conduct element of the offence. An example would be a case which depends on identification evidence, which is not so weak that the judge has been obliged to withdraw the case from the jury at the conclusion of the prosecution evidence.[161] Secondly, a qualified acquittal because of mental disorder will depend on the evidence of at least two medical practitioners, one of whom is duly approved under section 12 of the Mental Health Act 1983.[162] The accused should have a right to challenge the evidence without having to risk the prejudice which he or she may suffer if the jury hears evidence from psychiatrists.[163]

6.149 At the moment, however, it is sometimes considered appropriate for the jury to hear psychiatric evidence during the course of the section 4A hearing. This is because it is thought to be necessary for them to understand that a genuine belief on the part of the accused is not necessarily an accurate one, for example, if the belief is the result of a delusion brought about by mental disorder. In Appendix B we refer in detail to the case of *Sureda* where the issue on a charge of murder was self-defence. In this case, it was agreed between the trial judge and counsel that the jury should be made aware of the psychiatric evidence for this reason. The trial judge's directions to the jury are included in Appendix B.

6.150 In such a situation, if there was a further hearing as to the special verdict, the issue of whether or not the accused's belief was or may have been accurate would be addressed in that hearing. However, it is conceivable that there will be occasions when the accused's representative wishes medical evidence to be considered in the initial hearing (as to whether the accused committed the act and whether there are grounds for acquittal). This is because counsel may seek

---

[160] [2008] EWCA Crim 1997, [2009] 1 WLR 1545 where it was held that the hearing under section 4A in the case of an unfit accused and the trial of a fit defendant did not amount to separate issues.

[161] *Turnbull* [1977] QB 224.

[162] This is the requirement for special verdict of insanity: see s 1(1) of the 1991 Act.

[163] Until the Domestic Violence, Crime and Victims Act 2004 amended the 1964 Act to provide that "the question of fitness to be tried shall be determined by the court without a jury", where the issue was raised on arraignment it was determined by one jury and a second jury could be sworn to determine the s 4A hearing. This was so that the jury determining the s 4A hearing would not be prejudiced by the medical evidence.

an acquittal because the accused lacked the fault element for the offence with which he or she is charged.

6.151 We think that the possibility of a two-stage approach offers the following benefits. First, it offers the jury a very clear route through the various possible issues and on the facts of some cases, this may be of advantage to an accused person. Secondly, the opportunity for an acquittal because of mental disorder at the time of the alleged offence separates the issue of the accused's state of mind at the time of the offence from his or her ability to be tried. We recognise however that it may be thought to be unduly complex and that some consultees may think that the issues can all be resolved in one hearing which is why we referred to the New South Wales model at paragraphs 6.75 to 6.79 above. We have therefore asked questions 3 and 4 below.

6.152 In relation to the special verdict, we make the following provisional proposals:

> **Provisional Proposal 10: The further hearing should be held at the discretion of the judge on the application of any party or the representative of any party to the proceedings.**

> **Provisional Proposal 11: The special verdict should be determined by the jury on such evidence as has been heard or on any further evidence as is called.**

6.153 If consultees do not agree with the above provisional proposals, we would ask the following questions:

> **Question 3: Do consultees agree that we have correctly identified the options for reform in relation to the section 4A hearing? If not, what other options for reform would consultees propose?**

> **Question 4: If consultees do not agree that option 5 is the best option for reform, would they agree with any other option?**

Finding that the accused did an act other than the act specifically charged

6.154 The potential under option 5 for an acquittal because the accused lacked the fault element of the offence also raises the question of whether it should be possible in the first instance for the jury to return a finding that the accused has done an act and that there are no grounds for acquittal, in relation to an act other than that specifically charged.[164]

6.155 This would involve applying a similar procedure to the one which exists under section 6(3) and (4) of the Criminal Law Act 1967 to a finding that "the accused did the act or made the omission and that there are no grounds for acquittal". Under section 6(3) and (4) the jury are able to return a verdict of an alternative offence which is incorporated into the offence on the indictment. The provisions of section 6 are only applicable "on a person's trial on indictment" so, at the

---

[164] This was really the main issue in *Antoine* [2000] UKHL 20, [2001] 1 AC 340 in relation to diminished responsibility, leaving aside the wider issue of the scope of the act.

moment, they do not apply to a section 4A hearing. This makes sense given that an accused who is unfit to plead cannot be convicted.

6.156   However, as a matter of principle, we wonder whether, given that under option 5 all elements of the offence are to be considered, it should be possible for the jury to return a finding that the accused has done the act and that there are no grounds for an acquittal of a lesser offence than the one charged. In many cases, this may well have no practical effect. If, for example, it is not possible to find that the accused had the specific intent which is necessary to find that he or she has done the act in relation to an offence contrary to section 18 of the Offences Against the Person Act 1861, then it may not be any easier to make a finding that he or she had the requisite fault element in relation to section 20 of that Act.

6.157   Section 6(3) and (4) of the Criminal Law Act 1967 do not apply to a trial for an offence of treason or murder. In the case of murder, this is because section 6(2)(a) provides that a person found not guilty of murder may be found guilty of manslaughter. Similarly, section 6(2)(b) provides that he or she may be found guilty of any offence of which he or she may be found guilty under an enactment specifically so providing, or under section 4(2) of the Criminal Law Act 1967.[165] Section 6(2)(c) allows for the person to be found guilty of an attempt to commit murder, or of an attempt to commit any other offence of which he or she might be found guilty. However, he or she may not be found guilty of any offence not included in section 6(2).

6.158   If it were possible to apply the principle behind section 6(2) of the Criminal Law Act 1967 to a charge of murder under a section 4A hearing, it would mean, for example, that there could be a finding that the accused has done the act of manslaughter by reason of diminished responsibility and that there are no grounds for acquitting him or her. This would obviate the need for a hearing as to the special verdict (that an acquittal is because of mental disorder existing at the time of the offence). The court would be able to proceed to disposal in the same way as if there had been a finding that the accused did the act and that there are no grounds for acquittal in relation to any other offence.[166]

6.159   We therefore ask consultees the following question:

Question 5: Should a jury be able to find that an unfit accused has done the act and that there are no grounds for acquittal in relation to an act other than that specifically charged?

The burden of proof

6.160   A further matter which needs to be considered in the context of the possibility of alternative findings is the burden of proof. As we have indicated at paragraph 6.129 above, the prosecution will have the burden of proof (beyond reasonable doubt) in relation to whether or not the accused has done the act and whether there are grounds for an acquittal. However, some statutory defences place the burden of proof on the accused. The partial defence of diminished responsibility

---

[165] Which relates to assisting offenders.

[166] Any such finding would of course be subject to the fact that the burden of proof remains on the defence in cases of diminished responsibility.

which (at the time of writing) is provided for by section 2 of the Homicide Act 1957 is a case in point, where the defence has to prove the defence on the balance of probabilities. If the accused is unfit (or lacks decision-making capacity) then there is an obvious question as to how he or she is to be able to discharge this burden.

6.161 We stated at the outset of this Part that the procedure whereby a representative is appointed by the court to represent the interests of the accused in the section 4A hearing is one of the most successful and valuable aspects of section 4A. We see no reason why such a representative should not be able to raise a statutory defence on the accused's behalf as long as there is some factual or evidential basis for him or her doing so. Where diminished responsibility is relied on, it is the fact that medical evidence is required which necessitates a reversed burden of proof.[167] In a case of unfitness to plead or lack of decision-making capacity, there will have been a medical examination in order for the court to determine whether the accused lacks capacity to be tried. In theory, therefore, there is no obstacle to the accused's representative raising the defence of diminished responsibility if he or she thinks that it is appropriate.

6.162 More offences have recently been created in relation to which the statute providing for the offence provides for a defence to the charge where the burden of proof is on the defence. For example, sections 18, 38B and 57 of the Terrorism Act 2000, which we discussed in the context of interlinked conduct and fault elements, provide for defences where the burden of proof is on the defence.[168] In our view, it would be consistent with our provisional proposals for the accused's representative to be able to raise such defences as long as doing so is consistent with his or her ethical obligations and duty to the court.[169]

---

[167] See n 155 above.

[168] See para 6.28 above.

[169] We think that, at some stage, it might be appropriate for the Bar Standards Board and/or Bar Council Professional Conduct Committee, the Solicitors Regulation Authority and/or the Law Society to draw up guidelines on the subject of advocates' duties in representing defendants who are unfit or, under our proposed new test, lack decision-making capacity in criminal proceedings.

PART 7
MISCELLANEOUS ISSUES

INTRODUCTION

7.1   We have now provisionally proposed the abolition of the present legal test for determining whether or not an accused is unfit to plead. We have provisionally proposed a new test of decision-making capacity and have also recommended the adoption of a defined psychiatric test to assist the application of this legal test. We have provisionally proposed that the present section 4A procedure (for determining the facts of the offence with which the accused is charged) should be replaced by a new hearing at which the jury should be asked to consider all the elements of the offence in issue, with the possibility of a special verdict if an acquittal is because of mental disorder existing at the time of the offence.

7.2   In this Part, we deal with several miscellaneous issues. We explain the disposal regime under the 1964 Act, which has recently been addressed in the Domestic Violence, Crime and Victims Act 2004. Accordingly we do not have any proposals to make concerning this issue. We do however consider whether or not there should be reform of the procedure which enables the Secretary of State to refer a case back to court for trial where an unfit accused has been found to have done the act and then been detained by way of a hospital order with a section 41 restriction order.[1]

7.3   Later in this Part, we address two issues of procedure which have arisen relatively recently. First, we look at whether or not an accused who has been found to be unfit can continue to be dealt with at the same time as co-defendants who are fit and who are therefore undergoing a trial. The Court of Appeal has held that it is possible for the cases against the unfit accused and the fit defendant to be heard simultaneously in the same proceedings. We agree that there are some difficulties with this approach as the law stands at the moment, but for reasons which we will explain we think that these difficulties will not exist under the reformed procedure we have provisionally proposed in this CP.

7.4   Secondly, we look at the issue of whether or not the Court of Appeal should be given the power to remit a case for a re-hearing under section 4A as opposed to simply having the power to remit a case for trial, which is the extent of its powers at present. We conclude that there is presently an unacceptable lacuna in the law in this regard and therefore provisionally propose an amendment to the present procedure.

DISPOSALS

7.5   At present, disposals are relevant if an unfit accused following a section 4A hearing is found by the jury to have done the act or, in other words, committed the conduct element of the offence with which he or she is charged.

---

[1]   See paras 7.14 onwards below.

7.6 Under our provisional proposals the question of disposal will become relevant if:

(1) there is a finding that the accused has done the act or made the omission and that there are no grounds for acquitting him or her; or

(2) the accused is acquitted because of mental disorder existing at the time of the commission of the offence with which he or she is charged.

7.7 We have not previously addressed the issue of disposals in the case of an accused who has been found to have done the act. As we explain below, there has been recent reform in this area which means that there is no need for us to propose any changes.

Availability of disposals

7.8 The 1991 Act introduced flexibility of disposal in relation to an unfit accused. It provided for four possible disposals when a person was found to be unfit and to have done the act: a hospital order, a supervision order, a guardianship order and an order for an absolute discharge. The Domestic Violence, Crime and Victims Act 2004 amended the powers of the court to deal with persons who are either not guilty by reason of insanity[2] or where a finding that they are under a disability and that they have done the act has been recorded.[3] There is no longer a power to make a guardianship order. The court now has the power to make a hospital order[4] with or without a restriction order,[5] a supervision order[6] or an order for the accused's absolute discharge.[7] Research which we have commissioned by Professor Mackay to assist us in this project shows that between 2002 and 2008 out of a total of 473 hospital orders imposed, 257 of these were imposed together with section 41 restriction orders without limit of time and a further 6 of these hospital orders were imposed with restriction of time.[8]

7.9 Further, "hospital order" now has the same meaning as hospital order under section 37(2) of the Mental Health Act 1983. This is with the exception that, where the special verdict or the finding is in relation to an offence which is fixed by law (for example, murder)[9] and the court has the power to make a hospital order, then the court has to make a hospital order with a restriction order[10]

---

[2] 1964 Act, s 5(1)(a).

[3] Above, s 5(1)(b).

[4] Hospital order has the meaning given in s 37 of the Mental Health Act 1983: s 5(4) of the 1964 Act.

[5] 1964 Act, s 5(2)(a). See further Appendix A.

[6] Above, s 5(2)(b).

[7] Above, s 5(2)(c).

[8] See Appendix C. The Mental Health Act 2007 however amended s 41 of the Mental Health Act 1983 so that the court no longer has the power to make a restriction order with a time limit – all restriction orders are now without limit of time: see Appendix A.

[9] Section 37(1A) of the Mental Health Act 1983 refers to other offences fixed by law in the sense that they attract minimum mandatory terms in relation to which an order under s 37 (1) can be imposed.

[10] Restriction order has the meaning given to it by s 41 of the Mental Health Act 1983.

regardless of whether it would otherwise have the power to make a restriction order.[11]

7.10 This change was necessary because the original "admission orders" under the 1964 Act mandated hospitalisation of those accused who were charged with murder and found unfit to plead but who did not necessarily have a mental disorder. It was therefore potentially in breach of article 5(1)(e) of the European Convention on Human Rights, which requires the existence of a mental disorder before a person can be detained in hospital.[12] It should be noted that in *Grant*, the Divisional Court and the Court of Appeal held that there was no such violation.[13] This finding, however, did not preclude a possible future violation of article 5 in other circumstances.

7.11 The reason for the amendments made by the Domestic Violence, Crime and Victims Act 2004 was the need for "alignment of hospital-based disposals with the regime of the Mental Health Act"[14] for those found unfit to plead. The amendments were essentially aimed at ensuring that the detention in hospital of an unfit accused who is found to have done the act will be compatible with article 5. The result is therefore that the court has no power to make a hospital order unless the conditions of section 37 of the Mental Health Act 1983 are satisfied. Under section 37 there must be medical evidence that justifies hospital detention, in other words, a mental disorder as defined by the Mental Health Act 1983 which makes treatment in hospital appropriate.[15] This satisfies the requirement for "objective medical expertise" to justify detention under article 5(1)(e).[16]

7.12 The conditions which are set out in the Mental Health Act 1983[17] have to be met before either a hospital order or a hospital order with a restriction order can be

---

[11] Section 5(3) of the 1964 Act.

[12] Article 5(1) provides that no one shall be deprived of his or her liberty. There are limited exceptions to this right which include the lawful detention of "persons of unsound mind". In *HL v United Kingdom* (2005) 40 EHRR 32 (App No 45508/99) the court ruled that a man diagnosed with autism was deprived of his liberty and that this was in breach of article 5.

[13] [2001] EWCA Crim 2611, [2002] QB 1030. It was held that on the facts under consideration in that case, the order made under the pre-2004 legislation did not violate the rights of the accused under article 5 because article 5(1)(e) specifically allows for the detention of those of unsound mind and there was ample evidence that the accused was suffering from mental impairment that was treatable.

[14] RD Mackay, "AAPL Practice Guideline for the forensic psychiatric evaluation of competence to stand trial: an English legal perspective" (2007) 35 *Journal of the American Academy of Psychiatry and the Law* 501, 503.

[15] Section 1(2) of the 1983 Act originally provided for four categories of mental disorder: "mental disorder", "severe mental impairment", "mental impairment" and "psychopathic disorder". Section 1 of the 2007 Act replaced the four categories in s 1(2) with a single definition of mental disorder as "any disorder or disability of the mind". The new s 1(2) is therefore arguably considerably wider.

[16] *Winterwerp v Netherlands* (1979) 2 EHRR 387 (App No 6301/73).

[17] The Mental Health Act 2007 makes the following changes to Mental Health Act 1983. First, there is a new definition of mental disorder as "any disorder or disability of the mind", and some exclusions to the Mental Health Act 1983 have been removed. Second, the "treatability test" is replaced by an "appropriate treatment test". A further discussion of these changes can be found in Appendix A.

made. This applies to murder as well as all other offences.[18] If therefore a person is unfit through physical disability[19] and is found to have done the act of murder then the only option would be a supervision order.

7.13   It is likely in practice that the unfit accused who is found to have done the act of murder will come within the provisions of the Mental Health Act 1983. Certainly those who are found unfit because of, for example, a learning disability which on its own is excluded from the definition of mental disorder will come under the exception of displaying "irresponsible or abnormally aggressive conduct".[20] This means that they will be eligible for "appropriate medical treatment".

POWERS TO REMIT THE ACCUSED FOR TRIAL

7.14   If an unfit accused person is found to have done the act and is detained by a hospital order by virtue of section 5(1)(b) with a section 41 restriction order[21] which has not ceased to have effect, then under section 5A(4) of the 1964 Act the Secretary of State, if satisfied after consultation with the "responsible clinician", may remit the accused for trial.[22] We do not have data on how often this has happened.

7.15   These are the only circumstances in which a case can be remitted for trial and but for this provision, the finding that an accused has done the act remains for all time.

7.16   It is not clear what the rationale is for limiting the procedure for remission to a case which involves a section 41 restriction order. However, our research shows that section 41 restriction orders without limit of time tend to be imposed (as one would expect) in those cases where the offences with which the accused is charged are particularly harmful.[23] We infer that section 41 orders without limit of time are imposed in the most serious of cases and that the public interest is therefore best served by the case being resolved by the court at a later stage if this is possible.

7.17   There will undoubtedly be occasions on which it is appropriate for a previously unfit accused to be remitted for trial, as is the case in the following example:[24]

---

[18]   Although if a hospital order can be made in the case of an unfit accused found to have done the act of murder, then the court must impose a restriction order: s 5(3) of the 1964 Act.

[19]   For example, if he or she was unable to concentrate on the evidence because he or she was suffering from cancer: see TP Rogers et al, "Reformulating the law on fitness to plead: a qualitative study" (2009) 20(6) *Journal of Forensic Psychiatry and Psychology* 815, 824.

[20]   See s 1(2A) of the Mental Health Act 1983 as amended.

[21]   Under the Mental Health Act 1983.

[22]   The "responsible clinician" is the practitioner with overall responsibility for the patient's case: see Appendix A.

[23]   See Appendix C table 11. It should be noted that the court no longer has the power to impose restriction orders with time limits – all restriction orders are now without limit of time: see Appendix A.

[24]   This example is based on the case of *Grey* which was heard at Bristol Crown Court on 4 July 2008 after being remitted.

> **Example 7A**
>
> The defendant killed a person when he (the defendant) was suffering from mental disorder. He is suffering from mental disorder at the time of the trial and is found to be unfit to plead. He is found to have done the act and given a hospital order with a restriction order attached. He is treated in Broadmoor for 10 years until he is considered to be well. He is then referred back to the court where he tenders a plea of guilty to manslaughter by way of diminished responsibility.

7.18   The above example demonstrates the way in which the present system can work to the advantage of relations of victims, witnesses and the defendant who, having received treatment for his or her disorder, is able to take responsibility for his or her actions.

7.19   The procedure can, however, have some disadvantages. If an accused is dealt with by way of a hospital order and a section 41 restriction order as a result of an adverse finding under section 4A and is then treated for his or her mental disorder, it may not be in his or her interest to be referred back to court. Moreover, it may not be in the public interest. The problems include unnecessary expenditure, delay and possible adverse effects on the evidence of witnesses. Once a case has been referred back by the Secretary of State, then there is nothing that the Crown Court can do about the decision.[25] The accused person must be retried even if it then transpires that he or she clearly still has a mental disorder. This may mean that the issue of whether or not the accused is unfit to plead needs to be re-determined. If it is and the accused is found to be under a disability so as to be unfit to plead, then there is no discretion to obviate a second hearing of the facts under section 4A. The process must be gone through again.

7.20   The case law and empirical or anecdotal evidence suggests that there can be adverse consequences as a result of this inflexibility. The mental health of the accused can deteriorate as a result of the stress occasioned by court proceedings. Even if this happens, at present, the court has no choice but to embark on the determination of the issue and thereafter a hearing under section 4A which is both expensive and unnecessary.[26]

7.21   We therefore provisionally propose that:

> **Provisional Proposal 12: Where the Secretary of State has referred a case back to court pursuant to the accused being detained under a hospital order with a section 41 restriction order and it thereafter becomes clear beyond doubt (and medical evidence confirms) that the accused is still unfit to plead, the court should be able to reverse the decision to remit the case.**

---

[25]   Legal advisors for the accused may be able, subject to the facts, to judicially review the decision.

[26]   See *R (Julie Ferris) v DPP* [2004] EWHC 1221 (Admin). See also anecdotal evidence of His Honour Judge Jeremy Roberts QC concerning the case of *Sureda*, which is the subject of a case study in Appendix B.

Provisional Proposal 13: In the event of a referral back to court by the Secretary of State and where the accused is found to be unfit to plead, there should not be any need to have a further hearing on the issue of whether the accused did the act. This is subject to the proviso that the court considers it to be in the interests of justice.[27]

7.22 During the time in which we have been researching this project, it has been brought to our attention that a possible problem with the limitation of the present procedure for referral of a case back to the court is that it does not enable a person who has been found to be unfit to plead and to have done the act to request referral of his or her own case back to court.[28] This is thought to occasion possible injustice given the limitation of consideration of facts to the conduct element of the offence only.[29]

7.23 However, as we have seen in Part 6, we are now provisionally proposing that all the elements of the alleged offence should be considered for the purpose of our reformed section 4A hearing. In addition to this, we have pointed out that the appointment of a representative for the accused means that all possible avenues which may lead to an acquittal should be explored within the context of this hearing. We therefore think that it would be unlikely that an accused who is found to have done the act and in respect of whom it is also found that there are no grounds for an acquittal would benefit from a trial at a later stage when his or her mental disorder has been treated.

7.24 Over and above this, there will be the question of whether or not the prosecution are able to marshal witnesses given the possible delay which may have occurred.

7.25 Furthermore, research on the system in Scotland which is provided for by the Criminal Procedure (Scotland) Act 1995[30] reveals that some people express reservations about the fact that in Scotland a person who is found unfit to plead may be subjected to a trial upon recovery.[31] Semi-structured interviews conducted with lawyers and psychiatrists revealed:

---

[27] We assume that this would involve consent on the part of the representative of the accused.

[28] Meeting of the Law Commission working group on unfitness to plead, 14 December 2009.

[29] Conversely if an accused recovers after a finding that he has done the act or made the omission charged but before the case is disposed of under the provision of ss 5(2) and (3) of 1964 Act, the Divisional Court has held that the judge must re-determine the issue under s 4: see *R (Hasani) v Crown Court at Blackfriars* [2005] EWHC 3016 (Admin), [2006] 1 WLR 1992.

[30] C Connolly, "Unfitness to Plead and Examination of the Facts Proceedings: A Report Prepared for the Law Commission of England and Wales" (March 2010).

[31] Where the facts are held to have been established at the examination of the facts procedure, this finding is not classed as a conviction and it is competent for a person to be subsequently charged, on either a complaint or an indictment, with an offence arising out of the same act or omission as was considered at the examination of the facts and found to have been established.

Lawyers were generally of the view that trial upon recovery was necessary especially when a serious crime had been established at the EOF [examination of the facts]. Psychiatrists, who would have more on-going contact with patients, referred to the possibility of trial upon recovery as causing distress to patients. One psychiatrist referred to a case where a patient had waited for four years concerned that charges would be brought against them on recovery. When they did recover adequately to be tried, the psychiatrist was asked to provide a report indicating a suitable disposal following conviction. In this case the psychiatrist had indicated that the disposal would be a restricted compulsion order. The Crown then indicated that they would not proceed with a prosecution as the accused was already being detained on such an order. It was suggested that this example is representative of a normal procedure.[32]

7.26 We would welcome views from consultees on this point:

Question 6: Are there circumstances in which an accused person who is found to have done the act and in respect of whom there are no grounds for an acquittal should be able to request remission for trial?

JOINT TRIALS

7.27 The 1964 Act does not provide for a situation where there are proceedings involving more than one defendant.[33] This is problematic in joint trials where one accused becomes unfit to plead after the jury has been put in charge. The 1964 Act makes no provision for co-defendants when the trial against an unfit defendant must stop (so that there can be a section 4A hearing in respect of him or her).

7.28 The issue recently arose at appellate level[34] in *B and others*.[35] In that case the Court of Appeal heard an interlocutory application from a preparatory hearing.[36] The case involved allegations on a 32-count indictment of sexual abuse against ten people over a period of 40 years.

7.29 Eight of the ten defendants had been arraigned and pleaded not guilty to all counts. Two (A1 and A3)[37] had not been arraigned, however, and had been found unfit to plead under section 4 of the 1964 Act. Seventeen of the counts on

---

[32] C Connolly, "Unfitness to Plead and Examination of the Facts Proceedings: A Report Prepared for the Law Commission of England and Wales" (March 2010), p 13.

[33] The 1964 Act as amended makes no provision for a situation which could arise by virtue of a joint trial. A reading of Hansard reveals that the issue did not arise during the passage of the 1991 Act. The Act refers only to "the defendant", which seems to imply that it was intended that an unfit defendant would always be alone in a jury hearing as to whether he or she did the acts alleged.

[34] There have been at least two cases at first instance where the issue was decided differently but this is the first case on this point to reach appellate level.

[35] [2008] EWCA Crim 1997, [2009] 1 WLR 1545.

[36] Criminal Procedure and Investigations Act 1996, s 29.

[37] A1 had severe mental problems and A3 had recently suffered a stroke.

the indictment were against A1. A3 faced one count only in which he was jointly charged with D4.

7.30 At the plea and case management hearing (which was in fact treated as the preparatory hearing)[38] the judge addressed the question:

> Whether there can be one jury that decides the guilt or innocence of all the defendants who are fit to stand trial and can also decide whether the two defendants who are not fit to stand trial did the act.

He held that it would be "inappropriate" and "entirely wrong" for there to be a single jury to determine both issues and that it was an "inescapable" fact that there would have to be two separate hearings. This was of course unfortunate in the sense that it would involve witnesses having to give evidence twice. The prosecution appealed the ruling by leave of the judge.

7.31 The Court of Appeal held that the judge had jurisdiction to conduct the preparatory hearing to decide whether the case against the fit defendants should properly proceed either separately or jointly with the determination of whether the unfit accused did the acts that were alleged against them. In the view of the Court of Appeal, this involved a question of law which would affect the management of the trial. It would also impinge upon the question of severance because it would reduce the number of counts on the indictment.

7.32 The Court of Appeal stated that it had to consider two questions. First, was it permissible for the trial of fit defendants and the determination of whether unfit defendants did the acts alleged to be heard simultaneously? Secondly, if the answer to the first question was in the affirmative, then should the court interfere with the judge's ruling that the matters should be heard separately?

7.33 The Court of Appeal referred to a possible situation where a defendant is found to be unfit during the course of a trial which involves several defendants and asked itself what would have happened in the hypothetical situation where D8 (the eighth of the defendants on the indictment) had suffered from a stroke towards the end of the trial when he was about to give evidence. Under the 1964 Act as amended the question of whether he did the act that was charged had to be decided by the jury by whom he was being tried.[39] Given this, the jury could not be discharged. At the end of the trial they would either acquit or make the relevant finding of fact in relation to whether he had done the act. Of the fit co-defendants the court held that, "it would be most unfortunate if the law required the jury to be discharged from giving their verdicts in their cases and there had to be a re-trial."[40] It was held that neither the 1964 Act nor the Juries Act 1974 required that to happen.

7.34 The relevance of the Juries Act 1974 is that section 11(4) provides:

---

[38] See para 7.28 above.

[39] Section 4A(5).

[40] *B and others* [2008] EWCA Crim 1997, [2009] 1 WLR 1545 at [17] by Toulson LJ.

Subject to section (5) below, the jury selected by any one ballot shall try only one issue (but any juror shall be liable to be selected on more than one ballot).[41]

7.35 It was stated that in principle it should not make any difference at what stage the determination of unfitness occurred, although it was also stated that "it could be argued that, on a literal reading, that section 11(4) would prohibit a jury from determining more than one count against one defendant".[42] However the joinder of different defendants in a single indictment and the inclusion of more than one count in an indictment "is not only everyday practice but has a long pedigree".[43] The court looked at the legislative origins of section 11 of the Juries Act 1974. Referring to section 26 of the Juries Act 1825,[44] it was held:

> We are satisfied that section 11(4) of the Juries Act when it speaks of one issue is to be interpreted in this way. When a jury is empanelled to decide whether allegations contained in an indictment are proved by the evidence presented to a jury, that is the relevant issue for the purposes of section 11(4). What may properly be contained in the indictment is governed by other legislation and case law, so there is no irreconcilable conflict. Where a jury has been empanelled to decide whether a person is guilty of a charge in the indictment, that necessarily includes finding whether he committed the *actus reus* … it is a more limited issue than that which the jury was originally empanelled to decide but … the greater includes the less. The same principle must in our judgment apply if the unfitness occurs before the commencement of the proceedings before a jury.[45]

Some problems with the decision in *B and others*

7.36 The first problem with the decision in *B and others* is that it does not appear to take account of the decision of the Court of Appeal in *O' Donnell*.[46] In that case it

---

[41] There are exceptions under s 11(5)(a) and (c) for the hearing of special pleas. A previous exception under s 5(b) which applied to a jury which had previously been trying an accused who becomes unfit has been repealed by the Domestic Violence, Crime and Victims Act 2004, s 58(1) and Sch 10 para 8. As we explained in Part 2, the court can no longer direct that a jury can decide whether the accused is unfit to plead.

[42] Although it was observed that "it may be pertinent when considering the question": *B and others* [2008] EWCA Crim 1997, [2009] 1 WLR 1545 at [18] by Toulson LJ.

[43] Above at [18] and [19] by Toulson LJ.

[44] Where it was provided that jurors who had been balloted and who had returned their verdict could have their names returned to the box there to be kept with the other names remaining at that time undrawn so *toties quoties* as long as any issue remains to be tried. This was with the proviso that:
> where no objection shall be made on behalf of the king or any other party it shall be lawful for the court to try any issue with the same jury that shall have previously tried or been drawn to try any other issue without their names being returned to the box and re drawn … and so *toties quoties* as long as any issue remains to be tried.

[45] [2008] EWCA Crim 1997, [2009] 1 WLR 1545 at [24] by Toulson LJ.

[46] [1996] 1 Cr App R 286.

was held that guilt or the lack of guilt[47] was a different issue from the issue as to whether an unfit accused had done the act.

7.37 The two findings (guilty or has done the act) have distinct consequences and as we explained in Part 2,[48] can lead to different disposals. This distinction is further reflected in the fact that there is different legislative provision for appeal. Appeal against conviction is by way of appeal under section 1 of the Criminal Appeal Act 1968 and an appeal against an adverse decision under section 4A is by way of an appeal under section 15 of that Act.

7.38 The reference to joinder[49] is also a little misleading. Whereas there can be no dispute that defendants can be properly joined[50] in the same indictment, the actual rationale behind joinder of defendants was stated in *Lake*[51] as

> not merely the saving of time and money; it also affects the desirability that the same verdict and the same treatment shall be returned against all those concerned in the same offence; if joint offences were widely to be tried as separate offences, all sorts of inconsistencies might arise.

7.39 In the present context we are starting, as it were, from a position of inconsistency between the co-accused. This is because there can be no question of "joint verdicts".

7.40 If found to have done the act charged, the unfit accused will be subject to the disposal regime under the 1964 Act.[52] Under section 5A of the 1964 Act the Secretary of State may order a new trial if the accused subsequently recovers.[53] By force of circumstance this will not be a joint trial.

7.41 In the initial trial, in which the accused is joined with the co-accused, both the unfit and fit accused will have an interest in obtaining an acquittal. This would be of particular concern in the context of a "cut-throat"[54] defence, in which a number of issues arise.

> (1) The unfit accused may, through counsel, put a case adverse to the co-accused. However, the unfit accused will not be required to give evidence to support it before the jury, as he or she may be presumed to be incapable of giving evidence.

[47] Which as we have explained previously, tends to be referred to as the general issue.

[48] See paras 2.28 to 2.31 above.

[49] See para 7.35 above.

[50] In other words, tried together.

[51] (1977) 64 Cr App R 172 at 175, by Lord Widgery CJ.

[52] Possible disposals include a hospital order with or without restrictions on release; a supervision; or absolute discharge which we have previously set out in para 7.8 above.

[53] See discussion at paras 7.14 onwards above.

[54] A cut-throat defence is where one defendant seeks to prove his or her own innocence by implicating a co-defendant.

(2) The unfit accused's silence will not be subject to the adverse inference in section 35 of the Criminal Justice and Public Order Act 1994,[55] unlike a co-accused who decides not to give evidence at trial.

(3) The unfit accused will not be available for cross-examination to a fit co-accused who may have hoped to elicit advantageous evidence. Equally, he or she will not be able to defend him or herself in the event that the fit co-accused seeks to blame him or her. It is conceivable that in a cut-throat defence, the unfit accused may unfairly be found to have done the act because a fit co-accused can give evidence and say that that is the case. Although a positive finding does not result in a conviction it can result in disposals with significant consequences: for example the accused being placed on the sex offenders register.[56]

(4) It is possible that the jury may think that the fit accused is taking advantage of the situation by making an allegation against the unfit accused which he or she cannot refute.

7.42 Arguably there is another problem which was not considered by the Court of Appeal in *B and others*. As observed in Part 6 at paragraph 6.42 above, article 6 of the European Convention on Human Rights does not presently apply to the hearing under section 4A.[57] We have made it clear that we think that it should do so and in our view, our provisional proposed changes to the section 4A hearing will make the case for this stronger.

7.43 If this were not the case then we would think that it is surely inequitable for one accused to the proceedings to have the advantage of the procedural fairness which article 6 confers and another accused to be disadvantaged in this respect. It is also potentially likely to lead to a situation where a defendant may seek to blame an unfit accused for the offence with which he or she (the defendant) is charged.

7.44 However, on the basis of our reasoning in Part 6 for the reform of the section 4A hearing, and on the basis of the fact that we set great store by the appointment of

---

[55] Section 35(2) of the Criminal Justice and Public Order Act 1994 provides that:

Where this subsection applies, the court or jury, in determining whether the accused is guilty of the offence charged, may draw such inferences as appear proper from the failure of the accused to give evidence or his refusal, without good cause, to answer any question.

[56] Although the court in *B and others* [2008] EWCA Crim 1997, [2009] 1 WLR 1545 stated that the four sets of interests to be considered were those of the unfit defendants, the fit defendants, witnesses and the public (at [36]), the court relied on the fact that none of the fit defendants had "suggested that it would be in any way prejudicial to them for the jury simultaneously to consider the issue whether he did the acts alleged". It is however conceivable that in a different case there may well be objections from either the fit defendants or the unfit accused.

[57] *H* [2003] UKHL 1, [2003] 1 WLR 411.

a person to represent the acccused's interests in a section 4A hearing,[58] we do not believe that under our proposed scheme, the problems that we have identified with *B and others* would persist. Therefore, we do not think that we need to make any proposal in relation to the need for separate trials of the fit and the unfit co-accused. Given some of the concerns with the decision raised in the above paragraphs however, we invite consultees' views on this point.

> **Question 7: Should an accused who is found to be unfit to plead (or to lack decision-making capacity) be subject to the section 4A hearing in the same proceedings as co-defendants who are being tried?**

POWERS OF THE COURT OF APPEAL TO REMIT FOR A RE-HEARING

7.45   As stated at paragraph 7.37 above, the power to appeal an adverse finding under section 4A is by leave of the Court of Appeal under section 15[59] of the Criminal Appeal Act 1968. At present there is however no power for the Court of Appeal to remit for a re-hearing under section 4A of the 1964 Act; it can only enter an acquittal.[60]

7.46   We believe that this is potentially problematic in a situation where there is a need to protect the public interest.

7.47   In the case of *Norman*[61] the accused was alleged to have committed an offence under the Child Abduction Act 1984. After charge he was remanded in custody and committed for trial on 5 June 2006. At the plea and case management hearing on the 27 July 2006, the issue of the accused's unfitness was raised. The

---

[58]   On which point, the Court of Appeal in *Norman* [2008] EWCA Crim 1810, [2009] 1 Cr App R 13 held that it should be someone experienced in mental health matters as well as criminal matters.

[59]   Section 15 provides:

   (1)   Where there has been a determination under section 4 of the Criminal Procedure (Insanity) Act 1964 of the question of a person's fitness to be tried, and there have been findings that he is under a disability and that he did the act or made the omission charged against him, the person may appeal to the Court of Appeal against either or both of those findings.

[60]   Section 16(3) of the Criminal Appeal Act 1968 provides:

   Where the Court of Appeal allow an appeal under section 15 of this Act against a finding that the appellant is under a disability –

      (a) the appellant may be tried accordingly for the offence with which he was charged; and

      (b) the Court may, subject to section 25 of the Criminal Justice and Public Order Act 1994, make such orders as appear to them necessary or expedient pending any such trial for his custody, release on bail or continued detention under the Mental Health Act 1983.

   Section 16(4) provides:

   Where, otherwise than in a case falling within subsection (3) above, the Court of Appeal allow an appeal under section 15 of this Act against a finding that the appellant did the act or made the omission charged against him, the Court shall, in addition to quashing the verdict, direct a verdict of acquittal to be recorded (but not a verdict of not guilty by reason of insanity).

[61]   [2008] EWCA Crim 1810, [2009] 1 Cr App R 13.

accused suffered from Huntington's disease. Three psychiatrists were of the view that the accused was not fit to plead.

7.48 On 27 January 2007, the matter was again listed at Lewes Crown Court for the extension of custody time limits. As the accused's mother had written to complain about the delay the judge decided to determine the issue of the accused's unfitness to plead. The reports of the psychiatrists were in agreement and the court was entitled to proceed under section 4(6) of the 1964 Act. Accordingly the accused was found unfit to plead.

7.49 The accused had been subject to unpleasant treatment by his fellow prisoners and so the judge directed that the section 4A hearing should take place as soon as possible. The issue was heard a week later by a judge and jury, and the jury found that the accused had committed the act. No order was made and the accused appears to have remained in custody until he was admitted on 15 May 2007 to a medium secure psychiatric unit. On 20 September 2007 under section 37 of the Mental Health Act 1983 the judge made a hospital order with a section 41 restriction order.

7.50 The background to the decision to prosecute the accused was that in light of allegations against the accused of sexual misconduct in relation to a child ("CM"), a written notice had been served on the accused forbidding him to see CM. The evidence against the accused had been that a few days later CM's father had taken him to Brighton where they had met the accused on the pier. They returned to the accused's flat and CM's father had left him there. CM's father and mother were divorced but shared control of CM. The mother gave evidence that in the early hours of the next morning CM had telephoned her and that the accused had snatched the phone and said that he was in love with CM and was keeping him there.

7.51 The trial judge directed the jury that if they were satisfied that the telephone call had taken place then the act of abduction was made out.

7.52 The appellant appealed by way of leave from the single judge[62] against the verdict of the jury that he did the act charged and renewed an application for leave to appeal the orders made on disposal.

7.53 The initial ground of appeal against the finding appears to have been that the judge should have allowed the evidence of a witness from the Huntingdon's Disease Association as to the nature of the appellant's disability. A fresh witness statement was prepared and an application made to call the evidence as fresh evidence under section 23 of the Criminal Appeal Act 1968.

7.54 The Court of Appeal itself however raised the question of whether the summing up had been adequate on the basis that it did not draw the jury's attention to the question of what act could or was said to constitute the abduction. The court therefore invited further submissions from prosecution counsel on this point. It was also directed that counsel experienced in mental health issues be assigned by the Registrar to put the case for the defence on the appeal by way of discharging the court's duty under section 4A(2) of the 1964 Act.

---

[62] One of the persons who has the power to grant leave to appeal.

7.55 The Crown contended that the direction that the judge had given was in fact sufficient to cover the questions which had been raised by the Court of Appeal. The Court of Appeal did not agree that the direction was adequate because the judge told the jury that they were to find that the act of abduction had taken place if they were satisfied merely that the telephone call took place. For the direction to have been satisfactory the judge would first have had to point out to the jury that they had to be sure of the precise words spoken. Second, they would have had to be sure that CM had heard the words and that they had in fact amounted to an inducement for him to stay with the appellant. Third, they would have had to be sure that the words were the effective cause of the child remaining with the appellant.[63]

7.56 The direction which had been given did not touch on any of the above because the Crown had not set out its case in the way that it had for the Court of Appeal. The finding of the jury was therefore unsafe and was quashed on this basis. The ground in relation to the fresh evidence[64] was not decided.

7.57 The Court of Appeal observed that under section 16(4)[65] of the Criminal Appeal Act 1968 it was obliged to direct a verdict of acquittal, as it had not been a case where there was any procedural irregularity which would permit a re-hearing.[66] The appellant's welfare was being adequately safe-guarded as he had been transferred to a specialised home for those suffering from Huntingdon's disease under section 17 of the Mental Health Act 1983.

7.58 In light of the growing number of cases concerning unfitness to plead the Court of Appeal made a number of observations.

> Once it is clear that there is an issue, such cases need very careful case management to ensure that full information is provided to the court without the delay so evident in this case.

---

[63] The Court referred in this regard to the decisions in *A* [2000] 1 WLR 1879 and *Leather* (1994) 98 Cr App R 179.

[64] [2008] EWCA Crim 1810, [2009] 1 Cr App R 13 at [29]. It was submitted that as the appellant could not speak for himself, then the jury should have heard the evidence of a witness (which spoke to the fact that because of his disability, the appellant was never confrontational and tended to agree with everything that was said to him) to challenge the mother's evidence. It was submitted that the evidence was admissible because there was no other way in which the mother's account of the conversation could have been challenged. The court decided that it was not necessary to decide this "cogent" submission.

[65] Which provides:
> Where, otherwise than in a case falling within subsection (3) above, the Court of Appeal allow an appeal under section 15 of this Act against a finding that the appellant did the act or made the omission charged against him, the Court shall, in addition to quashing the verdict, direct a verdict of acquittal to be recorded (but not a verdict of not guilty by reason of insanity).

[66] See *O'Donnell* [1996] 1 Cr App R 286, *Hussein* [2005] EWCA Crim 3556.

When full information is available, the court will need carefully to consider whether to postpone the issue of trial of fitness to plead under section 4(2), given the consequences that a finding of unfitness has for the defendant.[67]

If the court determines that the appellant is unfit to plead, then it is the court's duty under section 4A(2) [of the 1964 Act] carefully to consider who is the best person to be appointed by the court to put the case for the defence. The court was of the view that it should not necessarily be the same person as had represented the defendant to date.

Finally, Parliament might like to give consideration to "the lacuna in the statutory provisions and consider granting this court power to order a re-trial of the issue as to whether the defendant did the act with which he is charged". [68]

7.59 This is an obvious technical lacuna and we therefore make a further provisional proposal:

Provisional Proposal 14: In circumstances where a finding under section 4A is quashed and there has been no challenge to a finding in relation to section 4 (that the accused is under a disability) there should be a power for the Court of Appeal in appropriate circumstances to order a re-hearing under section 4A.

---

[67] Referring to *M (Edward)* [2001] EWCA Crim 2024, [2002] 1 WLR 824.

[68] *Norman* [2008] EWCA Crim 1810, [2009] 1 Cr App R 13 at [34].

PART 8
UNFITNESS TO PLEAD AND THE MAGISTRATES' COURTS AND YOUTH COURTS

8.1 In this Part we address the situation concerning unfitness to plead[1] in the magistrates' courts and in the youth courts. We analyse the case law and ask consultees whether our provisional proposals in this CP should be applied to courts of summary jurisdiction.

UNFITNESS TO PLEAD AND THE MAGISTRATES' COURTS

8.2 As we explain below, there is currently no procedure in the summary jurisdiction that reflects the unfitness to plead procedure applicable in the Crown Court. We think it is arguable that the provisional proposals made in this CP in relation to proceedings on indictment should have equal application in the summary jurisdiction. We set out our reasoning for this and seek consultees' views. Our reasoning on the procedures in the adult magistrates' courts applies equally to the youth courts. However, there are additional considerations as far as youth courts are concerned and we address these below. As we explained in Part 1, the scope of this CP does not address the issue of insanity and therefore we do not consider the defence of insanity in relation to the magistrates' courts.[2]

Powers of the magistrates' courts

8.3 The procedure in the 1964 Act for unfitness to plead presently only has application to the Crown Court because the terms of the 1964 Act extend only to proceedings before the Crown Court. It has been held that the Crown Court procedure is "entirely inappropriate" for the determination of issues in the summary jurisdiction.[3]

8.4 The magistrates' powers to deal with defendants with a mental or physical condition derive from section 37(3) of the Mental Health Act 1983 ("the 1983 Act") and section 11(1) of the Powers of Criminal Courts (Sentencing) Act 2000 ("the 2000 Act").

---

[1] Which of course is not called unfitness to plead in the summary jurisdiction.

[2] On the basis of current authority insanity applies to offences in the magistrates' court other than offences of strict liability (in other words, where there is no fault in relation to one or more elements). The court cannot however return the special verdict of not guilty by reason of insanity as s 2(1) of the Trial of Lunatics Act 1883 provides that a special verdict may only be provided by a jury. Neither can it commit a defendant who has been acquitted of an offence by reason of insanity to the Crown Court for the imposition of a hospital order with a s 41 restriction order under the Mental Health Act 1983. We think that it is unlikely that there is any justification for precluding the application of the defence of insanity to offences of strict liability. However, we will look at this in the course of our forthcoming project on insanity.

[3] *R (P) v Barking Youth Court* [2002] EWHC 734 (Admin), [2002] 2 Cr App R 19 at [8].

8.5 Section 37(3) of the 1983 Act provides:

> Where a person is charged before a magistrates' court with any act or omission as an offence and the court would have power, on convicting him of that offence, to make an order [hospital or guardianship] under subsection (1) above in his case, then, if the court is satisfied that the accused did the act or made the omission charged, the court may, if it thinks fit, make such an order without convicting him.

8.6 Section 37(3) gives the magistrates' court the power to make a hospital order without convicting the accused and obviates the need to hold a trial.[4] Moreover, it has been held that, where the conditions of section 37 of the 1983 Act[5] are satisfied, the magistrates' court has the power to impose a hospital order in circumstances where an accused has elected trial on indictment.[6]

8.7 Further to this, section 11(1) of the 2000 Act provides:

> If, on trial by a magistrates' court of an offence punishable on summary conviction with imprisonment the court
>
> (a)   is satisfied that the accused did the act or made the omission charged, but
>
> (b)   is of the opinion that an inquiry ought to be made into his physical or mental condition before the method of dealing with him is determined,
>
> the court shall adjourn the case to enable a medical examination and report to be made, and shall remand him.

---

[4]   *R v Lincolnshire (Kesteven) Justices, ex parte O'Connor* [1983] 1 WLR 335. Here the accused, who was charged with assault occasioning actual bodily harm, was unable to consent to summary trial due to his mental disorder. His representative asked the examining magistrates to make a hospital order (under s 60(2) of the Mental Health Act 1959, the predecessor to s 37(3) of the 1983 Act) without convicting the accused. The justices refused, believing that a trial was necessary, and proceeded to committal. On an application for judicial review of the decision to commit, the Divisional Court held that a trial was not a necessary precondition for the purposes of s 60(2) of the Mental Health Act 1959. In an exceptional case such as the one in question and where the accused was represented and there was no issue as to the assault, the justices could conclude without evidence that the offence had occurred and there was jurisdiction to make a hospital order. Matters will not always be this straightforward. See for example, A Samuels, "Hospital orders without conviction" [1995] *Criminal Law Review* 220, 222 where it was stated:

> The meaning of the "act" seems to be unclear. The issue is important. The mentally ill need protection, more so than ordinary people; but they are not to be deprived of their liberty simply because of mental illness. The public must be protected. A proper balance is required. Clarification from the judiciary and from Parliament would be welcome.

Obviously, this pre-dates the decision of the House of Lords in *Antoine* [2000] UKHL 20, [2001] 1 AC 340.

[5]   Under subsection (2), for a hospital order to be made there must be written or oral evidence from at least two registered medical practitioners that the accused is suffering from a mental disorder of a nature or degree which makes it appropriate for him or her to be detained in hospital and that appropriate medical treatment is available.

[6]   *R v Ramsgate Justices ex parte Kazmarek* (1985) 80 Cr App R 366.

8.8   Section 11(1) therefore empowers the magistrates' court to order a medical report on a defendant's physical or mental condition when he or she is being tried for a summary offence and the court is satisfied that he or she did the act or made the omission charged. This of course assumes that the defendant is being tried or is about to be tried at the time the disorder is, or becomes, apparent.[7] There is now some authority that a trial can be converted to a fact-finding exercise under the 2000 Act.[8]

8.9   The power to order medical reports under the 2000 Act, and the power to make a hospital order under section 37(3) of the 1983 Act, both depend merely on the court being satisfied that the accused committed the external elements of the offence. Although there is no direct authority on the point,[9] it appears that the test for satisfying the court that the accused has done the act or made the omission charged is that which was set down by the House of Lords in *Antoine*,[10] namely that the prosecution need to prove the conduct element of the offence only.

8.10   It is therefore open to the magistrates' court to cause a not guilty plea to be entered on behalf of the accused and to hear the prosecution evidence. If that evidence proves the external elements of the offence charged, the court may then adjourn for reports under section 11(1) of the 2000 Act. If on the basis of the reports, the medical criteria are satisfied, the court may then go on to make a hospital order under section 37(3) of the 1983 Act without convicting the accused. Taken together, section 11(1) and section 37(3) allow the magistrates' court to decide whether a defendant has done the act alleged before considering whether a hospital order should be made. It has been held that these two provisions provide:

> A complete statutory framework for the determination by the magistrates' court ... of all the issues that arise in cases of defendants who are or may be mentally ill or suffering from severe mental impairment in the context of offences which are triable summarily only.[11]

---

[7]   The wording of s 11(1) is clear: "if, on *the trial* ... the court shall adjourn the case" (emphasis added).

[8]   *Crown Prosecution Service v P* [2007] EWHC 946 (Admin), [2008] 1 WLR 1005 by Smith LJ. See below at paras 8.42 to 8.54 for a discussion of this decision.

[9]   In *Bartram v Southend Magistrates' Court* [2004] EWHC 2691 (Admin), [2004] MHLR 319 at [6] it was said:

> I should say that the requirement to establish that the accused did the act does not import any question of *mens rea*. It is purely directed at the *actus reus* of the offence. As it happens, and this will be material subsequently, the offence with which he was charged was an offence of absolute liability. There is no mental element involved. Provided that the accused did cause the unnecessary suffering, he is guilty of that offence. Accordingly, satisfaction that he did the act would amount to satisfaction that he committed the offence charged in the circumstances of this case. That is because, as Mr Clark on his behalf accepts, the defence of insanity would not have been open to him because there was, as I say, no mental element involved in the commission of this offence.

[10]   *Antoine* [2000] UKHL 20, [2001] 1 AC 340 which is discussed in detail in Part 6 above.

[11]   *R (P) v Barking Youth Court* [2002] EWHC 734 (Admin), [2002] 2 Cr App R 19 at [10].

8.11   Where a defendant is convicted by a magistrates' court (either after a trial or on a plea of guilty) of an offence punishable on summary conviction with imprisonment, section 37(1) of the 1983 Act provides that the court can make a hospital order if the conditions in subsection (2) are satisfied.[12] Unlike section 37(3) which only has application in the magistrates' courts, section 37(1) also has application in the Crown Court.

Committal to the Crown Court in the case of an offence which is triable either way

8.12   Magistrates may commit an accused who has been charged with an offence which is triable either way[13] to the Crown Court. The issue of unfitness to plead may then be raised in the Crown Court by invoking the procedure laid down in the 1964 Act.[14]

8.13   There is no power to commit the accused to the Crown Court to decide the issue of fitness on a charge which is triable only summarily.[15] In this situation the case of an accused who is suffering from a mental or physical condition at the time of the hearing must, as in every other summary only case, be dealt with in the magistrates' court.

PROBLEMS WITH THE APPROACH IN SUMMARY HEARINGS

8.14   There are at least five potential problems with the resolution of an accused's fitness to plead in the summary jurisdiction. First, it is unclear what will trigger an inquiry into whether an accused is unfit to plead. Secondly, there is no declared test to be applied to determine unfitness to plead.[16] Thirdly, the disposal powers that exist under the legislation referred to in paragraphs 8.4 to 8.7 above are not suitable for all cases. Fourthly, the unsuitability of the disposal powers means that a proper trial may be likely to be held when there is good evidence that an accused is unfit. A concomitant problem which we explore at paragraph 8.33 is that the accused who is dealt with in the magistrates' court does not have the same opportunity of being acquitted as the accused who is tried in the Crown Court. Fifthly, in the youth courts there is no possibility of a *doli incapax*[17] plea. We will now examine the first four problems which apply to the magistrates' courts. In paragraphs 8.38 to 8.69 we will address the further problems which arise in the youth courts.

---

[12]   See n 5 above.

[13]   This of course presupposes that the accused is able to give instructions that no representations should be made in relation to summary trial.

[14]   Once the transfer provisions are extended to either way offences (see s 41 of and Sch 3 to the Criminal Justice Act 2003), this is likely to speed up the unfitness to plead procedure in relation to cases which are presently subject to committal procedures.

[15]   *R v Metropolitan Stipendiary Magistrates Tower Bridge, ex parte Aniifowosi* (1985) 149 JP 748.

[16]   In reality these issues are conflated because without a declared test it can be difficult to see what would trigger an enquiry except in the most extreme cases.

[17]   This is explained at para 8.38 below.

Lack of procedure to determine the issue

8.15 The first of the problems identified in paragraph 8.14 is caused by the limited provision[18] for dealing with mentally or physically impaired offenders.[19] Inherent in this is the question of who will decide whether there is a potential issue of unfitness to plead and who will benefit from the procedure under section 11(1) of the 2000 Act read together with section 37(3) of the 1983 Act. In the magistrates' court there is no procedure akin to the common law test in the Crown Court.[20] Accordingly, whether or not an accused who is actually unfit to plead will benefit from an assessment is arbitrary. It is unlikely that there would be sufficient information regarding an accused's mental state following charge. There may, in the future, be improved early detection of mental disorder with the implementation of the recommendations of the Bradley Report for improved screening measures.[21]

The procedure to determine fitness

8.16 Although magistrates have the power under these sections to determine whether the accused has done the act or made the omission charged, there is no explicit statutory or common law test of how to determine the prior question of whether the defendant is unfit. The defence and the court may need to know at the outset whether what is in issue is guilt or merely the question of whether the accused has committed the external elements of the offence. In other words, the defence will need to know what they are defending: whether they are proceeding to trial or aiming for a section 37(3) disposal. It is not possible to decide what is best for a defendant if there is no procedure by which to assess his or her condition.

8.17 The difficulty in not having a procedure to determine the preliminary issue of unfitness to plead is apparent from a series of cases which originated in the youth courts. The matter was raised in *R (P) v Barking Youth Court*[22] where the 16-year-old accused was charged with offences of harassment and damage. However, as a result of a history of mental problems and learning difficulties (99.9% of children his age had a higher IQ than him), his solicitors instructed an educational psychologist to examine and report on him. The psychologist reported that P was incapable of understanding the nature of the offence with which he was charged and would be unable to give instructions, follow the course of proceedings or understand the evidence. In light of this report, P's solicitors indicated to the youth court that they wished to raise the issue of P's unfitness to plead as a preliminary issue. Any suggestion that this was not the appropriate course was not raised either by the prosecution or the court itself, and the issue was accordingly heard. However, the justices found P to be fit to plead, apparently on the basis of their own observations of his behaviour, and did not

---

[18] As provided by s 37(3) of the 1983 Act and s 11(1) of the 2000 Act. We say "limited" on the basis of the case law which we cite at paras 8.17 onwards below.

[19] In other words those accused who might be under a disability so that they cannot be tried.

[20] The *Pritchard* test, discussed in detail in Part 2 above.

[21] See The Bradley Report: Lord Bradley's review of people with mental health problems or learning disabilities in the criminal justice system (April 2009) p 53.

[22] [2002] EWHC 734 (Admin), [2002] Cr App R 294. Although concerned with the youth court it was made clear that the issue is equally relevant to a hearing before the adult magistrates' court.

consider the *Pritchard* criteria (by which the psychologist had considered his opinion) to be relevant.[23]

8.18 P sought judicial review of the justices' decision that he was fit to plead on the basis that their approach indicated a lack of understanding of the relevant law and that they had taken the wrong matters into account. In the Divisional Court, Mr Justice Wright expressed the view that, even if the procedure that the justices were following had been an appropriate one, their determination would have to be quashed on the basis that they allowed their own subjective and lay view to override the expert evidence, and that the fact that they regarded *Pritchard* as "irrelevant" indicated a lack of understanding of the relevant law.

8.19 However, Mr Justice Wright concluded that the correct procedure had not in fact been followed. Expressing surprise that the appropriateness of considering unfitness as a preliminary issue had not been questioned, he determined that the procedure to be followed in the adult magistrates' court[24] should also apply in the youth court.

> It will be seen that these two provisions [section 37(3) of the 1983 Act and section 11(1) of the 2000 Act] provide a complete statutory framework for the determination by the magistrates' court ... of all the issues that arise in cases of defendants who are or may be mentally ill or suffering from severe mental impairment in the context of offences which are triable summarily only.[25] It will also be noted that the criteria for exercising the powers vested in the magistrates' court under section 37(3) are considerably less strict and more flexible than the common-law rules governing the issue of fitness to plead in the Crown Court. It is true that in the context of cases triable either way there may be an unresolved problem when considering whether a defendant faced with such an allegation is capable of making a valid election as to the mode of trial ... . In the present case, however, as all the matters which P faces are to be tried in the youth court, and thus summarily, that problem does not arise.[26]

8.20 According to Mr Justice Wright, the correct course to be followed, therefore, was to determine first whether or not P did the acts alleged against him and if so then to consider whether or not a hospital order was suitable on the basis of medical reports.

8.21 The decision in *R (P) v Barking Youth Court* has been criticised[27] for failing to take account of the point that the court cannot hold a trial without first determining whether or not a trial can take place. It seems to us that a logical approach dictates a need for (1) a test for fitness (2) a test for whether an accused

[23] Above at [6].

[24] As described at paras 8.5 to 8.8 above.

[25] It might be argued that this is misleading. This is because although there is a test to determine whether D did the act if he or she is potentially unfit, there is no test to determine fitness.

[26] [2002] EWHC 734 (Admin), [2002] Cr App R 294 at [10].

[27] A Turner, "Capacity to stand trial, especially in the youth court" (2008) 172 *Justice of the Peace* 364.

performed the acts and (3) disposal powers. In other words, the question is whether there should be an initial procedure to determine the issue of fitness. We know from the way in which the 1964 Act works in the Crown Court that the starting point should be the determination of unfitness to plead, or under our provisionally proposed new test, a lack of decision-making capacity. Only then is it logical for the court to inquire into whether the accused performed the external elements of the offence alleged. We will address the question of whether or not a test is needed in the magistrates' courts.

Is there a need for a capacity based test in the magistrates' court?

8.22 This is the question which pertains to the second problem identified in paragraph 8.14 above. The principles of legal clarity and fairness support the adoption of a capacity based test in the magistrates' court. Whether there is, in practice, also a sufficient volume of deserving cases is a matter on which we seek consultees' views.[28]

8.23 Although in *R (P) v Barking Youth Court* the present legislative scheme was described by Mr Justice Wright as a comprehensive system, it does seem to us to have some limitations. Although it is comprehensive in terms of applying to all cases, nevertheless we suggest that it fails to provide a clear test and an adequate range of disposals. In our view, it is desirable to have a procedure, akin to the procedure which currently only has application in the Crown Court, so that magistrates can deal effectively with defendants who are unfit to plead (or lack decision-making capacity under a new legal test).

8.24 Once it is known whether or not an accused is unfit or lacks decision-making capacity, it should, in principle, then be possible to know with certainty what procedure needs to be followed and what the consequences will be in terms of disposal. This leads us to the third problem identified in paragraph 8.14 above.

The disposal powers are not suitable for all cases

8.25 Taken together, section 37(3) of the 1983 Act and section 11(1) of the 2000 Act provide powers for disposal by means of a hospital or guardianship order or for the provision of medical reports with a view to making such orders. As discussed elsewhere in this CP however, a hospital order may not be the most appropriate disposal in the sense that it is not the correct medical response to the accused's symptoms. As an obvious example, if an accused has severe learning disabilities which affect his or her ability to understand the proceedings, it may not be appropriate to impose a hospital order. It would seem (on current authorities) that if this is the case, there may not be any point in a fact-finding exercise as contemplated by section 11(1) of the 2000 Act. This is particularly true given the wide range of conditions that might be sufficient to render an accused unfit. In the magistrates' court, the absence of a clear test for unfitness exacerbates this problem because a potentially wider range of disorders might be regarded by the court as sufficient to trigger section 37 and section 11.

---

[28] See para 8.37 below.

The unsuitability of the disposal power can mean that a proper trial is more likely to be held where there is good evidence that a defendant is unfit

8.26   If the court recognises that it is not appropriate to make a hospital order then the accused is potentially exposed to a trial even though he or she may not be able to participate effectively in that trial. In *Blouet v Bath and Wansdyke Magistrates Court*[29] the Divisional Court refused leave for an application for judicial review of the magistrates' court decision not to order a fact-finding hearing with a view to ascertaining whether D (the claimant) had done the act or made the omission charged.

8.27   D suffered from Asperger's syndrome. There were conflicting psychiatric reports on his fitness to plead. Although it is not clear from the report, it is a reasonable inference that a hospital order would not have been appropriate in this case. The Divisional Court held, citing *R (Singh) v Stratford Magistrates Court*,[30] that in these circumstances the correct procedure was to proceed to trial. A fact-finding hearing under section 11(1) of the 2000 Act should only be held where there is a possibility of making a hospital order under section 37(3) of the 1983 Act.[31]

8.28   A contrary view to that in *Blouet* was expressed in *R (Varma) v Redbridge Magistrates' Court*.[32] In that case the defendant had learning difficulties and behavioural problems. The Divisional Court held that in light of four reports which concluded that he was unfit to plead and one report which concluded that he was fit, a trial should not have taken place. The apparent conflict between *Blouet* and *Varma* cannot be reconciled by suggesting that in one case but not the other a hospital order was an appropriate disposal. The cases appear therefore to stand in direct conflict. The Divisional Court in *Blouet* may have been unduly influenced by the decision in *Singh* where insanity[33] was the issue. In *Crown Prosecution Service v P*[34] (a hearing concerned with the correct procedure in the youth court), it was said that there may be advantages to having a fact-finding hearing even if it was unlikely that a hospital order would be imposed.[35]

[29]   [2009] EWHC 759 (Admin).

[30]   [2007] EWHC 1582 (Admin), [2007] 1 WLR 3119, where it was said at [35]:
> In all cases where an order under section 37(3) is a possibility, the court should first determine the fact-finding exercise. That may be concluded, as here, on admissions or it may involve hearing evidence. If the court is not satisfied that the act/omission was done /made, an unqualified acquittal must follow, whatever the anxieties may be about the accused's state of health …

> If it is clear that no section 37(3) order is going to be possible on the evidence whatever happens, then in the absence of some other compelling factor the case must proceed to trial.

[31]   [2009] EWHC 759 (Admin) at [9].

[32]   [2009] EWHC 836 (Admin).

[33]   It may be that insanity is more likely to mean that a hospital order is appropriate but this is really no more than general supposition.

[34]   [2007] EWHC 946 (Admin), [2008] 1 WLR 1005.

[35]   The conflicting cases referred to above were not cited in *CPS v P* (above). For a further discussion of this case, see paras 8.42 to 8.54 below.

8.29   In *R (Varma) v Redbridge Magistrates' Court*[36] the accused was committed to the Crown Court on unrelated charges[37] and thereafter found to be unfit to plead. This serves as a powerful illustration of the fact that as long as there is a distinction between the procedures in the two jurisdictions, there is also the unseemly possibility that the same accused may be found unfit in one jurisdiction and fit in another. This might also be perceived as sending out the unfortunate message that summary justice is less important than justice in the Crown Court.

8.30   The arguments against exposing an accused to trial when he or she is unable to effectively participate in a trial are set out in detail in Part 2 of this CP. These arguments apply regardless of whether the appropriate disposal in the circumstances of the particular case would be a hospital order. We can see no reason why they are any less compelling in the context of the summary jurisdiction. In our view, the question of whether an accused has the necessary decision-making capacity should be separate from the question of the appropriate disposal. However, the current procedure in the magistrates' court may mean that an accused who lacks decision-making capacity nonetheless faces a trial because it is thought that a hospital order is not an appropriate disposal.

ADVANTAGES AND DISADVANTAGES OF THE PRESENT SYSTEM

8.31   The advantage of the present system which allows for the obtaining of medical reports in the case of those accused whom it is thought are suffering from some mental or physical condition is that they can be dealt with quickly through the services of the duty psychiatrist who will check on the availability of appropriate hospital services.

8.32   If a two tier process such as exists under the 1964 Act were adopted, it may take considerably more time for matters to be resolved and there might be undesirable delay in securing treatment for those accused who need it.

8.33   A problem which results from the problems identified above is the possible unfairness in the magistrates' court for the accused with a potential lack of capacity. It is arguable that the accused does not have the same opportunity of being acquitted in a magistrates' court as he or she does in the Crown Court. If a legal representative acting for the accused at summary trial decided not to oppose the imposition of a hospital order under section 37(3) of the 1983 Act then the accused will receive treatment for his or her disorder. However, he or she may have been wrongly accused of an offence and unless that offence could be proved to the criminal standard, he or she is entitled to be acquitted. If the accused's solicitor takes the view that the accused could be acquitted on the facts, then he or she would be expected to opt for a trial in which only the conduct element will be in issue.[38] This would be with a view to testing the evidence in the course of a summary trial during which it would be possible to make a submission of no case to answer (if appropriate). This will depend on whether acquittal will be likely on the basis of a denial of the acts or a denial of the fault element or a claim

---

[36]   [2009] EWHC 836 (Admin).

[37]   Charges that are founded on the same facts or fall within specified categories can be committed or sent to the Crown Court at the same time as the charges which are triable either way under the provisions of ss 40 and 41 of the Criminal Justice Act 1988.

[38]   As indicated in s 11(1) of the 2000 Act.

of defence. So for example, if the case depends on the correctness of identification evidence then a trial is feasible but if it is a case involving duress it is likely that a representative will wish to avoid a hearing. This means that the outcome is arbitrary. In a case where a hospital order is the predicted outcome, there is a danger that the accused's legal representative may be willing to accept that disposal via the section 37(3) route, and by that decision, deny the accused the opportunity for an acquittal.

8.34 An initial procedure whereby unfitness to plead or lack of capacity can be determined as a preliminary issue in the magistrates' courts would offer clear benefits. Although it is possible to stay proceedings in the magistrates' courts[39] this is not something which is likely to happen at the outset. The authorities suggest that a stay will be countenanced when it is clear that a fair trial cannot take place. Case law on unfitness in the youth courts reveals that magistrates have the power to stay the proceedings (the trial) as an abuse of process if the defendant is incapable of effective participation in his or her trial. This might be a way of avoiding having to try an individual who is unfit but for whom a hospital order would be an inappropriate disposal. However, it generates its own problems. In our view, this approach would not be the most satisfactory way of dealing with the problem in adult cases in the magistrates' court. It is much less satisfactory than adopting a test of unfitness or decision-making capacity with appropriate procedures for resolution of the facts. It is less satisfactory because it depends on a purely discretionary and exceptional remedy, and because it does not lead to the appropriate disposal of the case in terms of providing treatment for the accused. In addition, a stay tends to be regarded as an exceptional course to remedy an unfairness which cannot be put right by the trial process. This highlights the need to remedy the trial process.

8.35 A stay is a final resort (once a trial has been embarked on and found to be problematic). Time will therefore have been expended on a trial before proceedings can be stayed.[40] Further, we are not aware of whether or not this solution has actually been adopted in the magistrates' courts. We suspect that it has not.

8.36 We are unaware of published material indicating whether practitioners believe that a test for determining unfitness to plead (or decision-making capacity as it would be under our provisionally proposed test for the Crown Court) is necessary in relation to cases which are triable summarily. The lack of authority on the point might be taken as an indication that the present system works quite well.

8.37 Accordingly, we do not at present think that it would be right to make any explicit proposals in relation to summary proceedings but in light of the criticisms which we have made in this Part, we ask consultees a range of questions which will inform our view on whether proposals are necessary and what form they might take.

---

[39] The possibility of a stay of the proceedings has emerged from the youth court cases which we consider below at para 8.38 and the following paragraphs.

[40] See para 8.47 below.

Question 8: Do consultees think that the capacity based test which we have proposed for trial on indictment should apply equally to proceedings which are triable summarily?

Question 9: Do consultees think that if an accused lacks decision-making capacity there should be a mandatory fact-finding procedure in the magistrates' court?

Question 10: If consultees think that there should be a mandatory fact-finding procedure, do they think it should be limited to consideration of the external elements of the offence or should it mirror our provisional proposals 8 and 9?

YOUTH COURTS

8.38 We turn now to examine the procedure in youth courts and, in doing so, address the fifth problem identified at paragraph 8.14 above: the lack of a *doli incapax*[41] defence and its relationship with developmental immaturity and decision-making capacity. Youth court cases raise issues which are different from cases involving adult defendants.[42] Problems caused by developmental immaturity or which are attributable to a lack of ready access to psychiatric diagnosis and help for children and young people[43] factor into the equation. Notwithstanding the above however, it seems that the youth courts do not suffer from all of the problems which are associated with the adult magistrates' courts.[44]

8.39 The reasons for any distinction in the approach between adults and young people involve difficult questions pertaining to matters such as developmental immaturity.

8.40 In *R (TP) v West London Youth Court*,[45] a 15-year-old who had the intellectual capacity of an 8-year-old (TP) was charged with robbery and attempted robbery. TP sought judicial review of the decision of the youth court not to stay the proceedings as an abuse of process. The Divisional Court in dismissing the application stated that the question for the court was whether the accused would be able effectively to participate in his trial in order to ensure that the trial did not breach article 6 of the European Convention on Human Rights. It upheld the minimum requirements of a fair trial as being the following:

---

[41] *Doli incapax* refers to the rebuttable presumption that a child aged fourteen or under is incapable of committing a criminal offence. This imposed an obligation on the prosecution to prove, in addition to the usual elements of the offence, the fact that the child knew that what he or she was doing was seriously wrong. Although the presumption was abolished by s 34 of the Crime and Disorder Act 1998, Smith LJ doubted, in part of the judgment that is non-binding, whether the defence itself was abolished. The House of Lords has however since said that it has been abolished: see *JTB* [2009] UKHL 20, [2009] 1 AC 1310. We address this issue in more detail at paras 8.55 to 8.57 below.

[42] At the very least, the issues are more acute than in the trial of adults.

[43] Referrals to psychiatrists have to be through the CAMHS system.

[44] See *R (TP) v West London Youth Court* [2005] EWHC 2583 (Admin), [2006] 1 WLR 1219 cited at para 8.51. The last of the essential requirements of a fair trial is an explicit acceptance of an unfitness to plead test in the youth courts.

[45] [2005] EWHC 2583 (Admin), [2006] 1 WLR 1219.

(a)   the accused had to understand what he or she is said to have done wrong;

(b)   the court had to be satisfied that the accused when he or she had done wrong by act or omission had the means of knowing that was wrong;

(c)   the accused had to understand what, if any defences were available to him or her;

(d)   the accused had to have a reasonable opportunity to make relevant representations if he or she wished; and

(e)   the accused had to have the opportunity to consider what representations he or she wished to make once he or she had understood the issues involved.[46]

8.41   In Part 2 of this CP, we looked at the development of the rules governing the availability of special measures and noted that these measures had largely been developed in relation to how children were dealt with in the Crown Court. We highlighted the importance of the decision of the European Court of Human Rights in *SC v UK*[47] where it was held that there had been a breach of article 6 despite the fact that special measures had been put in place for trial of a child in the Crown Court. *SC* was distinguished in *R (TP) v West London Youth Court* on the basis that in the latter case, the trial venue was the youth court. The decision in *SC* suggested that in order to ensure compatibility with article 6, children must be tried before a specialist tribunal, and the Divisional Court in the *West London* case made it clear that the youth court (where procedures could be adapted) was the appropriate venue for trial of children.[48] It was also made clear in this case that the test for capacity was one of effective participation.

8.42   In *Crown Prosecution Service v P*[49] (another youth court case) Lady Justice Smith addressed the question of when, if at all, in the context of unfitness to plead, proceedings should be stayed by the magistrates as an abuse of process. The case was an appeal by way of case stated against a decision of a District Judge sitting in the Bishop Auckland Youth Court in which he stayed, as an abuse of process, criminal proceedings brought against the respondent P.

8.43   At the age of seven, P had been diagnosed as having Attention Deficit Hyperactivity Disorder (ADHD) and was prescribed a stimulant medication. In 2002, aged 9, he was assessed as having special educational needs. In 2003, it was noted that his behaviour was not well controlled despite his medication. In 2004, he appeared before the youth court charged with a number of serious offences and was committed for trial at the Teesside Crown Court. Having been provided with a number of psychiatric and psychological reports (on the basis of

---

[46]   Above at [7].

[47]   (2004) 40 EHRR 10 (App No 60958/00), discussed in detail in Part 2 above.

[48]   Except in circumstances where the charge and the facts of the case required that it be committed or sent to the Crown Court.

[49]   [2007] EWHC 946 (Admin), [2008] 1 WLR 1005.

which the prosecution accepted that P was unfit to plead) the judge decided to stay the proceedings.[50]

8.44 In April 2006, P appeared before the Bishop Auckland Youth Court where the District Judge was provided with the same expert evidence which had been provided to the Crown Court. He was also provided with an up to date psychological report from the consultant adolescent psychologist who had reported at the earlier proceedings. This report made it clear that P had a conduct disorder as well as ADHD. Further:

> [P] would not be capable of understanding the nature of court proceedings. He would not be able to concentrate on the evidence and argument in a court room. His memory capacity was so impaired that he would not remember what had gone before. He would not understand much of what was going on during the proceedings.[51]

8.45 It was contended that P did not have a sufficient level of maturity or intellectual capacity to participate effectively in the proceedings. The experts opined that P had been correctly diagnosed as having ADHD and, in addition, had a full scale IQ level of 65 which went to place him in the lowest centile of the population. At the age of eleven he had a mental age of seven. All the experts agreed that P did not have the capacity to participate effectively in a criminal trial. Importantly, one psychiatrist took the view that P was so "disengaged from any process from which he could learn effectively or accept advice" that he would be unable to cope with or follow the proceedings. She added to her report a section on the subject of disposal which would be relevant in the event that the court went on to find that P had committed the external elements of the offence. In effect, she opined that his mental health difficulties did not warrant the making of an order under the 1983 Act (but rather recommended that a "multi-agency package should be put together").[52]

8.46 The prosecution submitted that the correct procedure to be followed by the youth court, in circumstances where the defendant's unfitness to plead or capacity to understand the proceedings was raised, was provided for in section 37(3) of the 1983 Act read together with section 11(2) of the 2000 Act. In other words, if the court was of the view that P should not face trial because of his disability then it should proceed to consider whether or not P had done the acts alleged. If satisfied that he had, the court should then consider the medical evidence and all the circumstances of the case before deciding whether a hospital order could be made under the 1983 Act.[53] As already indicated, a hospital order was not thought to be appropriate.

8.47 The District Judge stayed the proceedings and one of the questions for the Divisional Court was:

---

[50] It is not clear why the procedure provided for by the 1964 Act as amended was not followed.

[51] *Crown Prosecution Service v P* [2007] EWHC 946 (Admin), [2008] 1 WLR 1005 at [10].

[52] Above at [8]. As was pointed out by Smith LJ, it is not clear under what provision such an order could be made.

[53] Above at [13].

Whether [the District Judge] erred in concluding on the evidence that the defendant did not have the mental capacity to effectively participate in the proceedings and accordingly stayed the proceedings on that basis?[54]

8.48 Lady Justice Smith acknowledged the apparent deficiency in the procedures provided for by the 1983 Act and the 2000 Act in so far as the youth court is concerned.

> It seems to me that, although the provisions of section 11(1) [of the 2000 Act] and section 37(3) [of the 1983 Act] may provide a complete statutory framework for the determination of "all the issues that arise in cases of defendants who are or may be mentally ill or suffering from severe mental impairment", they do not provide the solution to all the problems which may confront a youth court before which a young person of doubtful capacity appears.[55]

8.49 She suggested that there were a number of overlapping capacity issues in cases involving young people. First there was the test for fitness to plead, secondly, the ability to take part in the trial and thirdly, (possibly) the issue of *doli incapax*.[56]

> The test for deciding upon fitness to plead bears some resemblance to the criteria set out in *SC* ... as those relevant to the question of whether a defendant is capable of effective participation in the trial. The criteria are also similar, although not identical, to those set out in the *West London* case ... relating to the essential elements of a fair trial. It should be noted however, that one of the listed requirements of a fair trial is that the defendant should know that what he is alleged to have done is wrong, which is in effect the test for *doli incapax*. Thus it appears to me that there is a large measure of overlap between the issues of "sufficient understanding of right from wrong", "fitness to plead", "ability to participate effectively in a trial" and the "fairness of the trial".[57]

8.50 She went on to say that it was "unfortunate that there is no statutory procedure laid down by which the youth court should approach these overlapping capacity issues".[58] She set out what, in the absence of such procedure, she thought the youth court should do. First, she noted that, although the jurisdiction to stay proceedings exists in cases where an accused's fitness or capacity[59] is in issue, this solution should only be exercised before any evidence is heard in exceptional circumstances. This is because medical evidence "will rarely provide the whole

---

[54] *Crown Prosecution Service v P* [2007] EWHC 946 (Admin), [2008] 1 WLR 1005 at [23].

[55] Above at [16].

[56] See paras 8.59 to 8.65 below.

[57] Above at [48]. She observed that a child who, because of immaturity or a lack of understanding, did not know right from wrong may well also be unable to participate effectively in a trial.

[58] Above at [50].

[59] In the broad sense.

answer to whether the child ought to be tried for a criminal offence".[60] Her Ladyship offered examples of other matters relevant to the decision such as evidence of the way in which the child reacted to arrest and interview. She also indicated that the child's understanding should be assessed in a stage-by-stage way, which may involve direct exchanges between the child and the bench. Medical evidence therefore needs to be considered in the context of the evidence as a whole "and not as the sole evidence on a free standing application".[61]

8.51   Secondly, as was noted in *R (TP) v West London Youth Court*,[62] the court has a duty to keep under continuing review whether the criminal trial ought to continue.[63] If the court concludes at any stage that "the child is unable to participate effectively, it may decide to call it to a halt".[64] The court may however consider that it is in the child's interests to allow the trial to continue. Further, if the prosecution case is weak there may be no case to answer. The defendant's representative may decide (on the basis of what Lady Justice Smith had said in her judgment about the availability of *doli incapax*) to invite the court to acquit on the basis that the child did not know that what he or she had done was seriously wrong.

8.52   Thirdly, if the court decides that the criminal proceedings should cease on the basis that the child cannot effectively participate in the proceedings, it should then consider whether to switch to a fact-finding hearing and consider whether the child has done the act of which he or she is accused.[65]

8.53   In relation to this aspect of the procedure, Lady Justice Smith stated that, whereas the possibility of making a hospital order was the main advantage of switching to a fact-finding process, there may be other advantages to continuing to complete the fact-finding process. If the child had done the act, it may be appropriate to alert the local authority to the fact with a view to consideration of care proceedings.[66]

8.54   Finally, Lady Justice Smith accepted that if it is clear before any evidence is called that the defendant will not be able to participate effectively in a trial, in these circumstances it would be right to stay the proceedings.[67]

Abolition of the defence of *doli incapax*

8.55   Since Lady Justice Smith gave her judgment in *Crown Prosecution Service v P* it has been held by the House of Lords in *JTB*[68] that section 34 of the Crime and

---

[60]   *Crown Prosecution Service v P* [2007] EWHC 946 at [10] (Admin), [2008] 1 WLR 1005 at [51] and [52].

[61]   Above at [53].

[62]   [2005] EWHC 2583 (Admin), [2006] 1 WLR 1219.

[63]   *Crown Prosecution Service v P* [2007] EWHC 946 (Admin), [2008] 1 WLR 1005 at [54].

[64]   Above.

[65]   Above at [55].

[66]   Above at [56].

[67]   See our observation at para 8.34 on whether it is appropriate to extend this procedure to adults.

[68]   [2009] UKHL 20, [2009] 1 AC 1310.

Disorder Act 1998 abolished the defence (and not just the rebuttable presumption) of *doli incapax* in the case of a child between the ages of 10 and 14 years.[69]

8.56 The developmental status of juveniles may well justify the distinctive approach which was analysed in *Crown Prosecution Service v P* and which could be encapsulated in a reappraisal of the age of criminal liability. Although the age of criminal responsibility is a discrete area it could, as Lady Justice Smith observed, come into play in questions of capacity.[70]

8.57 This decision raises some questions in the light of developing research on developmental maturity in children and adolescents which is possibly relevant to the issue of decision-making capacity generally. In particular, there may be sound policy reasons for looking afresh at the age of criminal responsibility.[71] Commentators have observed a "net widening" in terms of the way in which children and young people are dealt with in the criminal justice system which is said to be attributable to a "shift in the transfer of the locus of decision-making from the police station (in the form of both informal warnings and formal cautioning) to the youth court in a substantial proportion of cases."[72] Clearly this is something which lies outside the scope of this CP. However we intend to look briefly at some aspects of the research into the age of criminal responsibility in so far as that research has any bearing on the question of the likely capacity of a child or a young person to participate effectively in a criminal trial.

The age of criminal responsibility

8.58 It might be argued by some that any reform of the law in relation to the capacity of children and young people to stand trial is best approached in the context of a review of the age of criminal responsibility. It seems to us that the issue of criminal responsibility can be readily divided into three areas. First, there is the irrebuttable presumption that a child under the age of 10 cannot be criminally liable. Secondly, there is the area of *doli incapax* which as we have indicated at paragraph 8.57 is intrinsically linked to the question of developmental immaturity and thirdly, there is the question of how this factors in to the issue of decision-making capacity. Only the third of these areas is directly relevant to this project but it will assist to place it in context.

---

[69] Crime and Disorder Act 1998, s 34 provides:

> Abolition of rebuttable presumption that a child is doli incapax
>
> The rebuttable presumption of criminal law that a child aged 10 or over is incapable of committing an offence is hereby abolished.

[70] See paras 8.58 onwards below.

[71] See H Keating, "Reckless Children?" [2007] *Criminal Law Review* 546, 549 where referring to the judgment of Mr Justice (now Lord Justice) Laws in *C (A Minor) v DPP* and the Home Office CP *Tackling Youth Crime* (1997) (which preceded s 34 Crime and Disorder Act 1998) both of which relied on arguments put forward by Glanville Williams, it is said:

> It is deeply unfortunate that arguments designed to ensure that young offenders could receive treatment (in a more welfare oriented era) have been influential, almost 50 years later, in developing a strongly punitive approach.

[72] M Telford, "Youth Justice : new shoots on a bleak landscape - *Director of Public Prosecutions v P*" [2007] *Child and Family Law Quarterly* 505, 507.

8.59   The irrebuttable presumption that a child under the age of 10 cannot be criminally liable is not founded on any logical or principled basis. The cut-off point of 10 years is arbitrary. At 10, the age of criminal responsibility in England and Wales falls well below that in France, Germany and Spain where it is 13, 14 and 16 respectively. In October 2008 the UN Committee on the Rights of the Child specifically criticised the low age of criminal responsibility in Scotland and England and Wales.[73] In addition to the requirements set by the United Nations Convention on the Rights of the Child,[74] rule 4.1 of the Beijing rules provides:

> In those legal systems recognising the concept of the age of criminal responsibility for juveniles, the beginning of that age shall not be fixed at too low an age level bearing in mind the facts of emotional, mental and intellectual maturity.[75]

8.60   The results of the (US) MacArthur Juvenile Competence Study found that "compared to adults, a significantly greater proportion of juveniles in the community who are fifteen and younger, and an even larger proportion of juvenile offenders this age are probably not competent to stand trial in a criminal proceeding."[76]

8.61   There have been expressions of public concern over the question of the low age of criminal responsibility in England and Wales and particularly in the light of one recent high profile trial.[77]

8.62   The European Convention on Human Rights and the Children Act 1989 refer to children and young people as children until the age of 18. Experts have claimed that this definition of a "child" is indicative of an assumption of developmental immaturity which will persist until the age of 18 and that because it is not reflected in criminal procedure, a child defendant's human rights are not protected accordingly.[78]

---

[73]   http://www2.ohchr.org/English/bodies/crc/docs/AdvanceVersions/CRC.C.GBR.CO.4.pdf at para 77(a) (last accessed 19 August 2010), cited by Professor Andrew Ashworth in his commentary on T [2009] UKHL 20, [2009] 1 AC 1310 in [2009] Criminal Law Review 581. Section 52 of the Criminal Justice and Licensing (Scotland) Act 2010 when it comes into force will raise the age of criminal responsibility in Scotland to 12.

[74]   Article 40.1 was cited by Lord Steyn in G [2003] UKHL 50, [2004] 1 AC 1034 at [53]. Article 40(3)(a) requires that each signatory state establish a minimum age below which children shall be presumed not to have capacity to infringe the criminal law.

[75]   Cited in M Ashford, A Chard and N Redhouse, Defending Young People in the Criminal Justice System (3rd ed 2006) at para 6.5.

[76]   MacArthur Foundation Juvenile Competence Study: Summary at p 3.

[77]   In the light of the child rape case (two 10-year-old boys convicted of the attempted rape of an 8-year-old girl at the Central Criminal Court in 2010) the former Director of Public Prosecutions Sir (now Lord) Ken MacDonald said: "We are making demons of our children ... very young children do not belong in adult criminal courts. They rarely belong in criminal courts at all". See F Bennion, "The Legal Age of Discretion" (2010) 174 Criminal Law and Justice Weekly 357, 358. On the issue of the age of criminal responsibility generally, see also "Child Defendants" Occasional Paper 56 (March 2006) Royal College of Psychiatrists London Executive Summary p 7.

[78]   See "Child Defendants" Occasional Paper 56 (March 2006) Royal College of Psychiatrists London Executive Summary p 7.

8.63   In our work on murder we recommended that in relation to diminished responsibility there should be a separate defence of developmental immaturity for persons under the age of 18.[79] This was not adopted by the Government however.[80] The fact that it did not receive Government support in the context of murder suggests that without more, it is unlikely to receive support in the more general context of other offences. It did however receive support from other quarters. For example, Lord Phillips has said:

> The Government has not accepted this argument for two reasons. The first is that they do not believe that the absence of such a provision is causing serious problems in practice. The second is, I quote: "[W]e think that there is a risk that such a provision would open up the defence too widely and catch inappropriate cases. Even if it were to succeed only rarely (as the Law Commission suggest), we think it likely that far more defendants would at least try to run it, so diverting attention in too many trials from the key issue." I believe that there is something of a paradox in this reasoning. At present natural developmental immaturity in a child who has reached the age of 10 does not constitute a defence. That may be why developmental immaturity is not causing problems in practice. But it is surely offensive to justice that a child whose brain has not yet developed to the extent necessary to provide the self-control that is found in an adult should be unable to pray this fact in aid, at least as a partial defence. Children develop at different speeds. If (and it may be a big if) some are sufficiently mature at the age of 10 to have full criminal responsibility, those who are not should, I feel be entitled to pray this in aid.[81]

8.64   The importance of developmental immaturity cannot be ignored. In addition to the point made about the research referred to in paragraph 8.66 below, one of the most obvious reasons for issues of developmental psychology to inform criminal justice policy making is that it is arguable that, infancy apart, "there is probably no period of human development characterised by more rapid or pervasive transformation in individual competencies" than adolescence.[82] Further, it is a period of malleability during "which experience in the family, peer group, school and other settings have a great deal of influence over the course of development".[83] It is a unique time of intellectual, emotional and social development.

8.65   This CP is, of course, focused on the specific question of capacity to be tried. We acknowledge that the issue of the age of criminal responsibility touches on the

[79]   Murder, Manslaughter and Infanticide (2006) Law Com No 304 at 5.125:
> It should be possible to bring in a verdict of diminished responsibility on the grounds of developmental immaturity of an offender who was under 18 at the time he or she played his or her part in the killing.

[80]   It was not included in the Coroners and Justice Act 2009.

[81]   Lord Phillips, Essex University/Clifford Chance lecture on Reforming the Law of Homicide delivered on 6th November 2008, at p 14.

[82]   L Steinberg and R G Schwartz, "Developmental Psychology Goes to Court" in T Grisso and R G Schwartz (eds) Youth on Trial (2000) p 23.

[83]   Above, p 23.

subject of this CP because "the multiple transitions and influences that converge are likely to influence the capacities of adolescents to make decisions".[84] Therefore if the emphasis is to be on decision-making capacity with the aim of increasing participation, then the issue of developmental maturity cannot be disregarded entirely.

8.66 It has been suggested that offending youths have much higher rates of mental disorders (which will affect decision-making abilities) than do adolescents generally.[85] Research has suggested that various disorders in adolescents (such as conduct disorders, ADHD, learning disability, psychoses and autism) can have variable effects on decision-making depending on when the disorder emerges. Significantly, "changes in disorders over the course of childhood and adolescence are not well charted".[86] It has been suggested that empirical research is needed to further understand the decision-making capacity of offending youths as, in addition to affecting decision-making capacity itself, the presence of mental disorder can indicate other factors which may go to influence decision-making capacity.

Conclusion

8.67 If our provisional proposals for a decision-making capacity test[87] are adopted then in so far as trials on indictment[88] are concerned, it may be that juveniles who are presently found to be fit to plead are in future found to lack decision-making capacity.

8.68 In addition to the questions which we have asked in relation to the magistrates' courts, we consider that an additional question is raised by the way in which the legislation has been interpreted in youth court proceedings. That is whether there is a justification for the court to have a *discretion* to switch to fact-finding hearing or whether that process should be mandatory. In the Crown Court, the fact-finding process under section 4A of the 1964 Act is mandatory following a finding that the accused is unfit to plead. It is on the basis of the inadequacy of the

---

[84] AE Kazdin, "Adolescent Development, Mental Disorders and Decision Making of Delinquent Youths" in T Grisso and R G Schwartz (eds) *Youth on Trial* (2000) p 33.

[85] Above, p 34.

[86] Above, p 41.

[87] Which we discussed in Part 3 of this CP.

[88] Very serious matters can be committed from the youth court for trial on indictment: see s 24(1) of the Magistrates' Courts Act 1980 which provides that persons under the age of 18 years charged with indictable offences shall be tried summarily unless the offence is one which comes within the provisions of s 91 of the Powers of Criminal Courts (Sentencing) Act 2000, that is to say one for which a young person sentenced on indictment could be sentenced to be detained for a long period or he or she is charged jointly with a person over the age of 18 and it is thought to be in the interests of justice to commit them both for trial.

legislation applying in the magistrates' courts that Lady Justice Smith in *Crown Prosecution Service v P* inferred that the court had a discretion to switch to a fact-finding hearing.[89] As we have seen in Part 2, the accused who is found unfit to plead in the Crown Court is protected from conviction; there can only be a finding that he or she did the act.[90] It seems to us that the arguments which we cited in relation to the same process being desirable in adult magistrates' courts[91] apply equally (if not more so) to youth courts. The discretionary nature of the imposition of a fact-finding process in the youth court means that at the moment, a child is not necessarily guaranteed the same protection as an adult.

> **Question 11: Do the matters raised in questions 8, 9 and 10 merit equal consideration in relation to the procedure in the youth courts?**

8.69 For the purpose of this CP (project on unfitness to plead), we also wish to ask consultees the following question:

> **Question 12: How far if at all, does the age of criminal responsibility factor into the issue of decision-making capacity in youth trials?**

---

[89] [2007] EWHC 946 (Admin), [2008] 1 WLR 1005 at [56]. See also *C v Sevenoaks Youth Court* [2009] EWHC 3088, [2010] 1 All ER 735 at [30] where it was implied that the switch to a fact-finding hearing is optional as opposed to being mandatory:

> The CPS and the court are under a continuing duty to review whether "C" was and remains fit effectively to participate in the trial and if it were to become clear that he was not then the procedure *could* change to an enquiry under section 37(3)of the Mental Health Act 1983 read together with section 11(2) of the Powers of Criminal Courts (Sentencing) Act 2000, as to whether he had done the acts alleged. All these are perfectly proper reasons for deciding to proceed with the charge (our emphasis).

[90] See para 2.26 above.

[91] See paras 8.14 to 8.37 above.

PART 9
LIST OF PROVISIONAL PROPOSALS AND QUESTIONS

PROVISIONAL PROPOSALS

9.1 We provisionally propose that:

(1) The current *Pritchard* test should be replaced and there should be a new legal test which assesses whether the accused has decision-making capacity for trial. This test should take into account all the requirements for meaningful participation in the criminal proceedings.

[Paragraph 3.41]

(2) A new decision-making capacity test should not require that any decision the accused makes must be rational or wise.

[Paragraph 3.57]

(3) The legal test should be a revised single test which assesses the decision-making capacity of the accused by reference to the entire spectrum of trial decisions he or she might be required to make. Under this test an accused would be found to have or to lack decision-making capacity for the criminal proceedings.

[Paragraph 3.99]

(4) In determining the defendant's decision-making capacity, it would be incumbent on the judge to take account of the complexity of the particular proceedings and gravity of the outcome. In particular the judge should take account of how important any disability is likely to be in the context of the decision the accused must make in the context of the trial which the accused faces.

[Paragraph 3.101]

(5) Decision-making capacity should be assessed with a view to ascertaining whether an accused could undergo a trial or plead guilty with the assistance of special measures and where any other reasonable adjustments have been made.

[Paragraph 4.27]

(6) Where a defendant who is subject to a trial has a mental disorder or other impairment and wishes to give evidence then expert evidence on the general effect of that mental disorder or impairment should be admissible.

[Paragraph 4.31]

(7) A defined psychiatric test to assess decision-making capacity should be developed and this should accompany the legal test as to decision-making capacity.

[Paragraph 5.17]

(8) The present section 4A hearing should be replaced with a procedure whereby the prosecution is obliged to prove that the accused did the act or made the omission charged and that there are no grounds for an acquittal.

[Paragraph 6.140]

(9) If the accused is acquitted provision should be made for a judge to hold a further hearing to determine whether or not the acquittal is because of mental disorder existing at the time of the offence.

[Paragraph 6.140]

(10) The further hearing should be held at the discretion of the judge on the application of any party or the representative of any party to the proceedings.

[Paragraph 6.152]

(11) The special verdict should be determined by the jury on such evidence as has been heard or on any further evidence as is called.

[Paragraph 6.152]

(12) Where the Secretary of State has referred a case back to court pursuant to the accused being detained under a hospital order with a section 41 restriction order and it thereafter becomes clear beyond doubt (and medical evidence confirms) that the accused is still unfit to plead, the court should be able to reverse the decision to remit the case.

[Paragraph 7.21]

(13) In the event of a referral back to court by the Secretary of State and where the accused is found to be unfit to plead, there should not be any need to have a further hearing on the issue of whether the accused did the act. This is subject to the proviso that the court considers it to be in the interests of justice.

[Paragraph 7.21]

(14) In circumstances where a finding under section 4A is quashed and there has been no challenge to a finding in relation to section 4 (that the accused is under a disability) there should be a power for the Court of Appeal in appropriate circumstances to order a re-hearing under section 4A.

[Paragraph 7.59]

QUESTIONS

9.2 In addition to the above proposals, we also ask the following questions:

(1) Do consultees agree that we should aim to construct a scheme which allows courts to operate a continuum whereby those accused who do not have decision-making capacity will be subject to the section 4A hearing and those defendants with decision-making capacity should be subject to a trial with or without special measures depending on the level of assistance which they need?

[Paragraph 4.27]

(2) Can consultees think of other changes to evidence or procedure which would render participation in the trial process more effective for defendants who have decision-making capacity but due to a mental disorder or other impairment require additional assistance to participate?

[Paragraph 4.31]

(3) Do consultees agree that we have correctly identified the options for reform in relation to the section 4A hearing? If not, what other options for reform would consultees propose?

[Paragraph 6.153]

(4) If consultees do not agree that option 5 is the best option for reform, would they agree with any other option?

[Paragraph 6.153]

(5) Should a jury be able to find that an unfit accused has done the act and that there are no grounds for acquittal in relation to an act other than that specifically charged?

[Paragraph 6.159]

(6) Are there circumstances in which an accused person who is found to have done the act and in respect of whom there are no grounds for an acquittal should be able to request remission for trial?

[Paragraph 7.26]

(7) Should an accused who is found to be unfit to plead (or to lack decision-making capacity) be subject to the section 4A hearing in the same proceedings as co-defendants who are being tried?

[Paragraph 7.44]

(8) Do consultees think that the capacity based test which we have proposed for trial on indictment should apply equally to proceedings which are triable summarily?

[Paragraph 8.37]

(9)   Do consultees think that if an accused lacks decision-making capacity there should be a mandatory fact-finding procedure in the magistrates' court?

[Paragraph 8.37]

(10)   If consultees think that there should be a mandatory fact-finding procedure, do they think it should be limited to consideration of the external elements of the offence or should it mirror our provisional proposals 8 and 9?

[Paragraph 8.37]

(11)   Do the matters raised in questions 8, 9 and 10 merit equal consideration in relation to the procedure in the youth courts?

[Paragraph 8.68]

(12)   How far if at all, does the age of criminal responsibility factor into the issue of decision-making capacity in youth trials?

[Paragraph 8.69]

APPENDIX A
MENTAL HEALTH LEGISATION

INTRODUCTION

A.1 The Mental Health Act 1983 ("the 1983 Act") is an Act which contains the law relating to the detention and treatment of mentally disordered persons. It establishes a framework for the legal detention of persons with mental disorders in hospital for assessment and/or treatment, which may be without a person's consent if necessary. In some circumstances it also allows patients to be treated in the community under varying degrees of coercion. There is some overlap between the 1983 Act and the Mental Capacity Act 2005, in that those individuals who require treatment for mental disorder but who lack the capacity to make decisions about that treatment could be covered by either statute. However, as Professor Richardson has highlighted:

> The two statutes are designed for very different jobs. The Mental Health Act 1983 is primarily concerned with the reduction of the risks flowing from mental disorder, both to the patient and to others. While the Mental Capacity Act 2005 is designed to "empower people to make decisions for themselves wherever possible, and to protect people who lack capacity", it is governed by principles which ensure that decisions reflect the individual's best interests and that the least restrictive intervention is used.[1]

A.2 There are three main routes through which a person can be detained in hospital under the 1983 Act:

(1) civil admission, where the decision to detain is taken by mental health professionals or the police;

(2) admission to hospital from the courts, either when he or she is on remand or following his or her conviction; and

(3) transfer from prison to hospital.

A.3 The Mental Health Act 2007 ("the 2007 Act") amended the 1983 Act, primarily in relation to the provisions dealing with civil admission. However certain amendments affect the detention in hospital of mentally disordered offenders.[2] Most importantly, the 2007 Act changed the definition of "mental disorder" and replaced the "treatability" test with a new "appropriate medical treatment" test as a criterion for the use of longer-term powers of detention under the 1983 Act.

---

[1] G Richardson, "Mental capacity at the margin: the interface between two Acts" (2010) 18 *Medical Law Review* 56, 57; citing the foreword to the Mental Capacity Act 2005 Code of Practice.

[2] Most of these amendments came into force on 3 November 2008.

Article 5 of the European Convention on Human Rights

A.4   The detention of a person because of his or her mental disorder must be compatible with article 5 of the European Convention on Human Rights. Article 5(1) provides that no one shall be deprived of his or her liberty, unless one of the limited exceptions applies which includes the lawful detention of "persons of unsound mind".[3]

A.5   In determining whether the detention of a person of unsound mind is compatible with article 5(1), the European Court of Human Rights relies on what it refers to as the "*Winterwerp* criteria".[4] These were described in *Kolanis v United Kingdom*[5] as follows:

- there must be reliable objective medical expertise showing the patient to be suffering from a mental disorder;

- the disorder must be of a "kind or degree" warranting compulsory confinement; and

- the validity of any continued detention depends upon the persistence of a true mental disorder of a kind or degree warranting compulsory detention, established upon objective medical expertise.[6]

A.6   The court's jurisprudence on article 5(1)(e) suggests that national law will be compatible with the Convention as long as it requires some objective medical evidence which establishes that the person is suffering from a mental disorder warranting compulsory detention.

THE DEFINITION OF MENTAL DISORDER

A.7   In order for the provisions of the 1983 Act to apply, a person must be shown to be suffering from a mental disorder. The definition of mental disorder therefore acts as the gateway to the powers available under the Act.

A.8   Section 1(2) of the 1983 Act originally provided for four categories of mental disorder: "mental illness", "severe mental impairment", "mental impairment" and "psychopathic disorder". Depending on the category of mental disorder that a person suffered from, different criteria for detention and treatment could apply.[7]

---

[3]   Article 5(1)(e).

[4]   The requirements of article 5 were considered in *Winterwerp v Netherlands* (1979) 2 EHRR 387 (App No 6301/73).

[5]   (2006) 42 EHRR 12 (App No 517/02).

[6]   Above at [67].

[7]   For example, where an offender was suffering from a psychopathic disorder or mental impairment, s 37 of the 1983 Act provided for an additional criterion that medical treatment had to be "likely to alleviate or prevent a deterioration" of the offender's condition. This was referred to as the "treatability" test: see paras A.19 to A.27 below.

A.9   Section 1 of the 2007 Act replaced the four categories in section 1(2) of the 1983 Act with a single definition of mental disorder as "any disorder or disability of the mind". This change was justified by the then Government on the basis that it would ensure that the patient's "needs and risks" determine when the powers under the 1983 Act are used, and that it would make it "easier for clinicians to use and for others to understand".[8]

A.10   In effect, the 2007 Act broadened the definition of mental disorder for the purpose of longer-term detention powers. For example, the 1983 Act could now cover forms of personality disorder which would not legally be considered as "'mental illness' and which do not fall within the [previous] definition of psychopathic disorder because they do not result in abnormally aggressive or seriously irresponsible conduct."[9]

Compatibility with article 5

A.11   This broader definition of mental disorder must however be compatible with the interpretation given by the European Court of Human Rights to the phrase "persons of unsound mind" in article 5(1)(e).

A.12   In *Winterwerp v Netherlands*[10] the court stated that the term "persons of unsound mind" could not be given a definitive interpretation:

> It is a term whose meaning is constantly evolving as research in psychiatry progresses, an increasing flexibility in treatment is developing and society's attitude to mental illness changes, in particular so that a greater understanding of the problems of mental patients is becoming wide-spread.[11]

A.13   The court went on to emphasise, however, that article 5(1)(e) does not permit "the detention of a person simply because his views or behaviour deviate from the norms prevailing in a particular society".[12] The purpose of article 5(1) is to "ensure that no one should be dispossessed of his liberty in an arbitrary fashion", and therefore the exceptions listed in article 5(1) should be interpreted narrowly.[13]

---

[8] *Hansard* (HL), 28 November 2006, vol 687, col 657.

[9] Explanatory notes to the 2007 Act, para 19.

[10] (1979) 2 EHRR 387 (App No 6301/73).

[11] Above at [37].

[12] Above.

[13] Above.

Learning disabilities

A.14 People with a learning disability have always been included within the definition of a mental disorder under the 1983 Act mainly, but not exclusively, under the categories of "mental impairment" or "severe mental impairment". But for certain provisions of the 1983 Act, a person with a "mental impairment" could only be detained if the impairment was associated with "abnormally aggressive or seriously irresponsible conduct".[14] This requirement did not, however, apply to "severe mental impairments".

A.15 The amendments introduced by the 2007 Act have preserved this general effect, despite the removal of the categories of mental disorder. Thus, people with learning disabilities[15] continue to fall within the scope of the 1983 Act. However, section 2 of the 2007 Act inserts a new subsection (2A) into section 1 of the 1983 Act. This provides that, for certain provisions of the 1983 Act,[16] a person with a learning disability shall not be considered by reason of that disability to be suffering from a mental disorder "unless that disability is associated with abnormally aggressive or seriously irresponsible conduct".

The exclusions from the definition of mental disorder

A.16 The 1983 Act originally provided that a person could not be considered as having a mental disorder "by reason only of promiscuity or other immoral conduct, sexual deviancy or dependence on alcohol or drugs".[17]

A.17 Section 3 of the 2007 Act amends these exclusions so that it is now only "dependence on alcohol or drugs" which is not considered to be a disorder or disability of the mind for the purpose of the 1983 Act. This may be seen as an odd exclusion on the basis that alcohol and drug dependency are recognised as treatable mental conditions.[18] However, the exclusion does not prevent a person being categorised as mentally disordered if, in addition to their dependency on alcohol or drugs, he or she is suffering from an unrelated mental disorder, or a mental disorder which arises from dependency on alcohol or drugs or withdrawal from alcohol or drugs.[19]

---

[14] Civil admission under s 3, remand for reports or treatment (ss 35 and 36); hospital orders and interim hospital orders (ss 37 and 38); hospital and limitation directions (s 45A); and transfer directions (ss 47 and 48).

[15] Learning disability is defined as a "state of arrested or incomplete development of the brain which includes significant impairment of intelligence and social functioning": see s 1(4) of the 1983 Act, as inserted by s 2(1), (3) of the 2007 Act.

[16] Subsection (2A) applies in relation to civil admission under s 3. It also applies in relation to provisions concerning mentally disordered offenders: remand for reports or treatment (ss 35 and 36); hospital orders and interim hospital orders (ss 37 and 38); hospital and limitation directions (s 45A); transfer directions (ss 47 and 48).

[17] Section 1(3).

[18] R Jones, *Mental Health Act Manual* (12th ed 2009) at para 1-026.

[19] Above. See also the Mental Health Act 1983 Code of Practice (revised 2008) at para 3.10; explanatory notes to the 2007 Act at paras 25 to 27.

A.18   As for the removal of the "promiscuity or other immoral conduct" and "sexual deviancy" exclusions, this may make little difference in practice in terms of the scope of the 1983 Act, as none of these things are in themselves regarded as mental disorders. However, some disorders of sexual preference (such as paedophilia) are clinically recognised as mental disorders and therefore may now come within the 1983 Act.[20] Concern has been expressed that the removal of the sexual deviancy exclusion could inappropriately bring all sexual preferences and behaviours classified as psychiatric disorders within the scope of compulsory powers.[21]

THE "TREATABILITY" TEST

A.19   Under the 1983 Act as originally enacted (both in relation to civil detention for treatment under section 3 and hospital orders made by the court under section 37), a person could only be detained in hospital for treatment if his or her mental disorder was of a nature or degree[22] which made it appropriate for him or her to receive medical treatment in hospital and it was necessary for the health and safety of the patient or for the protection of others that he or she should receive such treatment and it could not be provided unless they were detained under this section. This applied in relation to all four categories of mental disorder.

A.20   However, for persons suffering from psychopathic disorder or mental impairment, the treatability test applied so that, in order for the longer-term powers of detention to be used, medical treatment had to be "likely to alleviate or prevent a deterioration of [the patient's] condition".[23]

A.21   The 2007 Act removed as a criterion for the use of longer-term powers of detention under the 1983 Act the requirement that medical treatment must be "likely to alleviate or prevent a deterioration of [the patient's] condition", known as the "treatability" test. Instead, it must now be shown that "appropriate medical treatment" is available, where the purpose of such treatment is to "alleviate, or prevent a worsening of, the disorder or one or more of its symptoms or manifestations".[24]

---

[20]   Explanatory notes to the 2007 Act, para 24.

[21]   See Joint Committee on Human Rights, Legislative Scrutiny: Mental Health Bill, Fourth Report of Session 2006-07, HL Paper 40, HC 288 referring to concerns expressed by JUSTICE: pp 8 to 9.

[22]   "Nature" refers to the diagnosis of the patient's particular mental disorder. "Degree" refers to the patient's current symptoms.

[23]   Section 3(2)(b) of the 1983 Act as originally enacted.

[24]   Section 145(4) of the 1983 Act, which sets out the definition of "medical treatment" for the purposes of the Act.

A.22   Section 4 of the 2007 Act replaced the treatability test with the requirement that "appropriate medical treatment" must be available for the patient. Given that the four categories of mental disorder have been abolished, the new test now applies to every person with a mental disorder dealt with under section 3 or the other relevant provisions of the 1983 Act. Medical treatment must actually be available for the patient, and it must be both clinically appropriate and more generally appropriate given all the circumstances of the case.[25]

A.23   The removal of the treatability test was highly contested in the policy process leading to the 2007 Act. On the one hand, there was concern that the test was used to avoid treatment of some patients by labelling their type of disorder "untreatable". This could be both detrimental to patients and "sometimes dangerous to the public".[26] The removal of the treatability test could bring, for example, psychopaths more clearly within the scope of the 1983 Act.

A.24   On the other hand, the treatability test meant that the longer-term powers of detention could not be used unless a patient was likely to receive some medical benefit, and the removal of this constraint was of particular concern given the broader definition of mental disorder following the 2007 Act. Those who opposed the removal of the treatability test were largely concerned that the new appropriate medical treatment test could mean that a person could be detained simply for preventative purposes without any medical benefit. However, the main reason given for abolishing the old treatability test is that case law had rendered it so broad as to be almost meaningless. Similar claims have been made of the appropriate treatment test.[27]

A.25   Arguably, protections are available under the new test. A doctor could be said to act unethically if he or she admitted a patient to hospital knowing that the patient would receive no therapeutic benefit from treatment.[28] There has however been concern that the new test could allow issues of public protection to override any possible therapeutic benefit to the accused.[29]

---

[25] Mental Health Act 1983 Code of Practice (revised 2008), paras 6.7 to 6.14; explanatory notes to 2007 Act, para 30.

[26] *Hansard* (HL), 28 November 2006, vol 687, col 658.

[27] R Jones, *Mental Health Act Manual* (12th ed 2009) at para 1-054.

[28] Above.

[29] R Daw, "The Mental Health Act 2007 – the defeat of an ideal" [2007] *Journal of Mental Health Law* 131, 141.

A.26   Nonetheless, it is unlikely that the removal of the treatability test means that the 1983 Act is incompatible with article 5(1),[30] particularly given the amended definition of medical treatment under the 1983 Act.[31] The European Court of Human Rights has held, in relation to a provision similar to the treatability test,[32] that article 5(1)(e) does not require that detention in hospital must be conditional on the mental disorder being of a nature or degree amenable to medical treatment.[33] Instead, the court emphasised that its case law refers to a person "being properly established as suffering from a mental disorder of a degree warranting compulsory confinement".[34]

A.27   Moreover, the court went on to state that confinement is not only necessary where a person needs treatment to cure or alleviate his or her condition, "but also where the person needs control and supervision to prevent him, for example, causing harm to himself or other persons".[35] In this particular case the applicant, who was suffering from a form of psychopathic personality disorder, had derived benefit from a hospital environment, even though his condition was not perceived as being curable or susceptible to treatment. His detention was therefore justified.[36]

Definition of medical treatment

A.28   Section 7 of the 2007 Act changes the definition of medical treatment under the 1983 Act.[37] Section 145 now provides that "medical treatment" includes nursing, psychological intervention and specialist mental health habilitation, rehabilitation and care and any reference to medical treatment should be "construed as a reference to medical treatment the purpose of which is to alleviate, or prevent a worsening of, the disorder or one or more of its symptoms or manifestations". This applies to *all* references in the 1983 Act to medical treatment, including references to "appropriate medical treatment".[38]

---

[30]   The Joint Committee on Human Rights concluded that in terms of the European Convention on Human Rights, "there would appear to be no obstacle to replacing 'treatability' with 'availability of appropriate treatment' as a condition of detention". See Joint Committee on Human Rights, Legislative Scrutiny: Mental Health Bill, Fourth Report of Session 2006-07, HL Paper 40, HC 288, p 11.

[31]   See paras A.28 to A.30 below.

[32]   Section 17 of the Mental Health (Scotland) Act 1984 provided that where the mental disorder is one which is manifested only by abnormally aggressive or seriously irresponsible conduct (ie a psychopathic or anti-social personality disorder), a person could only be detained where "medical treatment was likely to alleviate or prevent a deterioration of his condition".

[33]   *Reid v United Kingdom* (2003) 37 EHRR 9 (App No 50272/99) at [51].

[34]   Above.

[35]   Above.

[36]   Above at [54] to [55].

[37]   Under the 1983 Act as amended, medical treatment includes "nursing, psychological intervention and specialist mental health habilitation, rehabilitation and care" (s 145(1)).

[38]   Explanatory notes to 2007 Act, para 40.

A.29 This change to the definition of medical treatment has been described as a "compromise amendment" given the controversy surrounding the removal of the treatability test.[39] The 1983 Act, in both its original and amended form, links medical treatment to the alleviation of the patient's mental disorder. The difference is that the 1983 Act originally required that treatment be *likely* to alleviate the disorder, whereas it now only requires that this is the *purpose* of the treatment. Thus while the treatability test may have been modified, it has not been entirely removed by the 2007 Act.[40] However, the emphasis on the availability of the treatment rather than its efficacy may widen the scope of the 1983 Act in relation to the use of longer-term powers of detention.[41]

A.30 Moreover, the Code of Practice for the 1983 Act states that medical treatment may still be appropriate even if the patient's mental disorder is likely to persist or get worse despite that treatment.[42] For example, for patients with persistent mental disorders "management of the undesirable effects of their disorder may be all that can realistically be hoped for".[43]

MENTALLY DISORDERED OFFENDERS

A.31 Part 3 of the 1983 Act contains the provisions relating to the detention and treatment in hospital of patients concerned in criminal proceedings or under sentence. Although dealt with under different provisions of the 1983 Act, according to the Code of Practice people subject to criminal proceedings have "the same right to psychiatric assessment and treatment as anyone else".[44]

A.32 Different provisions apply pre-sentence, at the sentencing stage, and where a person is already in custody. These provisions have been left largely intact by the 2007 Act. However, their scope has been affected by the change to the definition of mental disorder and the replacement of the treatability test with the appropriate medical treatment test.

Pre-sentence

A.33 The 1983 Act provides the courts with three options for the detention in hospital of a mentally disordered defendant who is awaiting trial, at any stage of his or her trial, or awaiting sentence:

(1) remand the accused to hospital for a report;

(2) remand the accused to hospital for treatment; or

---

[39] R Daw, "The Mental Health Act 2007 – the defeat of an ideal" [2007] *Journal of Mental Health Law* 131, 141.

[40] W Bingley, "The Mental Health Act 2007" [2007] *Archbold News* 6, 8.

[41] D Hewitt, "Treatment shock" (2007) 157 *New Law Journal* 1258. Although the emphasis is now on the purpose of the treatment rather than its likely effect, Hewitt suggests that the weakening of the treatability test is not as great as some may have feared since it has always been interpreted broadly by the courts.

[42] Mental Health Act 1983 Code of Practice (revised 2008), para 6.6.

[43] Above, para 6.15.

[44] Above, para 33.2.

(3)　where the accused is remanded in custody, transfer him or her to hospital.[45]

Remand to hospital for a report

A.34　Under section 35 of the 1983 Act, the court has the power to remand an accused[46] to hospital for a report on his or her mental condition. Subsection (3) provides that the court may exercise this power if:

(a)　the court is satisfied, on the written or oral evidence of a registered medical practitioner, that there is reason to suspect that an accused person is suffering from mental disorder; and

(b)　the court is of the opinion that it would be impracticable for a report on his mental condition to be made if he were remanded on bail.

A.35　This is an alternative to remanding the accused person in custody for a medical report, and is not an alternative to remand on bail. The consent to treatment provisions in Part 4 do not apply and therefore a person is entitled to consent to, or refuse treatment in the same way as any informal patient.

Remand to hospital for treatment

A.36　Under section 36, the Crown Court has the power to remand an accused[47] to hospital for medical treatment. Following the changes under the 2007 Act to the definition of mental disorder and the new appropriate treatment test, in order to exercise its powers under section 36, the court must now be satisfied on the written or oral evidence of two medical practitioners that:

(a)　the accused is suffering from mental disorder of a nature or degree which makes it appropriate for him to be detained in a hospital for medical treatment; and

(b)　appropriate medical treatment is available for him.

A.37　Prior to the single definition of mental disorder under the 2007 Act, the Crown Court had only been able to remand an accused to hospital for treatment if he or she was suffering from "mental illness" or "severe mental impairment". Given that there is now a single definition of mental disorder, the court may be able to use its powers under section 36 in relation to a wider range of accused.

---

[45]　For the transfer of an accused remanded in custody to hospital, see para A.57 below.

[46]　Under s 35(2), "accused" is defined in relation to the Crown Court as any person who is awaiting trial or has not yet been sentenced for an offence punishable with imprisonment. In relation to the magistrates' court, "accused" is defined as any person convicted by the court of an offence punishable on summary conviction with imprisonment, or any person charged with such an offence if the court is satisfied that he or she did the act or made the omission charged or has consented to the exercise of the court's powers under s 35.

[47]　Defined in subsection (2) as "any person who is in custody awaiting trial before the Crown Court for an offence punishable with imprisonment (other than an offence the sentence for which is fixed by law) or who at any time before sentence is in custody in the course of a trial before that court for such an offence".

A.38 Under the original section 36, the only requirement was that it was "appropriate for [the patient] to be detained in hospital for medical treatment"; the treatability test[48] did not apply. The 2007 Act inserted into section 36 the new requirement that "appropriate medical treatment be available".

A.39 Section 36 is an alternative to remand in custody. It can be used where a person may otherwise be found unfit to plead, enabling the accused to receive treatment prior to the trial. The trial may proceed at a later date when his or her condition has improved.

At the sentencing stage

Hospital and guardianship orders

A.40 If a person who is unfit to plead is found to have done the act or made the omission, section 5 of the Criminal Procedure (Insanity) Act 1964 provides that the court can make a hospital order. Following the Domestic Violence, Crime and Victims Act 2004, "hospital order" under section 5 is to be given the same meaning as hospital order under section 37 of the 1983 Act.[49] Therefore, an unfit accused who is found to have done the act cannot be detained in hospital unless he or she could be detained under section 37 of the 1983 Act.

A.41 Under section 37 the court can order that an offender suffering from a mental disorder should be admitted to hospital for treatment or placed under the guardianship of a local service authority (or a person approved by such an authority).[50] Section 37 can only be used as an alternative to a prison sentence.

A.42 In order for the court to make a hospital order, the court must be satisfied on the written or oral evidence of two medical practitioners that:

(a) the mental disorder from which the offender is suffering is of a nature or degree which makes it appropriate for him or her to be detained in hospital; and

(b) appropriate medical treatment is available.[51]

A.43 Prior to the 2007 Act, section 37 referred to the four categories of mental disorder, and the treatability test applied in relation to those suffering from a psychopathic disorder or mental impairment. The requirement that appropriate medical treatment be available now applies to all offenders suffering from a mental disorder.

---

[48] See paras A.19 to A.21 above.

[49] See s 5(4) of the Criminal Procedure (Insanity) Act 1964, as inserted by s 24(1) of the Domestic Violence, Crime and Victims Act 2004.

[50] A guardianship order gives the guardian the power, for example, to require the person to live in a specific place or to attend specific places, for example, for medical treatment or education.

[51] See s 37(2)(a)(i).

A.44   The Crown Court can exercise the section 37 power if the accused is convicted of an offence punishable with imprisonment (other than murder). The magistrates' court can make an order under section 37 if the accused is convicted of an offence punishable on summary conviction with imprisonment, or has been charged with such an offence and the court is satisfied that the accused did the act or made the omission.[52] There must be evidence that arrangements have been made for the accused's admission to hospital, and admission must take place within 28 days.[53]

A.45   Under a guardianship order, the offender is placed under the responsibility of a local authority or a person approved by the local authority. Like a hospital order, this can be made by a magistrates' court or Crown Court following conviction, or by a magistrates' court without conviction if the court is satisfied that the offender committed the act or omission.

A.46   Under section 38 of the 1983 Act, the court also has the power to make an interim hospital order, prior to making a hospital order under section 37 or dealing with the convicted offender in some other way. The offender must be suffering from mental disorder, and there must be reason to suppose that the mental disorder is such that it may be appropriate for a hospital order to be made. An interim hospital order can be made by the Crown Court or a magistrates' court after conviction, when the court needs more time to decide whether to impose a hospital order or to use an alternative disposal.

Restriction orders

A.47   Where the Crown Court makes a hospital order under section 37 of the 1983 Act, it may "further order that the offender shall be subject to special restrictions" set out in section 41. This is known as a restriction order. A restriction order can also be given where an unfit accused, found to have done the act, is given a hospital order. The main effect of a restriction order is that the patient cannot be given leave of absence, transferred to another hospital or discharged without the approval of the Secretary of State.

A.48   In deciding whether to impose a restriction order, the court must consider whether, having regard to the nature of the offence, the antecedents of the offender and the risk of reoffending if set at large, it is necessary for the protection of the public from serious harm that the court restrict the offender's discharge from hospital.

A.49   The Secretary of State can direct that the patient no longer be subject to a restriction order, or discharge the patient during the time a restriction order is in force, either absolutely or subject to conditions.[54]

---

[52]   Section 24(1) of the Domestic Violence, Crime and Victims Act 2004 inserted s 5A into the Criminal Procedure (Insanity) Act 1964, which provides that s 37 of the 1983 Act can have effect as if the reference to a person being convicted before the Crown Court included a reference to the case where an unfit accused is found to have done the act.

[53]   Section 37(4).

[54]   Section 42 of the 1983 Act. While the restriction order is in force, the Secretary of State can order the recall of a conditionally discharged patient.

A.50   Prior to the 2007 Act, the Crown Court could impose time-limited restriction orders. Section 40 of the 2007 Act amends section 41 of the 1983 Act so that the court no longer has the power to make restriction orders for a limited period. Restriction orders now imposed by the court will remain in force until they are discharged by the Secretary of State or the Mental Health Review Tribunal.

A.51   The magistrates' court has no power to make a restriction order. However, if it is satisfied that the conditions exist to make a hospital order, and feels that a restriction order should also be made, it may commit a convicted offender to the Crown Court under section 43.

Hospital and limitation directions

A.52   Section 45A of the 1983 Act[55] provides that the Crown Court can give both of the following directions:

> (a)   a direction that, instead of being removed to and detained in prison, the offender be removed to and detained in hospital (a "hospital direction"); and

> (b)   a direction that the offender be subject to the special restrictions set out in section 41 (a "limitation direction").

A.53   These directions can only be given after the court has imposed a fixed-term sentence of imprisonment. The court must also have considered making a hospital order under section 37 before imposing the sentence of imprisonment. Previously, a direction could only be made if the offender was suffering from psychopathic disorder. Following the 2007 Act, a direction can be made under section 45A for any offender suffering from mental disorder. The mental disorder must be of a nature or degree which makes it appropriate for the offender to be detained in a hospital for medical treatment, and appropriate medical treatment must be available.

A.54   The offender can only be discharged before the end of the prison sentence by the Secretary of State, who may order a return to prison.

Transfers from prison to hospital

A.55   Under section 47 of the 1983 Act, the Secretary of State may direct that a person serving a prison sentence should be transferred to and detained in hospital for all or part of his or her sentence. There must be reports from at least two medical practitioners that the accused is suffering from a mental disorder which makes it appropriate for them to be detained in hospital and that appropriate medical treatment is available. When making such a transfer direction, the Secretary of State can also direct that the person be subject to certain restrictions.[56]

A.56   If the Secretary of State makes a transfer direction and a restriction direction, under section 50 he or she can later direct that the person be remitted to any prison or other institution in which he or she might have been detained if he or she had not been removed to hospital.

---

[55]   As inserted by s 46 of the Crime (Sentences) Act 1997.

[56]   See s 49 of the 1983 Act.

A.57   Section 48 also allows the Secretary of State to order the transfer of certain unsentenced prisoners to hospital, for example, prisoners on remand, where the person is in "urgent need" of medical treatment.

PROFESSIONAL ROLES

A.58   The 2007 Act amends the 1983 Act so that the functions previously carried out by the "responsible medical officer" will now be carried out by the "responsible clinician". Under the 1983 Act, the responsible medical officer was the registered medical practitioner in charge of the treatment of the patient. He or she had various functions, including deciding when the patient could be discharged. Although the identity of the registered medical officer was a question of fact in the circumstances, in practice registered medical officers were usually consultant psychiatrists.[57] However, a responsible clinician does not have to be a doctor – it can be anyone who is approved to undertake the role. Such an approved clinician could be a nurse, psychologist, occupational therapist or social worker.[58] The 1983 Act therefore now recognises a broader range of mental health professionals as having the necessary expertise to take clinical responsibility for a particular patient.

A.59   Under the 2007 Act, the responsible clinician does not however assume all of the functions previously reserved to the responsible medical officer. For some functions medical input remains necessary. The initial detention of a person in hospital still requires reports from two registered medical practitioners. This is to ensure that there is objective medical expertise, as required by article 5(1)(e), to justify initial detention. However, a person can only be initially detained for up to 28 days under section 2 or six months under section 3. Under the latter, detention can be renewed for another six months and then for a further one year, and subsequently for periods of one year at a time.[59] It is the responsible clinician who is responsible for approving this renewal of detention but only after consulting at least one other member of the multi-disciplinary team.

---

[57]   Explanatory notes to the 2007 Act, para 47. See also W Bingley, "The Mental Health Act 2007" [2007] *Archbold News* 6, 7.

[58]   Explanatory notes to the 2007 Act, para 48.

[59]   Section 20 of the 1983 Act.

A.60 Concerns were raised by the Joint Committee on Human Rights about the wider range of practitioners who are now able to carry out many of the functions previously reserved to responsible medical officers.[60] Of particular concern was the Government's view that objective medical expertise "means relevant medical expertise, and not necessarily that of a registered medical practitioner".[61] This could therefore extend to, for example, evidence from a psychologist with the relevant skills and ability to identify the presence of a mental disorder.[62] The Joint Committee disagreed with this broad interpretation, emphasising that the European Court of Human Rights had given "every indication ... that objective medical expertise involved reports from psychiatrists who are doctors" and that "the opinion of a medical expert who is a psychiatrist is necessary for a lawful detention on grounds of unsoundness of mind".[63]

---

[60] See Joint Committee on Human Rights, Legislative Scrutiny: Mental Health Bill, Fourth Report of Session 2006-07, HL Paper 40, HC 288.

[61] Above, para 23.

[62] Above.

[63] Above, para 26. The Joint Committee relied on the case of *Varbanov v Bulgaria* Judgment of 5 October 2000 (App No 31365/96), where the European Court of Human Rights stated at [47] that "no deprivation of liberty of a person considered to be of unsound mind may be deemed in conformity with article 5(1)(e) of the Convention if it has been ordered without seeking the opinion of a medical expert". The court went onto state that "in the absence of an assessment by a psychiatrist" there was no justification for the applicant's detention: see [48].

APPENDIX B
CASE STUDY

INTRODUCTION

B.1 In Part 6 we referred to a recent case at the Central Criminal Court: *R v Patrick Sureda*. The accused was diagnosed as suffering from paranoid schizophrenia. In 2000, he was on home leave from a psychiatric hospital when he murdered his mother by strangling her. On returning to hospital, he said that he had had to do it because she was an MI6 agent and that she had been trying to kill him with a knife in order to stop him divulging information about MI6. A knife with the accused's blood on it was found next to the deceased's body and he had some fairly superficial knife tip grazes to his arm.

B.2 The case first came before the Central Criminal Court in 2001 and the accused was found to be unfit to plead and after a section 4A hearing was found to have done the act. A hospital order together with a restriction order was imposed and he was sent to Broadmoor.

B.3 In 2008, the responsible medical officer decided that the accused had recovered sufficiently to be able to plead to the charge. The Secretary of State was therefore notified of this and the accused was remitted to the Central Criminal Court. It rapidly became apparent that the accused had not in fact recovered. However, as the process of remitting the accused had been instigated, it was not possible to reverse it.[1] It was apparent to the judge (His Honour Judge Jeremy Roberts QC) and the jury that the resurrection of the court proceedings was having a hugely damaging effect on Mr Sureda's mental health which disintegrated completely as the hearing progressed.[2]

B.4 He was accordingly found unfit to plead and the matter was set down for a section 4A hearing. The hearing illustrates some of the difficulties which can arise in a trial of the facts hearing. As we explained in Part 6, these difficulties arise from:

> (a) the fact that sometimes the act alleged is something which is not in itself unlawful (any unlawfulness arises, if at all, from the state of mind with which it is done); and

> (b) the fact that, conversely, sometimes an act which is on its face unlawful, (for example punching or kicking someone else) may in fact be rendered perfectly lawful by a legally recognised justification or excuse.

---

[1] In Part 7 we explained that there is no power to do this once the case has been remitted to court.

[2] The accused informed the jury from the dock that his counsel were useless and had been paid by MI6 to make a mess of his case. The jury sent a note to the judge detailing their concerns about the accused's mental health.

B.5 In *Antoine*,[3] Lord Hutton stated that if there is some objective evidence of a legal justification for the act or omission charged, the prosecution must negative that justification beyond reasonable doubt, otherwise the defendant will be found not to have "done the act or made the omission charged" against him or her. So as we explained in Part 6, "the act" means the unlawful act charged.

B.6 Moreover, this means that at the moment, it is not easy to see how the issue of lawful self-defence can be approached without any reference to the defendant's state of mind. In the normal course of events,[4] a defendant's state of mind is a relevant factor in determining whether the defence of self-defence succeeds. This is because under section 76 of the Criminal Justice and Immigration Act 2008, a defendant is entitled to be judged on the facts as he or she genuinely (even if mistakenly) believes them to be, so that his or her belief as to the factual situation and danger in which he or she was placed is relevant (a) in determining whether he or she was justified in using any force at all and (b) if so, in determining whether the force he or she used went beyond what was reasonably necessary in the circumstances.

B.7 If these two questions must be judged purely on the objective facts then a genuine but mistaken belief as to those facts would have to be ignored. Such an approach is arguably unfair to an accused. On the other hand, it would not necessarily be satisfactory if an accused had to be acquitted in a case where his or her genuine but mistaken belief as to the facts was the result of a delusion caused by mental disorder.

B.8 In the section 4A hearing against Mr Sureda, counsel agreed that, although Mr Sureda could not be called as a witness in the trial, the jury should hear evidence of his account at the time to the hospital staff and the police. The presence of the knife and Sureda's injuries amounted to "objective evidence" within the ambit of what Lord Hutton had referred to in *Antoine*.

B.9 The written directions which were given to the jury in this case are reproduced below. As can be seen, they were designed to strike a fair balance between the considerations which are referred to above. They were read out by the judge once before counsels' speeches and again in the summing up.

B.10 The jury in this case concluded that Mr Sureda did "do the act". They therefore came to the same conclusion to which the previous jury had come in 2001.

---

[3] [2000] UKHL 20, [2000] 2 All ER 208.

[4] In other words, in a trial.

B.11 It can be seen that paragraphs 8 to 10 of these directions, unusually, deal with the consequences of the jury's decision.[5] These paragraphs were included at the request of counsel appointed to present the case for the accused, to allay concern that the jury might have had that a decision in favour of Mr Sureda might have resulted in his being at liberty to kill again. The responsible medical officer had made it clear that in the event of a finding that he did not "do the act", he would still continue to be detained under the Mental Health Act 1983.[6]

THE QUEEN v PATRICK SUREDA

EXPLANATION OF ISSUES FOR THE JURY TO DECIDE

Introduction

1. This is a special kind of trial being conducted under section 4A of the Criminal Procedure (Insanity) Act 1964 (as amended). That section applies where, as in this case, a defendant has been found "unfit to plead" (i.e. unfit to participate in a normal trial).

2. A trial under section 4A does not result in a verdict of guilty or not guilty of the offence charged (in this case the murder of Mrs Geraldine Sureda) and consequently cannot result in a prison sentence.

3. The purpose of the trial is to decide whether the defendant, in the words of section 4A, "did the act charged against him as the offence".

4. Most offences (including murder) involve two ingredients: (a) the doing of a specified act and (b) the existence of a specified state of mind at the time of doing that act. In a trial under section 4A it is immaterial whether the defendant had the state of mind required to make him guilty of the offence charged: all that matters is whether he did the act alleged.

5. The ingredients of murder are (a) any unlawful act which causes the death of another person and (b) an intention, at the time of doing that act, either to kill that other person or to cause him/her some "grievous bodily harm" (i.e. some really serious harm).

6. It follows from the above that, in a trial under section 4A where the offence charged is murder, the question is whether the defendant did some unlawful act which caused the death of another person: if he did, the intention with which he did that act is immaterial.

---

[5] Since the abolition of capital punishment, (before which it was permissible to refer to the fact that the accused was on trial for his life) it has not been permitted for counsel to refer the jury to the likely consequences of an adverse decision.

[6] As to this point, in Scotland, undertakings from psychiatrists that they will use civil procedures to detain some accused appear to mean that the procedure for examination of the facts is used less than one might suppose: C Connolly, "Unfitness to Plead and Examination of the Facts Proceedings: A Report Prepared for the Law Commission of England and Wales" (March 2010).

7. When you have reached your decision and return to court to deliver it, the clerk of the court will ask your foreman "Do you find that Patrick Sureda did the act charged against him as the act of murder?" Your foreman will reply simply "Yes" or "No".

8. If the answer is "Yes" Mr Sureda will not be sent to prison but an order will be made for his continued detention in Broadmoor Hospital for treatment for his paranoid schizophrenia until he has recovered sufficiently to be discharged into the community (no doubt subject to certain conditions).

9. If the answer is "No" he will also, but under a different procedure, continue to be detained in Broadmoor Hospital. The mechanism by which he may ultimately be discharged from hospital will then be a different one.

10. However, whichever is the basis on which he continues to be detained in hospital, the fundamental factor which will determine the date of his ultimate discharge into the community will be whether he has recovered sufficiently for it to be considered safe to discharge him (subject, as I say, to appropriate conditions).

The burden and standard of proof

11. The burden of proving that Mr Sureda did the unlawful act alleged rests on the prosecution. In no way does any burden rest on Mr Sureda to prove that he did not.

12. The prosecution have not succeeded in proving their case unless they have succeeded in making you sure, after hearing all the evidence and all the arguments, that Mr Sureda did "the act charged against him", i.e. that he unlawfully killed his mother.

The killing

13. Everybody agrees that on 19 August 2000 Mr Sureda did in fact kill his mother by strangling her.

14. What you have to decide is, therefore, whether his act in strangling her was lawful or unlawful. It is always unlawful to strangle another person unless one of a small number of legal justifications applies. The only one of those justifications which might apply in this case is lawful self-defence.

Lawful self-defence: the legal principles

15. Lawful self-defence, where it applies, is a complete defence to any criminal charge (including murder). A person who was acting in lawful self-defence is, in a normal trial, entitled to be acquitted altogether; and in a trial under section 4A he is entitled to be found not to have done the unlawful act alleged (he may have done the act, but it was not unlawful).

16. It is for the prosecution to disprove lawful self-defence (to the high standard explained in paragraph 12 above), not for the defence to prove it. This applies in a trial under section 4A just as it applies in a normal trial.

17. The general principle is this: if you are in what I call a "self-defence situation" (i.e. if you are being attacked, or if you are about to be attacked, or if you genuinely believe you are being attacked or about to be attacked) you are entitled to use whatever force is reasonably necessary in the circumstances (as you believe them to be) to

defend yourself.

18. It follows that as a general rule a person who genuinely but mistakenly believes that he is being attacked or about to be attacked, and who uses no more force than is reasonably necessary to defend himself against that perceived attack, is entitled to be acquitted (in a normal trial) or found not to have done the unlawful act (in a trial under section 4A), even though he was not in fact, as it turns out, being attacked or about to be attacked at all.

19. To that general rule there is one exception, which applies both in a normal trial and in a trial under section 4A.

20. In a normal trial, if the defendant's genuine belief that he was being attacked or about to be attacked was a delusion caused by a mental illness from which he was suffering, the law provides him with a defence, but that defence is not lawful self-defence, and it is only a partial defence.

21. If the allegation is one of murder, there are two possible partial defences, known as insanity and diminished responsibility. If either of those succeeds, the result is a special verdict ("not guilty by reason of insanity" or "guilty of manslaughter by reason of diminished responsibility"). Following either of those special verdicts the defendant will not be liable to be sentenced to life imprisonment (the sentence fixed by law when someone is found guilty of murder) but will be ordered to be detained in a mental hospital until he has recovered sufficiently to be released into the community.

22. The reason for this exception to the general rule that a defendant is entitled to be judged on the facts as he genuinely believed them to be is that, if a person suffers from a mental illness which has caused him to have deluded ideas as a result of which he has killed or injured somebody else, he presents a danger to the public and ought not simply to be acquitted: he needs to be detained and treated in hospital for his own and other people's safety.

23. Just as in a normal trial a genuine but deluded belief that you are being attacked or about to be attacked, if it is caused by a mental illness, does not result in an acquittal on the ground of self-defence, so in a trial under section 4A such a belief does not result in a finding that the defendant did not do "the act charged against him". He will be found to have done that act, and ordered to be detained and treated in hospital.

24. You will see that in a trial under section 4A (where the offence charged is, as here, murder) there is no need to consider insanity or diminished responsibility. The purpose of those defences, where they apply, is to avoid the necessity to pass a sentence of life imprisonment on a defendant who has killed because of a deluded belief caused by a mental illness, and to enable the court to order him to be detained and treated in a mental hospital. Where there is a trial under section 4A, there is no question of the defendant being sent to prison: if he is found to have done "the act charged against him", he will be ordered to be detained and treated in hospital just as if, following a normal trial, he had succeeded in a defence of insanity or diminished responsibility.

Two possible ways of disproving self-defence

25. The first way in which the prosecution might be able to disprove lawful self-defence in this case is by making you sure:

A. that Mrs Sureda was not in fact attacking or about to attack Mr Sureda with a knife; <u>AND</u>

B. <u>EITHER</u> that he did not genuinely believe that she was attacking him or about to attack him with a knife OR, if you think he did believe or may have believed that, that his mistaken belief must have been the result of a delusion caused by his paranoid schizophrenia.

26. If the prosecution fail to disprove lawful self-defence in that way, the other way in which they might be able to do so is by making you sure that the force Mr Sureda used against his mother went beyond what was reasonably necessary in the circumstances.

"Reasonably necessary in the circumstances"

27. What was or was not reasonably necessary in any particular circumstances is for you, as representatives of public opinion, to judge.

28. You should judge that question in the light of the circumstances as you think Mr Sureda genuinely believed (or may have believed) them to be, except that you should disregard any belief of his which you are sure must (if it existed) have been the result of a delusion caused by his paranoid schizophrenia.

29. In judging what was or was not reasonably necessary, you will want to bear two points in mind:

(1) The law does not require a person who is acting in self-defence to judge his response to a nicety. If a person is or believes himself to be under imminent attack, he does not have a lot of time to decide what to do. If he seems generally to be a reasonable person, and if he reacts in a way which he honestly and instinctively thinks is appropriate, that would be good evidence that what he did was reasonably necessary, even if with the benefit of hindsight it can be seen that there might have been a better way of dealing with the situation.

(2) On the other hand self-defence is to be distinguished from retaliation; and once the defendant has successfully defended himself against the attack, it cannot normally be said to be reasonably necessary to continue to use force against (e.g. to continue to strangle) the other person.

The key questions

30. I have attached to this document a "flow chart" of the questions which, applying the principles I have set out, you will need to work your way through in order to come to your final decision.

KEY QUESTIONS

I am going to ask you to consider the following questions in the order in which I have set them out. Your answers to the questions will lead you to your final decision.

QUESTION 1: Have the prosecution proved so that you are sure that Mrs Sureda was not attacking or about to attack Mr Sureda with a knife?

If NO, go straight to Question 4. If YES, go on to Question 2.

QUESTION 2: Have the prosecution proved so that you are sure that Mr Sureda did not genuinely believe that Mrs Sureda was attacking him or about to attack him with a knife?

If YES, you need go no further: you will find that Mr Sureda was acting unlawfully, and therefore that he did "the act charged against him".
If NO, go on to Question 3.

QUESTION 3: Have the prosecution proved so that you are sure that, if Mr Sureda believed or may have believed that Mrs Sureda was attacking or about to attack him with a knife, his belief must have resulted from a delusion caused by his paranoid schizophrenia?

If YES, you need go no further: you will find that Mr Sureda was acting unlawfully, and therefore that he did "the act charged against him".
If NO, go on to Question 4.

QUESTION 4: Have the prosecution proved so that you are sure that the force which Mr Sureda used against Mrs Sureda went beyond what was reasonably necessary in the circumstances (as to which see paragraphs 27-29 of my explanatory notes)?

If YES, you will find that Mr Sureda was acting unlawfully, and therefore that he did "the act charged against him".
If NO, you will find that he was acting lawfully, and therefore that he did not do "the act charged against him".

APPENDIX C
DATA ON FINDINGS OF UNFITNESS TO PLEAD

INTRODUCTION

In this Appendix we provide the results of research conducted by Professor Mackay into findings of unfitness to plead between 2002 and 2008.

UNFITNESS TO PLEAD – DATA ON FORMAL FINDINGS FROM 2002 TO 2008

By RD Mackay[1] Professor of Criminal Policy and Mental Health, Leicester De Montfort Law School, De Montfort University.

Introduction

Prior to 1991 little was known about the operation of unfitness to plead (UTP) other than that the number of those found "under disability in relation to the trial" was small. This was confirmed in a first empirical study which revealed that unfitness to plead was rarely used which in the light of the mandatory disposal of indeterminate hospitalisation under the Criminal Procedure (Insanity) Act 1964 was hardly surprising.[2] This was followed by two other empirical studies both of which were conducted after the introduction of flexibility of disposal under the Criminal Procedure (Insanity and Unfitness to Plead) Act 1991. They revealed a gradual but steady increase in findings of unfitness to plead during the ten year period 1992 to 2001. In the first such study the following conclusion was reached:

After a period in decline the number of findings of UTP has begun to rise. The increase from 13 findings in 1993 to 31 findings in 1994 strongly suggests that the legislative changes contained in the 1991 Act are having an effect. As with insanity the introduction of flexibility of disposal (except in murder cases)[3] removed a central disincentive to use UTP and in this context it is of note that although hospital based disposals predominate in UTP (77.4%, n=85), many (31.9%, n=35) were imposed without restrictions.[4]

This was echoed in the second study which also concluded:

---

[1] With thanks to the Law Commission for commissioning this research and to the Nuffield Foundation for their continued support of my research into unfitness to plead.

[2] RD Mackay "The Decline of Disability in Relation to the Trial" [1991] *Criminal Law Review* 87.

[3] On 31 March 2005 these disposals were reduced to three by virtue of s 24 of the Domestic Violence, Crime and Victims Act 2004. This provision abolished Guardianship as an option and now permits the court to make:
- a hospital order (with or without a restriction order);
- a supervision order;
- an order for an absolute discharge.

The hospital order is now identical to one made under the Mental Health Act 1983 and where the unfit to plead accused is charged with murder and the court has the power to make such an order, it must impose restrictions. These changes were prompted by concerns that the 1991 Act disposal regime was not compliant with the Human Rights Act 1998.

[4] RD Mackay and G Kearns "An upturn in unfitness to plead? Disability in relation to the trial under the 1991 Act" [2000] *Criminal Law Review* 532, 546.

The number of findings of UTP has continued to rise. The increase from 35 findings in 1997 to a peak in 1999 of 80 findings suggests that the legislative changes contained in the 1991 Act are having an ongoing effect. Although, unlike insanity, hospital based disposals still predominate in UTP (62.9%, n=207), with 38.9% (n=128) being imposed with restrictions, these percentages have fallen from 77.4% and 45.5% respectively with an increase in the use of Supervision and Treatment Orders from 13.6% to 17.9%. This shows that, as with insanity, the judiciary is continuing to make full use of the flexible disposal powers contained in the 1991 Act. Although it remains to be seen what the impact of the new disposal regime under the Domestic Violence, Crime and Victims Act 2004 will have, the fact that admission to hospital with restrictions in murder charges is no longer mandatory but rather can only be made if the court has the power to make a hospital order under the Mental Health Act 1983[5] removes a further disincentive to use both UTP and the insanity defence.[6]

What follows is a study of formal findings of unfitness to plead during the seven year period from 2002 to 2008 in order to assess the continued impact of flexibility of disposal together with the effect of the changes implemented by the Domestic Violence, Crime and Victims Act 2004 referred to above. At the outset, however, the limitations to this current study need to be emphasised for unlike the three earlier studies on this occasion access to court files, and in particular relevant psychiatric reports, was unavailable. Despite this however, it is hoped that the following research will give an up to date picture relating to unfitness to plead findings in England and Wales. Although the Statistics of Mentally Disordered Offenders continue to give the number of unfitness to plead cases annually in relation to restricted patients,[7] no official statistics are published on the use of unfitness to plead where other disposals are given. A final caveat, therefore, relates to the consistency of the data which were collected for this study using three major sources, namely two statistical returns from the Ministry of Justice and one from the Mental Health Casework Section. Inevitably, although some disparity has been found in relation to these three sources as complete a picture as seems possible of UTP findings has emerged for the purpose of this research for which grateful thanks is acknowledged to the agencies and personnel involved for all the assistance given.

---

[5] See s 24 Domestic Violence, Crime and Victims Act 2004 substituting s 5 of the Criminal Procedure (Insanity) Act 1964.

[6] RD Mackay, BJ Mitchell and L Howe "A continued upturn in unfitness to plead - More disability in relation to the trial under the 1991 Act" [2007] *Criminal Law Review* 530, 544.

[7] See Statistics of Mentally Disordered Offenders in England and Wales 2008 (Ministry of Justice Statistics Bulletin – Published 29 January 2010) at Table 5 which does not distinguish between restriction orders given with and without limit of time. Although it should be noted that the possibility of a time limited restriction order has been removed by s 40(1) of the Mental Health Act 2007. It should also be noted that the Ministry of Justice figures are based on the date of the hospital warrants rather than the date of the finding. Although this may have led to minor inconsistency in relation to the actual number of annual findings it is important to note that the total number of unfitness findings which resulted in hospital orders with restrictions recorded by the Ministry of Justice in the above bulletin for the seven year period 2002 to 2008 is almost identical to the number contained in this study for the same seven years, namely 264 by the Ministry of Justice compared to 263 (257 without limit of time and 6 with limit of time), see Table 10c below.

Table 1- Findings of UTP by 5 Year Periods from 1987-2006

la 1964 Act Final 5 years		1b 1991 Act 1st 5 years		1c 1991 Act 2nd 5 years		1c 1991 Act 3rd 5 years	
Year	Number	Year	Number	Year	Number	Year	Number
1987	16	1992	11	1997	50	2002	115
1988	13	1993	13	1998	53	2003	93
1989	11	1994	31	1999	80	2004	86
1990	13	1995	35	2000	70	2005	118
1991	10	1996	33	2001	76	2006	109
Total	63	Total	123	Total	329	Total	521

THE RESEARCH FINDINGS

The Number of UTP findings

Table 1 above gives the annual number of findings of UTP for the last 5 years of the operation of the original 1964 Act, the first 5 years, the second 5 years and the third 5 years of the 1991 Act. The picture is of a continuing steady rise in the number of UTP findings. In the third 5 years there was an annual average of 104.2 findings of UTP compared an average of 65.8 and 24.6 findings in the second and first five year periods respectively. This compares to an average of 12.6 from 1987-91 (although in the previous 11 years from 1976-1986 the average was 19.8) with an overall total of 973 UTP findings for the first fifteen years of the 1991 Act, giving an annual average of 64.9 findings.

Table 2a below gives the annual number of findings of UTP for the research period for this study, namely the seven years from 2002 to 2008. The total of UTP findings during this period was 725, giving an annual average of 103.6. In essence, therefore, the annual average number of UTP findings has now reached over one hundred for the first time. Table 2b shows the annual percentage of UTP findings.

Table 2a - Findings of UTP 2002-2008

	Frequency	Percent	Cumulative Percent
2002	115	15.9	15.9
2003	93	12.8	28.7
2004	86	11.9	40.6
2005	118	16.3	56.8
2006	109	15.0	71.9
2007	100	13.8	85.7
2008	104	14.3	100.0
Total	725	100.0	

year of decision

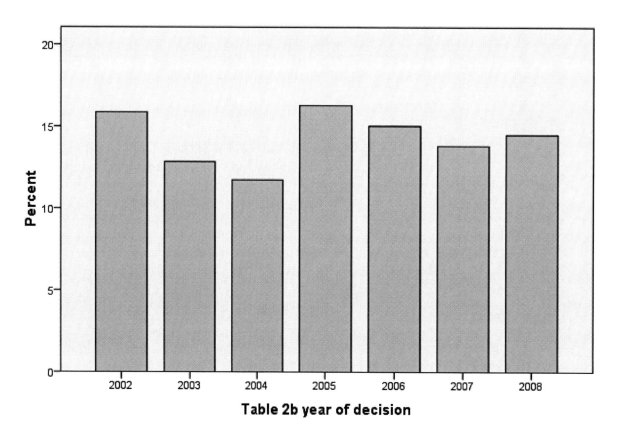

Table 2b year of decision

Some demographic data

As far as sex and age distribution are concerned, Table 3a shows that the vast majority of those found UTP continue to be males at 91 per cent (n=680), compared to only 9 per cent for females (n=65). Table 3b gives the age ranges as a percentage. The mean age at the time of the offence was 34.6 (range 12 to 84), with males having a mean age of 34.5, whilst females had a higher mean age of 36. The most prevalent age range for both males and females is 20-29 (n=222, 31.5%) with the vast majority of those found UTP falling within the age ranges of 20-29 or 30-39 (n=403, 55.6%). The available data for ethnicity is presented below in Table 4. However, this information is very sketchy as in the majority of cases it was either unavailable or not recorded. Neither was any information available on criminal records, psychiatric history or psychiatric diagnoses.[8]

Table 3a – sex/age distribution

		sex of accused		
		male	female	Total
age range of accused	up to 15	11	1	12
	15-19	73	7	80
	20-29	207	15	222
	30-39	168	13	181
	40-49	102	24	126
	50-59	42	3	45
	60-69	34	2	36
	70-79	18	0	18
	80-89	3	0	3
	not known	2	0	2
	Total	660	65	725

---

[8] For data relating to these issues see my earlier studies referred to above at notes 4 and 6.

age range of accused

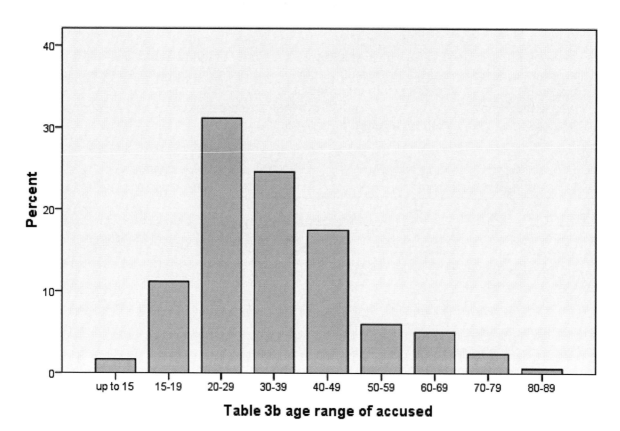

Table 3b age range of accused

Table 4 – ethnicity

	Frequency	Percent	Cumulative Percent
white	186	25.7	25.7
black	43	5.9	31.6
asian (Indian sub-continent)	34	4.7	36.3
other	19	2.6	38.9
not known/not recorded	443	61.1	100.0
Total	725	100.0	

The courts involved in UTP proceedings

Table 5 below gives a breakdown of the Crown Courts which were involved in the UTP proceedings. It can be seen from this that there was a wide geographical distribution with Snaresbrook Crown court the most frequent venue with 45 cases (6.3%).

Table 5 crown court

	Frequency	Percent	Cumulative Percent
Not known	110	15.2	15.2
Aylesbury	2	.3	15.4
Barnstaple	1	.1	15.6
Basildon	7	1.0	16.6
Birmingham	32	4.4	21.0
Blackfriars	16	2.2	23.2
Bolton	13	1.8	25.0
Bournemouth	2	.3	25.2
Bradford	16	2.2	27.4
Bristol	8	1.1	28.6
Burnley	5	.7	29.2
Cambridge	2	.3	29.5
Canterbury	8	1.1	30.6
Cardiff	14	1.9	32.6
Carlisle	1	.1	32.7
CCC	16	2.2	34.9
Chelmsford	4	.6	35.4
Chester	2	.3	35.7
Coventry	3	.4	36.1
Croydon	15	2.1	38.2
Derby	6	.8	39.0
Doncaster	3	.4	39.4
Durham	1	.1	39.6
Exeter	5	.7	40.3
Gloucester	8	1.1	41.4
Great Grimsby	2	.3	41.7
Guildford	2	.3	41.9
Guilford	6	.8	42.8

Harrow	17	2.3	45.1
Haverford West	1	.1	45.2
Hull	2	.3	45.5
Inner London	11	1.5	47.0
Ipswich	4	.6	47.6
Isleworth	15	2.1	49.7
Kingston	21	2.9	52.6
Knutsford	3	.4	53.0
Lancaster	2	.3	53.2
Leeds	14	1.9	55.2
Leicester	6	.8	56.0
Lewes	14	1.9	57.9
Lincoln	7	1.0	58.9
Liverpool	8	1.1	60.0
Luton	6	.8	60.8
Maidstone	9	1.2	62.1
Manchester	25	3.4	65.5
Merthyr Tydfil	5	.7	66.2
Middlesex	10	1.4	67.6
Newcastle	11	1.5	69.1
Newport	2	.3	69.4
Northampton	2	.3	69.7
Norwich	3	.4	70.1
Nottingham	17	2.3	72.4
Oxford	7	1.0	73.4
Peterborough	1	.1	73.5
Plymouth	1	.1	73.7
Portsmouth	6	.8	74.5
Preston	5	.7	75.2
Reading	5	.7	75.9
Sheffield	12	1.7	77.5
Shrewsbury	5	.7	78.2
Snaresbrook	46	6.3	84.6
Southampton	2	.3	84.8

212

Southend	1	.1	85.0
Southwark	7	1.0	85.9
St Albans	9	1.2	87.2
Stafford	4	.6	87.7
Swansea	5	.7	88.4
Swindon	5	.7	89.1
Taunton	1	.1	89.2
Teesside	16	2.2	91.4
Truro	1	.1	91.6
Warrington	3	.4	92.0
Warwick	4	.6	92.6
Weymouth	1	.1	92.7
Winchester	5	.7	93.4
Wolverhampton	17	2.3	95.7
Wood Green	9	1.2	97.0
Woolwich	7	1.0	97.9
Worcester	8	1.1	99.0
York	7	1.0	100.0
Total	725	100.0	

The offences charged

Table 6 gives the main offence charged which in each case led to a finding of UTP. It can be seen from this that although there was a wide spread of offences, the most prevalent continues to be indecent/sexual assault (n=140, 19.3%). Table 7 gives a breakdown of the broad types of offence.

Table 6 main offence charged

	Frequency	Percent	Cumulative Percent
murder	32	4.4	4.4
attempted murder	20	2.8	7.2
manslaughter	6	.8	8.0
GBH	85	11.7	19.7
ABH	61	8.4	28.1
arson	82	11.3	39.4
criminal damage	7	1.0	40.4
robbery	52	7.2	47.6
burglary	36	5.0	52.6
rape	38	5.2	57.8
indecent/sexual assault	140	19.3	77.1
threats to kill	15	2.1	79.2
kidnap/child abduction	5	.7	79.9
(death by)dangerous driving	8	1.1	81.0
possession/ importation/supply of drugs	10	1.4	82.3
threatening words/behaviour	4	.6	82.9
possession of firearm with intent	13	1.8	84.7
make explosive substance with intent	1	.1	84.8
breach restraining order	3	.4	85.2
affray	21	2.9	88.1
false imprisonment	3	.4	88.6
having article with blade	11	1.5	90.1
theft	14	1.9	92.0
obstruct engine on railway	1	.1	92.1
immigration offence	2	.3	92.4

racially aggravated assault	5	.7	93.1
bomb hoax	3	.4	93.5
Possess weapons designed for discharge of noxious liquid etc.	1	.1	93.7
child cruelty	2	.3	93.9
pervert course of justice	2	.3	94.2
make indecent photos of child	3	.4	94.6
possession offensive weapon	4	.6	95.2
putting people in fear of violence	6	.8	96.0
false accounting	3	.4	96.4
breach restraining order	1	.1	96.6
Cause/incite child prostitution	1	.1	96.7
obtain property/money transfer by deception	3	.4	97.1
forgery	2	.3	97.4
indecent exposure	6	.8	98.2
conspiracy to cheat public revenue	1	.1	98.3
blackmail	1	.1	98.5
Disqualified person managing company	1	.1	98.6
breach ASBO	2	.3	98.9
breach sex offence prevention order	1	.1	99.0
trespass w/i to commit sex offence	1	.1	99.2
harassment	1	.1	99.3
handling stolen goods	2	.3	99.6
possession false documents	2	.3	99.9
not known	1	.1	100.0
Total	725	100.0	

type of offence

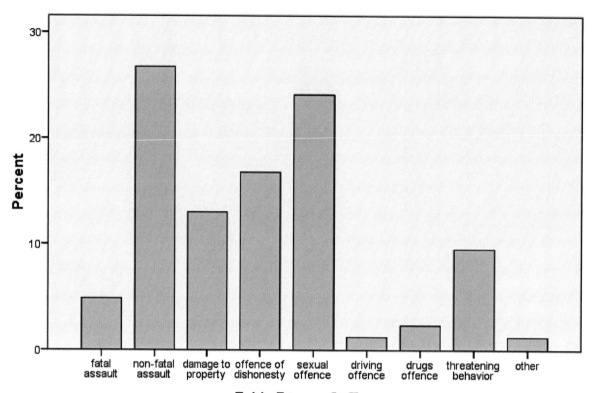

Table 7 type of offence

Table 8 gives a breakdown of the main offence charged cross tabulated with the broad types of offences involved. As in previous studies offences against the person (including robbery, kidnap/child abduction, false imprisonment and child cruelty) remain the most common type of offence with a total of 233 (32.1%), (n=271, 37.4% including rape) non-fatal and 38 (5.2%) fatal offences. There has also been an increase in arson from 8.1 per cent in the 1997-2001 study to 11.3 percent (n=82) making it the third highest single category of offence.

Table 8 main offence charged * type of offence Crosstabulation

		type of offence									
		fatal assault	non-fatal assault	damage to property	offence of dishonesty	sexual offence	driving offence	drugs offence	threatening behavior	other	Total
main offence charged	murder	32	0	0	0	0	0	0	0	0	32
	attempted murder	0	20	0	0	0	0	0	0	0	20
	manslaughter	6	0	0	0	0	0	0	0	0	6
	GBH	0	85	0	0	0	0	0	0	0	85
	ABH	0	61	0	0	0	0	0	0	0	61
	arson	0	0	82	0	0	0	0	0	0	82
	criminal damage	0	0	7	0	0	0	0	0	0	7
	robbery	0	52	0	0	0	0	0	0	0	52
	burglary	0	0	0	36	0	0	0	0	0	36
	rape	0	0	0	0	38	0	0	0	0	38
	indecent/sexual assault	0	0	0	0	140	0	0	0	0	140
	threats to kill	0	0	0	0	0	0	0	15	0	15
	kidnap/child abduction	0	5	0	0	0	0	0	0	0	5
	(death by)dangerous driving	0	0	0	0	0	8	0	0	0	8
	possession/ importation/supply of drugs	0	0	0	0	0	0	10	0	0	10
	threatening words/behaviour	0	0	0	0	0	0	0	4	0	4
	possession of firearm with intent	0	0	0	0	0	0	0	13	0	13
	make explosive substance with intent	0	0	0	0	0	0	0	1	0	1
	breach restraining order	0	0	0	0	0	0	0	3	0	3
	affray	0	0	0	0	0	0	0	21	0	21

Offence									
false imprisonment	0	3	0	0	0	0	0	0	0	3
having article with blade	0	0	0	0	0	0	0	11	0	11
theft	0	0	0	14	0	0	0	0	0	14
obstruct engine on railway	0	0	0	0	0	0	0	1	0	1
immigration offence	0	0	0	0	0	0	0	0	2	2
racially aggravated assault	0	5	0	0	0	0	0	0	0	5
bomb hoax	0	0	0	0	0	0	0	3	0	3
Possess weapons designed for discharge of noxious liquid etc.	0	0	0	0	0	0	0	1	0	1
child cruelty	0	2	0	0	0	0	0	0	0	2
pervert course of justice	0	0	0	0	0	0	0	0	2	2
make indecent photos of child	0	0	0	0	3	0	0	0	0	3
possession offensive weapon	0	0	0	0	0	0	0	4	0	4
putting people in fear of violence	0	0	0	0	0	0	0	6	0	6
false accounting	0	0	0	3	0	0	0	0	0	3
breach restraining order	0	0	0	0	0	0	0	1	0	1
Cause/incite child prostitution	0	0	0	0	1	0	0	0	0	1
obtain property/money transfer by deception	0	0	0	3	0	0	0	0	0	3
forgery	0	0	0	2	0	0	0	0	0	2
indecent exposure	0	0	0	0	6	0	0	0	0	6
conspiracy to cheat public revenue	0	0	0	1	0	0	0	0	0	1
blackmail	0	0	0	0	0	0	0	1	0	1
Disqualified person managing company	0	0	0	1	0	0	0	0	0	1
breach ASBO	0	0	0	0	0	0	0	0	2	2
breach sex offence prevention order	0	0	0	0	1	0	0	0	0	1
trespass w/i to commit sex offence	0	0	0	0	1	0	0	0	0	1

harassment	0	0	0	0	0	0	0	1	0	1
handling stolen goods	0	0	0	2	0	0	0	0	0	2
possession false documents	0	0	0	0	0	0	0	0	2	2
not known	0	0	0	0	0	0	0	0	1	1
Total	38	233	89	62	190	8	10	86	9	725

The 'trial of the facts' (TOF) follows the 'trial of the issue of UTP' and is mandatory once the accused has been found UTP in relation to the offence(s) charged. The result of the TOF is given below in Table 9a, although in 255 (35.2%) cases the result is coded as 'uncertain' as there was no information on this issue. As in the earlier study of UTP cases from 1997-2001 there were some cases where no TOF took place. The reasons were as follows. In 15 cases the prosecution offered no evidence. In nine cases the judge ordered the indictment to remain on file or stayed the proceedings (no further details are available as to why this was done). In one case a *nolle prosequi* was issued and in a final case the accused was certified insane prior to arraignment. In total therefore there were 26 cases where no TOF took place. In the vast majority of cases where some information about the TOF was available the accused was found to have done the act on all the charges (n=401, 55.3%). In only 17 cases was it clear that the accused had done the act on one or more offence but had been acquitted on other(s). In 26 cases (3.6%) the accused was acquitted of all offences. Table 9b below gives the main offence charged cross-tabulated with the TOF result. It can be seen from this that 11 of the 26 acquittals were in respect of indecent/sexual assault, which as mentioned above continues to be the most prevalent single offence. It is also of note, however, that there are three acquittals for burglary, and two for GBH. There are also single acquittals for murder, attempted murder, ABH, arson, robbery and rape. It seems clear, therefore, that acquittals are taking place in relation to some serious offences.

Table 9a result of trial of facts

		Frequency	Percent	Cumulative Percent
Valid	D did the act on all	401	55.3	55.3
	did the act on some, acquitted on others	17	2.3	57.7
	acquitted on all	26	3.6	61.2
	TOF did not take place as no evidence offered	15	2.1	63.3
	uncertain	255	35.2	98.5
	indictment to remain on file/stayed	9	1.2	99.7
	nolle prosequi	1	.1	99.9
	no TOF as certified insane before arraignment	1	.1	100.0
	Total	725	100.0	

Table 9b main offence charged * result of trial of facts Crosstabulation

		result of trial of facts								
		D did the act on all	did the act on some, acquitted on others	acquitted on all	TOF did not take place as no evidence offered	uncertain	indictment to remain on file/stayed	nolle prosequi	no TOF as certified insane before arraignment	Total
main offence charged	murder	17	0	1	0	14	0	0	0	32
	attempted murder	9	0	1	0	10	0	0	0	20
	manslaughter	3	0	0	0	3	0	0	0	6
	GBH	47	0	2	2	33	1	0	0	85
	ABH	37	1	1	0	22	0	0	0	61
	arson	43	2	1	3	32	0	0	1	82
	criminal damage	3	0	0	0	4	0	0	0	7
	robbery	36	0	1	0	14	1	0	0	52
	burglary	22	0	3	0	11	0	0	0	36
	rape	11	1	1	2	21	1	1	0	38
	indecent/sexual assault	74	5	11	3	43	4	0	0	140
	threats to kill	11	0	0	0	4	0	0	0	15
	kidnap/child abduction	2	0	0	0	3	0	0	0	5
	(death by)dangerous driving	6	0	0	0	2	0	0	0	8
	possession/ importation/supply of drugs	6	0	0	1	3	0	0	0	10
	threatening words/behaviour	1	1	0	0	2	0	0	0	4
	possession of firearm with intent	9	0	1	1	2	0	0	0	13
	make explosive substance with intent	1	0	0	0	0	0	0	0	1
	breach restraining order	1	0	0	0	2	0	0	0	3
	affray	11	2	0	0	8	0	0	0	21

false imprisonment	2	0	0	0	1	0	0	0	3
having article with blade	8	0	0	1	2	0	0	0	11
theft	10	0	1	0	3	0	0	0	14
obstruct engine on railway	0	1	0	0	0	0	0	0	1
immigration offence	1	0	0	0	1	0	0	0	2
racially aggravated assault	3	1	0	0	1	0	0	0	5
bomb hoax	2	0	0	1	0	0	0	0	3
Possess weapons designed for discharge of noxious liquid etc.	0	0	1	0	0	0	0	0	1
child cruelty	1	0	1	0	0	0	0	0	2
pervert course of justice	2	0	0	0	0	0	0	0	2
make indecent photos of child	0	1	0	0	2	0	0	0	3
possession offensive weapon	2	1	0	0	1	0	0	0	4
putting people in fear of violence	3	1	0	0	2	0	0	0	6
false accounting	3	0	0	0	0	0	0	0	3
breach restraining order	1	0	0	0	0	0	0	0	1
Cause/incite child prostitution	1	0	0	0	0	0	0	0	1
obtain property/money transfer by deception	1	0	0	1	1	0	0	0	3
forgery	2	0	0	0	0	0	0	0	2
indecent exposure	3	0	0	0	3	0	0	0	6
conspiracy to cheat public revenue	0	0	0	0	0	1	0	0	1
blackmail	0	0	0	0	1	0	0	0	1
Disqualified person managing company	0	0	0	0	1	0	0	0	1

breach ASBO	1	0	0	0	1	0	0	0	2
breach sex offence prevention order	1	0	0	0	0	0	0	0	1
trespass w/i to commit sex offence	1	0	0	0	0	0	0	0	1
harassment	1	0	0	0	0	0	0	0	1
handling stolen goods	2	0	0	0	0	0	0	0	2
possession false documents	0	0	0	0	1	1	0	0	2
not known	0	0	0	0	1	0	0	0	1
Total	401	17	26	15	255	9	1	1	725

The disposals

Earlier studies of UTP revealed that although hospital based disposals continue to dominate, many are imposed without restrictions leading to the conclusion that flexibility of disposal was being fully utilised. Indeed in the 1997-2001 study it was concluded that: "First, although the percentage of restriction orders (ignoring the 31 cases of "none given") has fallen from 45.5% to 38.9% what is equally noticeable is the increase in supervision and treatment orders from 13.6% to 17.9% (n=59). Taking account also of absolute discharges and guardianship orders this means that the overall percentage of hospital based disposals has fallen from 77.4% to 62.9%".[9]

Tables 10a, 10b and 10c below give the disposals for the current study. In 47 cases no disposal was given for the reasons indicated in Table 9a above. In addition, in five cases although a TOF took place, the accused was then discharged, as opposed to being given an absolute discharge under the 1964 Act as amended. With regard to the other disposals restriction orders have again fallen from 38.9 per cent to 36.2 per cent (n=264), although in contrast the percentage of hospital orders has risen from 24 per cent to 29 per cent (n=210). This means that there has been an overall increase in hospital based disposals from 62.9 per cent to 65.2 per cent. However, we must bear in mind that there were 31 murder cases (ignoring the murder acquittal) where after the TOF disposal flexibility was unavailable. In addition, although the percentage of supervision (and treatment) orders has fallen from 17.9 per cent to 15.7 per cent (n=114) there has been a marked increase in the use of absolute discharges from 3.6 per cent to 6.3 per cent (n=46). Overall therefore the percentage of non-hospital disposals has fallen from 27.6 per cent to 25.6 per cent. However, Table 11 below shows that both supervision (and treatment) orders and absolute discharges continue to be given for serious offences such as GBH (n=11), arson (n=6, although there are also 4 guardianship orders given for arson) and robbery (n=11). Finally, the percentage of guardianship orders has fallen from 6.1 per cent to 2.9 per cent (n=21) which is hardly surprising in view of the fact that this form of disposal was abolished by the Domestic Violence, Crime and Victims Act 2004. With this in mind it is now time to try to address the impact of the new disposal regime under the 2004 Act.

---

[9]   [2007] *Criminal Law Review* 530, 540 at Table 11.

Table 10a - disposals

		Frequency	Percent	Cumulative Percent
Valid	none given	47	6.5	6.5
	restriction order without limit of time	257	35.4	41.9
	restriction order with limit of time	6	.8	42.8
	hospital order	210	29.0	71.7
	guardianship order	20	2.8	74.5
	supervision (& treatment) order - 2 years	99	13.7	88.1
	supervision (& treatment) order -under 2 years	17	2.3	90.5
	absolute discharge	46	6.3	96.8
	D died prior to disposal	3	.4	97.2
	not known	15	2.1	99.3
	defendant discharged	5	.7	100.0
	Total	725	100.0	

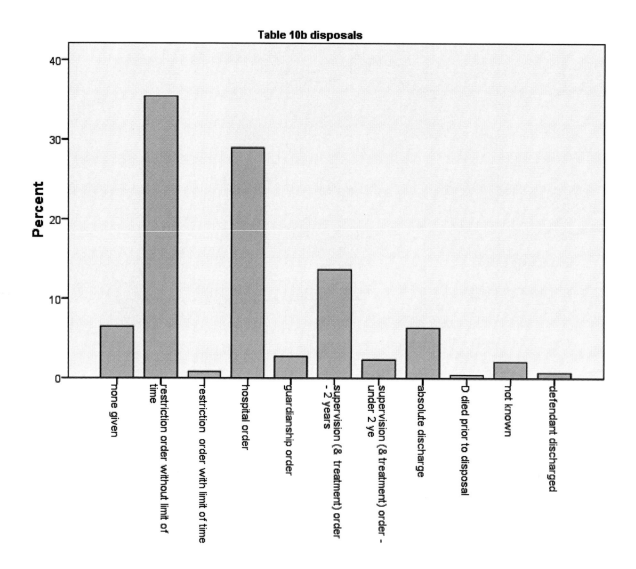

Table 10b disposals

Percent

- none given
- restriction order without limit of time
- restriction order with limit of time
- hospital order
- guardianship order
- supervision (& treatment) order - 2 years
- supervision (& treatment) order - under 2 ye
- absolute discharge
- D died prior to disposal
- not known
- defendant discharged

Table 10c disposals * year of decision Crosstabulation

		year of decision							
		2002	2003	2004	2005	2006	2007	2008	Total
disposals	none given	6	5	1	17	10	2	6	47
	restriction order without limit of time	43	39	44	38	36	34	23	257
	restriction order with limit of time	2	1	0	0	1	0	2	6
	hospital order	34	27	26	25	26	36	36	210
	guardianship order	4	7	0	8	1	0	0	20
	supervision (& treatment) order - 2 years	11	7	9	15	18	16	23	99
	supervision (& treatment) order -under 2 ye	1	2	1	3	1	3	6	17
	absolute discharge	7	5	4	8	11	5	6	46
	D died prior to disposal	0	0	0	1	1	1	0	3
	not known	6	0	0	1	2	3	3	15
	defendant discharged	1	0	0	2	2	0	0	5
	Total	115	93	85	118	109	100	105	725

225

Table 11 main offence charged * disposal Crosstabulation

		disposal											
		none given	restriction order without limit of time	restriction order with limit of time	hospital order	guardianship order	supervision (& treatment) order - 2 years	supervision (& treatment) order - under 2 ye	absolute discharge	D died prior to disposal	not known	defendant discharged	Total
main offence charged	murder	1	29	1	1	0	0	0	0	0	0	0	32
	attempted murder	1	17	0	2	0	0	0	0	0	0	0	20
	manslaughter	0	2	0	2	0	2	0	0	0	0	0	6
	GBH	3	45	0	22	0	4	1	6	0	2	2	85
	ABH	1	21	2	18	2	6	1	8	1	1	0	61
	arson	5	38	0	29	4	5	0	1	0	0	0	82
	criminal damage	0	4	0	3	0	0	0	0	0	0	0	7
	robbery	2	16	1	21	0	9	0	2	0	1	0	52
	burglary	3	8	0	20	0	4	0	1	0	0	0	36
	rape	3	15	1	7	1	6	0	0	1	2	2	38
	indecent/sexual assault	18	31	0	35	9	23	10	8	1	5	0	140
	threats to kill	0	7	0	7	0	0	0	1	0	0	0	15
	kidnap/child abduction	0	3	0	0	1	0	0	0	0	1	0	5
	(death by)dangerous driving	0	0	0	1	0	2	1	4	0	0	0	8

possession/ importation/supply of drugs	1	2	0	4	0	2	0	0	0	1	0	10
threatening words/behaviour	0	0	0	2	0	2	0	0	0	0	0	4
possession of firearm with intent	1	2	1	1	1	5	0	1	0	1	0	13
make explosive substance with intent	0	1	0	0	0	0	0	0	0	0	0	1
breach restraining order	0	2	0	1	0	0	0	0	0	0	0	3
affray	1	7	0	6	0	3	0	4	0	0	0	21
false imprisonment	0	0	0	2	0	1	0	0	0	0	0	3
having article with blade	0	2	0	6	0	2	0	1	0	0	0	11
theft	1	1	0	3	1	4	1	3	0	0	0	14
obstruct engine on railway	0	0	0	1	0	0	0	0	0	0	0	1
immigration offence	0	0	0	2	0	0	0	0	0	0	0	2
racially aggravated assault	1	0	0	1	0	3	0	0	0	0	0	5
bomb hoax	1	0	0	1	0	0	0	1	0	0	0	3
Possess weapons designed for discharge of noxious liquid etc.	1	0	0	0	0	0	0	0	0	0	0	1
child cruelty	1	0	0	0	0	1	0	0	0	0	0	2
pervert course of justice	0	0	0	0	1	0	1	0	0	0	0	2
make indecent photos of child	0	1	0	0	0	2	0	0	0	0	0	3

possession offensive weapon	0	0	0	1	0	2	0	0	0	1	0	4
putting people in fear of violence	0	1	0	1	0	4	0	0	0	0	0	6
false accounting	0	0	0	0	0	2	0	1	0	0	0	3
breach restraining order	0	0	0	0	0	1	0	0	0	0	0	1
Cause/incite child prostitution	0	0	0	0	0	0	1	0	0	0	0	1
obtain property/money transfer by deception	0	0	0	1	0	0	0	1	0	0	1	3
forgery	0	0	0	1	0	0	0	1	0	0	0	2
indecent exposure	0	1	0	3	1	1	0	0	0	0	0	6
conspiracy to cheat public revenue	1	0	0	0	0	0	0	0	0	0	0	1
blackmail	0	1	0	0	0	0	0	0	0	0	0	1
Disqualified person managing company	0	0	0	0	0	0	0	1	0	0	0	1
breach ASBO	0	0	0	1	0	0	0	1	0	0	0	2
breach sex offence prevention order	0	0	0	1	0	0	0	0	0	0	0	1
trespass w/i to commit sex offence	0	0	0	0	0	1	0	0	0	0	0	1
harassment	0	0	0	1	0	0	0	0	0	0	0	1
handling stolen goods	0	0	0	1	0	1	0	0	0	0	0	2
possession false documents	1	0	0	0	0	0	1	0	0	0	0	2
not known	0	0	0	1	0	0	0	0	0	0	0	1
Total	47	257	6	210	21	98	17	46	3	15	5	725

The Effect of the Domestic Violence, Crime and Victims Act 2004

The 2004 Act was implemented on March 31, 2005. Apart from abolishing the role of the jury in relation to findings of UTP, the Act reduced UTP disposals to three, namely:

- a hospital order (with or without a restriction order);[10]

- a supervision order;

- an order for an absolute discharge.

With regard to the present study which spans a period of seven years, 39 (46.4%) months of the research period were prior to the implementation of the 2004 Act and 45 (53.6%) months post implementation. However, with this in mind it must be made clear that only those defendants arraigned on or after March 31, 2005 are subject to the new disposal regime.[11]

The following tables give a split of these two respective periods in order to show something of the impact of the 2004 disposal regime. Table 12 below shows the numbers of UTP cases involved pre and post the 2004 Act. It can be seen from this that 378 (52.1%) of the UTP cases fell to be dealt with under the 2004 Act, compared to 347 (47.9%) dealt with before the Act.

Table 12 year of decision

Domestic Violence Act		Frequency	Percent	Cumulative Percent
pre2004Act	2002	115	33.1	33.1
	2003	93	26.8	59.9
	2004	85	24.5	84.4
	2005	54	15.6	100.0
	Total	347	100.0	
post2004Act	2005	64	16.9	16.9
	2006	109	28.8	45.8
	2007	100	26.5	72.2
	2008	105	27.8	100.0
	Total	378	100.0	

Table 13 below gives a breakdown of the main offences charged in the two periods pre and post the enactment of the 2004 Act. It can be seen from this that the pattern of offences has remained fairly consistent.

---

[10] The hospital order is now identical to one made under the Mental Health Act 1983 and where the unfit to plead accused is charged with murder and the court has the power to make such an order, it must impose restrictions.

[11] See *R v Hussein* [2005] EWCA Crim 3556 at para 14: 'The fact that the appellant was committed or sent to the Crown Court long before 31st March 2005 is nothing to the point.'

Table 13 main offence charged * Domestic Violence Act Crosstabulation

		Domestic Violence Act		
		pre2004Act	post2004Act	Total
main offence charged	murder	19	13	32
	attempted murder	13	7	20
	manslaughter	2	4	6
	GBH	47	38	85
	ABH	22	39	61
	arson	47	35	82
	criminal damage	3	4	7
	robbery	20	32	52
	burglary	20	16	36
	rape	15	23	38
	indecent/sexual assault	72	68	140
	threats to kill	8	7	15
	kidnap/child abduction	3	2	5
	(death by)dangerous driving	6	2	8
	possession/ importation/supply of drugs	7	3	10
	threatening words/behaviour	1	3	4
	possession of firearm with intent	5	8	13
	make explosive substance with intent	0	1	1
	breach restraining order	0	3	3
	affray	9	12	21
	false imprisonment	1	2	3
	having article with blade	7	4	11
	theft	5	9	14
	obstruct engine on railway	0	1	1
	immigration offence	0	2	2
	racially aggravated assault	2	3	5
	bomb hoax	0	3	3
	Possess weapons designed for discharge of noxious liquid etc.	0	1	1
	child cruelty	1	1	2

pervert course of justice		2	0	2
make indecent photos of child		1	2	3
possession offensive weapon		2	2	4
putting people in fear of violence		1	5	6
false accounting		0	3	3
breach restraining order		0	1	1
Cause/incite child prostitution		0	1	1
obtain property/money transfer by deception		2	1	3
forgery		1	1	2
indecent exposure		0	6	6
conspiracy to cheat public revenue		1	0	1
blackmail		1	0	1
Disqualified person managing company		1	0	1
breach ASBO		0	2	2
breach sex offence prevention order		0	1	1
trespass w/i to commit sex offence		0	1	1
harassment		0	1	1
handling stolen goods		0	2	2
possession false documents		0	2	2
not known		0	1	1
Total		347	378	725

Table 14 below gives the disposals for the two periods. The two Guardianship Orders in the post2004Act section of the table seem to have been given although the defendants were arraigned after 31 March 2005. In one case the committal date was February 2005 in which case the confusion referred to at note 11 in *R v Hussein* above may have operated. However, in the other case both the committal and arraignment dates were in 2006, in which case the Order is either a disposal or coding error. What is of note in Table 14 is the drop in restriction orders from 146 (42.1%) in the pre2004Act list to 111 (29.4%) in the post2004Act list. In addition, there is an increase in the post2004Act number of non-hospital disposals from 75 (21.4%) pre2004Act to 107 (28.2%) post2004Act.

231

Table 14 Disposals

Domestic Violence Act		Frequency	Percent	Cumulative Percent
pre2004Act	none given	19	5.5	5.5
	restriction order without limit of time	146	42.1	47.6
	restriction order with limit of time	3	.9	48.4
	hospital order	94	27.1	75.5
	guardianship order	18	5.2	80.7
	supervision (& treatment) order - 2 years	32	9.2	89.9
	supervision (& treatment) order -under 2 years)	6	1.7	91.6
	absolute discharge	19	5.5	97.1
	not known	7	2.0	99.1
	defendant discharged	3	.9	100.0
	Total	347	100.0	
post2004Act	none given	28	7.4	7.4
	restriction order without limit of time	111	29.4	36.8
	restriction order with limit of time	3	.8	37.6
	hospital order	116	30.7	68.3
	guardianship order	2	.5	68.8
	supervision (& treatment) order - 2 years	67	17.7	86.5
	supervision (& treatment) order -under 2 years)	11	2.9	89.4
	absolute discharge	27	7.1	96.6
	D died prior to disposal	3	.8	97.4
	not known	8	2.1	99.5
	defendant discharged	2	.5	100.0
	Total	378	100.0	

Concluding Remarks

As in my earlier studies the number of findings of UTP has continued to rise. The increase from a maximum of 80 findings in 1999 to a peak of 118 findings in 2005 strongly suggests that the legislative changes contained in the 1991 and 2004 Acts are having an ongoing effect. Although hospital based disposals still predominate in UTP (65.2%, n=474), with 36.2 per cent (n=264) being imposed with restrictions, the percentage of restriction orders has fallen from 38.9 per cent. In addition, although the percentage of supervision (and treatment) orders has fallen from 17.9 per cent to 15.7 per cent (n=114) there has been a marked increase in the use of absolute discharges from 3.6 per cent to 6.3 per cent (n=46). Overall, however, the percentage of non-hospital disposals has fallen from 27.6 per cent to 25.6 per cent.

With regard to the possible impact of the Domestic Violence, Crime and Victims Act 2004, what is of note is a reduction in restriction orders from 146 (42.1%) in the pre2004Act cases to 111 (29.4%) in the post2004Act cases. In addition, there is an increase in the post2004Act number of non-hospital disposals from 75 (21.4%) pre2004Act to 107 (28.2%) post2004Act. These differences could be indicative of an increasing awareness and use of flexibility of disposal as the number of unfitness to plead findings continues to rise.

APPENDIX D
IMPACT ASSESSMENT

THE IMPACT ASSESSMENT BEGINS ON THE NEXT PAGE

Title: **Impact Assessment of Unfitness to Plead Consultation Paper**	Impact Assessment (IA)
Lead department or agency: Law Commission	**IA No:** LAWCOM0003
	Date: 12/10/10
	Stage: Consultation
Other departments or agencies: Ministry of Justice	**Source of intervention:** Domestic
	Type of measure: Primary legislation
	Contact for enquiries: Clare Wade 02033340274

Summary: Intervention and Options

What is the problem under consideration? Why is government intervention necessary?

The common law (Pritchard) test used to determine whether an accused is unfit to plead is outdated and inappropriate in the light of modern psychiatric science. The limited scope of the section 4A hearing under the Criminal Procedure (Insanity) Act 1964 is also problematic in that it is not always possible to divide the conduct element from the fault element of an offence. This has led to uncertainty and inconsistency in how the law is applied. Government intervention is necessary to establish a more appropriate and comprehensive legal test. It is also necessary to reform the current legislation so as to remedy the problems with the section 4A hearing.

What are the policy objectives and the intended effects?

The objective of our proposals is to ensure that those accused who are unable to have any meaningful participation in their trial because of a mental or physical condition should not be subject to a trial. Further, those accused who are unable to participate in their trial should be dealt with in a fair and consistent manner. The proposals are intended to bring greater clarity, certainty and consistency to the law and to bring it into line with modern science and the modern trial process. The proposals should ensure a more efficient use of resources within the criminal justice system.

What policy options have been considered? Please justify preferred option (further details in Evidence Base)

Option 0: Do nothing.
Option 1: Comprehensive reform. This would involve a new legal test to determine whether an accused has decision-making capacity. The section 4A hearing would also be reformed so that the prosecution would have to prove that the accused did the act or made the omission and that there are no grounds for acquittal. There would be scope for a further hearing to determine whether the acquittal is because of mental disorder existing at the time of the offence. There would be other more miscellaneous reforms. Option 1 is our preferred option. The law on unfitness to plead has developed in a piecemeal way. Previous reforms have been aimed at specific difficulties and have been made without sufficient consideration of their wider implications or of commensurate reform of other aspects of the procedure. Comprehensive reform would address the problems with the current law while also ensuring that reform is coherent and consistent with relevant developments in other aspects of the law which govern crime and mental health.

When will the policy be reviewed to establish its impact and the extent to which the policy objectives have been achieved?	It will not be reviewed
Are there arrangements in place that will allow a systematic collection of monitoring information for future policy review?	No

Chair's Sign-off For consultation stage Impact Assessments:

I have read the Impact Assessment and I am satisfied that, given the available evidence, it represents a reasonable view of the likely costs, benefits and impact of the leading options.

Signed by the responsible Chair:... Date:......................................

Summary: Analysis and Evidence

Policy Option 1

Description:

Comprehensive Reform

Price Base Year 2009	PV Base Year 2009	Time Period Years 10	Net Benefit (Present Value (PV)) (£m)		
			Low: Optional	High: Optional	Best Estimate: £35.404

COSTS (£m)	Total Transition (Constant Price) Years	Average Annual (excl. Transition) (Constant Price)	Total Cost (Present Value)
Low	0	£16.429	**£153.069**
High	0	£43.755	**£407.690**
Best Estimate	0	£27.429	**£255.551**

Description and scale of key monetised costs by 'main affected groups'

Criminal justice system: increased number of hearings to determine whether the accused has decision-making capacity would incur costs in terms of obtaining expert evidence; there could also be costs as a result of an increase in the use of special measures; there would be a rise in the number of hospital based disposals and supervision orders.

Other key non-monetised costs by 'main affected groups'

BENEFITS (£m)	Total Transition (Constant Price) Years	Average Annual (excl. Transition) (Constant Price)	Total Benefit (Present Value)
Low	0	£18.804	**£175.187**
High	0	£39.404	**£367.107**
Best Estimate	0	£31.230	**£290.954**

Description and scale of key monetised benefits by 'main affected groups'

Criminal justice system: a reduction in the number of custodial sentences; a reduction in the number of transfers from prison to hospital, and the associated administrative costs.

Other key non-monetised benefits by 'main affected groups'

Criminal justice system: reduced burden on prison resources and staff; improvements in mental health of offenders; possible reduction in reoffending; positive application of the European Convention on Human Rights; more efficient use of resources; greater clarity, certainty and consistency to the law; enhanced public confidence in the criminal justice system.

Key assumptions/sensitivities/risks	Discount rate (%)	3.5

(1) A new test of decision-making capacity and a reformed section 4A hearing.
(2) For the best estimate we assume that there will be 500 additional cases where decisional capacity is raised. In 70% of cases (350) the accused will lack decision-making capacity and be subject to a section 4A hearing. 20% could have a trial assisted by special measures and 10% will have a normal trial. Of the 70% found to lack decision-making capacity, 90% will be subject to a disposal under section 5. 50% of these disposals will be hospital orders and 40% supervision orders. For benefits, the 315 receiving a disposal under section 5 would have had a custodial sentence. 70% of those receiving a hospital order would, if they had gone to prison, have been transferred to hospital. SEE PAGES 20 to 21.

Impact on admin burden (AB) (£m):			Impact on policy cost savings (£m):	In scope
New AB: 0	AB savings: 0	Net: 0	Policy cost savings: 0	No

Enforcement, Implementation and Wider Impacts

What is the geographic coverage of the policy/option?	England and Wales
From what date will the policy be implemented?	
Which organisation(s) will enforce the policy?	Criminal Justice System
What is the annual change in enforcement cost (£m)?	
Does enforcement comply with Hampton principles?	Yes
Does implementation go beyond minimum EU requirements?	Yes

What is the CO$_2$ equivalent change in greenhouse gas emissions? (Million tonnes CO$_2$ equivalent)	Traded: 0		Non-traded: 0	
Does the proposal have an impact on competition?	No			
What proportion (%) of Total PV costs/benefits is directly attributable to primary legislation, if applicable?	Costs:		Benefits:	

Annual cost (£m) per organisation (excl. Transition) (Constant Price)	Micro	< 20	Small	Medium	Large
Are any of these organisations exempt?	No	No	No	No	No

Specific Impact Tests: Checklist

Set out in the table below where information on any SITs undertaken as part of the analysis of the policy options can be found in the evidence base. For guidance on how to complete each test, double-click on the link for the guidance provided by the relevant department.

Please note this checklist is not intended to list each and every statutory consideration that departments should take into account when deciding which policy option to follow. It is the responsibility of departments to make sure that their duties are complied with.

Does your policy option/proposal have an impact on…?	Impact	Page ref within IA
Statutory equality duties[1] Statutory Equality Duties Impact Test guidance	Yes	22
Economic impacts		
Competition Competition Assessment Impact Test guidance	No	23
Small firms Small Firms Impact Test guidance	No	23
Environmental impacts		
Greenhouse gas assessment Greenhouse Gas Assessment Impact Test guidance	No	23
Wider environmental issues Wider Environmental Issues Impact Test guidance	No	23
Social impacts		
Health and well-being Health and Well-being Impact Test guidance	Yes	23
Human rights Human Rights Impact Test guidance	Yes	23
Justice system Justice Impact Test guidance	Yes	23
Rural proofing Rural Proofing Impact Test guidance	No	23
Sustainable development Sustainable Development Impact Test guidance	No	23

---

[1] Race, disability and gender Impact assessments are statutory requirements for relevant policies. Equality statutory requirements will be expanded in 2011, once the Equality Bill comes into force. Statutory equality duties part of the Equality Bill apply to GB only. The Toolkit provides advice on statutory equality duties for public authorities with a remit in Northern Ireland.

Evidence Base (for summary sheets) – Notes

Use this space to set out the relevant references, evidence, analysis and detailed narrative from which you have generated your policy options or proposal. Please fill in **References** section.

References

Include the links to relevant legislation and publications, such as public impact assessment of earlier stages (e.g. Consultation, Final, Enactment).

No.	Legislation or publication
1	The Criminal Procedure (Insanity) Act 1964
2	
3	
4	

+ Add another row

Evidence Base

Ensure that the information in this section provides clear evidence of the information provided in the summary pages of this form (recommended maximum of 30 pages). Complete the **Annual profile of monetised costs and benefits** (transition and recurring) below over the life of the preferred policy (use the spreadsheet attached if the period is longer than 10 years).

The spreadsheet also contains an emission changes table that you will need to fill in if your measure has an impact on greenhouse gas emissions.

Annual profile of monetised costs and benefits* - (£m) constant prices

	Y_0	Y_1	Y_2	Y_3	Y_4	Y_5	Y_6	Y_7	Y_8	Y_9
Transition costs	£0	£0	£0	£0	£0	£0	£0	£0	£0	£0
Annual recurring cost	£27.43	£27.43	£27.43	£27.43	£27.43	£27.43	£27.43	£27.43	£27.43	£27.43
Total annual costs	£27.43	£27.43	£27.43	£27.43	£27.43	£27.43	£27.43	£27.43	£27.43	£27.43
Transition benefits	£0	£0	£0	£0	£0	£0	£0	£0	£0	£0
Annual recurring benefits	£31.23	£31.23	£31.23	£31.23	£31.23	£31.23	£31.23	£31.23	£31.23	£31.23
Total annual benefits	£31.23	£31.23	£31.23	£31.23	£31.23	£31.23	£31.23	£31.23	£31.23	£31.23

* For non-monetised benefits please see summary pages and main evidence base section

Microsoft Office
Excel Worksheet

Evidence Base (for summary sheets)

Problem under consideration

The law on unfitness to plead is concerned with whether or not an accused is able to stand trial and, if not, the procedure that should be used to deal with that accused. Where it arises, the court does not consider the accused's guilt, but rather two distinct issues.

1. There is the question for the court of whether the accused is "under a disability" which prevents him or her from being tried – in other words, whether he or she is unfit to plead. "Disability" means any disability and can include both mental and physical impairments. Whether an accused is "under a disability" is determined by applying the legal test for unfitness to plead, which is known as the *Pritchard* test. This test is covered by the common law; its criteria have no statutory basis. For the court to make a finding of unfitness to plead, there must be oral or written evidence from two or more registered medical practitioners, at least one of whom is duly approved under section 12 of the Mental Health Act 1983 as having special expertise in the diagnosis or treatment of mental disorder.

2. If a person is found unfit to plead, there is the question for the jury of whether the accused did the act or made the omission of the offence charged against him or her. This is referred to as the "section 4A hearing". The House of Lords has held in *Antoine* [2000] UKHL 20, [2001] 1 AC 340 that the prosecution only has to prove the conduct element of the offence for the purposes of a section 4A hearing.

Following a finding that (1) the accused is unfit to plead and (2) that he or she did the act or made the omission, the court can make: a hospital order with or without a restriction order; a supervision order; or an order for absolute discharge. The procedure is governed by the Criminal Procedure (Insanity) Act 1964 ("the 1964 Act"), as amended by the Criminal Procedure (Insanity and Unfitness to Plead) Act 1991 and the Domestic Violence, Crime and Victims Act 2004.

The current law on unfitness to plead is unsatisfactory in the light of modern psychiatric science and the modern trial process. The legal test for unfitness to plead and the scope of the section 4A hearing are the two key areas of concern.

The problems with the legal test

The legal test currently used to determine whether someone is unfit to plead – the *Pritchard* test – is outdated and inconsistent with modern psychiatric understanding. The criteria which make up the test have their origins in nineteenth century cases, when the science of psychiatry was still in its infancy. The five basic criteria which emerged from these cases and that are still used today are the ability to: plead to the indictment; to understand the course of the proceedings; to instruct a lawyer; to challenge a juror; and to understand the evidence. An inability to do any one of these five things will result in a finding of unfitness to plead.

The criteria however focus on the intellectual abilities of the accused, and do not take into account his or her ability to make decisions in relation to the trial. There is a real danger that the *Pritchard* test is therefore under inclusive. The present law fails to catch some defendants who lack the capacity to participate meaningfully in the trial process, which in itself could be regarded as a breach of article 6 of the European Convention on Human Rights. The jurisprudence of the European Court of Human Rights makes it clear that article 6 includes a general right of "effective participation" (see *Stanford v United Kingdom* App No 16757/90). The underlying reasoning in the cases gives rise to a broad principle – namely, that effective participation requires active involvement on the part of the accused rather than just a passive presence. If the legal test is not broad enough to ensure that those accused who stand trial are capable of effective participation, then there is a clear risk that their trials will be trials incompatible with article 6. The *Pritchard* test is therefore outdated in the light of the jurisprudence on effective participation and other developments in relation to vulnerable defendants.

The unfairness of the test has been demonstrated, for example, in cases where a defendant is delusional but nonetheless found fit to plead because he or she has an underlying cognitive understanding of the trial. However, his or her delusions may be such as to impair his or her capacity to make decisions. For example, in *Murray* [2008] EWCA Crim 1792 the appellant suffered from paranoid schizophrenia. She had killed her five-year-old daughter by stabbing her with a kitchen knife more than fifty times. Even though she had a defence of diminished responsibility, she insisted on pleading guilty to the offence of murder. At the trial the consensus among psychiatrists had been that she was not unfit to plead in the legal sense but one observed that "psychiatric understanding and the law in relation to mentally ill defendants do not always sit comfortably together". *Murray* illustrates that the law does not have regard for the process by which a defendant comes to the decision to plead guilty and that, in this case, the law did not make sufficient allowance for the fact that the defendant's memory of her thoughts and emotions at the time of the killing were such that she simply wanted to be punished for what she saw as 'murder'. Cases such as *Murray* indicate a clear "mismatch between the legal test and psychiatric understanding" in relation to unfitness to plead (see *Murray* [2008] EWCA Crim 1792 at [6] by Lord Justice Toulson).

Ultimately the *Pritchard* test sets too high a threshold for finding an accused unfit to plead and is inconsistent with the demands of the modern trial process. It has the practical effect of limiting the number of people who are found unfit to plead and therefore could mean that many accused are not receiving a fair trial. It also leads to the danger of convicting those who might be innocent because they may not be able to rebut the allegations against them.

The problems with the section 4A hearing

Section 4A of the Criminal Justice (Insanity) Act 1964 provides that, following a finding of unfitness to plead:

> The trial shall not proceed or further proceed but it shall be determined by a jury … whether they are satisfied, as respects the count or each of the counts on which the accused was to be or was being tried, that he did the act or made the omission charged against him as the offence.

If the jury are so satisfied, then they make a finding that the accused did the act or made the omission. If they are not so satisfied, then they return a verdict of acquittal.

The problems with the section 4A hearing flow from a tension between the need to allow the accused a fair hearing as to the facts of the alleged offence and the need to protect the public from an accused who may be dangerous. The present legislation aims to provide for a fair hearing by giving the accused the opportunity to be acquitted if the prosecution cannot prove that he or she did the act. It aims to protect the public by ensuring that if there is evidence that the accused did the act, then a finding can be made to that effect and he or she will be subject to the disposal of the court.

The key issue in relation to the section 4A hearing is whether "the act" means that the prosecution has to prove only the conduct element of the offence, or whether both the conduct and fault elements must be proved. In *Antoine* [2000] UKHL 20, [2001] 1 AC 340 the House of Lords ruled that for the purposes of the section 4A hearing, only the conduct element of the offence must be proved.

This however depends on it being possible to divide the conduct element from the fault element of an offence. As the subsequent case law has shown, the problem with the ruling in *Antoine* is that it is not always possible to make such a division. The result in any given case will, to some extent, be arbitrary because it will depend on the nature of the charge.

This has an impact on cases involving secondary participation. Secondary participation is the common law doctrine which allows a person (D) who encourages or assists or in some circumstances, causes, another person (P) to perpetrate a criminal offence to be liable to the same extent as the perpetrator. If under a true construction of section 4A the jury is precluded from looking at the accused's knowledge and D's liability depends on what he or she knew P intended to do, then it is not possible to ascertain whether D is secondarily liable. An exclusive focus on the conduct element of the offence is also potentially problematic where the accused is charged with an inchoate offence. The current law is therefore uncertain and it is likely that it will continue to be applied inconsistently and somewhat arbitrarily.

Rationale for intervention

The problems with the current law can only be remedied through government intervention to amend the procedure under the existing legislation and to provide for a more comprehensive and appropriate legal test.

Intervention is necessary to clarify and modernise the law and therefore ensure that it is applied fairly and consistently.

Policy objectives

1. The law needs to be updated and clarified. The present legal test for unfitness to plead dates back to 1836 and is not consistent with the modern trial process in that it does not focus on the fact that effective participation requires the accused to make decisions relating to his or her trial. Further, it is not consistent with developments in psychiatry in that it does not take account of many types of mental disorder and places a disproportionate emphasis on cognitive ability.

2. The law must deal appropriately and fairly with those accused who have a mental or physical condition by finding a way of resolving an allegation against them which enables their representatives to test the evidence with a view to an acquittal. This must be done while simultaneously protecting the public against an accused who may be a danger.

3. All reform should be coherent and take account of the developments in relation to vulnerable defendants who may have difficulty in following the trial process but who are able to do so with the assistance of special measures.

4. The procedure should ensure that mentally disordered offenders are not inappropriately sentenced to custody but instead receive appropriate treatment either in hospital or in the community.

5. There needs to be certainty about the way in which the law is applied in relation to both the legal test and the resolution of the facts (the section 4A hearing) and results should not be arbitrary.

Achieving these policy objectives will enhance public confidence in the criminal justice system. It will also ensure greater fairness to people with a mental disorder, who are amongst the most vulnerable of society's citizens. This is of particular importance given the evidence that the numbers of mentally disordered persons encountering the criminal justice system are increasing and there is no reason to believe that the trend will reverse.

Scope and Scale

Studies of the prevalence of mental disorder in prison populations have consistently found a substantial level of disorder. Although over a decade old, the best guide to its prevalence remains the study conducted by the Office of National Statistics in 1997. Table 1 combines the results of this study and another study into psychiatric morbidity among the general population.

Table 1 – Prevalence of mental disorder in prisoners and the general population

	Prisoners	General population
Schizophrenia and delusional disorder	8%	0.5%
Personality disorder	66%	5.3%
Neurotic disorder	45%	13.8%
Drug dependency	45%	5.2%
Alcohol dependency	30%	11.5%

Source: N Singleton et al, *Psychiatric Morbidity among Prisoners in England and Wales* (1998) and *Psychiatric Morbidity among Adults Living in Private Households, 2000* (2001).

It has been estimated that at any one time 10% of the prison population have serious mental health problems. An estimated 72% of male and 70% of female sentenced prisoners have two or more mental health disorders, and 20% of all prisoners have four of the five major mental health disorders: see Prison Reform Trust, *Bromley Briefings Prison Factfile* (June 2009) at page 37.

These figures show that there are a significant number of offenders in prison who have mental health problems. In addition, it is estimated that 20% to 30% have learning difficulties or learning disabilities that interfere with their ability to cope within the criminal justice system: see The Bradley Report (April 2009) at page 98. The Prison Reform Trust reported that over half of prison Independent Monitoring Boards "frequently saw prisoners who were too ill to be in prison": see Prison Reform Trust, *Too little too late: an independent review of unmet mental health need in prison* (2009) at page 2. Further, HM Chief Inspector of Prisons has said that "prison has become, to far too large an extent, the default setting for those with a wide range of mental and emotional disorders": see HM Inspectorate of Prisons, *The mental health of prisoners, a thematic review of the care and support of prisoners with mental health* (2007) at page 7.

In light of this evidence, it has been observed that the numbers of findings of unfitness to plead remain low: see TP Rogers et al, "Reformulating the law on fitness to plead: a qualitative study" (2009) 20(6) *Journal of Forensic Psychiatry and Psychology* 815 at page 816. This is despite empirical research which shows that the average annual number of findings of unfitness to plead has been steadily increasing over the years: see table 2.

Table 2 – Annual average of findings of unfitness to plead, 1987-2006

5-year period	Annual average
1987-1991	12.6
1992-1996	24.6
1997-2001	65.8
2002-2006	104.2

Source: RD Mackay, Unfitness to plead – data on formal findings from 2002 to 2008 (research commissioned by the Law Commission).

Where an accused is unfit to plead and is subject to a section 4A hearing, the results of Professor Mackay's research suggest that in the majority of cases the accused is found to have done "the act": see table 3.

Table 3 – Outcome of section 4A hearings, 2002-2008

Result	Frequency	Percent
Did the act on all counts	401	55.3%
Did the act on some counts but acquitted on others	17	2.3%
Acquitted on all counts	26	3.6%
Section 4A hearing did not take place as prosecution did not offer any evidence	15	2.1%
Indictment to remain on file/proceedings stayed	9	1.2%
Nolle prosequi	1	0.1%
No section 4A hearing as accused certified insane before arraignment	1	0.1%
Uncertain (no information on outcome)	255	35.2%
Total	**725**	**100.0%**

Source: RD Mackay, Unfitness to plead – data on formal findings from 2002 to 2008 (research commissioned by the Law Commission).

Leaving aside the "uncertain cases", in approximately 90% of cases an unfit accused was found to have done the act on at least one count.

Following such a finding, the court can give a hospital order (with or without a restriction order), a supervision order or an order for absolute discharge. Professor Mackay's findings gives a break down of each type of disposal: see table 4.

Table 4 – Disposals, 2002-2008

Disposal	Frequency
Hospital order with a restriction order	263
Hospital order	210
Supervision order (2 years)	99
Supervision order (under 2 years)	17
Absolute discharge	46

Source: RD Mackay, Unfitness to plead – data on formal findings from 2002 to 2008 (research commissioned by the Law Commission).

It should be noted that during this period 20 guardianship orders were made, but following the Domestic Violence, Crime and Victims Act 2004 this is no longer an option available to the courts.

Figures from the Ministry of Justice show that the number of patients receiving a restriction order following a finding of unfitness to plead is a very small proportion of the total number of mentally disordered offenders who are admitted to hospital as restricted patients. Table 5 sets out the number of restricted patients admitted to hospital each year following a finding of unfitness to plead and the number of patients admitted after a hearing.

Table 5 – Restricted patients: annual admissions to hospital and admissions following a disposal from an unfitness to plead hearing, 2002-2008

	2002	2003	2004	2005	2006	2007	2008
Admissions to hospital	1,006	1,086	1,329	1,350	1,440	1,458	1,501
Admissions after hearing	50	39	51	31	32	31	30

Source: Ministry of Justice, *Statistics of mentally disordered offenders 2008* (January 2010).

Although only 30 restricted patients were admitted to hospital following a finding of unfitness in 2008, the total number of mentally disordered offenders admitted as restricted patients that year was 1,501. The number of admissions as a result of unfitness to plead hearings therefore represents a small proportion of the total number of admissions.

A significant proportion of admissions to hospital are as a result of a transfer from prison. The Ministry of Justice reported that in 2008, there were 926 restricted patients admitted to hospital as a result of a transfer from prison. This represented 62% of the total number of admissions to hospital in 2008: see Ministry of Justice, *Statistics on mentally disordered offenders 2008* (January 2010). Although some of these prisoners will have developed mental health problems, or their condition will have become significantly worse, during the period they spent in prison, anecdotal evidence strongly suggests that many of these offenders were suffering from significant mental disorder at the time of their trial which may have prevented their effective participation. This means that they will have been subjected to a trial and stigmatised with a conviction when they lacked the capacity to defend themselves. In addition, as a consequence of their not being diverted to hospital until a later stage their treatment will have been delayed, possibly resulting in longer and more costly intervention being required. The Sainsbury Centre for Mental Health (now the Centre for Mental Health) for example has suggested that savings for the NHS could be achieved through the earlier identification and treatment of mental health problems: see

Sainsbury Centre for Mental Health, *Diversion: a better way for criminal justice and mental health* (2009) at page 4.

Description of options considered

Two options for reform have been considered.

Option 0: do nothing. This option demonstrates the ongoing costs and benefits of non-intervention and is therefore the "base case" against which the other option for intervention is compared.

Option 1: comprehensive reform. This involves reforming both the legal test and the section 4A hearing, as well as reform in other miscellaneous areas such as the Secretary of State's power to refer cases back to court for trial.

Within option 1, alternatives have been considered for reform of the legal test and of the section 4A hearing.

Option 1

(a) A new legal test

Option 1 involves replacing the current *Pritchard* test with a test which assesses the decision-making capacity of the accused. This test would be broader than the current *Pritchard* test as it would not focus simply on the intellectual abilities of the accused but take into account his or her capacity to make decisions relating to the trial. It is envisaged that a wider range of mental disorders or other impairments would affect the accused's decision-making capacity than are currently found to affect the accused's fitness to plead.

In the consultation paper, we suggest that the new decision-making capacity test could operate as follows:

1. A unitary construct. This would mean that there would be a single test as to decision-making capacity which is in so far as is possible decided at the outset of the proceedings. This test would determine whether the accused has decision-making capacity for all purposes in relation to trial.

2. We have rejected a disaggregated approach, which would assess the accused's capacity to make each specific decision or do each task as it arises in his or her trial, taking into account the context of the case and the stage of and complexity of the proceedings. It would allow for a person to have capacity for one purpose but not for another.

A broad unitary construct reflects the underlying rationale for having any unfitness to plead procedure, namely that because of the accused's mental or physical condition a criminal trial is in itself an inappropriate process. Further, we think that a fully disaggregated approach would be unworkable in the criminal context. It would lead to uncertainty and could be complex and time-consuming and create unacceptable delays for victims and witnesses. The costs of this approach would be disproportionate to any benefits, and we believe that the problems with the current law can be remedied with a unitary construct which is broad enough to take into account the range of abilities required. In our view a unitary construct would be simpler to apply and more cost effective than a disaggregated approach.

We also consider the role of special measures within the structure of a new test of decision-making capacity. Special measures are put into place to ensure that vulnerable defendants can participate in the proceedings, for example, by seating the defendant next to his or her lawyer or providing for an intermediary when the defendant gives evidence (see section 33BA of the Youth and Criminal Evidence Act 1999, as inserted by section 104(1) of the Coroners and Justice Act 2009). We consider two options in relation to special measures.

1. The availability of special measures would be a factor in the new legal test. This would mean that in determining whether the accused has decision-making capacity, consideration would be given to the extent to which special measures could assist the accused to participate in his or her trial.

2. The availability of special measures would not be relevant to the new legal test of decision-making capacity. However, an accused who has decision-making capacity may still be vulnerable because of his or her mental or physical condition and therefore the use of special measures at

trial may be appropriate. This would be similar to the current position, where the availability of special measures is not part of the *Pritchard* test.

Our preferred option is that the availability of special measures should be a factor in the legal test. There is a significant disadvantage in not including special measures within the new decision-making capacity test in that it risks replicating the current situation where their availability is often overlooked. If special measures are ignored an accused who would be capable of being tried could be diverted unnecessarily into the section 4A procedure. In an appropriate case, however, special measures could allow an accused to enter a guilty plea even though he or she would not have the capacity to participate in a trial.

Research also suggests that judicial decisions to invoke special measures at the outset of a trial often lapse well before its conclusion: see TP Rogers et al, "Reformulating the law on fitness to plead: a qualitative study" (2009) 20(6) *Journal of Forensic Psychiatry and Psychology* 815. This has a negative impact in relation to protecting a vulnerable defendant's right to effective participation under article 6. By including the consideration of special measures in the capacity test it is anticipated that special measures will be secured for the whole of the trial.

Including special measures within the legal test could also make them more effective, as the measures used would be more targeted on the requirements of each individual defendant in order to ensure effective participation. A problem with the current situation has for example been that special measures do not focus on the specific needs of those defendants with learning difficulties: see Prison Reform Trust, *Vulnerable defendants in the criminal courts: a review of provisions for adults and children* (2009).

(b) Reform of the section 4A hearing

In relation to the section 4A hearing, we consider four options for reform.

1. Require the prosecution to prove all elements of the offence, as envisaged by the Butler Committee: see the Report of the Committee on Mentally Abnormal Offenders (1975) Cmnd 6244 paragraph 10.24.

2. Abolish the section 4A hearing. An unfit accused (or an accused lacking decision-making capacity) would undergo a trial, subject to the proviso that once he or she has been found to lack decision-making capacity then a legal representative would be appointed to represent his or her interests in the trial (as is currently done for the purposes of a section 4A hearing). This representative is not bound to follow the accused's instructions about the way in which the case should be run if he or she thinks that those instructions are not commensurate with the accused's interests.

3. Adopt the Scottish procedure which requires the prosecution to prove beyond reasonable doubt that the accused did the act or made the omission, but only on the balance of probabilities that there are no grounds for acquittal.

4. Replace the current section 4A hearing with a procedure whereby the prosecution has to prove that the accused did the act or made the omission and that there are no grounds for acquittal. This procedure could result in the following outcomes:

    (a) a finding that the accused has done the act or made the omission *and* that there are no grounds for acquittal;

    (b) an outright acquittal; or

    (c) an acquittal because the accused had a mental disorder at the time of the offence (along the lines of the special verdict of not guilty by reason of insanity).

    Following a finding under (a) or (c), the same disposals would be available as are currently available under section 5 of the Criminal Procedure (Insanity) Act 1964, namely a hospital order with or without a restriction order, a supervision order, or an order for absolute discharge.

Although abolishing the section 4A hearing has the advantage of simplicity, we believe that there is a strong case for retaining the section 4A hearing. This is because it would be wrong for an accused person to be found guilty and sentenced when he or she is not in a position to be able to meet the charge either by defending him or herself or providing instructions as to mitigation. The section 4A hearing provides an important protection from conviction for those who cannot participate meaningfully in a normal trial. In our view, the procedure outlined under option 4 above would continue to provide this protection and ensure greater fairness to the accused while avoiding the difficulties and uncertainties resulting from the decision in *Antoine*. However, given the possible greater scope for acquitting an accused, outcome (c) under that option provides an important protection for the public from harm.

(c) Miscellaneous issues

In addition to reform of the legal test and the section 4A hearing, we provisionally propose a number of other changes which we believe would improve the law in this area.

1. Where a defendant who is subject to a trial has a mental disorder or other impairment and wishes to give evidence, then expert evidence on the general effect of that mental disorder or impairment should be admissible.

2. A suitable instrument to assess decision-making capacity should be developed and this should accompany the legal test.

3. Where the Secretary of State has remitted an accused for trial under section 5A(4) of the Criminal Procedure (Insanity) Act 1964 pursuant to the accused being detained under a hospital order with a restriction order, and it thereafter becomes clear beyond doubt (and all the medical experts agree) that the accused is still unfit to plead (or still lacks decision-making capacity), the court should be able to reverse the decision to remit the case.

4. Where the Secretary of State has remitted an accused for trial and he or she is found to be unfit to plead (or to lack decision-making capacity) there should not be any need to have a further section 4A hearing. This is subject to the proviso that the court considers it to be in the interests of justice not to have a hearing.

5. In circumstances where a finding under section 4A is quashed and there has been no challenge or finding that the accused is unfit to plead (or lacks decision-making capacity) there should be a power for the Court of Appeal in appropriate circumstances to order a re-hearing under section 4A, rather than only being able to enter an acquittal as is the case under the current law (section 16 of the Criminal Appeals Act 1968).

Cost and benefit analysis

Option 0: do nothing

COSTS

There is an ongoing cost of doing nothing to address the problems identified in relation to the law on unfitness to plead.

The legal test

If the legal test for unfitness to plead remains unchanged it could mean that some accused who are unable to stand trial are nonetheless subject to trial. Subjecting these accused to trial runs the obvious risk of convicting those who might be innocent because they may not have the ability to rebut the allegations against them. Wrongful convictions involve significant costs to individuals and to society in general, and damage confidence in the criminal justice system as a whole.

Wrongful convictions also cost the criminal justice system time and money in appeals. The estimated cost of a day's sitting for the Court of Appeal (Criminal Division) in 2009-10 is £16,635. Further, if a wrongly convicted person is given a custodial sentence this would mean costs in terms of prison places.

A wrongful conviction can also have a detrimental impact on an individual's life. It can lead to stigmatisation, adversely affect the individual's mental health, or result in a loss of employment or home, and a wrongly convicted individual could seek compensation. It can also mean that the perpetrator of the crime is not punished, risking further harm to society in general.

An under inclusive unfitness to plead test also could also lead to trials which are incompatible with the right to a fair trial under article 6, in that it risks some defendants standing trial even though they are not able to effectively participate. This could incur additional costs in terms of appeals and further harm to public confidence in the criminal justice system.

The section 4A hearing

By doing nothing it is also likely that the problems with the section 4A hearing will not be resolved, leading to further uncertainty and inconsistency in the law. Uncertainty could increase the length of section 4A hearings, or result in more appeals. The law will continue to be applied arbitrarily leading to unfairness to individuals as well as harming public confidence in the criminal justice system.

Finally, without the miscellaneous reforms we provisionally propose, there could be unnecessary hearings to determine whether the accused is still unfit to plead (or lacks decision-making capacity) and unnecessary hearings under section 4A, with associated costs. Further, the limited options available to the Court of Appeal when a finding under section 4A is quashed could mean that a person is acquitted even though he or she presents a real danger to the public. This inefficient use of resources has an adverse effect.

BENEFITS

Because the do-nothing option is compared against itself, its costs and benefits are necessarily zero, as is its Net Present Value (NPV). The NPV shows the total net value of a project over a specific time period. The value of the costs and benefits in an NPV are adjusted to account for inflation and the fact that we generally value benefits that are provided now more than we value the same benefits provided in the future.

Option 1: comprehensive reform

The costs and benefits discussed below for option 1 are based on:

(i)   a new decision-making capacity test which is a unitary construct and for which the availability of special measures to aid participation is a relevant factor;

(ii)   a reformed section 4A hearing whereby the prosecution has to prove all elements of the offence and which can result in outcomes (a) to (c) discussed above; and

(iii)   the miscellaneous reforms outlined above.

TRANSITIONAL (ONE-OFF) COSTS

1. Developing a standardised instrument

We provisionally propose that a standardised instrument should be developed to assess decision-making capacity. Developing this instrument may incur transitional costs but until the form of such an instrument is known these costs cannot be estimated.

2. Training

Because we assume that both initial and ongoing judicial training in this area would not be unduly onerous and could therefore be incorporated within the Judicial Studies Board existing training programmes, there will be minimal if any additional costs as a result of judicial training.

With regards to training legal professionals, we would assume that training in this area would not add significant cost or time to the training required by the Solicitors Regulation Authority and the Bar Standards Board in order for barristers and solicitors to maintain their practising certificates. Any minimal costs would be borne by the practitioners (or their employers) if they choose to undertake training to assist their work.

ON-GOING COSTS

Criminal justice system

1. Court time

The length of an average hearing where the accused is found unfit to plead and is then subject to the section 4A procedure is likely to take approximately the same amount of time as an average Crown Court trial. If under our provisional proposals there is a rise in the number of decision-making capacity hearings, as this would represent a corresponding reduction in the number of trials, this would not generally represent any significant increase in costs in terms of court time.

Broadening the section 4A hearing may also increase the length of proceedings, although this may be counterbalanced by increased certainty as to what the prosecution must prove. In the event that an accused is acquitted following consideration of the facts in the section 4A hearing we provisionally propose that, at the judge's discretion, the jury should determine whether the acquittal is because the accused had a mental disorder at the time of the offence. This may marginally increase the overall time of the hearing.

2. Expert evidence required in more cases

Although there is currently an absence of data on the number of cases where unfitness to plead is raised, during the passage of the Domestic Violence, Crime and Victims Act in 2004 Vera Baird QC is reported in Hansard as stating that in 90% of cases where unfitness to plead was an issue there was no dispute between the prosecution and defence (*Hansard* (HC), 27 October 2004, vol 425 col 1525). The latest empirical research conducted by Professor Mackay shows that in the seven-year period from 2002 to 2008, the annual average number of findings of unfitness was 103.6. Assuming that all 10% of contested claims failed (which is unlikely) the current maximum average number of applications per year would be 115.1: see RD Mackay, Unfitness to plead – data on formal findings from 2002 to 2008 (research commissioned by the Law Commission).

A decision-making capacity test would be broader than the current *Pritchard* test as it would not focus simply on the intellectual abilities of the accused but take into account his or her capacity to make decisions relating to the trial. We therefore envisage that a wider range of mental or physical conditions would affect the accused's decision-making capacity than are currently found to affect the accused's fitness to plead. A possible impact of comprehensive reform therefore is that the accused's decision-making capacity will be raised in more cases than unfitness to plead is currently raised.

As discussed above, there is considerable evidence that a high number of prisoners suffer from one or more mental health problems. Further, Ministry of Justice data shows that in 2008, there were 926 offenders transferred from hospital as restricted patients, with 484 of these transfers taking place while the person was unsentenced or untried (*Statistics of mentally disordered offenders 2008* (January 2010) at page 7).

Additional hearings could incur additional costs in terms of obtaining medical evidence as to whether the accused lacks decision-making capacity. The Ministry of Justice has proposed rates for expert witnesses funded by legal aid. For psychiatrists and psychologists the rate would be £70 to £100 per hour for examination and the preparation of reports, and £346 to £500 for attendance in court for each full day: see Ministry of Justice, *Legal aid: funding reforms* CP 18/09 (November 2009). In the financial support to the Bradley Report, the cost of psychiatric court report was estimated at £738: see figure 20, page 22.

There could also be a need to obtain expert evidence in relation to a qualified acquittal (as under our provisional proposed reform of the section 4A hearing) which would incur additional costs.

Obtaining expert evidence could have financial implications for HM Court Service, the Crown Prosecution Service and other prosecuting authorities, individual defendants and the Legal Services Commission. The proportion of defendants in the Crown Court who are publicly funded is estimated to be between 91% and 97%: see Ministry of Justice, *Judicial and court statistics 2007* (September 2008) and *Judicial and court statistics 2008* (September 2009).

3. Increased use of special measures

We provisionally propose that when determining decision-making capacity the court should consider whether an accused who would otherwise lack decision-making capacity might be able to stand trial or plead guilty with the assistance of special measures. Special measures that might be deployed in this context might include the defendant giving evidence through a live television link or through an intermediary (likely to be a speech and language specialist).

We believe that there will be an increase in the use of special measures to support defendants with special needs as a result of these provisional proposals since (1) some individuals who are currently found unfit may, with the assistance of special measures, be found to have decision-making capacity to participate in trial, and (2) because it is anticipated that there will be an increase in cases where the accused's decision-making capacity is raised as an issue (see above) and some of these hearings will result in an order for a trial with special measures.

It is impossible to predict with any accuracy what proportion of cases considered under the decision-making capacity test would result in the accused being subject to a trial with special measures. Currently we assume that in 90% of cases where the issue is raised, an accused is found unfit to plead. However, a new test may mean that more accused might claim that they lack decision-making capacity speculatively, at least until the new test has become established, and this would likely increase the number of findings that the accused is able to stand trial with or without the assistance of special measures.

A scenario would be that in 70% of cases where the accused's decision-making capacity is raised as an issue, he or she will be found to lack decision-making capacity. In 20% of cases the accused would be found to have decision-making capacity but there would be an order for a trial with special measures. In 10% of cases he or she would be subject to a normal trial.

Little data is currently available on the costs of using special measures for defendants. In relation to a registered intermediary, an estimated cost for one day in court (including travel expenses) is £308[2]: see Office for Criminal Justice Reform, *Rates of remuneration for registered intermediaries* (November 2009).

4. Additional remissions for trial

Under the current system, and under our provisional proposals, in the event that an unfit accused who has been given a hospital order with a restriction order becomes fit he or she may be remitted to court to stand trial. Inevitably if more accused are found to lack decision-making capacity, there is the potential for an increase in the number of subsequent remissions for trial. However, it is impossible to anticipate how many additional cases would be remitted back to court as a result of our provisional proposals.

NHS

1. Increase in number of hospital based disposals

The most significant cost consideration arises from the additional hospital based disposals under section 5. The estimated average cost of a year in a medium secure hospital is an average of £165,000, and £300,000 for a high secure hospital: see Sainsbury Centre of Mental Health http://www.scmh.org.uk/criminal_justice/forensicservices.aspx). A small proportion of offenders go into high secure hospitals; most go into medium secure hospitals, and then later can be "stepped-down" to low secure facilities.

Above we highlighted that Professor Mackay's research suggests that in approximately 90% of cases (where the outcome was known), those subject to a section 4A hearing are found to have done the act on at least one of the counts on the indictment. An increase in the number of accused who are found to lack decision-making capacity could mean that more accused are subject to the disposals available under section 5 of the Criminal Procedure (Insanity) Act 1964 (a hospital order (with or without a restriction order), a supervision order or an order for absolute discharge). Under our revised section 4A hearing, these disposals would be available if there was either (1) a finding that the accused did the act or made the omission and that there were no grounds for acquittal or (2) an acquittal because the accused had a mental disorder at the time of the offence.

---

[2] This figure has been calculated using standard rates and on the assumptions that travel time is 3 hours (at £4 per 15 minutes) within London, and the cost of the train ticket is £8. The intermediary is at court for 7 hours (including lunch) at £36 pounds per hour. It has been brought to our attention that this estimate could be an over or under estimate if travel costs and travel time were higher or lower.

Although we anticipate more acquittals under our provisional proposals for reform of the section 4A hearing, many of these may be qualified on the basis that at the time of the offence the accused had a mental disorder. We would therefore expect that in the majority of cases an accused without decision-making capacity will be subject to a disposal under section 5. Given Professor Mackay's research, we think that a reasonable scenario would be that in 90% of the cases where an accused is found to lack decision-making capacity, he or she will be subject to a disposal under section 5; and in 10% of cases there will be an outright acquittal.

Professor Mackay's research shows that hospital orders continue to be the predominant disposal following a finding of unfitness to plead. In the period 1991 to 1996, hospital based disposals accounted for 77.4% of all disposals. This fell to 62.9% in the period 1997 to 2001, but increased to 65.2% in the period 2002 to 2008 (although during this period there were 31 murder cases where there was no flexibility as to disposal). However, a broader decision-making capacity test may mean that a hospital order is not an appropriate disposal in a greater proportion of cases. See RD Mackay, Unfitness to plead – data on formal findings from 2002 to 2008 (research commissioned by the Law Commission).

A scenario would be that, following our provisionally proposed reforms, 50% of disposals under section 5 would be hospital based disposals. An increase in the number of disposals under section 5 as a result of an increase in the number of accused found to lack decision-making capacity is therefore likely to have a significant impact on the numbers of hospital based disposals each year.

However, this may not necessarily mean that there will be a corresponding increase in the numbers of offenders in hospital. This is because, for example, a significant number of mentally disordered prisoners are transferred from prison to hospital every year: in 2008 there were 926 such transfers. Although some of these prisoners will have developed mental health problems in prison or suffered a worsening of their condition we anticipate that some of this number will have lacked decision-making capacity at trial. A reformulated test which picks up such offenders at an earlier stage could therefore reduce the number of transfers from prison to hospital: SEE PAGE 17.

2. Increase in number of supervision orders

An increase in the numbers of accused found to lack decision-making capacity could lead to an increase in the numbers of supervision orders, which could place additional burdens on the NHS to provide mental health treatment.

A supervision order under section 5 of the Criminal Procedure (Insanity) Act 1964 is an order which requires the person to be under the supervision of a social worker, an officer of a local probation board, or an officer of a provider of probation services for a specified period of not more than two years. A supervision order may require the person to submit during the whole or part of that period to treatment by or under the direction of a registered medical practitioner: see Part 1 of Schedule 1A to the Criminal Procedure (Insanity) Act 1964. This can include treatment as a non-resident at an institution specified in the order.

In 2002 to 2008 supervision orders represented 15.7% of the total number of disposals following a finding that the accused did the act under section 4A. This was a decrease from 17.9% in 1997 to 2001, but this could be explained by the fact that in 2002 to 2008 there were 31 murder cases where there was no flexibility as to disposal. Supervision orders have been given for serious offences including GBH, arson and robber. Professor Mackay's research also suggests that in cases where the Domestic Violence, Crime and Victims Act 2004 has come into force, there has been an increase in the number of non-hospital based disposals from 21.4% to 28.2%. Therefore, if more accused are found to lack decision-making capacity, then more could be given non-hospital based disposals, particularly given that the test may catch more accused for whom a hospital order would be inappropriate: see RD Mackay, Unfitness to plead – data on formal findings from 2002 to 2008 (research commissioned by the Law Commission).

A scenario could be that 40% of disposals following a decision-making capacity hearing would result in a supervision order. It is difficult however to predict how many of these disposals would include requirements as to medical treatment for the accused's mental condition.

The average cost per offender commencement for a stand alone supervision order is estimated at £652. For a community order involving access to mental health treatment, the average cost is estimated at £3,703: see Accenture, Final report costing community order requirements (October 2007).

BENEFITS

Criminal justice system

1. Reduction in number of custodial sentences

An increase in the number of findings that the accused lacks decision-making capacity (compared with the current number of findings of unfitness to plead) could lead to a reduction in the number of defendants receiving a custodial sentence. Comprehensive reform could therefore reduce the burden on the prison service. This is on the assumption that a new test would be more effective at identifying mentally disordered offenders at the point of trial which would be an increase in the number of disposals under section 5 and therefore a decrease in the number of custodial sentences.

An increase in the number of findings that the accused lacks decision-making capacity will however not necessarily lead to a commensurate decrease in the number of prison places required. This is because not all such accused would necessarily have been subject to a custodial sentence had they stood trial.

The estimated average total cost of a prison place as estimated by MoJ is £44,703 (in 2009-10 prices) and ranges between £31,374 and £69,885. The Sainsbury Centre has estimated that the average cost of keeping someone in prison is £39,000 a year. However, this does not include expenditure on health services, which is met by the Department of Health. Spending on mental health care in prisons is estimated at around £20 million a year. The Sainsbury Centre estimates therefore that up to £2,000 a year should be added to the average prison cost for someone with a severe mental illness: see Sainsbury Centre for Mental Health, *Diversion: a better way for criminal justice and mental health* (2009) at page 39.

2. Reduction in number of transfers from prison to hospital

If more people with a mental disorder are identified at the point of trial and do not therefore receive a custodial sentence, this could also potentially reduce the number of transfers of mentally disordered offenders from prison to hospital. This would reduce the administrative costs associated with such transfers. A reasonable scenario would be that out of those accused who are found to lack decision-making capacity under our proposed test and who are subsequently given a hospital order, 70% would have ended up in hospital if they had gone to prison beforehand as a result of a transfer. There is a medium risk that this is too conservative an estimate and therefore that we have underestimated the savings made as a result of fewer transfers.

Ministry of Justice data reveals that in 2008 there were 926 restricted patients transferred from prison to hospital. These figures only relate to restricted patients, and therefore it is likely that there could be many more patients, who are not under a restriction order, who have been transferred to hospital from prison. It has been estimated that at any one time up to 3,700 prisoners had a mental illness severe enough to require transfer to an appropriate NHS mental health service: Prison Reform Trust, *Too little too late: an independent review of unmet mental health need in prison* (2009) at page 6. It is reasonably likely that many people requiring a transfer could have had mental disorder at the time of their trial which affected their decision-making capacity.

Prisons have faced significant problems in transferring mentally disordered prisoners to hospital. An audit by the Department of Health indicated that at any one time there are on average 282 prisoners awaiting initial psychiatric assessment: see The Bradley Report (April 2009) page 105. According to figures given by Paul Goggins to Parliament in 2004, at any one time 40 people may have waited three months for transfer to an NHS hospital (*Hansard* (HC), 17 March 2004, vol 419, col 121WH). Although there is evidence that the process of transfers to hospital has improved, there are often still considerable delays. Such delays can cause significant distress to the patient, their family, and the people charged with their care: see The Bradley Report (April 2009) at page 105. It can also lead to the misuse of segregation units: see Prison Reform Trust, *Troubled inside: responding to the mental health needs of men in prison* at page 43. Given the adverse impact of such delay, this could mean that longer and therefore possibly more costly treatment will ultimately be required when they reach hospital. By detecting those with severe mental disorder at the time of the trial and dealing with them using an appropriate disposal, treatment could start at an earlier stage and reduce the costs of transfers from prison to hospital.

3. Reduced burden on prison service

A new decision-making capacity test could provide one means of more effective diversion of mentally disordered accused away from prison. This could have a positive impact for the prison service, given that there is considerable evidence that prisons are struggling to deal with the high level of mental disorder among prisoners.

A review by Lord Bradley of people with mental health problems or learning disabilities in the criminal justice system concluded that evidence suggests that "prisons are currently struggling to provide [effective treatment], and in particular that certain elements of the prison population with mental health problems are not receiving any treatment at all": see The Bradley Report (April 2009) at page 98. The high numbers of mentally disordered offenders within prisons have placed considerable strain on prison staff and resources. There is also evidence that prisons must devote disproportionate resources to looking after prisoners with mental health problems. Mentally ill prisoners can also have a negative impact on staff who have insufficient training. Source: Prison Reform Trust, *Too little too late: an independent review of unmet mental health need in prisons* (2009) at pages 4 to 8.

4. Improvements in mental health and reductions in reoffending

If the decision-making capacity test identifies people with mental disorder at an earlier stage, this could ensure that they receive treatment earlier. Earlier intervention could improve mental health and reduce the economic costs of mental health treatment. We do not however have sufficiently robust information to monetise this benefit, which could mean that we have underestimated the overall benefit of comprehensive reform.

A wider decision-making capacity test which results in fewer mentally disordered prisoners in custody could have a positive impact in improving mental health. A high prevalence of mental disorder in prison can have a substantial negative impact on individual offenders. In 2007, there were 22,459 recorded incidents of self-harm in prison. There were 61 apparent self-inflicted deaths in custody in 2008. It is estimated that men recently released from prison are eight times more likely, than the general population, to commit suicide, and women are 36 times more likely: see Prison Reform Trust, *Bromley Briefings Prison Factfile* (June 2009) at page 40. If more mentally disordered accused are receiving appropriate care, this could reduce the occurrence of self-harm and number of suicides in custody.

Prison can be seriously detrimental to mental health. The World Health Organisation and International Red Cross have listed the following factors as contributing to poor mental health among prisoners:

- overcrowding;

- various forms of violence;

- enforced solitude;

- lack of privacy;

- lack of meaningful activity;

- isolation from social networks;

- insecurity about future prospects (work, relationships etc); and

- inadequate health services, especially mental health services in prisons.

See *Information Sheet Mental Health and Prisons* (2005) http://www.who.int/mental_health/policy/mh_in_prison.pdf

A study into the experiences of prisoners by the Sainsbury Centre showed that many prisoners found similar factors as adversely affecting their mental health, as well as other factors such as bullying, poor diet and limited psychical activity, difficulties in accessing services particularly health care and counselling: see Sainsbury Centre for Mental Health, *From the inside: experiences of prison mental health care* (2008) at page 18.

The use of segregation in prisons was reviewed after the European Court of Human Rights decision in *Keenan v United Kingdom* (2001) 33 EHRR 38 (App No 27229/95) which found that the prison service was in breach of article 3 (inhumane and degrading treatment) over the suicide of a prisoner in a segregation unit. Nonetheless, the Prison Reform Trust has concluded that "in the absence of adequate mental health care for acutely ill prisoners, there is a risk that use of segregation for their management is being sanctioned under prison rules": see Prison Reform Trust, *Troubled inside: responding to the mental health needs of men in prison* (2005) at page 36. Independent Monitoring Boards have also expressed concern that segregation units are used as a place of containment for seriously disturbed prisoners when their behaviour becomes too difficult to manage. Further, it is estimated that prisoners with learning disabilities or difficulties are five times as likely as prisoners without such impairments to be subject to control and restraint techniques and more than three times as likely to spend time in segregation: see Prison Reform Trust, *Bromley Briefings Prison Factfile* (June 2009) at page 36.

Further, a study commissioned by the Home Office has suggested that diversion from the prison system can be significantly more effective in improving mental health and reducing re-offending: see D James et al, *Outcome of psychiatric admission through the courts* (2002). The two year reconviction rate of defendants admitted to hospital by the courts was 28%. The standard two year reconviction rate for people with a similar age and offence profile who were given a custodial sentence was 56% (and 58% for a community penalty). The reconviction rate for people admitted to hospital from the courts was therefore half the reconviction rate of people sent to prison. As a result, the study concluded that "psychiatric admission through the courts may be effective as a crime prevention measure": see page 50. Comprehensive reform could therefore have a positive impact in reducing both the economic and social costs of crime if it leads to more people being admitted to hospital rather than sent to prison.

5. Ensure compatibility with article 6 and efficient use of court resources

The proposed decision-making capacity test would modernise the law and ensure that those who are unable to participate meaningfully in a trial are not subjected to an inappropriate trial process and sentence. This will ensure compatibility with article 6 of the European Convention on Human Rights. A more up to date and comprehensive legal test will therefore significantly reduce the risk of appeals brought on the ground that a defendant who was found fit and therefore stood trial in fact lacked the capacity to participate effectively as required under the right to a fair trial under article 6.

In addition, our provisional proposal for the section 4A procedure would make its scope much more comprehensive and certain which would significantly reduce the risk that appeals would be brought, like that in *Antoine*, as to its scope. Our provisional proposals will also ensure that article 6 applies to the section 4A hearing, which is important given that under our proposals there is the possibility that the accused to be acquitted by a qualified verdict (in a way similar to the special verdict of insanity).

We also provisionally propose that where the Secretary of State has remitted a case to court pursuant to the accused being detained under a hospital order with a restriction order, the court can reverse this decision if it is clear (and medical experts agree) that the accused is unfit to plead. Further, where there is a hearing as to unfitness to plead and the accused is again found unfit to plead (or to lack decision-making capacity under the new test), we suggest that there should not be any need to have a further hearing on the issue of whether the accused did the act, subject to the proviso that the court considers it to be in the interests of justice. Both these proposals could reduce unnecessary hearings and therefore reduce the financial burden on the court service, prosecuting authorities, individual accused and the Legal Services Commission.

6. Improved public confidence

Comprehensive reform would be likely to have a positive impact in relation to the general public, and would enhance public confidence in the criminal justice system as a whole. This is because it would ensure that vulnerable accused are treated fairly while continuing to ensure that the public is protected from harm. It would also bring clarity, certainty and consistency to the law.

SUMMARY OF COST AND BENEFIT ANALYSIS

Given the limited available data, we will work with three possible scenarios whereby the number of additional cases each year where the accused's decision-making capacity is raised as an issue under our proposed test would be 300, 500 and 800.

Table 6 – Cost of option 1 using different scenarios (in 2009 prices):

(Based on 300, 500, 800 additional hearings in relation to decision-making capacity)

	300	500	800
Expert evidence: Psychiatric court report: (300, 500, 800) @ £1476	£442,800	£738,000	£1,180,800
Special measures: (60, 100, 160) @ £1540	£92,400	£154,000	£246,400
Disposals: Hospital orders: (95, 158, 252)@ £165,000	£15,675,000	£26,070,000	£41,580,000
Supervision order with mental health treatment: (76, 126, 202)@ £3703	£218,428	£466,578	£748,006
Total cost	£16,428,628	£27,428,578	£43,755,206

Explanation of table

Assumptions:

- The cost of obtaining expert evidence 70% of applications will result in a finding that the accused lacks decision-making capacity; 20% will result in a finding that the accused has decision-making capacity but an order for a trial with special measures will be made; and 10% will result in the accused being found to have decision-making capacity and being subject to a normal trial: SEE PAGE 15. For example, if there are 500 additional applications this will result in 350 findings that the accused lacks decision-making capacity and 100 trials with special measures.

- The cost of special measures is based on the cost of having an intermediary for a week trial (the cost for one day is £308: SEE PAGE 15). While we consider special measures other than intermediaries we do not have accurate costs for these. We have used the estimated costs for intermediaries as a proxy for the costs of all special measures. A pre-trial hearing would be needed only in the case of an intermediary being used as a special measure. For the majority of special measures a pre-trial assessment would not be necessary and hence we have not included it in the estimated cost for special measures.

- Where an accused is found to lack decision-making capacity, in 90% of cases he or she will be subject to a disposal under section 5 (either because of a finding under section 4A that he or she did the act and that there are no grounds for acquittal or because of a qualified acquittal): SEE PAGE 15. For example, 350 findings that the accused lacks decision-making capacity would result in 315 disposals under section 5.

- Hospital based disposals will represent 50% of disposals under section 5: SEE PAGE 16. Supervision orders will represent 40% of disposals: SEE PAGE 16. For example, out of a total of 315 disposals, there would be approximately 158 hospital based disposals and 126 supervision orders.

- The cost of a hospital place is £165,000 on the assumption that most places required will be in medium secure hospitals: SEE PAGE 15.

- All supervision orders will include a requirement for mental health treatment.

Table 7 – Benefit of option 1 using different scenarios (in 2009 prices):

(Based on 300, 500, 800 additional hearings in relation to decision-making capacity)

	300	500	800
Less prison spaces: (189, 315, 504)@ £41,000	£7,749,000	£12,915,000	£20,664,000
Reduction in number of hospital places required as a result of transfer from prison: (67, 111, 176) @ £165,000	£11,055,000	£18,315,000	£29,040,000
Total	£18,804,000	£31,230,000	£49,704,000

Explanation of table

Assumptions:

- Those accused who are found to lack decision-making capacity and subject to a disposal under section 5 would have received a custodial sentence if they had stood trial. For example, 350 findings that the accused lacks decision-making capacity will result in 315 disposals under section 5 and therefore 315 fewer prison places.

- The average cost per year for a prison place is £41,000, which takes into account the estimated additional £2,000 that needs to be added to the average cost of a prison place (£39,000) for mentally disordered offenders: SEE PAGE 17.

- Out of those accused who lack decision-making capacity and who are given a hospital order, 70% would have ended up in hospital if they had gone to prison before hand as a result of a transfer. For example, if as a result of 500 applications as to decision-making capacity, 158 accused receive a hospital order, we assume that if these 158 had gone to prison, 111 would have been transferred to hospital.

Risks

1. We have incorrectly estimated the level of take-up as measured by the number of cases where decision-making capacity is raised as an issue. This is a high risk given the insufficient data currently available as to in how many cases unfitness to plead is raised and the difficulties in predicting how often the new test will be used.

2. We have incorrectly estimated the number of people who will be found to lack decision-making capacity (which we have estimated as 70%). We have some data on how many people are currently found to be unfit to plead (SEE PAGE 8) but there is a medium risk that 70% is an incorrect estimate given the difficulties in predicting who will be found to lack decision-making capacity, particularly as it will not be the case that every accused with a particular mental disorder will be found to lack decision-making capacity.

3. We have incorrectly estimated the cost for special measures (£1,540 per week). This is a medium risk, and it could result in higher or lower costs.

4. We have incorrectly estimated the number of people who will be subject to a disposal under section 5 (which we have estimated at 90%). Professor Mackay's research showed that in approximately 90% of cases where the result of the section 4A hearing was known, the accused was found to have done the act on at least one count: SEE PAGE 9. However, there is a risk that this may be too high an estimate given that in many of the cases the result of the hearing was unknown.

5. We have incorrectly estimated the proportions of hospital based disposals, supervision orders and absolute discharges: SEE PAGES 15 TO 16. This is a medium risk given that it is difficult to predict in what cases each disposal will be appropriate.

6. We have overestimated the saving in terms of prison places. This is a high risk because we have assumed that all those receiving a disposal under section 5 would have received a custodial sentence had they stood trial. However, in many cases they may have received a non-custodial sentence.

7. We have incorrectly estimated the reduction in the number of hospital places required as a result of a transfer from prison to hospital. We have estimated that out of those accused who lack decision-making capacity and who are given a hospital order, 70% would have ended up in hospital if they had gone to prison beforehand as a result of a transfer. This figure could be higher given that it is reasonably likely that many people requiring a transfer could have had mental disorder at the time of their trial which affected their decision-making capacity: SEE PAGE 17.

8. The costs and benefits have been determined using the average annual cost of a place in hospital or prison (in other words, there is the assumption that each prison sentence or hospital order will last one year). However, this does not take into account the fact that the length of time that a person will spend in either hospital or prison will vary from case to case.

Questions

We would appreciate consultees' views on the following questions, the risks and assumptions outlined above and any other material in this Impact Assessment.

1. Is it reasonable to assume that a pre-trial assessment will not be required before the use of special measures in the majority of cases? Do consultees agree that the estimated cost of £308 a day for special measures is reasonable?

2. We have used an estimate that in 90% of cases where the result of the section 4A hearing was known, the accused was found to have done the act on at least one count. Do consultees agree?

Specific Impact Tests

An impact assessment must consider the specific impacts of a policy option upon various groups within society.

Statutory equality duties

- **Gender**

The Corston Report concluded that "mental health problems are far more prevalent among women in prison than in the male prison population or in the general population": see Home Office, *The Corston Report: a review of women with particular vulnerabilities in the criminal justice system* (2007) at page 3. The Sainsbury Centre similarly found that "female prisoners have higher rates of severe mental illness (psychosis) and of common mental health problems such as depression and anxiety than male prisoners" but that "male prisoners are more likely to have personality disorder and substance dependency": see Sainsbury Centre for Mental Health, *Diversion: a better way for criminal justice and mental health* (2009) at page 45. Statistics show that women accounted for about 54% of the total self-harm incidents, even though they form only around 5% of the prison population: Prison Reform Trust, *Bromley Briefings Prison Factfile* (June 2009) at page 38. Reforms aimed at diverting people away from prison would therefore be particularly beneficial for female defendants.

- **Disability**

We do not foresee any adverse impact on people with disabilities. Our proposals may aid people with mental health problems, some of whom may be considered disabled.

- **Race**

The Prison Reform Trust reported that on 30 June 2008, 27% of the prison population was from a minority ethnic group. This compares to one in eleven of the general population: see Prison Reform Trust, *Bromley Briefings Prison Factfile* (June 2009) at page 24. Statistics also show that Black people are significantly more likely to have ever been in custody than other ethnic groups: see Home Office Online Report 33/55, Minority ethnic groups and crime: findings from the Offending, Crime and Justice Survey 2003 at page 22. Similarly, Ministry of Justice statistics show that in 2007/08 custodial sentences were given to a greater proportion of Black offenders (67%) and those in the 'Other' category (67%) than White (54%) or Asian (57%) offenders: see Ministry of Justice, *Statistics on Race and the Criminal Justice System 2007/08* (2009) at page 136.

There is also evidence that mental health problems are more prevalent among minority ethnic groups. For example, Black Caribbean, Black African and other Black groups seem to be over-represented in psychiatric hospitals. Further, results from the 2005 'Count me in' census showed that men from Black and White/Black mixed groups were two or more times more likely than the general population to be admitted to a psychiatric hospital. They represent the group with the highest rates of admission. Figures from the 2009 census suggest the position is still the same. However, it has been suggested for example that although more Black Caribbean people are treated for psychosis, this may not indicate that they are more likely to have such an illness. Moreover, research indicates that their initial contact with the mental health services has lead to more African Caribbean and other Black people with psychosis to be admitted to hospital for treatment. For example, it is more likely they have been in contact with the police prior to admission: see Mind, *Race, culture and mental health statistics.*

(http://www.mind.org.uk/help/people_groups_and_communities/statistics_3_race_culture_and_mental_health)

Nonetheless, the apparent disproportionate representation of some ethnic groups in both psychiatric hospitals and the criminal justice system suggests that there is a possibility that they may be particularly affected by reform in this area.

Competition Assessment

The recommendations are not expected to have any effect on competition.

Small Firms Impact Test

The recommendations are not expected to have any effect on small firms.

Carbon Assessment

The recommendations are not expected to have any effect on carbon emissions.

Other Environment

The recommendations are not expected to have any effect on the environment.

Health Impact Assessment

The recommendations are expected to have beneficial health impacts as the adverse impact of delay in accessing treatment for mental health problems (through inappropriate placement in prisons rather than hospitals) is reduced. People with mental health problems are less likely to require longer and therefore possibly more costly, treatment when they ultimately reach hospital. By detecting those with severe mental disorder at the time of the trial and dealing with them using an appropriate disposal, treatment could start at an earlier stage and reduce the costs of transfers from prison to hospital. Fuller detail is provided on PAGES 15 AND 17.

Human Rights

The recommendations will ensure compatibility with article 6 of the European Convention on Human Rights. The impact is discussed in further detail on PAGE 19.

Justice Impact Test

The recommendations are expected to impact on the criminal justice system at several levels. In particular it is anticipated that expert evidence will be required in more cases, there will be an increased use of special measures in keeping with the anticipated increase in cases where the accused decision-making capacity is raised as an issue. It is also expected that there will be a reduction in prison spaces as individuals are transferred directly to hospital from the courts as against being sent to prison then subsequently being transferred to hospital.

Detailed consideration of the justice impact is embedded throughout the impact assessment, see in particular PAGES 16 TO 19.

Rural proofing

The recommendations are not expected to have any differential impact on rural areas.

Sustainable Development

The recommendations are not expected to impact on sustainable development.

Annexes

Annex 1 should be used to set out the Post Implementation Review Plan as detailed below. Further annexes may be added where the Specific Impact Tests yield information relevant to an overall understanding of policy options.

Annex 1: Post Implementation Review (PIR) Plan

A PIR should be undertaken, usually three to five years after implementation of the policy, but exceptionally a longer period may be more appropriate. A PIR should examine the extent to which the implemented regulations have achieved their objectives, assess their costs and benefits and identify whether they are having any unintended consequences. Please set out the PIR Plan as detailed below. If there is no plan to do a PIR please provide reasons below.

Basis of the review: [The basis of the review could be statutory (forming part of the legislation), it could be to review existing policy or there could be a political commitment to review];

Review objective: [Is it intended as a proportionate check that regulation is operating as expected to tackle the problem of concern?; or as a wider exploration of the policy approach taken?; or as a link from policy objective to outcome?]

Review approach and rationale: [e.g. describe here the review approach (in-depth evaluation, scope review of monitoring data, scan of stakeholder views, etc.) and the rationale that made choosing such an approach]

Baseline: [The current (baseline) position against which the change introduced by the legislation can be measured]

Success criteria: [Criteria showing achievement of the policy objectives as set out in the final impact assessment; criteria for modifying or replacing the policy if it does not achieve its objectives]

Monitoring information arrangements: [Provide further details of the planned/existing arrangements in place that will allow a systematic collection systematic collection of monitoring information for future policy review]

Although the Law Commission is not planning a PIR, we can however suggest further information that could be useful. This includes: data on the number and outcome of unfitness to plead applications; more detailed information about transfers from prison to hospital including the nature of any mental health problems at the time of going to prison; data on the number of remissions for trial of accused who had been found unfit to plead and subject to a restriction order; information on the costs of special measure for vulnerable defendants.

Reasons for not planning a PIR: [If there is no plan to do a PIR please provide reasons here]

The Law Commission's role is to review areas of law and recommend, where necessary, reform of those areas to government. It is not the role of the Law Commission to implement legislation and therefore it is inappropriate for us to plan a PIR.